T0278267

VINTAGE

1947–1957, INDIA

Chandrachur Ghose is an author, researcher and commentator on history, economics and the environment. He graduated from Visva Bharati and the University of Sussex. His book *Bose: The Untold Story of an Inconvenient Nationalist* was published by Penguin Random House India in 2022 and is a national bestseller. He has also co-authored *Conundrum: Subhas Bose's Life after Death*, which features among the bestsellers on Amazon. He is one of the founders of the pressure group Mission Netaji, which has been the moving force behind the declassification of secret documents related to Netaji Subhas Chandra Bose. His activism led to the declassification of over 10,000 pages in 2010.

Celebrating 35 Years of
Penguin Random House India

1947-1957 INDIA

THE BIRTH OF A REPUBLIC

CHANDRACHUR
GHOSE

VINTAGE
An imprint of Penguin Random House

VINTAGE

USA | Canada | UK | Ireland | Australia
New Zealand | India | South Africa | China | Singapore

Vintage is part of the Penguin Random House group of companies
whose addresses can be found at global.penguinrandomhouse.com

Published by Penguin Random House India Pvt. Ltd
4th Floor, Capital Tower 1, MG Road,
Gurugram 122 002, Haryana, India

Penguin
Random House
India

First published in Vintage by Penguin Random House India 2023

Copyright © Chandrachur Ghose 2023

All images courtesy of the Endangered Archives Programme, British Library

All rights reserved

10 9 8 7 6 5 4 3 2 1

The views and opinions expressed in this book are the author's own and the
facts are as reported by him which have been verified to the extent possible,
and the publishers are not in any way liable for the same.

ISBN 9780670097104

Typeset in Adobe Caslon Pro by Manipal Technologies Limited, Manipal
Printed at Thomson Press India Ltd, New Delhi

This book is sold subject to the condition that it shall not, by way of trade
or otherwise, be lent, resold, hired out, or otherwise circulated without the
publisher's prior consent in any form of binding or cover other than that in
which it is published and without a similar condition including this condition
being imposed on the subsequent purchaser.

www.penguin.co.in

Contents

1

The Transfer of Power

By 8.20 a.m. on 15 August 1947, the ministers-designate of the Dominion of India, led by Jawaharlal Nehru, had taken their seats on each side of the two red-canopied thrones placed at an elevated level in the Durbar Hall of the Government House (now the Rashtrapati Bhavan). The swearing-in ceremony began soon after Lord Mountbatten of Burma and his wife, preceded by ten Indian and British aides-de-camp, entered the hall at 8.30 a.m. sharp and walked up to the throne, with trumpets blowing from the upper gallery. The programme began with the home secretary, R.N. Banerjee, reading out the Royal Commission, the message from the king of England to Lord Mountbatten: 'We do by this our Commission under our sign manual appoint you Lord Mountbatten to be during our pleasure Governor–General of India.' It was then the turn of the chief justice of India, Hiralal J. Kania, to administer the oath to Mountbatten. 'I will well and truly serve His Majesty King George Sixth, his heirs and successors in the office of Governor–General of India,' Mountbatten swore. It was then his turn to administer the oath to the twelve ministers of the new dominion. On the dome of the Durbar Hall, fluttered the Indian national flag, the governor–general's deep-blue flag, the Star of India flag and Queen Victoria's standard.[1]

India was now free. The era of the British Raj was over.

Yet, uncomfortable questions that kept floating around couldn't be wished away. What made the Indian National Congress, India's largest and most representative political organization, sacrifice its long-held goals to accept a partitioned India and the status of being a dominion of the British Empire?

~

As 1941 prepared to make way for 1942, the Japanese war machine began the process of steamrolling the Allied military forces occupying the South-East Asian countries. 'Japs open war on U.S. with bombing of Hawaii,' screamed the frontpage of the *Los Angeles Times* on 8 December 1941. The Imperial Japanese Navy Air Service had launched a surprise attack on the naval base of the United States of America in Pearl Harbour early in the morning on 7 December. Both the US and Britain declared war on Japan.[2]

For Japan there was no looking back. After the attack on Pearl Harbour, the Japanese forces took Bangkok on 8 December, Hong Kong on 25 December, Borneo on 31 December, Manila on 3 January 1942, Singapore on 15 February, Rangoon on 7 March, Java on 8 March and Sumatra by 28 March.[3] According to historians Christopher Bayly and Tim Harper, there are 'few parallels in history to this sudden and dramatic humiliation of an old and complacent supremacy—the British Empire in Asia—by an underrated and even despised enemy'.[4]

The unkindest cut was the fall of Singapore, where the British naval base and the fortress, considered impregnable, had been built at a cost of £30 million. Winston Churchill, the British prime minister, described it as a 'heavy and far-reaching military defeat'.[5]

With the fall of Singapore on 15 February 1942, Japanese premier, Hideki Tojo, referred to India in his speech to the House of Peers the very next day, arguing that the fall of Singapore was 'an excellent opportunity for India . . . to break off from Britain's callous domination and to join in the establishment of the Greater East Asia Co-Prosperity Sphere'. He continued:

> The Japanese Empire wishes India to be an Indians' India, and she is anxious to see that she is restored to past greatness. In this, Japan will offer her all help and assistance. If India abandons her tradition and history and forgets her missions under the spell of Britain's power and propaganda, and continues to follow her, then I shall feel very sorry for the Indian people for wasting this God-sent opportunity.[6]

The beginning of the war in September 1939 had already imparted a new momentum to the nationalist movement in India. Even before the war had started, radical leaders like Subhas Chandra Bose had raised the demand for a six-month ultimatum to the British Raj at the beginning of the year. Bose, with support from the leftists in the Congress and the youth organizations, escalated the pressure for a mass movement to set up a provisional national government and force the end of the Raj, as he saw a golden opportunity in the war situation. Not ready for such drastic measures, the Gandhian leaders of the Indian National Congress restricted themselves to announcing their opposition to the colonial government's decision to make India a party to the war and exploiting her manpower and resources to support the Allied war efforts. The Congress called upon the British government to clarify its stand on democracy and imperialism, because 'India cannot associate herself in a war said to be for democratic freedom when that very freedom is denied to her.'[7] 'If Great Britain fights for the maintenance and extension of democracy, then she must necessarily end imperialism in her own possessions, establish full democracy in India, and the Indian people must have the right of self-determination by framing their own constitution through a Constituent Assembly,' the Congress Working Committee (CWC) declared.[8] In response, the viceroy Marquess of Linlithgow reiterated on 17 October the British government's stated policy that India would gradually attain the status of a dominion in the British Empire. Towards that end, the British government would be willing to hold consultations with Indians at the end of the war to further reform the Government of India Act of 1935. For the moment, the government could only offer to set up a consultative group comprising representatives of major Indian political parties and of the princes for 'association of public opinion in India with the conduct of the war and with questions relating to war activities'. This consultative committee would be presided over by the viceroy himself and meet at his invitation.[9] Unhappy with the government's response, the working committee directed the Congress ministries in the provinces to resign by the end of the month. At the same time, it warned Congressmen 'against any hasty action in the shape of civil disobedience, political strikes and the like'.[10] In keeping with the true spirit of Satyagraha, the Working Committee decided that it would 'continue to explore the means of arriving at an honourable settlement, even though the British Government has banged the door in the face of the Congress'.[11]

Consequent to the resignation of the Congress ministries, the administration in those provinces were taken over by the respective governors under Section 93 of the Government of India Act.[12] The Congress also refused to accept an offer from the viceroy to join his executive council (along with representatives of the Muslim League and other groups) in the absence of a declaration on India's freedom and the setting up of a Constituent Assembly based on adult suffrage.[13]

The British government continued to highlight the communal problem in India as the chief barrier to any progressive move. On 3 April 1940, the secretary of state for India, Marquess of Zetland, announced:

> I am convinced that no lasting settlement in India will prove possible without real reconciliation between Moslems and Hindus. Let me say, that whatever the difficulties standing in the way we shall continue to labour whole-heartedly and to the best of our ability for such a reconciliation. The goal we have set ourselves is to aid the people of India to acquire a measure of political unity which will enable her to take her place as a great self-governing dominion in the British Commonwealth of Nations.[14]

The idea of dominion status, however, was not acceptable to the Congress. At its annual session held at Ramgarh in March 1940, the Congress declared that 'Indian freedom cannot exist within the orbit of imperialism, and Dominion Status, or any other status within the imperial structure, is wholly inapplicable to India, is not in keeping with the dignity of a whole nation, and would bind India in many ways to British politics and economic structure'.[15] Explaining his individual position, Gandhi wrote in the *Harijan* that although the idea of dominion status with the right to secede from the British Empire was acceptable to him earlier, he now believed that it was no more suitable for India.[16]

Muhammad Ali Jinnah, in the meantime, continued to press his point harder that Hinduism and Islam were not only two different religions, but two 'distinct and separate civilisations', in fact, 'two different nations'.[17] Speaking at the twenty-seventh session of the Muslim League in Lahore on 22 March 1940, Jinnah proposed the partition of India. Arguing that 'Muslim India cannot accept any constitution which must necessarily result in a Hindu majority government', he declared, 'If the British Government are really in earnest and sincere to secure peace and happiness of the people of this sub-continent, the only course open to us all is to allow the major nations to separate the homelands by dividing India into autonomous national States.'[18]

Fazlul Huq, the premier of Bengal, moved the resolution the next day demanding that geographically contiguous units should be demarcated with necessary territorial readjustments so that 'areas in which the Muslims are numerically in a majority, as in the north-western and eastern zones of India, should be grouped to constitute "independent states" in which the constituent units shall be autonomous and sovereign'.[19]

A change in the government in the UK on 10 May, with Winston Churchill taking charge of a new coalition government, was soon followed by a renewed offer to expand the viceroy's executive council and establishment of a war advisory council. Announcing the new policy on 7 August 1940, the viceroy reiterated that no fundamental constitutional change was possible while the war lasted. However, the British government would 'most readily assent to the setting up after the conclusion of the war, with the least possible delay, of a body representative of the principal elements in India's national life in order to devise the framework of the new constitution'. In response to the Congress's demand for the immediate setting up of a national government and the Muslim League's opposition to it, Linlithgow stated that the British government could not transfer 'their present responsibilities for the peace and welfare of India to any system of government whose authority is directly denied by large and powerful elements in India's national life'.[20]

Leo Amery, the new secretary of state for India and Burma, explained in the House of Commons on 14 August that even if the major political parties did not agree to participate in these new initiatives, the viceroy would go ahead with prominent Indians who were prepared to work with him.[21] The process to expand the executive council began nearly a year later, in July 1941, when it was announced that the number of members would be increased from seven to twelve, with the number of Indians being increased from three to eight.[22]

Despite no visible signs of the government relenting, Gandhi refused to launch a mass civil disobedience movement. 'I cannot, will not, start mass civil disobedience so long as I am not convinced that there is enough discipline and enough nonviolence in Congress ranks,' he declared in March 1940. In his view, such a step would be 'suicidal'.[23] He went a step further in June, writing in the *Harijan*:

If the British Government will not suo motu declare India as a free country having the right to determine her own status and constitution, I am of opinion that we should wait till the heat of the battle in the heart of the Allied countries subsides and the future is clearer than it is. We do not seek our independence out of Britain's ruin. That is not the way of non-violence.[24]

After much deliberation, Gandhi decided to launch a limited, individual satyagraha, with Vinoba Bhave being the first satyagrahi chosen by him. The decision was approved by the Congress Working Committee in October 1940.[25] As the campaign was rolled out, several Congress leaders courted arrest one by one. The government was neither embarrassed nor worried.

In fact, within a month after Churchill and the US president Franklin D. Roosevelt accepted through the Atlantic Charter in August 1941 the 'right of all peoples to choose the form of government under which they will live', and desired 'sovereign rights and self-government restored to those who have been forcibly deprived of them', the British prime minister announced that the charter did not change anything in the British government's India policy. According to its stated goal, the British government would 'help India to obtain free and equal partnership in the British Commonwealth', but only on the condition of 'fulfilment of the obligations arising from our long connection with India and our responsibilities to its many creeds, races and interests'.[26]

The situation continued in a similar manner until the Japanese shook the British and Americans with their massive and rapid assault in South-East Asia, which brought the Japanese Army near the Indo–Burma border. At the same time, pressure was being built up on the British government by Roosevelt and the Chinese premier Chiang Kai-shek (who undertook a state visit to India in February 1942), to extend some gesture of self-determination to India.

On 11 March, the British prime minister Winston Churchill announced in the House of Commons that Stafford Cripps, the Lord Privy Seal and the leader of the House, would proceed to India to present proposals from the British government, which represented a 'just and final solution' of the Indian problem. The opening sentence of his speech left no doubt about the key trigger for this initiative: 'The crisis in the affairs of India arising out of the Japanese advance has made us wish to rally all the forces of Indian life, to guard their land from the menace of the invader.'[27]

After arriving in Delhi on 23 March and meeting several representatives of political parties, the princes and other interest groups, Cripps announced the details of the proposals in a press conference on 29 March.

The objective of the proposed cabinet decisions was to accord the full status of dominion to India, for which a constitution-making body would be set up immediately at the end of the war. However, if any province was not prepared to accept the constitution, it could frame its own constitution and would be accorded the same status as the Indian Union. The princely states would also have the freedom to decide whether or not they wanted to join the Indian Union. The constitution-making body would sign a treaty with the British government regarding complete transfer of power from British to Indian hands, which would make provisions for the protection of racial and religious minorities but would not impose any restriction on the Indian Union in terms of its relation with other members of the British Commonwealth. Until the constitution came into force, the British government would retain control of the defence of India, but 'leaders of the principal sections of the Indian people' were invited to offer their 'active and constructive help' in ensuring the defence of India. This included the possibility of offering Indian leaders positions in the viceroy's executive council.[28] In other words, while on one hand the proposal acknowledged India's right to move out of the British Commonwealth through its post-war constitution, it also sought to clear the way for a division of the country.

The initial euphoria emerging out of the general expectations from Cripps's visit soon gave way to disappointment. The Congress Working Committee passed a resolution on 2 April, rejecting Cripps's proposals, arguing that they belonged to an uncertain future and that some of the provisions were in negation of both democracy and self-determination. Moreover, the principle of non-accession for a province was a blow to the conception of the unity of India. The retention of the defence portfolio in the viceroy's executive council under British control, too, was not an acceptable proposition, and this became the bone of contention over which the negotiations broke down. The Congress's logic was that any proposal 'concerning the future of India must demand attention and scrutiny, but in today's grave crisis, it is the present that counts, and even proposals for the future are important in so far as they affect the present'.[29]

The rejection was followed by a lengthy correspondence between the Congress president, Maulana Abul Kalam Azad, and Cripps, which eventually reached a deadlock by 11 April. Azad wrote to Cripps that although the Congress had not accepted the proposals,

. . . we are yet prepared to assume responsibility provided a truly national government is formed. We are prepared to put aside for the present all questions about the future, though as we have indicated, we hold definite views about it . . . the National Government must be a cabinet with full power and must not merely be continuation of the Viceroy's Executive Council.

Despite opposing the principle of non-accession of provinces to an Indian Union, the Congress accepted the right of secession by territorial units unwilling to be a part of the Indian Union. The Working Committee declared that it

. . . cannot think in terms of compelling the people in any territorial unit to remain in an Indian Union against their declared and established will. While recognising this principle, the Committee feel that every effort should be made to create conditions which would help the different units in developing a common and cooperative national life.[30]

While the Hindu Mahasabha rejected Cripps's proposal, which 'had in it the danger of division of the country', Jinnah felt that the 'principle of Pakistan, which found a veiled recognition in the document should be conceded in unequivocal terms'.[31]

Bose, who had been imprisoned from July 1940 but succeeded in slipping out of India to reach Germany in April 1941, too opposed the Cripps Mission through his radio broadcasts. No sane Indian could be pleased with these proposals, he argued, nor be prepared to trust empty British promises. He added, 'Only one who lives in a fool's paradise could imagine that India still cares for Dominion Status.' The proposals were another attempt at the age-old British policy of divide and rule. Regarding Cripps's argument that the existing constitution could not be changed during the war, Bose reminded that in October 1939, he had suggested that a provisional national government commanding the confidence of the majority of Indians be set up and made responsible to the central Legislative Assembly—a suggestion that received support from the Congress too. Warning Indian leaders to not allow India become the next theatre of war, he emphasized that 'if India does not participate in Britain's war there is not the least possibility of India being attacked by any of the Axis Powers'.[32]

According to the Congress Working Committee, the failure of the Cripps Mission 'showed in the clearest possible manner that there was no change in the British Government's attitude towards India and that the British hold on India was in no way to be relaxed'. So the committee passed a resolution on 14 July in its meeting at Wardha, demanding an immediate withdrawal of British rule from India. Apart from its standard claim that immediate freedom would strengthen the anti-fascist war efforts, the Working Committee curiously found it necessary to impress that the Cripps Mission's failure

> . . . has resulted in a rapid and widespread increase in ill-will against Britain and a growing satisfaction at the success of Japanese arms. The Working Committee view this development with grave apprehension as this, unless checked, will lead to a passive acceptance of aggression. The Committee hold that all aggression must be resisted, for any submission to it must mean the degradation of the Indian people and the continuation of their subjection . . . The Congress would change the present ill-will against Britain into good-will and make India a willing partner in a joint enterprise of securing freedom for the nations and peoples of the world and in the trials and tribulations which accompany it.[33]

If this demand was ignored, the working committee declared, the Congress would then be compelled to launch a non-violent movement under Gandhi to attain the country's liberty. In view of the magnitude of its implications, the resolution was referred to the All India Congress Committee (AICC) for the final decision.

Explaining the resolution at the AICC meeting held at the Gowalia Tank Maidan in Bombay on 7 August, Azad said:

> What this resolution says is this: Let us not depend on promises. Let us have a declaration of Indian Independence forthwith and we, on our part, shall immediately enter in a Treaty of Alliance with the United Nations for the sole purpose of fighting and winning this war.[34]

The resolution, calling for 'a mass struggle on non-violent lines on the widest possible scale', was passed by an overwhelming majority on 8 August. 'I have pledged the Congress and the Congress will do or die,' Gandhi declared on the passing of the resolution.[35]

The government was prepared for this and immediately clamped down, arresting Gandhi and the members of the working committee before dawn on the next day. Within the week, almost all Congress leaders who mattered were in jail. The government succeeded in brutally repressing the largely violent and militant campaign that followed by the end of the year. No serious political campaign challenged the British Raj for nearly the next three years, until the end of the war. The absence of the Congress and the Left parties was utilized by the Muslim League to expand its support base and consolidate its communal politics that hinged on the demand for a separate Muslim state, or Pakistan.

After Gandhi was released on 6 May 1944, on the grounds of ill health, he entered into a correspondence with Archibald Wavell, who had taken over as India's new viceroy in October 1943.

In one of his letters written in July 1944 to Wavell, Gandhi repeated the Congress's demand:

> I am prepared to advise the Working Committee to declare that in view of the changed conditions, mass civil disobedience envisaged by the resolution of August 1942 cannot be offered and that full co-operation in the war-effort should be given by the Congress, if a declaration of immediate Indian independence is made and a national government responsible to the Central Assembly be formed subject to the proviso that, during the pendency of the war, the military operations should continue as at present but without involving any financial burden on India.[36]

The secretary of state, Leo Amery, was in no mood to listen to such demands. Asserting that the Cripps proposals still held good, Amery, referring to Gandhi's stand, told the House of Commons, 'So long as those are the basis for his proposals, they obviously do not form even the starting point for a profitable discussion either with Lord Wavell or with the interned Congress leaders.'[37]

Wavell's response to Gandhi's letter, which was sent on 15 August after much discussion in the British war cabinet, took the same line, telling him, 'no purpose would be served by discussion on the basis which you suggest'. Reminding Gandhi that the promise of 'unqualified freedom at the cessation of hostilities' in the Cripps offer was 'conditional upon the framing of a Constitution agreed by the main elements of India's national life and the negotiation of the necessary treaty arrangements' with the

British government, Wavell mapped out what he believed to be a progress in the current situation. A transitional government could be formed comprising Hindus, Muslims and other important minorities, within the present constitutional framework only after the different communities agreed in principle 'as to the method by which the new constitution should be framed'. The onus for constitutional progress, therefore, lay entirely with the Indians.[38]

Churchill was not happy with Wavell's correspondence with Gandhi, who, he thought, 'was released on the medical advice that he would not again be able to take part in active politics'. Wavell assured Churchill that he was not negotiating with Gandhi, but while reiterating the position of the British government as stated in the Cripps proposals, he believed that it would be wrong to adopt a negative attitude towards Gandhi's approach.[39]

While Churchill remained cold, even hostile, to the Indian question, Wavell felt that between the options to sit back and await events, or to make a positive move when the war with Germany ended, the latter was a better option. Bolstered with support from the governors of the provinces and the commander-in-chief (C-in-C),[40] Wavell articulated his prognostication about the end of the war situation in India in a letter to Amery. He was remarkably prescient in projecting the explosive scenario that was likely to emerge at the end of the war, primarily driven by 'the demobilization of the Indian Army, the dispersal of labour from war factories, and the winding up of large war establishments employing many thousands of clerks' at a time when the Congress leaders could not more be held in detention. 'If trouble is to be avoided we must find some outlet for the administrative and political energy of the Indian Parties, including the Congress and the Muslim League, and this can be done only by active steps to get the political problem solved,' he wrote to Amery on 5 September.[41] The situation, as we shall see, turned out to be worse than Wavell could imagine, chiefly because it wasn't possible for him to foresee the impact of Subhas Bose and his Indian National Army on Indian politics.

On 20 September, Wavell sent Amery a memorandum on what he thought should be done. The time was still not ripe for holding fresh elections in the provinces or for setting up a Constituent Assembly, but it was essential to form as soon as possible a transitional government at the centre, representative of the main political parties, until a new Constitution was framed. It would conduct administration under the existing Constitution, appoint representatives to the international conferences, and consider the composition of the body that would draft the new Constitution and negotiate the treaty with the British government relating to the transfer of power. To that end he would first hold informal talks with Gandhi and Jinnah and based on the outcome, would try to organize a formal conference of the principal political leaders.[42] Wavell's proposals failed to enthuse Amery, who detailed out a long list of problems that might arise out of the proposals, insisting that the existing executive council be retained during the duration of the war and that the National Defence Council be made use of for the conference proposed by Wavell.[43] An annoyed Wavell noted in his diary:

> Had a long telegram from S. of S. urging every possible objection and difficulty against my proposed political move, all of which I had of course considered before making it. He makes a fatuous counter-proposal which Linlithgow turned down with a bang nearly three years ago.[44]

An unrelenting Wavell brought up the matter again when he wrote to Churchill on the occasion of completing a year as viceroy on 24 October 1944, knowing that Churchill wouldn't like his ideas. He, however, changed his approach to the issue in his letter to Churchill, pivoting it more on the future of the British Commonwealth vis-à-vis India. Among other things, he wrote:

> I will begin by saying that my primary reason for writing is that I feel very strongly that the future of India is the problem on which the British Commonwealth and the British reputation will stand or fall in the post-war period. To my mind, our strategic security, our name in the world for statesmanship and fair dealing, and much of our economic well-being will depend on the settlement we make in India. Our prestige and prospects in Burma, Malaya, China and the Far East generally are entirely subject to what happens in India. If we can secure India as a friendly partner in the British Commonwealth our predominant influence in these countries will, I think, be assured; with a lost and hostile India, we are likely to be reduced in the East to the position of commercial bag-men.
>
> And yet I am bound to say that after a year's experience in my present office I feel that the vital problems of India are being treated by His Majesty's Government with neglect, even sometimes with hostility and contempt.[45]

'If our aim is to retain India as a willing member of the British Commonwealth, we must make some imaginative and constructive move without delay,' Wavell argued. He had no doubt that 'if we want India as a Dominion after the war, we must begin by treating her much more like a Dominion now.' Explaining the factors that were likely to turn into a 'fertile field for agitation,' Wavell warned Churchill:

> We cannot move without taking serious risks; but the most serious risk of all is that India after the war will become a running sore which will sap the strength of the British Empire. I think it is still possible to keep India within the Commonwealth, though I do not think it will be easy to do so. If we fail to make any effort now we may hold India down uneasily for some years, but in the end she will pass into chaos and probably into other hands.[46]

After repeated attempts by Wavell to place his proposals to the war cabinet were stonewalled by the British government, he was summoned to England in March 1945. His proposals, however, found little support from the government. When Wavell met Churchill at Downing Street on 29 March 1945, the prime minister told him bluntly that he had had no time to consider India and thought that the India issue 'could be kept on ice'.[47] A month later, as he was still struggling to make his way through the British cabinet, Wavell noted in his journal:

> I feel I have failed to make H.M.G. realise the importance and urgency of the Indian problem or the real facts of the position. We have been talking for 5 weeks, in a very disconnected way. The matter could have been settled in a week if they had really taken it seriously and wanted to. Now I think we have missed the bus in any case.[48]

With the British elections scheduled for July 1945 as the Labour Party resigned from the coalition ministry on 23 May, the caretaker government under Churchill finally agreed to go ahead with proposals on Indian constitutional reforms on 31 May. Amery explained in a statement issued on 14 June that the new proposals were interim in nature, to break the political deadlock and prepare the ground for the constitution to be formulated by the Indians themselves.[49] Wavell, too, broadcast the proposal the same day while ordering the release of the

Congress Working Committee members arrested during the Quit India movement. The proposals included the offer to set up a new executive council, which would be entirely Indian except for the viceroy himself and the commander-in-chief. 'Caste Hindus' and Muslims would have equal representation, the executive would work within the existing constitution, but the door would be kept open for discussion on a new constitution once the war was finally won.[50]

Wavell's talks with the leaders at the Simla Conference, which took place between 25 June and 14 July, broke down as the Congress objected to being branded as a purely 'caste Hindu' party, and over Jinnah's unwavering claim of the Muslim League being the sole party which could nominate Muslim members in the proposed executive council. Jinnah also insisted that the decisions opposed by Muslims in the council should require a two-thirds majority for adoption.[51]

Sources such as the journalist Durga Das and the then reforms commissioner, V.P. Menon, later claimed access to information that Jinnah was encouraged by an existing member of the viceroy's council and told that if he stuck to his position and wrecked the conference, he would achieve his goal of Pakistan. 'Am I a fool to accept this [the composition of the executive council] when I am offered Pakistan on a platter?' Jinnah told Durga Das after rejecting the conference's outcome.[52] Wavell's capitulation to Jinnah's stubborn insistence sharply increased the Muslim League's political stock by giving official recognition to Jinnah's standing as the sole arbiter of the political fate of India's Muslims. Coming at a time when the Muslim League was not in a commanding position even in Muslim-majority provinces of the North-West Frontier Province, Punjab and Bengal, this was seen as a blow to the Muslim leaders opposed to Jinnah.[53]

Following the failure of the Simla talks, the political atmosphere changed drastically in a very short span of time. As the official blackout policy regarding news on Subhas Bose and the Indian National Army (INA) was lifted, Indians started getting the details about Bose's armed campaign for the first time from May 1945 onwards. With the INA soldiers being brought back to India as prisoners, the government's decision to hold public trials created widespread resentment and, subsequently, a groundswell of public support for the soldiers, which soon assumed the form of a militant movement.

The state of mind of the Congress leaders at this time was described by Gandhi to a journalist. It was unfortunate, he said, 'that most of his colleagues had come out of jail tired and dispirited and without the heart to carry on the struggle. They wanted a settlement with Britain and what is more, hungered for power.'[54] Years later, in 1960, Nehru confirmed Gandhi's perception while talking to author Leonard Mosley:

> The truth is that we were tired men, and we were getting on in years too. Few of us could stand the prospect of going to prison again—and if we had stood out for a united India as we wished it, prison obviously awaited us . . . The plan for partition offered a way out and we took it.[55]

In 1945, Gandhi was seventy-six years old, Patel seventy, Rajagopalachari sixty-seven, Govind Ballabh Pant fifty-eight, Azad and Kripalani fifty-seven, Nehru fifty-six and Prafulla Ghosh fifty-four. The Gandhian high command was indeed aged and tired. The leaders who held more aggressive and radical views at the time were much younger. For instance, Subhas Bose was forty-eight, Jayaprakash Narayan forty-three and Ram Manohar Lohia only thirty-five.

With the Labour government coming to power in July 1945, Viceroy Wavell conveyed to the secretary of state Frederick Pethick-Lawrence the near-unanimous decision of the provincial governors for holding elections to the provincial and central legislatures. The meeting of the India and Burma Committee of the British cabinet agreed on 17 August that the viceroy should begin the preparations for the central and provincial elections. Pethick-Lawrence informed Wavell that the cabinet was looking at the 'whole Indian problem' with greatest urgency. Three days later, he authorized Wavell to announce that elections would be held during the winter of 1945–46 and invited him to visit London for further discussions with the cabinet.[56] Wavell arrived in London five days after announcing the elections on 21 August. At subsequent meetings of the India and Burma Committee, while Wavell argued for holding discussions with Indian leaders after the elections to reach an agreement over the procedure for constitution-making, Cripps (now president of the Board of Trade) and Prime Minister Clement Attlee felt that the only hope for making any progress was to hold the parties against a definite plan of action that would compel them to come to an agreement in the face of the realities.

After much deliberation, the British government decided to go with Wavell's plan of holding discussions with the elected representatives after the elections to ascertain whether a modified Cripps scheme or some other formula was acceptable to them.[57]

On his return, Wavell declared on 19 September that, as a preliminary step towards the formation of a constitution-making body, immediately after the elections he would be holding discussions with the representatives of the legislative assemblies of the provinces to ascertain if subsequent negotiations could be based on the Cripps proposals of 1942. In addition, he would take required steps for the formation of a new executive council that would have the support of India's main political parties.[58]

The failure of 1942 was such a shattering blow that the AICC, which met in Bombay from 21–23 September 1945, at the same place where the Quit India resolution was adopted in August 1942, saw little hope for independence at that time. Vallabhbhai Patel moved a resolution on 23 September, which read:

> Neither the end of the War nor the change of Government in Britain appears to have resulted in any real change in British policy towards India, which seems to be based on delaying every advance and in attempting to create new problems and fresh complications. It is significant that there is no mention in these [British] broadcasts of the Independence of India.[59]

Despite pointing out several constraints, such as the lack of universal adult franchise, ban on several organizations affiliated to the Congress and continued detention of a great number of leaders and workers, the Congress decided to participate in the elections. The Congress's election manifesto articulated that 'in these elections, petty issues do not count nor do individual or sectarian cries—only one thing counts: the freedom and independence of our motherland'.[60] The Muslim League decided to contest the elections on the issue of Pakistan and the party's claim to represent all the Muslims in India.[61] At this crucial juncture, the government announced holding public trials against the INA soldiers, the first to be held at the Red Fort from November.

The INA trials became the campaign issue that the Congress had been so desperately looking for—an issue that could cut across communities and classes and arouse their enthusiasm. Thus, despite branding Bose and his INA as 'mistaken', the Congress decided to set up a committee to defend the soldiers in their trial. Soon after the first trial at Red Fort started on 5 November, Jawaharlal Nehru wrote to Abul Kalam Azad, on 16 November, saying that the 'Indian situation is developing very rapidly, perhaps too rapidly, and the temperature of the country is rising'.[62] He informed Patel that he had asked the three heroes of the INA trials, Shah Nawaz Khan, P.K. Sehgal and G.S. Dhillon, whether they would agree to contest the forthcoming elections on Congress tickets. All three agreed.[63] Patel raised the question that 'if the British government are sincere about giving India self-Government why don't they make the National Army created by Subhas Chandra Bose the nucleus of the new National Army to be raised?'[64]

The countrywide eruption of popular discontent in the form of riots and demonstrations continued well into 1946, until the government decided to discontinue the trials at the end of April. The sentiments generated by the trial of the INA soldiers led to unprecedented mutinies, first in the Royal Indian Air Force (RIAF) and then in the Royal Indian Navy (RIN), from 18 February 1946.

The nationalist fervour in the country had reached such levels by that time that it erased the differences between the Hindus and the Muslims. Violence had broken out in many states. The *New York Times* reported on 17 February 1946:

> In spite of the uncompromising struggle between the two factions, last week for the first time since 1921, Moslems and Hindus together staged street protests and riots against the British in Calcutta, Bombay and New Delhi. The catalytic agent in this case was the Indian National Army, organized by a Japanese collaborator named Subhas Chandra Bose.

On 20 November, the Government of India's home department forwarded a report by the Intelligence Bureau to the India Office that noted that the 'situation in respect of the Indian National Army is one which warrants disquiet. There has seldom been a matter which has attracted so much Indian public interest and, it is safe to say, sympathy.'[65]

The developments made Wavell panic. He started sending his reports to Pethick-Lawrence, painting a grim picture of the possibility of large-scale violence. On 9 October 1945, he wrote to Pethick-Lawrence:

> Nehru is very bitter against the British regime in India and against the Muslim League, and the adoption for the campaign of the I.N.A.

war cries is significant . . . Some people believe that Nehru's plan is to make use of the I.N.A.—large quantities of arms are said to have been smuggled into India from the Burma front—both to train Congress volunteers and as a Congress striking force; and also possibly to tamper with the Indian Army. He is said to have had conversations about the use of the I.N.A. for subversive purposes during his visit to Lahore . . . Nehru's uncompromising attitude implies that he is not opposed to a violent mass movement of some kind.[66]

A week later, he wrote:

Nehru continues his intemperate speeches and statements, and is now on tour in the Eastern Districts of the United Provinces. It is difficult to explain his conduct and that of the other Congress leaders except on the assumption that Congress wish to bring about communal rioting and anti-Government disturbances . . . Attempts by the politicians to enlist popular interest in, and sympathy for, the I.N.A. are fully maintained; and the first trials by Court Martial, which are expected to begin here next month, will cause considerable excitement.

. . . Several Governors and my Colleagues in the Executive Council are apprehensive about the law and order situation . . . Now that the people are being told daily in the Press, and in the speeches of their political leaders, that the Members of the Executive Council are a contemptible set of crooks; that the administration is corrupt, incompetent, and oppressive; that those who took part in the disturbances and sabotage of 1942 are martyrs and heroes; and that within a year or two there will be Independence, under which the official 'war criminals' of India will be punished, there is good reason for apprehension amongst the loyalists.[67]

Wavell was particularly worried about the morale of officers in the administration, as the Congress leaders started declaring their intention for reprisal when in power. After meeting Nehru on 3 November to express his displeasure about provocative political speeches, Wavell reported back to Pethick-Lawrence, 'I have no doubt that he is bent on serious trouble and that it will be very difficult indeed to divert him from his purpose except by repressive action.'[68] On 12 November, Wavell advised Pethick-Lawrence, 'I feel that not only should the Cabinet be informed of what is happening and is likely to happen, but that the general position should be disclosed to the country by a statement in Parliament,' while describing the situation in an accompanying memorandum:

We are now faced in India with a situation of great difficulty and danger, in which I require support and guidance from His Majesty's Government.

Since the session of the All India Congress Committee (21st-23rd September) the Congress leaders everywhere, but particularly Vallabhbhai Patel in Bombay and Nehru and [Govind Ballabh] Pant in the United Provinces, have been making statements and speeches which can only be intended to provoke or pave the way for mass disorder. They began by taking the credit of the 1942 disturbances; asserting that the British could be turned out of India within a very short time; denying the possibility of a compromise with the Muslim League; glorifying the I.N.A.; and threatening the officials who took part in the suppression of the 1942 disturbances with trial and punishment as 'war criminals'. From these general attempts to excite racial and communal hatred, they have now passed to a disclosure of their programme, which is, briefly, to contest the elections, to serve an ultimatum on H.M.G., and, in default of its acceptance, to organise a mass movement on the 1942 lines but on a much larger scale.

The Congress, as a body, would almost certainly deny, in spite of the speeches of members of the Working Committee, that violence is any part of their official creed. But either there is a secret policy which includes use of violence, or the more extreme leaders are out of control.

. . . In order to make sure that there was no misunderstanding I saw Nehru on 3rd November, and pointed out to him the danger of the course he and other leaders were advocating. He made it clear that he thought violence inevitable, and shortly after our interview delivered an inflammatory speech of the usual kind. I believe that the Congress are counting on the I.N.A. as the spear-head of their revolt; they would suborn the Indian Army if they could, and they hope that their threats will impair the loyalty and efficiency of the Police.

. . . The object of the rising the Congress leaders have in mind would be the expulsion of the British. Whatever the leaders themselves might say publicly, there would be organised attacks on the railways and public buildings, treasuries would be looted and records destroyed. In fact Congressmen would attempt to paralyze the administration, as they did in 1942; they would also attack and possibly murder any officials, British and Indian, on whom they could lay their hands.

. . . It is in my judgment unlikely that the Congress leaders will attempt their coup until all the Provincial elections are completed, unless events force their hand. I doubt if they are much interested in the elections as such; what is more important to them is the opportunity afforded by the elections to revive and re-organise the Party, and they are already taking full advantage of this opportunity.[69]

In the same memorandum, Wavell suggested the suppression of Congress 'with great thoroughness' involving British troops, declaring martial law and detention of 'a large number of persons without trial or trial by special courts'. Although he believed that the government would be justified in taking these measures immediately, he was ready to wait for the present as it would 'invite criticism all over the world'. The best course was 'to wait for the present, and prepare to act quickly as soon as we are compelled to do so'.[70]

On his part, Pethick-Lawrence tried to calm Wavell down by postulating that the stance taken by the Congress leader only reflected their anxiety to 'keep their organisation together in the stress of the election. He would, however, be surprised if the Congress actually plunged into a mass movement instead of cooperating in the next round of negotiations planned after the elections. Pethick-Lawrence believed that it was nonetheless a possibility if Jinnah maintained 'the kind of attitude he adopted at Simla' and the British government accepted it. He wanted Wavell's opinion on whether Jinnah could be brought around to accept a modified form of Pakistan.[71] On 14 November, Pethick-Lawrence informed the British cabinet that although he did not take all Nehru's speeches at face value, he couldn't 'take the Viceroy's warning lightly, particularly as I am told for the first time that there are signs of a demoralising effect not only among the civil services but also in the Indian Army'.[72]

In its meeting on 19 November, the India and Burma Committee took up for consideration some suggestions made by Rajkumari Amrit Kaur to Cripps for defusing the current situation. These suggestions included sending a parliamentary delegation to India, inviting Nehru and Jinnah to the UK for discussions, a meeting between Gandhi and the viceroy, and a clear declaration that the British government wasn't seeking any excuses for delay in granting independence. The idea of sending a parliamentary delegation to India was strongly supported by the Committee.[73] Pethick-Lawrence hoped that the delegation would help in demonstrating the sympathy of the British parliament with Indian aspirations and 'assure Indian opinion of the sincerity of British intentions' by means of personal contact.[74]

Arriving in India on 5 January 1946, the ten-member parliamentary delegation spent about a month in the country, meeting almost all important political leaders. However, on their return, when they met Attlee on 13 February 1946, to brief him on their impressions, one of the members bluntly put forward that

> There are two alternative ways of meeting this common desire (a) that we should arrange to get out, (b) that we should wait to be driven out. In regard to (b), the loyalty of the Indian Army is open to question; the INA have become national heroes under the boosting of the Congress; the possibility cannot be excluded that Congress could form an 'Independent Indian Army' . . .[75]

There was a noticeable change in the attitude of the Congress leaders by early December, largely due to assurances from personal interactions with the viceroy and governors of provinces such as Bengal, the government's public announcements and Gandhi's renewed efforts reinforced by Congress president Azad and sections within the organization. Nehru and Patel still appeared intractable. Gandhi's confidante Sudhir Ghosh told the Bengal governor Richard Casey on 4 December that 'Nehru and Patel have lost faith in the "Gandhian way"', and that 'they do not conceal their determination that if they do not get their way there will be bloodshed in India on a wide scale'.[76] Wavell believed that the Congress leaders wouldn't launch a mass movement until after the elections.[77]

The Congress Working Committee, at its 7–11 December meeting in Calcutta , felt it was necessary 'to affirm for the guidance of all concerned that the policy of non-violence adopted in 1920 by the Congress continues unabated and that such non-violence does not include burning of public property, cutting of telegraph wires, derailing trains and intimidation'.[78] Further effort to calm the nerves was made by Pethick-Lawrence when, in his New Year's broadcast, he announced that the British government and the British people 'earnestly wish to see India rise quickly to the full and free status of an equal partnership in the British Commonwealth'. He reassured that 'we present no obstacles to India's attaining that position', and hence there was 'no longer any need for denunciations or organised pressure to secure recognition of India's due position in the world'.[79]

Yet, serious clashes continued to erupt around the issue of the INA, with two major ones taking place in Calcutta in November 1945, in Bombay in January 1946 and, finally, during the mutiny in the RIN in February. Significantly, these large-scale clashes took place despite the non-involvement of Congress leaders and even their categorical discouragement. Patel played a particularly active role in quelling the RIN uprising, asking the ratings to surrender.

The results of the Central Legislative Assembly became available towards the end of December 1945. Congress won massively in the general (that is, non-Muslim) constituencies, capturing fifty-seven out of 102 seats in the Central Assembly (increased from thirty-six in 1934), and 91.3 per cent of non-Muslim votes. While the Hindu Mahasabha was routed, the Communists won only a handful of provincial seats (three in Bengal, two in Bombay and two in Madras). The Muslim League, on the other hand, won all thirty reserved constituencies in the Centre, with 86.6 per cent of Muslim votes, and 442 out of 509 Muslim seats in the provinces. The nationalist Muslims performed poorly, forfeiting their deposit in many constituencies.[80]

Without losing time, Wavell proposed the next course of action to the secretary of state for India on 27 December. Presenting an assessment of the situation, Wavell argued that the Congress—being the strongest organization without any opposition other than the Muslim League, which represented only sectional interests—was undoubtedly in a position to 'bring about a very serious revolt against British rule'. Such a revolt could be suppressed 'after a considerable amount of bloodshed', but it would 'certainly not be wise to try the Indian Army too highly in the suppression of their own people'. 'As time goes on, the loyalty of Indian officials, the Indian Army and the police might become problematical,' he pointed out. What worried him was that the suppression of the Congress would result in 'an almost entirely official rule', a situation that would be further complicated by the fact that for such a rule 'the necessary number of efficient officials do not exist'. 'We shall be placed in a quite untenable position, unless we find a solution,' Wavell pleaded.[81]

Wavell's proposed solution was to form a central executive as soon as possible, even before ministries were formed in the provinces, if possible by the first week of April. If this plan materialized, Wavell wanted the new executive to consider the composition of and the agenda for the preliminary conference to convene the constitution-making body. The conference, he hoped, could be summoned sometime in May 1946.[82]

Pethick-Lawrence saw several practical problems in being able to implement the viceroy's programme as sequentially envisaged in watertight compartments. He recommended an alternative approach. On 14 January 1946, a meeting of the India and Burma Committee, chaired by Attlee, decided to send a mission of three cabinet ministers to India towards the end of March, when the results of the elections would be fully known.[83] The Cabinet Mission, comprising Pethick-Lawrence, Stafford Cripps and A.V. Alexander, was formally announced in the House of Commons and the House of Lords on 19 February 1946.

The 19 February announcement of the Cabinet Mission in the British parliament laid down the steps to be followed:

> . . . first, preparatory discussions with elected representatives of British India and with Indian states in order to secure the widest measure of agreement as to the method of framing a Constitution.
>
> Second, the setting up of a Constitution-making body and third, the bringing into being of an Executive Council having the support of the main Indian parties.[84]

The three members of the Cabinet Mission, along with Viceroy Wavell, began their discussions and negotiations with the Indian leaders a week after their arrival on 23 March, which continued until June 1946. At a press conference on 25 March in New Delhi, Pethick-Lawrence clarified:

> Our talks will not be concerned with the question of whether India shall determine her own destiny that is already decided—but with how she will do so.
>
> . . . We cannot of course at this meeting express any views either on the shape of the machinery that should be devised for determining a solution, or on the merits of any particular constitutional plan. These are matters which must await the discussions with Indian representatives. We have come with only one fixed intention, and that is to play our full part as representing His Majesty's Government in helping Indians to achieve their independence.[85]

Speaking in the House of Commons on 15 March 1946, Attlee held out hope that 'India may elect to remain within the British Commonwealth. I am certain that she will find great advantage in doing so, but if she does, she must do it of her own free will . . . If on the other hand she elects for independence—and in our view she has a right to do so—it will be for us to help make the transition as smooth and easy as possible.'[86]

Just how much the ongoing unrest originating from the INA trials and the RIN mutiny was troubling the minds of the British decision-makers is also made clear from Wavell's note to the cabinet delegation, where he stated, 'We are going into these negotiations with an extremely difficult hand to play, owing to the necessity to avoid the mass movement or revolution in India which it is in the power of the Congress to start, and which we are not certain that we can control.'[87]

Nearly a decade later, in a February 1955 interview with BBC's Francis Watson, Dr Bhimrao Ambedkar wondered, 'I don't know how Mr Attlee suddenly agreed to give India independence. That is a secret that he will disclose in his autobiography. None expected that he would do that.' Ambedkar told the BBC that from his 'own analysis' he had figured out what had convinced the Labour Party to take the decision to free India:

> The national army that was raised by Subhas Chandra Bose. The British had been ruling the country in the firm belief that whatever may happen in the country or whatever the politicians did, they could never be able to change the loyalty of soldiers. That was one prop on which they were carrying on the administration. And that was completely dashed to pieces.

In October 1956, two months before Ambedkar passed away, Attlee himself disclosed the reason to Phani Bhusan Chakravartti, chief justice of the Calcutta High Court and acting governor of West Bengal, in a private conversation. Chakravartti recounted what he'd heard from Attlee in a handwritten letter to historian Ramesh Chandra Majumdar:

> The INA activities of Subhas Chandra Bose, which weakened the very foundation of the British Empire in India, and the RIN mutiny which made the British realise that the Indian armed forces could no longer be trusted to prop up the British.

Justice Chakravartti, the first Indian to become permanent chief justice of India's oldest court, also asked Attlee about the extent of Gandhi's influence upon the British decision to quit India. In Chakravartti words: 'Hearing this question, Attlee's lips became twisted in a sarcastic smile as he slowly chewed out the word, "m-i-n-i-m-a-l"!'[88] In 1960, in Nuffield College, Oxford, Attlee repeated the same statement to historian Barun De.[89]

The assessment reports of the country's situation at the end of 1945 and early 1946 by the viceroy and the commander-in-chief provide a clear insight into why the Attlee government was in a rush.

Commander-in-chief of the British Indian Army, Field Marshal Claude Auchinleck's 24 November 1945 report on the internal situation in India clearly stated, 'It is a reasonable assumption, therefore, that widespread trouble either communal or anti-government or both is to be expected in the late Spring.' He expected the scale of disturbances to be much greater than what was seen in 1942. He pointed out the uncertainties around the army in such an eventuality—uncertainties that largely were triggered by the INA. 'I consider that there must be doubt as to the continued loyalty of the Armed Forces unless Government produce a strong and unequivocal statement of policy comprehensible by the rank and file.' He said that the government must declare that 'any armed insurrection will be put down, by force if necessary and the leaders punished'. Auchinleck went to the extent of asking the British government to be prepared with plans for sending British reinforcement troops to India for its reconquest.

> If the Indian forces as a whole cease to be reliable, the British Armed Forces now available are not likely to be able to control the internal situation or to protect essential communications, nor would any piecemeal reinforcements of these forces be of much avail. To regain control of the situation and to restore essential communications within the country, nothing short of an organised campaign for the reconquest of India is likely to suffice . . . The situation in India is, therefore, extremely delicate . . . I request, therefore, that plans may be prepared for the despatch to India of such British Formations as could be made available.[90]

Auchinleck sent a similar assessment report to the British chiefs of staff about a month later.[91]

As the national demand was overshadowed gradually by the communal issues, there too, the Government of India saw critical problems regarding the armed forces. On 18 January 1946, Wavell wrote to the chiefs of staff asking for three brigade groups to send to India with the 'object of providing steadying effect during Provincial elections and in period immediately after them'.[92] The chief of the imperial general staff, Field Marshal Viscount Alanbrooke, informed Auchinleck on 4 February about the difficulties in meeting that demand as the British troops worldwide had reached an 'irreducible minimum' due to an 'acute UK manpower situation'.[93] On 14 February 1946, Auchinleck explained the need for more British troops in India to Alanbrooke:

> . . . no one can forecast with any certainty the extent or degree of the hostile action with which we may have to deal. Such action may vary from complete rebellion aided by the whole or great majority of the Indian Armed Forces . . . to isolated civil disturbances . . .
>
> In addition to the above possibilities of anti-Government action there is the equally if not more serious possibility of a religious war on a large scale . . . it is more than likely that it will be impossible to rely on either the Police or the Indian Armed Forces to take action for the restoration of law and order if this means firing on their own co-religionists. This means that British troops alone would be available to restore the situation and the use of British troops in such circumstances would almost certainly result in turning communal strife into anti-Government action by both parties. In this event we would again be faced by the risk of the Indian Armed Forces throwing in their lot with the insurgent elements . . .[94]

The commander-in-chief had lost faith in his forces, but the viceroy was fairly confident that the Congress leadership saw more value in acting as a check on popular upsurges in order to ensure smooth negotiations leading to a quick transfer of power.

Unable to find a common ground between the Congress and the Muslim League in its deliberations, the cabinet delegation proposed its own basic formula for a new constitution on 16 May 1946:

1. There should be a Union of India, embracing both British India and the States, which should deal with the following subjects: Foreign Affairs, Defence, and Communications; and should have

the powers necessary to raise the finances required for the above subjects.

2. The Union should have an Executive and a Legislature constituted from British Indian and States representatives. Any question raising a major communal issue in the Legislature should require for its decision a majority of the representatives present and voting of each of the two major communities as well as a majority of all the members present and voting.

3. All subjects other than the Union subjects and all residuary powers should vest in the Provinces.

4. The States will retain all subjects and powers other than those ceded to the Union.

5. Provinces should be free to form Groups with executives and legislatures, and each Group could determine the Provincial subjects to be taken in common.

6. The constitutions of the Union and of the Groups should contain a provision whereby any Province could, by a majority vote of its Legislative Assembly, call for a reconsideration of the terms of the constitution after an initial period of 10 years and at 10 yearly intervals thereafter.[95]

Although the delegation felt that the ideal scenario would be to elect a Constituent Assembly on the basis of adult franchise, but to attempt that at this stage would result in 'a wholly unacceptable delay in the formulation of the new Constitution'. The only practicable alternative, therefore, was to have the recently elected provincial legislative assemblies elect the members of the Constituent Assembly. But there were complications in that approach, too. Firstly, the strengths of the provincial assemblies were not in the same proportion to the population of the provinces. Secondly, the strengths of several communities were not in proportion to their population in each province due to the weightage given to minorities by the Communal Award of 1932. The delegation therefore proposed:

that the fairest and most practicable plan would be—

a. to allot to each Province a total number of seats proportional to its population, roughly in the ratio of one to a million, as the nearest substitute for representation by adult suffrage.

b. to divide this provincial allocation of seats between the main communities in each Province in proportion to their population.

c. to provide that the representatives allotted to each community in a Province shall be elected by the members of that community in its Legislative Assembly.[96]

On the basis of these calculations, the whole of British India was to have a maximum number of 292 representatives, and the Indian states were to have a maximum number of ninety-three representatives in the Constituent Assembly.[97]

The representatives thus chosen should meet at New Delhi as soon as possible. The Indian states should, in the preliminary stage, be represented by a negotiating committee. A preliminary meeting would be held at which the general order of business would be decided, a chairman and other officers elected and an advisory committee on the rights of citizens, minorities and tribal and excluded areas set up.[98]

Thereafter, the provincial representatives would split into three sections: A (Madras, Bombay, United Provinces, Bihar, Central Provinces and Orissa, and representatives of the chief commissioners' provinces of Delhi, Ajmer-Merwara and Coorg), B (Punjab, North-West Frontier Province and Sind) and C (Bengal and Assam). These sections would proceed to settle the constitutions for the provinces included in each section, and decide whether any group constitution should be set up for those provinces and, if so, what provincial subjects the group should deal with.[99]

The representatives of the sections and the Indian states would reassemble for the purpose of settling the Union constitution. As soon as the new constitutional arrangements come into operation, it should be open to any province to elect to come out of any group in which it had been placed. Such a decision would be taken by the new legislature of the province after the first general election under the new constitution. The provinces were therefore to proceed with electing their representatives and the states to set up a negotiating committee.

In addition, a treaty would be negotiated between the Union Constituent Assembly and the UK regarding matters related to the transfer of power.

The results of the elections in all the provinces became available by the spring of 1946. The Congress formed governments in Assam, the

North-West Frontier Province, Bihar, UP, Bombay, Central Provinces and Punjab (a coalition government with the Unionist Party and the Akali Sikhs). The Muslim League was able to form ministries in only two of the provinces it claimed for Pakistan—Sind and Bengal. In Sind, the governor invited the Muslim League to form the government despite the Congress-led coalition of nationalist Muslims, a breakaway group of the League and an independent labour member being in a majority of one. In terms of votes, the Muslim League polled about 74 per cent of the Muslim votes in the contested seats.[100]

The Cabinet Mission delegation recommended, while the constitution-making proceeded according to its own schedule, it was important to set up at once an interim government to carry on with the administration of India. In the delegation's view, the only alternative to accepting the plan would be 'a grave danger of violence, chaos and civil war', which would be 'a terrible disaster for many millions of men, women and children'.[101]

Both the Congress and the Muslim League accepted the plan after some initial reservations. While the Congress argued that compulsory grouping of provinces contradicted the principle of provincial autonomy, Jinnah felt that the plan had several lacunas, but the Muslim League, on 6 June, decided to accept it, since it implicitly provided the basis and foundation of Pakistan through the grouping of the six provinces in sections B and C. The party hoped that the plan 'would ultimately result in the establishment of complete sovereign Pakistan' on the basis of 'the opportunity and the right of secession of provinces or groups from the Union which have been provided in the Mission's plan by implication'. On 25 June, the Congress Working Committee decided to participate in the Constituent Assembly elections. The Sikhs rejected the plan on the grounds that it would place them as a minority without adequate safeguards in a Muslim-majority in Punjab.[102]

Wavell's efforts to set up an interim government also failed due to differences between the Congress and the League over the representation of communities. After some back and forth, the viceroy announced on 16 June that the proposed executive council would have fourteen members, of which six would be from the Congress (including one scheduled-caste member), five from the Muslim League and one each from the Sikh, Indian Christian and the Parsi communities. The Congress refused to accept the proposed parity between Hindus and Muslims in the Council and that despite being a non-communal nationalist party it was not allowed to

nominate a Muslim member. It also rejected the plan, which proposed that
no decision could be taken by the council on any major communal issue
if the majority of either community was opposed to it. With the failure of
the negotiations to form an interim government, the cabinet delegation
left India on 29 June. As a result, Wavell set up a caretaker government of
officials on 4 July.[103]

It was thus a curious deadlock, where the Congress and the Muslim
League had accepted the long-term plan of the Cabinet Mission
announced on 16 May, but the Congress had rejected the interim
proposals announced on 16 June. In a meeting with Wavell on 25 June,
Jinnah expressed doubt if the Congress truly accepted the long-term plan
in view of their declared reservations, whereas his party had accepted the
proposal of a Union constitution making 'substantial concessions' on his
previous demand of settling the Pakistan question first.[104] Events reached a
breaking point when Nehru declared at a press conference on 10 July after
an AICC meeting (where leftist leaders Jayaprakash Narayan and Swami
Sahajananda Saraswati demanded a total rejection of the Cabinet Mission
plan) that the only commitment made by the Congress was to participate
in the Constituent Assembly elections. 'The big probability is that . . .
there will be no grouping,' he said, as the NWFP and Assam would have
objections to joining sections B and C. The League responded on 29–30
July by withdrawing its earlier acceptance of the long-term plan and calling
on the 'Muslim nation' for 'Direct Action' to achieve Pakistan and assert
the just rights of the Muslims from 16 August to achieve Pakistan.[105]

The Muslim League's call for direct action resulted in a chain of large-
scale communal massacres, starting with Calcutta from 16 August, followed
by Noakhali in East Bengal and Bihar in October, UP's Garmukteswar in
November and throughout Punjab from March 1947.[106]

The elections to the Constituent Assembly for the British Indian
provinces had been completed by the end of July, with the Congress
winning all but one of the general seats and the Muslim League all but
five. At the same time, the viceroy wrote again on 22 July, on a 'strictly
personal and secret basis', to Nehru and Jinnah, seeking their cooperation
in the formation of the interim government. The offer was again rejected
by both the parties. Although the Congress was opposed to the manner
of forming the interim government by Wavell, it still stood in acceptance
of the long-term offer of 16 May. In contrast, the Muslim League had
rejected both the long-term and interim proposals. Wavell therefore

made an offer to Nehru on 6 August to form the interim government, also giving the latter the choice to discuss with Jinnah the possibility of forming a coalition government. The viceroy's offer was accepted by the Congress Working Committee on 8 August. Although it expressed hope that the Muslim League will join the interim government, the Congress felt that the better course of action would be to approach the League after the viceroy announced the Congress's acceptance of his offer. The viceroy announced on 13 August that he had invited the Congress to form the interim government.[107]

With further negotiations between the Congress, the Muslim League and the viceroy yielding no results, Wavell announced on 24 August the names of the new executive council members, comprising six Congressmen, a Sikh, an Indian Christian, a Parsi and three Muslims (out of the five allotted to the community). The members were Nehru, Patel, Rajendra Prasad, Asaf Ali, C. Rajagopalachari, Sarat Chandra Bose, John Matthai, Baldev Singh, Shafaat Ahmad Khan, Jagjivan Ram, Syed Ali Zaheer and C.H. Bhabha. On 2 September 1946, the interim government, headed by Nehru, was sworn in.[108]

After prolonged negotiations, Wavell succeeded in persuading Jinnah to join the interim government. It was agreed that Jinnah would nominate a scheduled-caste member while allowing the Congress to nominate a nationalist Muslim for the new executive council. It was also made clear to Jinnah by the viceroy that the Muslim League's participation in the interim government was conditional upon reversing the party's earlier rejection of the long-term plan. Thus, the League was allowed to join the interim government without giving up its Direct Action programme, its rejection of the Cabinet Mission long-term plan or its insistence on compulsory grouping with decisions taken by the majority vote by a section as a whole. The five members nominated by the League were Liaquat Ali Khan, I.I. Chundrigar, Abdur Rab Nishtar, Ghazanfar Ali Khan and Jogendra Nath Mandal (the scheduled-caste member). The new members replaced Sarat Chandra Bose, Shafaat Ahmad Khan and Syed Ali Zaheer.[109]

When the viceroy issued invitations to the elected members to attend the Constituent Assembly on 20 November, Jinnah, resenting the move without resolving the objections raised by the Muslim League regarding interpretations of the clauses of the long-term plan, announced that the party would not participate in the Assembly and that it stood by its declaration of direct action. Thus the Constituent Assembly started meeting from 9

December without the participation of the Muslim League. The Congress, in response, demanded at its annual session at Meerut in November that the Muslim League should resign from the interim government if the party wasn't ready to accept the long-term plan. A meeting of Nehru, Baldev Singh, Jinnah and Liaquat Ali Khan with the British government in London, between 2 and 6 December, also failed to break the deadlock.[110] The assembly passed the 'Objectives Resolution', drafted by Nehru on 22 January 1947, which stated the ideal of India as an independent, sovereign republic with autonomous units, adequate minority safeguards, and social, political and economic democracy.

The demand for resignation of the Muslim League members was raised again by the Congress and minority members of the interim government in early February 1947, which was followed by a letter with the same demand from Nehru on 13 February, and a statement from Patel a couple of days later. The Muslim League, however, refused to budge, arguing that the Congress, too, had not accepted the long-term plan in its totality. To get around the stalemate Attlee announced on 20 February 1947 the replacement of Wavell by Louis Mountbatten and set a fixed date for the transfer of power by June 1948, since the 'present state of uncertainty is fraught with danger and cannot be indefinitely prolonged'. In his statement, Attlee threw the challenge that if the Indians failed by June 1948 to make their own constitution through a 'fully representative Assembly', the British government would

> . . . have to consider to whom the power of the Central Government in British India should be handed over, on the due date, whether as a whole to some form of Central Government for British India, or in some areas to the existing Provincial Governments, or in such other way as may seem most reasonable and in the best interests of the Indian people.[111]

Attlee later explained why he set a specific time limit, till June 1948, for the transfer of power. He told Francis Williams:

> I'd come to the conclusion from my own experience of Indians that there was a great deal of happiness for them in asking for everything, and putting down everything that was wrong in India to British rule, and then sitting pretty. I thought that most of them were not really keen on responsibility. They would talk and talk and talk, and as long

as they could put the responsibility on us they would continue to quarrel among themselves. Therefore I concluded the thing to do was to bring them right up against it and make them see they'd got to face the situation themselves. I decided that the only thing to do was to set a time-limit and say: 'Whatever happens, our rule is ending on that date.' It was of course, a somewhat dangerous venture. But one had also to remember that inevitably the machine of administration in India was running down.[112]

The speed of negotiations for the transfer of power entered a new phase with the arrival of Mountbatten. However, at a meeting of the India Committee of the British government, nine days before his arrival on 22 March 1947, Mountbatten came across a document that Gandhi's emissary Sudhir Ghosh had discussed with Cripps on 3 March and had presented to Pethick-Lawrence a week later. The document, believed to have emanated from Patel, contained a plan for the transfer of power to the existing interim government on the basis of dominion status, as it was felt that a constitution acceptable to both Congress and the League would not be ready by June 1948. A Congress Working Committee resolution of 8 March also raised a similar demand.[113]

The CWC demanded that the 'transfer of power, in order to be smooth, should be preceded by the recognition in practice of the Interim Government as a Dominion Government with effective control over the services and administration, and the Viceroy and Governor-General functioning as the constitutional head of the Government'.[114] The demand for complete independence had gone out of the window. Dominion status was no more a taboo.

Attlee issued a set of guidelines to Mountbatten on 18 March about the objectives of the British government and about the approach he was to take regarding the transfer of power. Among other things, the directive specified that the key objective was 'to obtain a unitary Government for British India and the Indian States, if possible within the British Commonwealth, through the medium of a Constituent Assembly, set up and run in accordance with the Cabinet Mission's plan', and that Mountbatten should do the utmost 'in your power to persuade all Parties to work together to this end'. Mountbatten should, Attlee suggested, 'impress upon the Indian leaders the great importance of avoiding any breach in the continuity of the Indian Army', and 'the need for continued collaboration in the security of the Indian Ocean area for which provision might be made in an agreement between the two countries'.[115]

Mountbatten, increasingly convinced that it was impossible to reach an agreed solution, drew up an alternative plan in consultation with his advisers. This plan envisaged transfer of power to the provinces or groups of provinces and proposed that both Bengal and Punjab should be partitioned if the representatives of the Muslim-majority and the non-Muslim-majority areas of these two provinces, meeting separately, decide upon it.[116]

When Nehru met Mountbatten on 8 April 1947, he conveyed that the provinces and partitioned provinces 'should have the right to decide whether to join a Hindustan Group, a Pakistan Group or possibly even remain completely independent', with the proviso that the whole plan 'revolved around having a strong Centre'. Mountbatten developed his plan based on this input from Nehru and called it 'Plan Balkan', cautioning a meeting of the provincial governors on 15–16 April that it could be 'helping towards the "Balkanisation" of India and going against everything that Congress stood for'.[117] On 28 April, Rajendra Prasad cautioned the Constituent Assembly about the possibility of a division, not only of India but also of some provinces. Earlier, Patel too had assured V.P. Menon, the reforms commissioner, that if power was transferred immediately on the basis of Dominion Status, Patel would use his influence to ensure its acceptance by the Congress.[118]

Mountbatten also used Jinnah's agreement for retaining Pakistan within the Commonwealth to influence the Indian leaders. He impressed upon Defence Minister Baldev Singh that if India left the Commonwealth, the consequent withdrawal of British officers would deprive the armed services of effective leadership. Singh, incidentally, was himself keen that India remained within the Commonwealth and retained British officers as advisers for as long as possible. Nehru, however, wasn't too bothered by the argument. Contrary to Singh's logic, he argued that severance of the Commonwealth connection would rather strengthen India's security, as alone she faced no threat from any major power. Nehru wrote to Singh bluntly, 'Under no conceivable circumstances is India going to remain in the British Commonwealth whatever the consequences.' The prospect of the departure of all the British officers didn't bother him. On the other end of the spectrum were C. Rajagopalachari and Brigadier K.M. Cariappa, who believed that the Indianization of the armed forces should be spread out over five years. Mountbatten brought in the Orissa governor, Chandulal Trivedi, to try and convince Nehru and Patel.[119]

Mountbatten's most valuable conversion was that of Krishna Menon, Nehru's confidant who claimed to have drafted the phrase 'independent sovereign republic' in the Objectives Resolution of the Constituent Assembly. Menon now suggested that 'if the British were voluntarily to give us now Dominion Status, well ahead of June 1948, we should be so grateful that not a voice would be heard in June 1948 suggesting any change, except possibly to the word dominion if that had been actually used up to that date'.[120]

According to V.P. Menon, the reforms commissioner, the continuous deterioration in the country worried Mountbatten that if there were delays in the transfer of power, in some parts of the country there might not be any authority to hand over power to.[121] To discuss his plans further, Mountbatten, along with Eric Miéville and V.P. Menon, reached Simla on 6 May. Nehru and Krishna Menon joined them at the viceregal lodge two days later. In the meantime, Jinnah rejected the idea of partitioning Bengal and Punjab in a statement issued on 30 April, and reiterated his demand for a Muslim state comprising the six provinces of the NWFP, Punjab, Bengal, Assam, Sind and Baluchistan.

In its meeting on 1, 2 and 4 May, the CWC also accepted the principle of Partition based on self-determination. Gandhi, however, remained opposed to Partition, and in his meeting with Mountbatten on 4 May he appealed for an immediate transfer of power to either a Congress or a League government on a dominion-status basis, with Mountbatten remaining as governor–general until June 1948. Following another round of CWC meeting on 7 May, Gandhi, Nehru and Patel separately issued statements demanding an interim government on a dominion-status basis for all of India. The interim government would preside over the eventual secession of those areas that rejected the constitution formulated by the existing Constituent Assembly, and during the interim period the minorities would enjoy special judicial safeguards.[122]

Amending his plan on the basis of consultation with his advisers and discussions with the Indian leaders, Mountbatten sent it to London on 2 May for consideration by the British cabinet. After receiving the further amended and approved plan from the cabinet on 10 May, Mountbatten announced that he would meet Nehru, Jinnah, Liaquat Ali Khan and Baldev Singh in Delhi on 17 May to discuss the plan with them. However,

Mountbatten showed the plan approved by the cabinet to Nehru on the night of 10 May itself. Nehru immediately turned it down, arguing that such a plan—which he, too, believed would lead to the balkanization of India—would not be accepted by the Congress under any circumstances. In view of Nehru's vehement opposition, Mountbatten asked V.P. Menon to present a plan which had been developed by the latter earlier in the year and shared with Patel and the secretary of state. Menon's plan envisaged transfer of power to two central governments on the basis of dominion status. On seeing a draft of the alternative plan, Nehru told Mountbatten that it wouldn't be unacceptable to the Congress. Patel, too, informed Menon that there would be no difficulty in the Congress accepting dominion status. The meeting with the leaders proposed for 17 May, in the meantime, was postponed to 2 June.[123]

The new plan for the transfer of power to only two successor dominions, without giving the choice to the provinces for standing out independently, was sent to London for consideration by the India Committee on 14 May, which subsequently summoned Mountbatten to London. His meetings with the Committee between 19 and 28 May sealed the deal. While Attlee secured the support of the Opposition leaders, Mountbatten insisted that power must be transferred not later than the early autumn of 1947. It was also decided that power should be transferred to a Pakistan dominion, which might secede at once if it wished, and that the princes must be told that their relations with the Crown will have to be through one or the other governors-general of the dominions.

On 2 June Mountbatten presented the final plan to seven prominent leaders in India—Nehru, Patel, J.B. Kripalani, Jinnah, Liaquat Ali Khan, Abdur Rab Nishtar and Baldev Singh, assuring them of the immediate transfer of power, for which necessary legislation would be undertaken by the British parliament in its current session. While the Congress and the Sikhs agreed to accept the plan through their written responses, Jinnah only agreed verbally. Mountbatten broadcast the developments on All India Radio on the evening of 3 June, and Attlee made his announcement on the same day in the House of Commons.

2

Framing the Constitution

The Cabinet Mission's statement of 16 May 1946 had provided the broad procedural guidelines for the Constitution-making body. Each of the eleven British Indian provinces, divided into three sections, as well as the Indian states were allocated specific number of seats in the Constituent Assembly, calculated roughly on the basis of one member per million population. Seats were distributed among the three main communities—Muslims, Sikhs and General (all communities other than Muslims and Sikhs) in each province on the basis of their proportion to total the provincial population. The members representing the provinces in the Constituent Assembly were to be elected by the provincial legislative assemblies, but the method of selection of the states' representatives was left to further consultation. Until the method was finalized, the states were to be represented by a negotiating committee. The number of seats allotted to the provinces and the Indian states were 292 and ninety-three, respectively.

The process of Constitution-making was to begin with a meeting of the representatives in New Delhi, where they would elect a chairperson and other officers, and appoint an advisory committee on the rights of citizens, minorities and tribal and excluded areas. In the next phase, they would regroup in the three sections to settle the constitutions for the provinces in each section and decide whether any group constitution needed to be set up. After settling the question of constitutions for the provinces and groups, the members of the Constituent Assembly from the British Indian provinces and the Indian states were to meet and frame the Union constitution.[1]

While the Muslim League accepted the Cabinet Mission plan on 6 June, the Congress Working Committee (CWC) announced its acceptance of only the long-term plan involving the Constituent Assembly on 25 June, immediately issuing instructions to the Congress premiers in the provinces to start the process of selecting suitable candidates. The CWC also decided to nominate about fifty candidates from outside the party fold and those who were not members of state legislatures.[2] The CWC's decision was ratified by the All India Congress Committee (AICC), which met on 6 and 7 July. To prepare material and draft proposals for the Constituent Assembly, the CWC appointed a sub-committee under Nehru, the other members being Asaf Ali, K.M. Munshi, N. Gopalaswami Ayyangar, K.T. Shah, K. Santanam, Humayun Kabir and D.R. Gadgil. The key objectives of the committee (which functioned from July 1946 to December 1948) were to suggest rules of procedure for the assembly and prepare general directives in the form of resolutions on a wide range of topics to be discussed by the assembly.[3]

Announcing the elections to be held in July, Viceroy Archibald Wavell appointed B.N. Rau as the constitutional adviser to oversee the setting up of the Constituent Assembly.[4] The Pratinidhi Panthic Board announced on 9 July that the Sikhs would boycott the Constituent Assembly, but the decision was reversed in response to an appeal by Jawaharlal Nehru.[5] However, in another reversal, the Sikh candidates withdrew their nominations within the next few days.[6] The leftist parties such as the Congress Socialist Party also decided not to participate in the assembly.[7]

The results of the elections to the Constituent Assembly were available by the end of July 1946. Out of the 216 general seats, the Congress won in 207, with the remaining seats going to independent candidates such as B.R. Ambedkar, Jwala Prasad Srivastava, Padampat Singhania and Kameshwar Singh, the maharajadhiraj of Darbhanga, and Somnath Lahiri, the sole Communist elected from Bengal. The Muslim League won seventy-three seats, losing out five seats to the Congress candidates such as Maulana Abul Kalam Azad, Khan Abdul Ghaffar Khan, the Krishak Praja Party leader Fazlul Huq and a Unionist candidate from Punjab.[8] Due to their boycott, there was no Sikh representative in the Constituent Assembly.

The Congress had given space to eminent jurists, lawyers and constitutional experts such as Tej Bahadur Sapru, Alladi Krishnaswami Ayyar and M.R. Jayakar, but its overwhelming majority ensured that there was no effective opposition to the line taken by the organization. Some members (such as Shibban Lal Saxena) accused that the Constitution reflected the Congress's point of view disproportionately.[9] The Muslim

League described the Constituent Assembly as 'a packed committee of individuals chosen by the Congress', which had destroyed all fundamentals of the Cabinet Mission's statement. The League denounced further meetings of the Constituent Assembly as 'void, invalid and illegal'.[10]

Although the original plan of the Cabinet Mission was to convene the Constituent Assembly at the earliest, the rejection of the Mission's 16 May plan by the Muslim League on 27 July over Congress's interpretation of the grouping provision for the provinces in the assembly led to continued postponement. On 27 August, Wavell told Nehru and Gandhi that he could not convene the Constituent Assembly unless this point of contention was settled.[11] Nehru wrote to Wavell on 8 September that 'it is obvious that the Assembly cannot wait indefinitely because some of its members are not prepared to participate in it'.[12] When Jinnah continued to refuse to retract the party's rejection of the Cabinet Mission plan even after joining the interim government, by convening a meeting of the council of the All India Muslim League, Wavell felt the same way as Nehru. He told Nehru on 19 November that he was ready to issue invitations to the elected members to convene the Constituent Assembly if Nehru advised him to do so. According to Nehru's assessment, if the assembly was postponed any further, the earliest that it could meet was in April 1947, by which time, he feared, everybody would have lost interest in it. He therefore advised Wavell to issue the invitations immediately. The invitations were sent out the next day for the first meeting of the Constituent Assembly to be held on 9 December.[13]

Gandhi, however, held a completely different point of view and told Wavell that if the Muslim League did not join, 'it would be of no use for the Constituent Assembly to meet, and it would be quite honourable for the British Government' to drop the idea altogether.[14]

Even before the assembly met, substantial background work was being carried on. Apart from the sub-committee formed by the CWC, B.N. Rau prepared a number of leaflets and pamphlets, which Nehru found so useful that he wanted them to be printed as a book and circulated among the members of the assembly.[15] Rau continued to provide background material on a variety of constitutional questions facing the assembly.[16]

As the Assembly formally began its business at 11 a.m. in the presence of 207 members, Congress president Kripalani spoke briefly in Hindustani before introducing the seventy-five-year-old temporary chairman Sachchidananda Sinha, who was the oldest member of the

Assembly. After reading messages of good wishes from Australia, China and the United States, Sinha delivered a short inaugural address in which he dealt briefly with the precedents provided by Europe's oldest republic, Switzerland, and by France on the making of constitutions. He laid most stress on the Constitutional Convention that took place in Philadelphia in 1787, when Americans, 'having thrown off their allegiance to the British King in Parliament met and drew up what has been regarded, and justly so, as the soundest and most practical and workable republican constitution in existence'. Commending the United States Constitution, Sinha said, 'It may possibly be that in some such scheme, skilfully adapted to our requirements, a satisfactory solution may be found for a Constitution for an independent India which may satisfy reasonable expectations and legitimate aspirations of almost all leading political parties in the country.'[17][18]

Sinha ended his inaugural speech by remembering the poet Iqbal and the Bible:

Let us not forget to justify the pride of the great Indian poet, Iqbal, and his faith in the immortality of the destiny of our great, historic, and ancient country, when he summed up in these beautiful lines:

Yunan-o-Misr-o-Roma sab mit gaye jahan se,
Baqi abhi talak hai nam-o-nishan hamara.
Kuch bat hai ke hasti mit-ti nahin hamari,
Sadion raha hai dushman daur-e-zaman hamara.

It means: 'Greece, Egypt, and Rome, have all disappeared from the surface of the Earth; but the name and fame of India, our country, has survived the ravages of Time and the cataclysms of ages. Surely, surely, there is an eternal element in us which had frustrated all attempts at our obliteration, in spite of the fact that the heavens themselves had rolled and revolved for centuries, and centuries, in a spirit of hostility and enmity towards us.' I particularly ask of you to bring to your task a broad and catholic vision, for as the Bible justly teaches us—'Where there is no vision the people perish.'

Frank Anthony, leader of the Anglo-Indian community was nominated the deputy chairman.

On 11 December, Rajendra Prasad was elected the chairman, amid cries of 'Inquilab Zindabad' (Long Live Revolution), 'Jai Hind' (Victory to India) and 'Rajendra Babu Zindabad'. The office was later designated as president of the Assembly. Mindful of the absence of the Muslim League members in the Assembly, Prasad mentioned in his speech:

> Our brethren of the Muslim League are not with us and their absence increases our responsibility. We shall have to think at each step what would they have done if they were here? We have to proceed keeping all these things in view. We hope they will soon come and take their places and share in the deliberations for framing a constitution for their country . . . But if unfortunately these seats continue to remain unoccupied, it will be our duty to frame a constitution which will leave no room for complaint from anybody.[19]

On 13 December, while moving the Objectives Resolution, Nehru observed, 'It [the Constituent Assembly] has come into being under particular conditions and the British Government has a hand in its birth. They have attached to it certain conditions.' The resolution was similar to 'a plan for the structure that one wishes to erect'. 'It defines our aims, describes an outline of the plan and points the way which we are going to tread.' Nehru laid out the plan:

(1) This Constituent Assembly declares its firm and solemn resolve to proclaim India as an Independent Sovereign Republic and to draw up for her future governance a Constitution;

(2) WHEREIN the territories that now comprise British India, the territories that now form the Indian States, and such other parts of India as are outside British India and the States as well as such other territories as are willing to be constituted into the Independent Sovereign India, shall be a Union of them all; and

(3) WHEREIN the said territories, whether with their present boundaries or with such others as may be determined by the Constituent Assembly and thereafter according to the Law of the Constitution, shall possess and retain the status of autonomous Units, together with residuary powers, and exercise all powers and functions of government and administration, save and except such

powers and functions as are vested in or assigned to the Union, or as
are inherent or implied in the Union or resulting therefrom; and

(4) WHEREIN all power and authority of the Sovereign Independent
India, its constituent parts and organs of government, are derived
from the people; and

(5) WHEREIN shall be guaranteed and secured to all the people of
India justice, social, economic and political; equality of status, of
opportunity, and before the law; freedom of thought, expression,
belief, faith, worship, vocation, association and action, subject to law
and public morality; and

(6) WHEREIN adequate safeguards shall be provided for minorities,
backward and tribal areas, and depressed and other backward classes;
and

(7) WHEREBY shall be maintained the integrity of the territory of the
Republic and its sovereign rights on land, sea, and air according to
Justice and the law of civilised nations; and

(8) this ancient land attains its rightful and honoured place in the world
and make its full and willing contribution to the promotion of world
peace and the welfare of mankind.[20]

Nehru argued that although the resolution did not mention the word
'democratic', the use of the word 'republic' implied it and went beyond in
including the 'content of economic democracy'. He stood for socialism,
Nehru announced, and hoped that India would adopt a socialist constitution
but refrained from using the term so as not to make the resolution
controversial. 'Therefore, we have laid down, not theoretical words and
formulae, but rather the content of the thing we desire,' he explained. As
far as the Indian states were concerned,

... I do not wish, and I imagine this Constituent Assembly will not like, to
impose anything on the States against their will. If the people of a particular
State desire to have a certain form of administration, even though it might
be monarchical, it is open to them to have it. There is no incongruity
or impossibility about a certain definite form of administration in the
States, provided there is complete freedom and responsible Government
there and the people really are in charge. If monarchical figure-heads are
approved by the people of the State, of a particular State, whether I like it
or not, I certainly will not like to interfere.

The Resolution, seconded by Purushottam Das Tandon, was debated till 19 December. M.R. Jayakar contested the moving of the resolution on the grounds that it was against the Cabinet Mission plan of 16 May, which had stipulated that the purpose of the preliminary meeting of the Constituent Assembly was limited to deciding the general order of business, election of the chairperson and other officials, and appointment of an advisory committee. He argued that such a resolution that laid down fundamental principles of the future constitution could be taken up only after settling the provincial constitutions, especially when the Muslim League and the representatives of the Indian states had not joined the Assembly yet. The debate went on for four days in view of the strong support from the members to continue the consideration of the resolution, when the president of the Assembly had to put it on hold in order to take up other more immediate business. He hoped that the Muslim League would join by the time the debate was resumed in the next session, to be held in January 1947. The resolution was adopted at the next session, which took place from 20–25 January 1947, after two more days of debate, when it was decided to not wait any longer for the League to join the assembly.

For the remaining days of this short second session, the Assembly focused on election of the vice-president, the Steering Committee, to oversee the regular functioning of the Assembly and coordinate its activities, and the Business Committee, to guide the Assembly by recommending the manner in which to proceed for framing the Constitution. In its January session, the Assembly, apart from setting up these administrative committees, also set up two more committees to deal with the content of the Constitution. The first one was the formation of an Advisory Committee on the rights of citizens, minorities and tribal and excluded areas, as stipulated by the Cabinet Mission statement of 16 May 1946. In order to deal with the issues with all the diligence they deserved, the assembly made provision for a sub-committee each to prepare schemes for the administration of the north-western tribal areas, the north-eastern tribal areas, and the territories marked as excluded and partially excluded areas under the Government of India Act, 1935. The Advisory Committee was asked to submit its final report within three months.[21] The excluded and partially excluded areas were the tribal areas where federal or provincial laws were not applicable and were administered directly by the governor.

The assembly also decided to appoint another committee to examine the scope of the subjects assigned to the Union (defence, communications and foreign affairs, and powers necessary to raise the finances required for these subjects) by the Cabinet Mission statement and list interconnected subjects, so that there were no overlaps or conflicts with the provincial constitutions. This committee, which came to be known as the Union Subjects Committee, was asked to submit its report by 15 April 1947.[22]

The third session of the Constituent Assembly was another short one that sat for five days from 28 April to 2 May. The British government's statement of 20 February, announcing the transfer of power by June 1948, imparted a sense of urgency to the work of the assembly. Rajendra Prasad envisaged that the constitution could be made ready in its final form by October 1947. The idea was to be ready with the Constitution before the transfer of power took place.[23] Unfortunately, it would take over two years to finalize the Constitution.

One of the most significant developments of this session was the participation of the representatives from the Indian states of Baroda, Bikaner, Cochin, Jaipur, Jodhpur, Patiala and Rewa. More states continued to join the assembly subsequently.[24] On 28 April, Nehru presented the report of the committee, which was appointed to confer with the States Negotiating Committee on the two key points of distribution of the ninety-three seats among the Indian states and the method of selecting their representatives. While the two committees arrived at an agreement on the distribution of the seats, it was also agreed that at least 50 per cent of the total representatives of states were to be elected by the elected members of legislatures or, where such legislatures did not exist, of other electoral colleges.[25]

On the same day, N. Gopalaswami Ayyangar presented an interim report of the Committee on Union Subjects, but it was not taken up for discussion during this session, as the committee wanted the members of the assembly to fully study the report before debating on its findings. Moreover, it was felt that it would be better to take it up when the house had more representation from the Indian states and the elected members of Muslim League joined in (which was still a possibility).[26] An interim report of the Order of Business Committee, which was presented in the assembly on 30 April, recommended setting up two more committees: a committee for drawing up the principles of the Union Constitution and another for drawing up a model constitution for the provinces.[27]

The preliminary report on fundamental rights was presented in the Assembly on 29 April by Vallabhbhai Patel on behalf of the Advisory

Committee. Introducing the report, Patel explained that the committee divided the fundamental rights into two categories—justiciable and non-justiciable. While the justiciable rights were enforceable by appropriate legal process, the other category consisted of 'directive principles of social policy which, though not enforceable in Courts, are nevertheless to be regarded as fundamental in the governance of the country'. The preliminary report introduced in the assembly contained only the justiciable rights, which were incorporated after rigorous consideration by the Fundamental Rights Sub-Committee, the Minorities Rights Sub-Committee and the Advisory Committee. The key justiciable rights included in the report, which generated a spirited debate spread over three days, were the rights of equality, rights of freedom, rights relating to religion, cultural and educational rights, rights to constitutional remedies and other miscellaneous rights.[28]

The Constituent Assembly as well as the Constitution-making process underwent significant changes with the announcement of the 3 June plan, which decided on the partition of India. The Indian Independence Act stipulated that the Constituent Assembly would double up as the new Central Legislative Assembly. Bengal and Punjab, the two provinces which were partitioned, were required to elect new members to the assembly, as the sitting members lost their seats as a result of Partition. When the fourth session of the assembly commenced on 14 July 1947, thirty-seven new representatives from the Indian states, twenty-three (out of twenty-eight) members of the Muslim League from the Indian Union who had so far abstained from attending the assembly, and the new members from Punjab and Bengal joined in. B.R. Ambedkar, who, as a representative from Bengal, lost his seat, was re-elected from Bombay. Somnath Lahiri, the sole communist member of the assembly, wasn't re-elected.[29]

Rajendra Prasad was still hopeful that the Constitution could be given the final shape by October. The Order of Business Committee, too, made the same recommendation.

While presenting another report of the Order of Business Committee, K.M. Munshi clarified that 'the fetters that were imposed upon this Constituent Assembly by the plan of May 16 have fallen'. With the passage of the Indian Independence Act there would be 'no sections and groups to go into . . . nor more provinces with residuary powers, no opting out, no revision after ten years and no longer only four categories of powers for the Centre'.

While the Constituent Assembly was in recess, the Provincial Constitution Committee and the Union Constitution Committee had drafted their reports to be placed in the Assembly, along with the revised report of the Union Powers Committee, which had to re-examine the subjects allocated to the Union government in view of the changed circumstances. These reports, after being discussed and adopted by the assembly, would be sent to a Drafting Committee to frame the necessary provisions of the Constitution of India. In contrast, the reports of the sub-committees under the Advisory Committee, which was expected to complete their work by August, might go straight to the Drafting Committee. They would be presented in the assembly only after the Drafting Committee drew up the relevant provisions for the Constitution. However, based on objections from a large number of members, the assembly decided that the principles related to the minorities should be discussed within the assembly before being sent to the Drafting Committee.[30]

Out of the fourteen days that the Constituent Assembly met for its fourth session (14–31 July), the discussion on the interim report of the Provincial Constitution Committee carried on for six days, and seven days were taken up by the discussion on the interim report of the Union Constitution Committee. Introducing the report on the provincial constitution on 15 July, Patel informed the assembly that because of differences in opinion among the members of the committee regarding the type of constitution, a joint meeting between the Provincial and the Union Constitution Committees decided that 'it would suit the conditions of this country better to adopt the parliamentary system of constitution, the British type of constitution with which we are familiar'.

The draft report on the provincial constitution dealt with the election, qualification, terms of office and powers of the governors in the provinces, council of ministers, the advocate general of a province, and the provincial legislature, judiciary and public service commission.[31]

The main and supplementary reports on the principles of the Union Constitution, which also incorporated the report of an ad hoc committee on the Supreme Court, was introduced by Nehru on 21 July 1947. The report of the committee was organized into a preamble and eleven parts covering federal territory and jurisdiction (Part I); citizenship (Part II); fundamental rights, including directive principles of state policy (Part III); the federal executive, the federal parliament, legislative powers of the president, the federal judicature, auditor general, services and elections

(Part IV); distribution of legislative powers between the federation and the units (Part V); administrative relations between the federation and the units (Part VI); finance and borrowing powers (Part VII); directly administered areas (Part VIII); miscellaneous provisions (Part IX); amendment of the constitution (Part X); and transitional provisions (Part XI).[32]

The fifth session of the Constituent Assembly convened on 14 August and sat for eleven days till 30 August. With India becoming independent on 15 August 1947, the Constituent Assembly became a sovereign body and also doubled as the legislature for the new state. It was responsible for framing the Constitution as well as making ordinary laws. While Governor-General Mountbatten, in his address to the Assembly, rued the absence of Gandhi, whom he referred to as 'the architect of India's freedom', the members shouted slogans like 'Mahatma Gandhi ki jai', 'Pandit Jawaharlal Nehru ki jai' and 'Lord Mountbatten ki jai'.[33]

The August session of the Constituent Assembly devoted a significant amount of time to discuss two reports: the second report of the Union Powers Committee and the report of the Advisory Committee on Minorities. Introducing the report of the Union Powers Committee in the assembly on 20 August 1947, N. Gopalaswami Ayyangar explained that the previous report which was presented in the assembly in April had been prepared keeping in view the limitations drawn by the Cabinet Mission plan and hence wasn't relevant any more. The current report under the changed circumstances attempted to establish a Federal Constitution, and one of the principal features was that 'it must provide for a method of dividing sovereign powers so that the Government at the Centre and the Governments in the Units are each within a defined sphere, co-ordinate and independent'. The committee attempted 'to bring into a Federation areas which were under British sovereignty before the 15th of August, as also areas which were in theory independent but which were under the suzerainty of the British Crown'. The challenge was 'to bring about a harmonious coordination of governmental activities in these two sets of areas'. The report prepared three lists enumerating subjects under the jurisdiction of the Central government, subjects to be dealt with by the provinces and concurrent subjects which were to be administered jointly. While in the case of the provinces any matter not covered under these three lists (residuary subjects) would be deemed to remain with the Centre, in the case of the Indian states all subjects not mentioned in the federal list remained with the states unless they voluntarily ceded those subjects to the Centre. After the transfer of power, the states which signed the instrument of accession to join the Indian Union ceded about eighteen to twenty subjects to the Union, in contrast to the three subjects stipulated by the Cabinet Mission in its 16 May plan.[34]

The report of the Advisory Committee on Minority Rights, Patel explained while introducing it in the assembly, was 'the result of a general consensus of opinion between the minorities themselves and the majority'. What made the task more challenging was that there were 'minorities within minorities' with 'conflicting interests among them'.[35] Patel also presented a Supplementary Report on Fundamental Rights, which included some of the rights that had not been covered in the first report, and the directive principles, 'which, though not cognizable by any court of law, should be regarded as fundamental in the governance of the country'.[36]

It was during this session that the Constituent Assembly appointed a committee 'to scrutinise and to suggest necessary amendment to the draft Constitution of India prepared in the Office of the Assembly on the basis of the decisions taken in the Assembly'.[37] B.N. Rau, the constitutional adviser, prepared an initial draft on the basis of the reports of the committees and his own research into the constitutions of other countries.

In its sixth session, the Constituent Assembly convened for a single day on 27 January 1948 to modify the number of representatives from West Bengal (increased from nineteen to twenty-one) and East Punjab (number of general and Sikh representatives increased by two each), and to amend the Constituent Assembly Rules.

The Constituent Assembly came together after a long gap of nearly ten months on 4 November 1948 and remained in session till 8 January 1949, sitting for thirty-six days. The assembly started considering the draft constitution prepared by the Drafting Committee from this session, an exercise that continued through the eighth session (16 May to 16 June 1949; twenty-four sittings), the ninth session (30 July to 18 September 1949; thirty-eight sittings), the tenth session (6–17 October 1949; ten sittings) and the eleventh session (14–26 November 1949; twelve sittings). Thus, the Constituent Assembly debated the draft constitution until its adoption for 115 days out of the total 167 days that it was in session.

The Drafting Committee was appointed by the Constituent Assembly on 29 August 1947 and began scrutinizing the draft prepared by B.N. Rau, the constitutional adviser, towards the end of October 1947. It made various changes Based on suggestions received not only from members of the

Assembly but also from various public bodies and provincial governments, and submitted the draft constitution to the president of the Assembly on 21 February 1948.[38]

Placing the draft formally in the Assembly for its article-wise consideration by the members, Ambedkar noted:

> The Draft Constitution as it has emerged from the Drafting Committee is a formidable document. It contains 315 Articles and 8 Schedules. It must be admitted that the Constitution of no country could be found to be so bulky as the Draft Constitution. It would be difficult for those who have not been through it to realize its salient and special features.[39]

He explained that the draft had proposed a parliamentary form of government, whereby the ministers would be members of the parliament and directly responsible to it, unlike the presidential system in the US, where the president and his secretaries are not members of the US Congress:

> The American Executive is a non-Parliamentary Executive which means that it is not dependent for its existence upon a majority in the Congress, while the British system is a Parliamentary Executive which means that it is dependent upon a majority in Parliament . . . Looking at it from the point of view of responsibility, a non-Parliamentary Executive being independent of Parliament tends to be less responsible to the Legislature, while a Parliamentary Executive being more dependent upon a majority in Parliament become more responsible . . . The Draft Constitution in recommending the Parliamentary system of Executive has preferred more responsibility to more stability.[40]

The draft constitution was also a combination of the two main types seen around the world—unitary as well as federal. 'This Dual Polity under the proposed Constitution will consist of the Union at the Centre and the States at the periphery each endowed with sovereign powers to be exercised in the field assigned to them respectively by the Constitution,' Ambedkar explained.[41]

Initially, the Constituent Assembly was not in favour of a strong central government. The Union Powers Committee of the Assembly, headed by Nehru, had, in its first report, provided for a very weak central government.

But once the plan was announced, on 3 June, the Constituent Assembly considered itself free of the restraints imposed by the Cabinet Mission Plan of 1946 and moved quickly in the direction of a federation with a strong Centre.

Ambedkar, while introducing the draft constitution, explained why the term 'Union of States' was preferred over 'Federation of States:

> The Drafting Committee wanted to make it clear that though India was to be a federation, the federation was not the result of an agreement by the States to join in a federation and that the federation not being the result of an agreement, no state has the right to secede from it. The federation is a Union because it is indestructible. Though the country and the people may be divided into different States for convenience of administration, the country is one integral whole, its people a single people living under a single imperium derived from a single source.

Thereafter, he addressed the criticisms levelled at the proposed Constitution:

> It is said that there is nothing new in the Draft Constitution, that about half of it has been copied from the Government of India Act of 1935 and that the rest of it has been borrowed from the Constitutions of other countries. Very little of it can claim originality.
>
> One likes to ask whether there can be anything new in a Constitution framed at this hour in the history of the world. More than hundred years have rolled over when the first written Constitution was drafted . . . Given these facts, all Constitutions in their main provisions must look similar. The only new things, if there can be any, in a Constitution framed so late in the day are the variations made to remove the faults and to accommodate it to the needs of the country. The charge of producing a blind copy of the Constitutions of other countries is based, I am sure, on an inadequate study of the Constitution. I have shown what is new in the Draft Constitution and I am sure that those who have studied other Constitutions and who are prepared to consider the matter dispassionately will agree that the Drafting Committee in performing its duty has not been guilty of such blind and slavish imitation as it is represented to be.
>
> As to the accusation that the Draft Constitution has produced a good part of the provisions of the Government of India Act, 1935, I make no apologies. There is nothing to be ashamed of in borrowing. It involves

no plagiarism. Nobody holds any patent rights in the fundamental ideas of a Constitution. What I am sorry about is that the provisions taken from the Government of India Act, 1935, relate mostly to the details of administration.[42]

The Preamble, which enunciates basic philosophy of the Constitution, was taken up for debate towards the very end of the tenure of the Assembly, on 17 October 1949, and adopted on the same day. The Preamble was claimed to have been based on the Objectives Resolution adopted on 22 January 1947.

It states that the people of India in the Constituent Assembly made a solemn resolve to secure to all citizens 'Justice, social, economic and political; Liberty of thought, expression, belief, faith and worship; Equality of status and of opportunity; and to promote among them all, Fraternity assuring the dignity of the individual and the unity of the nation.'

The first objection to the Preamble drafted by Ambedkar came from Maulana Hasrat Mohani, who moved two amendments. Mohani argued that the draft had deviated from the Objective Resolution in describing India as a 'Sovereign Democratic Republic', which should be substituted either by 'Sovereign Federal Republic' or 'Sovereign Independent Republic' or 'Union of Indian Socialistic Republics to be called UISR on the lines of USSR'. The amendments failed to garner support in the Assembly and were defeated.[43] Ambedkar had himself explained, in the Draft Constitution submitted to the president of the Constituent Assembly in February 1948, that the Drafting Committee 'adopted the phrase Sovereign Democratic Republic, because independence is usually implied in the word "Sovereign", so that there is hardly anything to be gained by adding the word "Independent"'.[44]

Hari Vishnu Kamath wanted to preface the Preamble with 'In the name of God' and suggested that instead of the gender-neutral 'its', 'her' should be used to refer to India the country, being considered the motherland. But Pandit H.N. Kunzru objected to this:

I recognise the sincerity of Mr. Kamath and of those who agree with him, but I do not see why in a matter that vitally concerns every man individually, the collective view should be forced on anybody. Such a course of action is inconsistent with the Preamble which promises liberty of thought, expression, belief, faith and worship to everyone.

While Ambedkar suggested that the amendment be withdrawn, Kamath insisted on a vote and a division on the question. The amendment lost, with forty-one voting in favour and sixty-eight against.[45]

Shibban Lal Saxena went a step further, asking to preface the Preamble with, 'In the name of God the Almighty, under whose inspiration and guidance, the Father of our Nation, Mahatma Gandhi, led the Nation from slavery into Freedom, by unique adherence to the eternal principles of Satya and Ahimsa and who sustained the millions of our countrymen and the martyrs of the Nation in their heroic and unremitting struggle to regain the Complete Independence of our Motherland.' However, on J.B. Kripalani's suggestion, he withdrew the motion.[46]

When Brajeshwar Prasad proposed that India be described as 'a cooperative commonwealth to socialist order and to secure all its citizens an adequate means of livelihood, free and compulsory education, free medical aid and compulsory military training', P.S. Deshmukh quipped, 'What about a camel and motorcycle?'[47]

In an earlier debate on 15 November 1948, K.T. Shah had moved that the words 'secular', 'federal' and 'socialist' be inserted, so that the clause read, 'India shall be a Secular, Federal, Socialist Union of States.' As far as the word 'secular' was concerned, Shah argued, 'We have been told time and again from every platform, that ours is a secular State. If that is true, if that holds good, I do not see why the term could not be added or inserted in the constitution itself, once again, to guard against any possibility of misunderstanding or misapprehension.' Calling the amendment 'purely superfluous', Ambedkar protested:

> What should be the policy of the State, how the Society should be organised in its social and economic sides are matters which must be decided by the people themselves according to time and circumstances. It cannot be laid down in the Constitution itself, because that is destroying democracy altogether.[48]

The motion lost.

While introducing the draft constitution, Ambedkar also elucidated the idea behind the Directive Principles:

> If it is said that the Directive Principles have no legal force behind them, I am prepared to admit it. But I am not prepared to admit that they have

no sort of binding force at all. Nor am I prepared to concede that they are useless because they have no binding force in law.

The Directive Principles are like the Instrument of Instructions which were issued to the Governor-General and to the Governors of the Colonies and to those of India by the British Government under the 1935 Act. Under the Draft Constitution it is proposed to issue such instruments to the President and to the Governors. The texts of these Instruments of instructions will be found in Schedule IV of the Constitution. What are called Directive Principles is merely another name for Instrument of Instructions. The only difference is that they are instructions to the Legislature and the Executive. Such a thing is to my mind to be welcomed. Wherever there is a grant of power in general terms for peace, order and good government, it is necessary that it should be accompanied by instructions regulating its exercise.[49]

Later, during the debate on the Constitution, when Kamath suggested that the word 'Directive' be substituted with 'Fundamental', Ambedkar stood up to explain the necessity of retaining the former:

. . . it is to be understood that in enacting this part of the constitution the Constituent Assembly, as I said, is giving certain directions to the future legislature and the future executive to show in what manner they are to exercise the legislative and the executive power which they will have . . . It is the intention of this Assembly that in future both the legislature and the executive should not merely pay lip service to these principles enacted in this part, but that they should be made the basis of all executive and legislative action that may be taken hereafter in the matter of the governance of the country.[50]

K.T. Shah argued in favour of inserting the word 'socialist':

I am fully aware that it would not be quite a correct description of the State today in India to call it a Socialist Union. I am afraid it is anything but Socialist so far. But I do not see any reason why we should not insert here an aspiration, which I trust many in this House share with me, that if not today, soon hereafter, the character and composition of the State will change, change so radically, so satisfactorily and effectively that the country would become a truly Socialist Union of States.[51]

The proposal found support from Kamath, who suggested the inclusion of these two terms in the Preamble, but was opposed by Ambedkar:

> If you state in the Constitution that the social organisation of the State shall take a particular form, you are, in my judgment, taking away the liberty of the people to decide what should be the social organisation in which they wish to live. It is perfectly possible today, for the majority people to hold that the socialist organisation of society is better than the capitalist organisation of society. But it would be perfectly possible for thinking people to devise some other form of social organisation which might be better than the socialist organisation of today or of tomorrow. I do not see therefore why the Constitution should tie down the people to live in a particular form and not leave it to the people themselves to decide it for themselves.[52]

Pointing to the Directive Principles, Ambedkar wondered, 'If these directive principles to which I have drawn attention are not socialistic in their direction and in their content, I fail to understand what more socialism can be.'

The inclusion of universal adult suffrage generated strong differences of opinion. The matter, however, was put to rest by Rajendra Prasad. Defending the measure, he said:

> Some people have doubted the wisdom of adult franchise. Personally, although I look upon it as an experiment the result of which no one will be able to forecast today, I am not dismayed by it. I am a man of the village and although I have had to live in cities for a pretty long time, on account of my work, my roots are still there. I, therefore, know the village people who will constitute the bulk of this vast electorate. In my opinion, our people possess intelligence and common sense. They also have a culture which the sophisticated people of today may not appreciate, but which is solid. They are not literate and do not possess the mechanical skill of reading and writing. But, I have no doubt in my mind that they are able to take measure of their own interest and also of the interests of the country at large if things are explained to them. In fact, in some respects, I consider them to be even more intelligent than many a worker in a factory, who loses his individuality and becomes more or less a part of the machine which he has to work.[53]

Ambedkar further elucidated the relation between the Centre and the states as a number of criticisms had been hurled at the draft constitution, claiming that the powers of the states had been reduced. Answering the criticism that the Centre had been given the power to override the states, Ambedkar clarified that although the 'charge must be admitted', 'these overriding powers do not form the normal feature of the Constitution. Their use and operation are expressly confined to emergencies only.'

Ambedkar told the Assembly:

> As to the relation between the Centre and the States, it is necessary to bear in mind the fundamental principle on which it rests. The basic principle of Federalism is that the Legislative and Executive authority is partitioned between the Centre and the States not by any law to be made by the Centre but by the Constitution itself. This is what Constitution does. The States under our Constitution are in no way dependent upon the Centre for their legislative or executive authority. The Centre and the States are co-equal in this matter. It is difficult to see how such a Constitution can be called centralism. It may be that the Constitution assigns to the Centre too large field for the operation of its legislative and executive authority than is to be found in any other Federal Constitution. It may be that the residuary powers are given to the Centre and not to the States. But these features do not form the essence of federalism. The chief mark of federalism as I said lies in the partition of the legislative and executive authority between the Centre and the Units by the Constitution. This is the principle embodied in our Constitution. There can be no mistake about it. It is, therefore, wrong to say that the States have been placed under the Centre. Centre cannot by its own will alter the boundary of that partition. Nor can the judiciary.[54]

On 25 November 1949, closing the debate on the adoption of the Constitution, Ambedkar made some incisive comments defending the work done by the Drafting Committee and the Constituent Assembly, and putting the onus of working the Constitution on the people of the country:

> I feel, however good a Constitution may be, it is sure to turn out bad because those who are called to work it, happen to be a bad lot. However bad a Constitution may be, it may turn out to be good if those who are called to work it, happen to be a good lot. The working of a Constitution

does not depend wholly upon the nature of the Constitution. The Constitution can provide only the organs of State such as the Legislature, the executive and the Judiciary. The factors on which the working of those organs of the State depend are the people and the political parties they will set up as their instruments to carry out their wishes and their politics. Who can say how the people of India and their parties will behave? Will they uphold constitutional methods of achieving their purposes or will they prefer revolutionary methods of achieving them?[55]

He had argued equally strongly while introducing the Draft Constitution in November 1948:

No Constitution is perfect and the Drafting Committee itself is suggesting certain amendments to improve the Draft Constitution. But the debates in the Provincial Assemblies give me courage to say that the Constitution as settled by the Drafting Committee is good enough to make in this country a start with. I feel that it is workable, it is flexible and it is strong enough to hold the country together both in peace time and in war time. Indeed, if I may say so, if things go wrong under the new Constitution, the reason will not be that we had a bad Constitution. What we will have to say is, that Man was vile.[56]

Rajendra Prasad referred to widespread public interest regarding the framing of the Constitution in his closing statement. He pointed out, '53,000 visitors were admitted to the visitors' gallery during the period when the Constitution has been under consideration.'[57]

The Constitution of India was finally adopted on 26 November 1949 and came into force on 26 January 1950.

3

Unification of India

The complex problem of the relation between the Indian states and the British Indian government assumed a new dimension with the Cabinet Mission's plan for the transfer of power.

An Indian state as distinct from a British Indian province was defined by the Government of India Act of 1935 as 'any territory, whether described as a State, an Estate, a Jagir or otherwise belonging to or under the suzerainty of a Ruler who is under the suzerainty of His Majesty and not being a part of British India'. The states came in a bewildering variety of area, population, economy, political institutions and the status of the ruler. At times, there were differences in estimating the number of such states. While the Indian States Committee (also known as the Harcourt Butler Committee), set up in 1927 to study the relationship of the Indian states with the British Crown and the British Indian government, estimated the number of states to be 562, according to the Joint Committee on Indian Constitutional Reforms the states numbered 600. Prior to Partition, the states accounted for 45 per cent of total Indian territory and 24 per cent of total Indian population (according to the 1941 census).[1]

Out of the fifteen states with an area of 10,000 square miles each, the largest ones were Kashmir (84,471 square miles) and Hyderabad (82,313 square miles). Sixty-seven states had an area of between 1000 and 10,000 square miles each, and 202 states were smaller than 10 square miles. Only sixteen states had a population of over a million.[2] Only nineteen states had an annual revenue of over Rs 1 crore, and the revenue in seven states was between Rs 50 lakh and Rs 1 crore.[3]

Every phase of constitutional reforms threw up the question of the status of the states under the new structure. The Butler Committee, formed in the face of the Congress's demand for dominion status for India, stated that the states would not be handed over to the Indian dominion, if formed, without their consent.[4]

In terms of institutions, the representative body of the states was the Chamber of Princes, which performed only advisory and consultative role, and was established by a Royal Proclamation on 8 February 1921. On the other hand, the All-India States People's Conference, which represented the political aspirations of the people in the states, came together to hold the first annual conference in December 1927. Although the Congress demanded fully responsible government and guarantee of civil liberty in the states, it only extended moral support and sympathy to the popular movements in the princely states and did not take part in them as an organization. In the annual session of 1938 at Haripura, the Congress passed a resolution stating that the 'burden of carrying on the struggle for freedom must fall on the people of the States', in order to 'produce self-reliance in them' without relying on 'extraneous help and assistance or on the prestige of the Congress name'.[5] Subhas Bose, the Congress president, however, held a different view. In his presidential address at the Haripura session Bose said, 'There is nothing to prevent individual Congressmen from actively espousing the cause of the states' subjects and participating in their struggle. There are people in the Congress like myself who would like to see the Congress participating more actively in the movement of the states' subjects.'[6] The Congress changed its stand in the next annual session at Tripuri, where it decided that in view of the 'great awakening that is taking place among the people of the States', it might remove the self-imposed restriction, 'thus resulting in the ever increasing identification of the Congress with the States People'.[7] Speaking at the annual session of the States People's Conference in Ludhiana in February 1939, Jawaharlal Nehru expressed his views on the treaties between the states and the British Crown by saying, 'We recognise no such treaties and we shall in no event accept them.' On the future of the states in an independent India, his views were categorical:

A new theory of the independence of the States has been advanced in recent years . . . There is no independence in the States, and there is going to be none, for it is hardly possible geographically and it is entirely opposed to the conception of a united free India. It is conceivable and desirable in the case of the larger States for them to have a great deal of autonomy within the framework of an Indian Federation. But they will have to remain integral parts of India and the major matters of common concern must be controlled by a democratic Federal Centre. Internally, they will have Responsible Government.[8]

The issue relating to treaties referred to by Nehru got addressed by the Cabinet Mission when it declared that with the transfer of power 'the relationship which has hitherto existed between the Rulers of the States and the British Crown will no longer be possible'. The strange position was that 'Paramountcy can neither be retained by the British Crown nor transferred to the new Government'. The Cabinet Mission pointed out that the new Union of India's power over foreign affairs, defence, and the communications and raising of finances required for these subjects would extend to the states just as to the British Indian provinces. The subsequent status of the states 'must be a matter of negotiation during the building up of the new constitutional structure'. To that end, it stipulated the states being represented by a Negotiating Committee during the preliminary stage of the Constituent Assembly and by ninety-three members in the final stages to frame the Union Constitution.[9] Welcoming the Cabinet Mission plan, the Nawab of Bhopal, who was the chancellor of the Chamber of Princes, announced on 10 June 1946 its decision to form the Negotiating Committee.[10] A committee appointed by the Constituent Assembly held a series of meetings with the States Negotiating Committee early February 1947 onwards, and representatives of some of the states started participating in the Constituent Assembly proceedings from April 1947.

In the meantime, Nehru sent out a clear message to the states in his speech at the All-India States People's Conference on 18 April 1947, when he said that any Indian state which did not come into the Constituent Assembly then would be treated as a hostile state by the country, and such a state would have to bear the consequences.[11]

The viceroy's statement of 3 June 1947, announcing the partition of India and transfer of power in August 1947, left the position of the states unchanged from what was stated in the Cabinet Mission plan. Answering questions from the rulers and other representatives of the states, whom he had met immediately before announcing the 3 June statement, Mountbatten clarified that joining the Constituent Assembly was a matter of free choice for the states, but until it was known what shape the two dominions of India and Pakistan would take, it was not possible to envisage the possible status of the states that decided not to join the assembly. However, Mountbatten explained, the first step for these states who wouldn't join the Constituent Assembly should be to enter into negotiations for administrative arrangements with either of the dominions, or both if necessary.[12]

After announcing the statement of the Cabinet Mission in a press conference on 16 May 1946, Stafford Cripps had explained, with reference to the Indian states, that they 'will therefore become wholly independent, but they have expressed their wish to negotiate their way into the Union and that is a matter we leave to negotiations between the States and the British Indian Parties'.[13] Soon after the announcement of the 3 June 1947 statement, the Nawab of Bhopal who had taken up a discouraging view on the states joining the Constituent Assembly, wrote to Mountbatten that Bhopal would be assuming an independent status as soon as paramountcy lapsed. The intention to declare themselves as independent sovereign states was also announced on 11 and 12 June, by Travancore and Hyderabad, respectively.[14]

In June 1947, the CWC passed a resolution, which was ratified by the All India Congress Committee (AICC), repudiating the right of any princely state to declare itself independent. Vallabhbhai Patel pointed out that the alternative to this was 'partition or complete Balkanisation and anarchy'.[15] The *Daily Telegraph* wondered a month before Independence, 'Will partition lead to fragmentation?'[16]

The issue of declaration of independence by the states and the handling of their relation with the new Union government came up at a meeting held on 13 June between Mountbatten, Nehru, Patel, Kripalani, Baldev Singh, Jinnah, Liaquat Ali Khan, Abdur Rab Nishtar, Hastings Ismay, E. Miéville, Conrad Corfield (the political adviser to the states) and Erskine Crum. While Nehru argued that the Cabinet Mission's memorandum did not allow any state to claim independence, both Jinnah and Corfield expressed the opposite view. Nehru insisted that if a state chose not to join either the Indian or Pakistani Constituent Assembly, it would have to come to some other arrangement, which could not be preceded by a declaration of independence. He argued that there were many rights and obligations apart from paramountcy, and with the lapse of paramountcy all the other matters which the British Crown representative and the political department in the states had to deal with should pass on to the Government of India. It was agreed that a new department, called the States Department, would be set up to deal with matters of common concern between the states and the Government of India.[17] Jinnah continued to publicly encourage his line of thought by declaring on 18 June 1947 that 'the States would be independent sovereign States on the termination of paramountcy' and were 'free to remain independent if they so desired'.[18]

The proposal for setting up the States Department was approved by the interim cabinet on 25 June 1947. Patel was nominated by Nehru to take charge as the minister for Congress, whereas Jinnah nominated Abdur Rab Nishtar as Patel's counterpart representing the Muslim League. Patel asked V.P. Menon, the viceroy's reforms commissioner, to join the department as its secretary. Mountbatten recorded his views in his personal report of 27 June: 'I am glad to say that Nehru has not been put in charge of the new States Department, which would have wrecked everything. Patel, who is essentially a realist and very sensible, is going to take over . . .'[19] According to Menon, it was he who brought up to Patel the idea of accession of the Indian states to the Indian Union by ceding only the three subjects mentioned in the Cabinet Mission plan—defence, foreign affairs and communications. Menon claimed that both Patel and Nehru were agreeable to the plan, albeit a little sceptical, and that they readily accepted his proposition to involve Mountbatten actively to secure the acceptance of the states. Mountbatten was only too happy to take up the role.[20] Jinnah came out in opposition to the policy of accession and announced that he would guarantee the independence of the states in Pakistan.[21]

Mountbatten told H.V. Hodson, constitutional adviser to the viceroy during 1941–42, who was given complete access to Mountbatten's papers and interviewed him extensively, that Patel told him not to bother about the states the first time Mountbatten discussed the states problem with him. Patel believed that after transfer of power, the states people would join the Congress movement and depose the rulers. Cautioning him that this would lead to a civil war, Mountbatten argued for a peaceful settlement by allowing the rulers to retain their titles and personal property in exchange for joining the dominion of India. After some reflection, Patel told him, 'I am prepared to accept your offer provided that you give me a full basket of apples.' Replying that it was not possible, Mountbatten asked, 'If I give you a basket with 560 apples [instead of 565 apples or states] will you buy it?' 'Well, I might,' replied Patel.[22]

On taking charge of the new department, Patel issued a conciliatory statement to the states on 5 July, asking them to join the Constituent Assembly:

The States have already accepted the basic principle that for defence, foreign affairs and communications they would come into the Indian Union. We ask of them no more than accession on these three subjects in which the common interests of the country are involved. In other matters we would scrupulously respect their autonomous existence . . .

. . . There appears a great deal of misunderstanding about the attitude of the Congress towards the States. I should like to make it clear that it is not the desire of the Congress to interfere in any manner whatever with the domestic affairs of the States. They are no enemies of the Princely order, but, on the other hand, wish them and their people under their aegis all prosperity, contentment and happiness. Nor would it be my policy to conduct the relations of the new department with the States in any manner which savours of the domination, of one over the other; if there would be any domination, it would be that of our mutual interests and welfare.[23]

Following this statement, Patel met with rulers and ministers of some of the leading states (Patiala, Gwalior, Baroda, Bikaner, Nawanagar) on 10 and 24 July.

Mountbatten had assured Nehru that he would assist with the integration of the Indian states to the dominions. Soon, he had a standard Instrument of Accession drafted to be put before the princes, to enable them to accede and hand over control of three subjects to the Indian government—those of foreign affairs, defence and communications. Mountbatten launched 'Operation Princes' on 25 July 1947, at a conference of the rulers and other representatives of the states.[24]

The Crown representative Mountbatten addressed the conference. Beginning by recounting his experience on conducting negotiations relating to the states, Mountbatten explained the implications of the present scenario and the future possibilities. Since the Indian Independence Act released the states from all their obligations, legally and technically they were independent. However, if the system of coordinated administration on all matters of common concern that had developed over the years of British rule was broken without a suitable replacement, it would result in a chaos that would hurt the states first. Reminding the representatives of their universal acceptance of the Cabinet Mission plan, Mountbatten tried to demonstrate how it would be beyond their capability to deal with the issues of defence, foreign affairs and communications. Presenting the draft Instrument of Accession as the basis for further discussion, he explained in no uncertain terms that accession to the appropriate dominion was on the basis of the three subjects only and absolutely without any financial liability. The instrument also made it clear, he pointed out, that the Central government would have no authority to encroach upon the internal autonomy or the sovereignty of the states. Mountbatten then announced the formation of a Negotiating Committee, comprising ten rulers and twelve ministers, split into two sub-committees, to consider the Instrument of Accession; and a stopgap measure called Standstill Agreement, which specified that all agreements and administrative arrangements regarding matters of common concern then existing between the states and the Crown would continue until new arrangements were made.[25] The *Amrita Bazar Patrika* reported that after Mountbatten's address, 'political circles here believe that the accession of all the States to the Union is practically certain'.[26]

Mountbatten kept up his outreach programme by hosting receptions and luncheons for the rulers and ministers. While Mountbatten and Patel were striving to have the states sign the Instrument of Accession, the Muslim League too was trying to rope in some of the states, especially those along the border, by offering big concessions. Menon was also informed that Corfield of the Political Department was instigating the nawab of Bhopal to create a 'Third Force' by trying to dissuade states from acceding to India.[27]

Towards the end of July, the announcement by Travancore that it was going to join the Indian Union, taking a U-turn from its previous position, came as much as a shot in the arm as a surprise. One newspaper editorial wondered if Patel's statement of 5 July, which was described by Mountbatten as 'most statesmanlike', had failed to convince the Maharaja: 'What is it then that did the trick?' It speculated that the most likely reason was Mountbatten's speech to the conference of the princes.[28] According to Menon's insider account, however, the trigger for this change was the series of meetings that both Menon and Mountbatten had with the dewan of Travancore, C.P. Ramaswami Iyer, which helped to dispel his misgivings about accession.[29] Travancore's decision undoubtedly influenced many of the other states that were yet to make up their mind.

K.M. Panikkar, dewan of Bikaner, wrote to Patel in the last week of July or early August, in an undated letter, that according to reliable sources 'the young Maharaja of Jodhpur has fallen a prey to [nawab of] Bhopal's intrigues and is likely to back out of the Instrument of Accession'. Panikkar informed Patel that Jinnah had offered the Maharaja full port facilities in Karachi, unrestricted import of arms, jurisdiction over the Jodhpur–Sindh railway and supply of gram from Sindh. A vital piece of information that Panikkar passed on to Patel was that the ruler of Jodhpur was scheduled to arrive in Delhi on 11 August and must be dealt with immediately.[30] The maharaja was picked up from Delhi's Imperial Hotel by V.P. Menon and taken to meet Mountbatten at the Government House. It was only after a gruelling session of explanation by both Mountbatten and Menon that the Maharaja signed the Instrument of Accession. By his persuasiveness, Mountbatten also succeeded in changing the attitudes of the nawab of Bhopal and maharaja of Indore, who signed the instrument by the first week of August. By 15 August 1947, the day of the transfer of power, all the states geographically contiguous to India had signed the Instrument of Accession, except Hyderabad, Junagadh and two small states in Kathiawar and Kashmir.[31] The tension in the air was palpable. The *Manchester Guardian* reported in mid-August that 'several princes have recently purchased enormous quantities of war material for possible use in emergencies later'.[32]

The accession of all these states, in contrast to the negotiated settlements with the other states that acceded, had to be accomplished with the involvement of armed forces. After protracted negotiations and intervention by armed forces, the regional commissioner took charge of the administration of Junagadh on 9 November 1947. The takeover of Junagadh was followed by a referendum on 20 February 1948 to ascertain the views of the people in the state. Referendums were also held at the same time in the smaller states of Mangrol and Manavadar, as well as in Babariawad, Bantwa and Sardargarh. The results at all the places were overwhelmingly in favour of accession to India.

In order to ensure an amicable settlement with Hyderabad, Patel made an exception in the case of Hyderabad by allowing the state to sign the Standstill Agreement first (in November 1947) without signing the Instrument of Accession. The Indian leaders were hopeful that Hyderabad would sign the Instrument of Accession before the expiry of the agreement, which was valid for one year. But events turned out quite to the contrary as the nizam's government began violating the terms of the agreement and showed no intention of acceding into India, resulting in a communal, political, diplomatic and ultimately a military conflict. The nizam finally signed the Instrument of Accession after India launched a military operation, named Operation Polo, as a result of which Major–General J.N. Chaudhuri took charge as the military governor on 18 September 1948. The administration headed by Maj. Gen. Chaudhuri continued till December 1949, when a civilian administration, with M.K. Vellodi as chief minister, took charge.

The state of Jammu and Kashmir, whose ruler, Maharaja Hari Singh, vacillated on the question of whether to remain independent or accede to one of the dominions, signed the Instrument of Accession on 26 October 1947, after being rendered helpless to defend his state, which was invaded by frontier tribesmen aided by the Pakistani military.

~

The accession of the states ensured the integrity of the country, but at the same time it created a new set of problems. Internal disturbances erupted in many of the states, or in some cases in Unions, where a number of small and medium states had joined together (for instance, the Eastern States Union formed by some states in Orissa and Chhattisgarh). Popular movements within the states demanding responsible government were also gaining strength, and the interlacing of the states within the territories of the provinces created administrative difficulties. The varied area, population and economic viability of the states compounded the problems. Situations like these clearly brought to the fore the fact that most of the states did not have the capability to deal with the adverse situations. It compelled the states ministry to intervene and take measures to integrate the states into the neighbouring provinces or to create unions of states.

The first instance of the Central government's intervention took place when the twenty-six states in Orissa agreed to be merged with the province of Orissa in December 1947. A simple form of 'merger agreement' was prepared, whereby the ruler in question ceded to the Government of the Dominion of India 'full and exclusive authority, jurisdiction and powers for and in relation to the governance' of his state. Though brief, the clauses of this agreement were framed to obviate any possibility of future dispute. The ruler gave up his authority on behalf not only of himself but also of his heirs and agreed that any controversy over what constituted private as distinct from state property should be settled by a judicial officer of the Government of India.[33]

In return, the rulers of the states were given tax-free allowances (named privy purses) for their maintenance, which were to be continued with their successors too, 'enjoyment of all private properties', and all personal privileges, dignities and titles enjoyed by them, whether within or outside their state. The agreement further guaranteed the succession according to law and custom. The quantum of the privy purses was determined on the basis of annual revenue of each state for 1945–46. The rulers were to get 15 per cent on the first lakh of their annual revenue, 10 per cent on the next Rs 4 lakh, and 7.5 per cent on all revenues above Rs 5 lakh, subject to a maximum allowance of Rs 10 lakh. This formula came to be known as the Eastern States Formula. The Government of India delegated to the Government of Orissa, under the Extra Provincial Jurisdiction Act, 1947, the power to administer the Orissa states in the same manner as the districts of the province. The only state that remained outside the process of merger—Mayurbhanj—agreed to be merged with Orissa, which was accomplished on 1 January 1949. The next round of merger to take place was with the states in Chhattisgarh, which was completed on 16 December.[34]

Table 1 provides a summary of the mergers of some states with the provinces as well integration of states into a larger union to make them administratively and economically viable.

Table 1: Rearrangements of Princely States in Independent India

Date	Region/State	Intervention
December 1947	Orissa	Merged with Orissa
December 1947	Central Provinces (Chhattisgarh states)	Merged with Central Provinces
February 1948	Bombay (Kathiawar states)	Integrated into United State of Kathiawar, later renamed Saurashtra
March 1948	Bombay (Deccan states)	Merged with Bombay
March 1948	Rajasthan (Alwar, Bharatpur, Dholpur and Karauli)	Integrated into Matsya Union (a union of states)
March 1948	Rajasthan (Banswara, Bundi, Dungarpur, Kotah, etc.)	Integrated into the Rajasthan Union (a union of states); Udaipur added to the union in April 1948

Date	Region/State	Intervention
April 1948	Central Provinces (Bundelkhand and Baghelkhand (Rewa) states)	Integrated into Vindhya Pradesh (a union of states, which was changed to a Centrally Administered Area in January 1950)
April 1948	Punjab Hill States	Integrated into a Centrally Administered Area (Chief Commissioner's Province); renamed as Himachal Pradesh
May 1948	Central India (Gwalior, Indore, Malwa states)	Integrated into Madhya Bharat (a union of states)
June 1948	Bombay (Gujarat states)	Merged with Bombay
June 1948	Kutch	Taken over as a Centrally Administered Area (Chief Commissioner's Province)
July 1948	East Punjab (Patiala, Nabha, Jind, Faridkot, Kapurthala, Malerkotla)	Integrated into the Patiala and the East Punjab States Union (PEPSU)
August 1948	Bilaspur	Taken over as a Centrally Administered Area (Chief Commissioner's Province); merged with Himachal Pradesh in 1954
October 1948	Manipur	Taken over as a Centrally Administered Area (Chief Commissioner's Province)
January 1949	Orissa (Mayurbhanj)	Merged with Orissa
January 1949	Bombay (Junagadh, Manavadar, Mangrol, Bantwa, Babariawad and Sardargarh)	Merged with United State of Kathiawar
January 1949	Rajasthan (Sirohi)	Merged with Bombay; in March, all of Sirohi except Abu Road and Dilawara tehsils merged with Rajasthan
March 1949	Bombay (Kolhapur)	Merged with Bombay
March 1949	Rajasthan (Rajasthan Union, Jaipur, Jodhpur, Bikaner and Jaisalmer)	Integrated into Greater Rajasthan Union (a union of states)

Date	Region/State	Intervention
May 1949	Baroda	Merged with Bombay
May 1949	Rajasthan	Matsya Union merged with Rajasthan Union
June 1949	Mysore	New Instrument of Accession handing over power to central legislature to legislate on all federal and concurrent subjects
June 1949	Bhopal	Taken over as a Centrally Administered Area (Chief Commissioner's Province);
July 1949	Travancore and Cochin	Integrated into Travancore-Cochin (a union of states)
October 1949	Tripura	Taken over as a Centrally Administered Area (Chief Commissioner's Province)

4

The Partition and the Refugees

In the story of India's partition and transfer of power, what appears inexplicable is why no one could foresee the gigantic magnitude of human tragedy in the form of communal holocaust and mass exodus. By the time the Mountbatten Plan of 3 June 1947 was announced, the fire of communal riots had been raging for nearly a year, although subdued and brought under control in many parts of the country. Yet, tragically, the early signs of plan's impact on population movement were either misread or ignored by those in power.

'The Hindus are, I think, resigned, a little hurt that the Congress has done so little for them,' the governor of Sind Francis Mudie wrote to Mountbatten four days after the plan for partition was announced. There was 'some movement of bank balances' to India, a fall in the value of real estate in the Hindu areas and some 'vague talk' about migration to India, but Mudie didn't think any of those to merit serious consideration. 'Some Gujeratis [sic], Kachhis and other Sindhis may retire to their original homes, but I don't expect many real Sindhis to leave the Province,' he concluded.[1] Towards the end of July, the situation in Sind had aggravated. A bulletin by the Congress party in the Sind Legislative Assembly claimed instances of forcible occupation of land and seizure of standing crops belonging to the minority communities. The bulletin also reported forcible expulsion of non-Muslims from their agricultural lands.[2] 'All ills and troubles of the Hindus of Sind are due to the huge wealth and the landed property they possess,' was the analysis of Congress president Kripalani when he arrived at Karachi in early August.[3]

Another letter to Mountbatten, written on the same day by Evan Jenkins, the governor of Punjab, painted a picture of hope. The 'Congress and Moslem [sic] League both claim that plan is master-stroke of their respective leaders and that all will be well in the end,' Jenkins wrote. However, his letter also sounded a warning note: the Sikhs were not ready to accept any 'western boundary short of Chenab'.[4]

In his radio broadcast of 3 June, Mountbatten indicated that although the partition of India would proceed on the basis of a provisional boundary drawn between Muslim-majority and non-Muslim-majority areas in Punjab, Bengal and parts of Assam, the final boundaries would be decided upon by a Boundary Commission. He particularly highlighted the problem of the Sikh population which was distributed across Punjab in a manner that any partition would inevitably divide them. In his response to the plan, Baldev Singh, the Sikh representative in the discussions on transfer of power and the defence minister in the interim government, pointed out that the Boundary Commission should take into account factors such as exchange of population with property and the religious and cultural institutions of the Sikhs. He asked Mountbatten to ensure 'that as large a percentage of Sikh population as possible is included in the Eastern Punjab'.[5] The necessity for a transfer of population and property of the Sikhs in Punjab was also expressed by V.P. Menon, the reforms commissioner, at the viceroy's staff meeting on 9 June.[6]

The United Provinces was seeing a different phenomenon. The assessment of the province's situation by its governor, Francis Wylie, was that the Muslim League leaders 'have been pretending to show their teeth' in their campaign for Partition under Jinnah's orders. The aim was to demonstrate that nothing short of a 'national home' for the Muslims would be acceptable. However, in Wylie's view, since 'Pakistan is of little use to the U.P.', the League members 'feel that they can drop out of the fight and look after their own local and more personal interests'.[7]

Mountbatten himself brought up the issue of population transfer in Punjab in a meeting with Nehru and Patel on 10 June. He was concerned that 'an enormous transfer of population would be required to build up even one district into a Sikh majority area', since the community accounted for only 13 per cent of Punjab's population. He suggested empowering the Boundary Commission to recommend such transfer of population. Nehru wasn't pleased. While he opposed any population transfer, Patel was unwilling to believe Jinnah's assurance to the Sikhs guaranteeing freedom of access to their religious places if they fell in Pakistan.[8]

The Akali Dal leader and member of the Punjab Legislative Assembly, Kartar Singh was one of the earliest to highlight the forced migration of the Sikhs. Already over a lakh people had migrated to Eastern Punjab as a result of the riots in Lahore, Amritsar, Rawalpindi, Multan and Jalandhar in March 1947, he wrote to Mountbatten. No one knew, he claimed, how much of the Sikh population would remain in West Punjab by the time the Boundary Commission announced its recommendations.[9]

By mid-June, Jenkins's report on Punjab was looking similar to that on Sind. The value of land was falling and stories about 'flight of capital' from Lahore were floating around. The announcement of the 3 June plan had not improved the communal situation. The average British official, Jenkins reported, believed that the new governments would not be fit to serve under. There was already a rush to move among the Indian officials—the Muslim officials 'parcelling out the more lucrative Pakistan appointments among themselves', and the non-Muslims hoping to be accommodated in India. As disturbances in Lahore and Amritsar continued, the 'old administrative machine is rapidly falling to pieces'.[10]

Nehru, too, noticed the refugee influx from Western Punjab during his late-June trip to Haridwar accompanied by Gandhi. On 22 June he wrote to Mountbatten that there were, 'till yesterday, about 32,000 refugees there from the Frontier Province and the Punjab', and that about 200 refugees were coming in daily. He suggested 'an organised and scientific approach to their problem', by appointing a relief officer with a few assistants to collect information on the refugees and report how to deal with their problems. At the same time, however, he also struck a philosophical note. 'Human beings have an amazing capacity to endure misfortune. They can bear calamity after calamity.'[11]

When he met Mountbatten a couple of days later, Nehru recommended immediate declaration of martial law in Lahore, Amritsar and any other riot-stricken areas. He suggested that 'the troops should be empowered to be utterly ruthless and to shoot at sight'. Jinnah, too, had a similar recommendation. 'I don't care whether you shoot Moslems or not, it has got to be stopped,' he told Mountbatten.[12] The 'expert advice' that Mountbatten received, however, was that martial law wouldn't be effective because the pattern of violence had undergone a change. Instead of large-scale open violence, Lahore and Amritsar were facing 'cloak and dagger activities' which were 'organised and carried into effect by a small body of well-trained men'. The only effective remedy in such a situation, according to Mountbatten, was direct contact with the people by political leaders, supported strongly by the respective party high commands.[13]

The two Boundary Commissions for Bengal and Punjab were announced on 30 June.

Meeting Mountbatten on 30 June, Kartar Singh repeated his earlier demand for transfer of population. The Sikhs wouldn't be satisfied, he said, unless at least 80 per cent of their population were brought into East Punjab by demarcating the boundary line appropriately. He demanded that Nankana Sahib, the birthplace of Guru Nanak, and the adjoining Hindu- and Sikh-majority areas in Lyallpur, Sheikhupura and Gujranwala districts, and a 'just share of the colony areas', should be included in East Punjab. Going a step ahead, he suggested separating the Hindi-speaking areas from non-Hindi-speaking areas in East Punjab.[14]

'The refugee problem has now assumed great proportions,' Mountbatten noted in the viceroy's personal report of the first week of July. The situation was particularly bad in Delhi, where over 70,000 refugees had taken shelter, with large numbers also having moved to the United Provinces and some neighbouring areas. The home department had started considering the appointment of a special officer with appropriate staff to provide relief in the form of food, clothing, medical facilities and sanitation in the refugee camps.[15]

By mid-July Jenkins was anticipating more trouble. After meeting Kartar Singh, he informed Mountbatten that the Sikhs meant 'to make trouble' if the decision of the Boundary Commission, which, headed by Cyril Radcliffe, had started its work. Yet, Jenkins believed that the claims of the Sikhs were not wholly unreasonable. Kartar Singh's 'idea that the Montgomery district should be allotted to the East is by no means as ridiculous as it sounds', he wrote. Concentrating the non-Muslims there and transferring Muslims to Lyallpur was not a bad proposition:

> . . . But with the Sikhs demanding the Chenab as the Western boundary and the Muslims hoping to stretch their tentacles as far east as Ambala, and everyone behaving as though they had just been at war and were going to have a new war within a few weeks, I see little hope of any solution . . .[16]

Jenkins' next encounter with another group of Sikh leaders should have been enough to take away whatever optimism he might have nurtured at that time. Repeating the demand for population exchange, Jathedar Mohan Singh and Sardar Harnam Singh of the Shiromani Gurudwara

Prabandhak Committee (SGPC) warned Jenkins of a violent retaliation towards the Muslims in East Punjab and subsequently inviting Sikhs from West Punjab to occupy the vacated properties. They claimed that the Muslims 'had already got rid of Sikhs in the Rawalpindi Division' and the evacuee land and property could be made available to the Muslims who would migrate from East Punjab. According to Jenkins, they disclosed a plan 'to act in a big way immediately after the transfer of power'.[17] Jenkins also shared with George Abell, the viceroy's private secretary, that the Hindus and the Sikhs were insistent on setting up the new provincial government in Lahore, as they believed that 'to move from Lahore would prejudice their claim to the city'. Abell requested Mountbatten to seek Nehru's or Patel's intervention to convince the Congress and the Sikhs to give up their claim on Lahore.[18]

It was clear to everyone that the future developments depended completely upon the final findings of the Boundary Commission. The Partition Council and the committees which were reporting to it on the administrative aspects of Partition had commenced their work on the basis of the provisional or 'notional' boundary. Uncertainty regarding the differences between the notional boundary and the actual boundary recommended by the commission created considerable confusion among the people of the two provinces which were being partitioned. Mountbatten therefore asked Radcliffe to present his reports before 15 August.

Anticipating further disturbances after the transfer of power, the commander-in-chief Claude Auchinleck proposed deployment of troops— largely Indian but with a number of British officers in command—in the neighbourhood of the boundaries between the two dominions. Mountbatten clarified that in the event of trouble, the full weight of the forces 'would be brought to bear for its suppression'. On 23 July the two governments announced the establishment of a special military command from 1 August, covering twelve districts of East and West Punjab. The Partition Council, however, did not expect 'very serious trouble in Bengal with the possible exception of the city of Calcutta'.[19] Organizations such as the Bengal Peace and Protection Committee, however, were explicit in expressing nervousness and insecurity of the Bengali Hindus and other non-Muslims living as minorities in East Bengal, the assurances of the Muslim League notwithstanding.[20]

Thus, the overarching focus of the government and the political parties remained on preventing riots during and after the transfer of power. The fear of the minorities as a trigger for starting a mass exodus was visible, and a large number of refugees had already started pouring in. Yet, the response of the government and the political leaders rarely measured up to the extent of the challenge. As a result, when the uncontrollable flood of refugees started rushing in, almost everyone was surprised. There were, of course, voices that urged the minorities to not panic. To the Hindus and Sikhs in West Pakistan, for instance, Gandhi appealed to 'rely on God's help' and 'avoid harbouring undue and unnecessary suspicion and fears against the Muslim League'.[21] A group of top Congress leaders of Bengal, including Arun Chandra Guha, Bhupati Majumdar, Bhupendra Kumar Dutta, Labanyaprava Dutta, Bina Das, Nalini Ranjan Sarkar, etc., urged Bengali Hindus in north and east Bengal to 'definitely abandon the idea of exodus'.[22] Jinnah himself announced on 12 July that minorities in Pakistan would not be discriminated against and would receive protection with regard to their religion, faith, life, property and culture, as long as they were loyal to the state.[23] Syama Prasad Mookerjee, in contrast, while appealing against mass exodus, argued that if Hindus in East Bengal did not wish to adopt Pakistani nationality, it was the duty of the West Bengal government to arrange for their transfer.[24] As the exodus from East Bengal started, he also issued a stern message for the Hindus of West Bengal. 'Ready response to East Bengal Hindus in times of need is the moral responsibility of West Bengal Hindus and any shirking of it would be an act of treachery,' Mookerjee said.[25] On hearing that Hindus were leaving East Bengal, a saddened A.K. Fazlul Huq, former premier of Bengal, declared in Barisal, 'I shall not hesitate to sacrifice my life for defending those whom I have always regarded as my brothers and sisters.'[26] Having expressed the hope that the two dominions were likely to reunite before long, Kripalani advised the minority communities in Pakistan 'to be loyal citizens of their State as we expect minority citizens in India to be loyal citizens of the Indian Union'.[27]

Yet, none of these proved enough to stop oppression of the minorities. Reports kept pouring in from both East and West Pakistan. On the other hand, Liaquat Ali Khan launched an attack on Kripalani, alleging failure of the Indian government and communal outrages on Muslims in India, and accusing Congress leaders of threatening Muslims. 'Let me tell Mr Kripalani and other Hindu leaders that they are playing with fire and trying to rekindle the embers of strife and hatred which we on our part, have sought assiduously to extinguish,' Khan said in a statement a few days before the transfer of power.[28]

Matters came to a head with the finalization of the reports of the Boundary Commissions for Bengal and Punjab. Radcliffe informed Mountbatten on 12 August that the final decisions or awards would be ready by noon of 13 August. The report on Bengal, however, reached Mountbatten by the evening of 12 August, but Mountbatten refrained from reading it. At the viceroy's staff meeting, he was told that the Bengal award allotted the Chittagong Hill Tracts (CHT) to Pakistan. V.P. Menon warned Mountbatten that Nehru and Patel would react vehemently to this, because not only had they been arguing in favour of including the area in India, but they had also gone ahead and assured so to a delegation from the Tracts. By this time, Mountbatten had changed his initial approach of publishing the boundary awards by 15 August, so that the new boundaries could take effect immediately, realizing that the awards couldn't have made any party happy, and, therefore, 'the later we postponed the publication, the less would the inevitable odium react upon the British'.[29]

Menon warned Mountbatten that if the details of the award were shared with Nehru and Patel, they might refuse to attend the meeting of the Constituent Assembly, which Mountbatten was scheduled to address, or refuse to attend the state banquet. Therefore, on 14 August, the day on which Mountbatten was leaving for Karachi, he wrote to Nehru and Jinnah that although Radcliffe was sending him the reports, they wouldn't reach him before he left for Karachi. He told them that he had no idea about their contents. Moreover, as he was not keen to publish the reports without first consulting the representatives of India and Pakistan, he called them for a meeting on 16 August. While Mountbatten was writing to Nehru, he received a letter from Patel, who claimed that if the CHT was awarded to East Bengal, the people would be justified in forcibly resisting the move and the Indian government would be bound to support them.

Despite the non-publication of the reports, widespread speculation had already started in Punjab, 'sufficient to start large scale rioting which would undoubtedly have been a real communal war on a big scale if it had not been for the Joint Punjab Boundary Force' set up by the Partition Council. Nehru told a press conference on 13 September that the death toll in Delhi had increased to a thousand. Official figures for deaths in East and West Punjab was 15,000, but he was sceptical about it, observing that the numbers appeared low and the real figures might even be double or triple.[30]

At the meeting of 16 August—which was attended by Fazlur Rahman, Baldev Singh and V.P. Menon, besides Mountbatten, Nehru, Khan and Patel—after much debate it was agreed that the awards would be published on the next day, accompanied by a communiqué stating that the prime ministers had considered the awards. Although Mountbatten suggested that the communiqué should specify that the unsatisfactory parts of the awards would be subsequently taken up at a governmental level for further action, the idea was dropped. On Nehru's suggestion, it was also decided that he and Khan would visit Lahore and Amritsar the next day.[31]

Returning from Pakistan, Nehru issued an appeal on 19 August to stop the carnage in Punjab:

> In both Amritsar and Lahore we heard a ghastly tale and we saw thousands of refugees, Hindu, Muslim and Sikh. There were some fires still burning in the city and reports of recent outrages reached us. We were all unanimously of opinion that we must deal firmly with the situation as we found it and not enter into acrimonious debate about the past, and that the situation demanded that crime must be put an end to immediately at whatever cost.[32]

Unfortunately, the exodus that had started wasn't going to stop so soon and so easily. On 18 November, the relief and rehabilitation minister K.C. Neogy informed the Constituent Assembly that the Military Evacuation Organisation had evacuated 2.01 million non-Muslims from West Punjab and the North-West Frontier Province (NWFP), and 2.4 lakh non-Muslims from Sind by sea and rail between 4 September and 11 November 1947. About 80,000 more had migrated from Bahawalpur. Some 1.3 million refugees had arrived before the setting up of the Military Evacuation Organisation. On 11 November, 9.76 lakh non-Muslims were living in West Punjab refugee camps.[33]

While Gandhi watched the mass exodus, in principle he remained a staunch opponent of the population exchange. In one of her letters, Sushila Nayyar recounted his thoughts at this time:

> Yesterday he [Gandhi] was saying that he would not be surprised if some of us might have to go the way of the leaders of the French

Revolution. The exchange of population is actually taking place however much we may dislike it. Will there be a mass exodus of Hindus from East Pakistan after the manner of West Pakistan? Bapu says it would be a catastrophe.[34]

In a discussion with Kripalani, Gandhi expressed his opinion that the Congress leaders of Sindh should be there and die if necessary. He believed that such examples would teach other non-Muslims to face the crisis with courage, faith and self-respect.[35]

In fact, as millions crossed the border between East and West Pakistan, the moral opposition of the Congress leaders reached almost a fanatical level. Gandhi told a prayer meeting that transfer of population would be a fatal snare and that it would mean nothing but greater misery.[36] Nehru put the blame on the mass exodus on the circumstances and almost casually admitted that the leadership had failed to foresee it. Speaking at a press conference on 12 October, he said, 'This business of exchange of populations was not of our seeking but, owing to various occurrences, it simply took place, and naturally we had to adapt ourselves to it . . . None of us envisaged a major transfer of population at any time . . . Perhaps this was lack of judgement on our part.'[37] It was probably only Kripalani, the Congress president, who admitted the failure squarely. 'We ought to have anticipated the contingency of a transfer of population being forced on us and should have provided for it in the June 3rd Agreement,' he said at the AICC session of 15 October.[38]

It also appeared that the story of horror in West Pakistan was not entirely known to the outside world. When Girdhari Lal Puri, former deputy speaker of NWFP, in arrived in Bombay on 12 October, he informed, 'As soon as the League Ministry assumed office in NWFP, a rigorous censorship on news was carried out with the result that the outside world is in complete darkness about the happenings in the province . . . Even telegrams sent by the Congress parliamentary secretary Lala Meherchand Khanna to premiers of India and Pakistan drawing their attention to the state of affairs were not allowed to pass.'[39] Dewan Shivsaran Lall, deputy commissioner of Dera Ismail Khan in NWFP, who had reached Delhi about a week before, told the press, 'It would be inhuman and insane on the part of the Government of India not to mobilise their transport to rescue the Hindus and Sikhs who are now counting their days in the Frontier Province like goats in the slaughter house.'[40]

The rural refugees were largely being settled in agricultural land evacuated by Muslim emigrants. By early February 1948, over 2 million refugees were settled in available agricultural land in East Punjab. Explaining that it was more difficult to settle urban refugees who were professionals, artisans, traders and industrial workers, Shanmukham Chetty, the finance minister, introduced a bill to establish the Rehabilitation Finance Administration. Although the East Punjab government had taken steps to provide grants of not more than Rs 500 and loans of not more than Rs 5000 to the urban refuges, Chetty argued that many among this particular class of refugees required much larger credit facilities which could not be provided by either commercial banks or the state government. The bill, therefore, was introduced as an intervention by the Central government to provide adequate credit facilities. The Central government was also planning to build new townships, in addition to acquiring sites for building 8000 houses in the neighbourhood of twelve towns in East Punjab.[41]

In contrast to the attention that the refugee problem in East Punjab got, the attention given to Bengal remained strikingly low-key. Surprisingly, when asked on 5 December 1947 about the number of people who had migrated from East Bengal into India, the government claimed ignorance. 'No figures for Baluchistan and East Bengal are available,' was the response of N. Gopalaswami Ayyangar.[42] Neogy repeated the same answer in response to a similar question on 7 February 1948.[43] The plan for rehabilitating displaced teachers, doctors and lawyers also did not include persons displaced from East Bengal.[44]

The status of the Central government's information on refugees from East Bengal didn't improve much even a year later. While the new rehabilitation minister Mohan Lal Saksena could provide a more or less accurate estimate of 5.5 million refugees from West Pakistan since Partition, in the case of refugees from East Pakistan, his response was that the number was 'not accurately known, but it may be roughly put at about' 1.8 million.[45] On 1 March 1949, Satya Narayan Sinha, the minister of state for parliamentary affairs, told H.V. Kamath in the Constituent Assembly that the influx of refugees from East Bengal had practically stopped.[46] The government also did not have specific figures of out-migration from West Bengal to East Bengal. Saksena told the Assembly on 16 March, 'No figures are available, but it is known that there has been no appreciable movement of population from West Bengal to East

Bengal.' He also informed that West Bengal was not covered under the Administration of Evacuee Property Act.[47]

Till the end of December 1948, the Central and the West Bengal governments had spent Rs 1.22 crore on refugees, Sinha told M. Ananthasayanam Ayyangar.[48]

Surendra Mohan Ghose, Congress member of Parliament from Bengal and president of the Bengal Congress, criticized the Central government's indecisiveness in dealing with refugees in Bengal, which he said was creating hurdles in their resettlement. During the general budget discussions in the Constituent Assembly on 5 March 1949, he bitterly complained that although the Central government had initially promised loans to the refugees, it changed its policy by stipulating that loans would be given only to cooperative societies and not to individual refugees, after several thousand applications from individual refugees had been collected.[49]

In order to find solutions to the unresolved issues concerning India's partition, the official representatives of both India and Pakistan held a series of inter-dominion conferences soon after the transfer of power. These conferences deliberated on a wide range of topics, including administration of evacuee property, ensuring the provision of equal rights and opportunities to the minorities in each dominion, and adoption of measures to ease trade and passenger traffic, etc.[50]

Despite the resolutions and the agreements, the situation in Bengal took a sharp turn for the worse from early 1950.

The impact of these developments was felt in Parliament, where the Nehru government faced scathing criticism from the members. During the debate on the President's address to Parliament on 2 February 1950, Thakur Das Bhargava raised the question, 'Today we hear from East Bengal that 10,000 Hindus have been driven out in a body from there. I cannot understand how the one crore Hindus of East Bengal would be able to live there.'[51] Speaking on a resolution for providing compensation to refugees, Renuka Ray, a Congress member from West Bengal, accused the government of turning its attention to Bengal's refugee problem at a late stage:

It was very surprising to many of us who come from Bengal . . . when we asked a question during the November Session of 1947 [and] were told by the then Minister of Rehabilitation that, neither the Central Government nor the Provincial Government, considered that there was any such problem. This was at a time when the streets of Calcutta were flooded with refugees and Sealdah station was crowded with them. When the Budget Session of 1948 was almost over, the new Premier of Bengal approached the Centre but very little funds were then available as allocations had already been made. Not till the 1949 Budget Session when more adequate finances were made available for the refugees from East Bengal was this problem properly tackled at all. We are still on the fringe of the problem and it is only in the last few months that there has been any intensified effort to deal with it. We are now faced with a new and grave problem, the new influx of refugees from Eastern Pakistan.

India is a secular state and we are going to maintain the secular character of our State. We have high ideals which we shall not discard. But whilst we follow a policy of patience and forbearance, across the border a hymn of hatred is being spread and the resultant effect on the minorities in East Bengal is terrible. I have neither the time nor even the power to describe some of the things that are happening. Many of us are receiving letters day after day from East Bengal Hindus which give evidence of the dreadful things happening there. It is easy to say why should they not have greater courage, why should they not try to resist this treatment? I want to tell this House that those who have stayed behind have shown a great deal of courage. They do not lack backbone but they are scattered and a few are now faced with an incredible and impossible position.[52]

Lala Achint Ram pushed the reaction a notch higher. During the debate on the Administration of Evacuee Property Bill, he passionately argued:

During the past two and a half years it has been repeatedly asked that the Hindus in East Bengal should stick to their places and need not run away. But what happens—they are forced to run away from there and they have become refugees. I would like to know that in case your policy is an appropriate one, then why does not it succeed? The problem is not facing merely a lac or two or even three or four lacs of them. Twenty lacs of people have crossed over to India from East Bengal. You have the liberty to hold your advice quite in keeping with the interests of the Hindus there and pass judgement on their incapacity to understand it.

East Bengal will have to be cut into two and a region made available to a crore and a half of people to live in. It will be a welcome thing if they surrender such region voluntarily, failing that we may proceed to have it in the way we have had Hyderabad because that is the only alternative . . . If you adopt the same attitude of vacillation as you did in the case of the Punjab, Bengal will suffer no dissimilar fate than the Punjab where the Hindus were killed in the land of their birth. I also desire that moral principles of Mahatma Gandhi should reign supreme in this land. But Mahatma Gandhi was a helpless spectator to witness all those ugly happenings and the migration of the Hindus from the West Punjab to India. Against his will and contrary to his principle of non-violence, the Mahatma had to accord his sanction to wage a war on the Kashmir issue and your armies did fight their Pakistan counterpart. Was that all a violation of Mahatma Gandhi's principles? I emphatically maintain that it was not. I don't want war and I am opposed to the idea of a war. I believe that the way of deliverance for the world lies ultimately in peace and reconciliation. I, however, see no other alternative that you can adopt. This vacillation will lead you nowhere. It must end.[53]

When Lakshmi Kanta Maitra moved an adjournment motion in the central legislature on the 'ruthless persecution of the minority Hindu community such as murder, loot, arson, abduction and outrage on women' in East Pakistan in February 1950, both the speaker and Nehru seemed reluctant to take it up for discussion. Responding that the matter had caused 'grave concern' to the Indian government and it had taken it up with the Pakistan government, Nehru held that it was not 'a fit subject for a motion for adjournment'. Faced with such objections and assurances, Maitra withdrew his motion.[54]

As the situation continued to deteriorate rapidly, an agreement was signed between Nehru and Liaquat Ali Khan, the prime minister of Pakistan, on 8 April 1950. Presenting the details of the agreement in Parliament, Nehru spoke with his usual eloquence, laying out his thoughts that led to this agreement:

During the past weeks and months, the whole country, and more particularly Bengal, have faced tragedy and disaster and it is not surprising that people's minds should have been excited and passion let loose . . . I saw an unending stream of unhappy, fear-stricken refugees, uprooted from their homes, facing a dark and unknown future. I experienced their sorrow and misery and I prayed for guidance as to how this could be stopped. All the ideals I had stood for since fate and circumstance pushed me into public affairs, appeared to fade away and a sense of utter nakedness came to me. Was it for this that we had laboured through the years? Was it for this that we had had the high privilege of discipleship of the Father of the Nation?[55]

The agreement, signed in Delhi, reiterated the principle of equal rights for the minorities, provided for the freedom of movement and protection in transit for migrants from East and West Bengal, Assam and Tripura, allowed migrants to return to their homelands when they chose and enabled the retention of ownership of property left behind, and the right to sell or exchange it. The two prime ministers also agreed to work towards restoring normal conditions, setting up agencies to recover abducted women, non-recognize forced conversions and punish the guilty. Commissions of inquiry would be set up to examine the causes and extent of disturbances, a minister would take the responsibility to remain in the disturbed areas and restore the confidence of the minorities, and minority commissions would be set up in West Bengal, Assam and East Bengal.[56]

A number of these provisions being reiterations of the agreements arrived at during the previous inter-dominion conferences, the effectiveness of the pact at this juncture was questioned by many, even within the cabinet.

N.V. Gadgil, the minister of power in Nehru's cabinet, later recalled how the pact was given its final shape:

. . . [the] temperament of Nehru made simple problems complex and gave cause for anxiety, particularly in the matter of the defence of the country. 1949 saw such unspeakable atrocities against Hindus in East Pakistan that it became almost imperative for India to go to their help. The Cabinet discussed the situation at great length and decided that some action should be initiated. But Nehru did not want it and the Hindu–Muslim riots in Howrah came timely to his rescue. In addition the Military authorities reported, or were persuaded to report that any action against Pakistan in those circumstances would be undesirable . . . Liaquat Ali came to Delhi in March 1950, had discussions with Nehru and one fine morning at 10 o'clock Nehru placed before the Cabinet a draft of his agreement with him. I am not sure if Vallabhbhai was consulted before the draft was agreed to.[57]

Gadgil claimed that the last two paragraphs of the draft agreed to the principle of reservation for Muslims in proportion to their population in both Central and state services. It was upon his vocal opposition that the provisions were dropped. He believed that signing the pact instead of taking military action encouraged Pakistan to continue with its minority persecution.

An insightful account has also been left by the then deputy director of the Intelligence Bureau, B.N. Mullik, in his memoirs. According to Mullik, 'Sardar Patel was so exercised over the treatment of the minority in East Pakistan that he wanted that Indian troops should move into East Pakistan to restore order.' When, after informing Mullik that on this matter Patel had the support of the defence minister as well as Syama Prasad Mookerjee, H.V.R. Iengar, the home secretary, asked for his opinion, Mullik opposed the idea on the grounds that sufficient Indian troops were not present in the eastern theatre to be able to sweep through East Pakistan. Intelligence reports showed, Mullik recalled, that even weeks after the pact came into force, oppression continued in East Bengal.[58]

The most sensational impact of Nehru's pact with Liaquat Ali Khan was the resignation of Syama Prasad Mookerjee from the cabinet. On 19 April 1950, in the course of explaining the reasons for his resignation from the provisional parliament, Mookerjee underscored the difference in approach towards the minorities by India and Pakistan:

> The vast majority of Muslims in India wanted the partition of the country on a communal basis, although I gladly recognise there has been a small section of patriotic Muslims who consistently have identified themselves with national interests and suffered for it. The Hindus on the other hand were almost to a man definitely opposed to partition . . . I along with others, gave assurances to the Hindus of East Bengal, stating that if they suffered at the hands of the future Pakistan Government, if they were denied elementary rights of citizenship, if their lives and honour were jeopardised or attacked, Free India would not remain an idle spectator and their just cause would be boldly taken up by the Government and people of India . . . Today I have no hesitation in acknowledging that in spite of all efforts on my part, I have not been able to redeem my pledge and on this ground alone—if on no other—I have no moral right to be associated with the Government any longer . . .[59]

Mookerjee argued that the Nehru–Liaquat pact offered no solution to the 'basic problem' as he believed that the 'establishment of a homogeneous Islamic State is Pakistan's creed and a planned extermination of Hindus and Sikhs and expropriation of their properties constitute its settled policy'. The agreement, he argued, ignored 'the implications of an Islamic State'. Mookerjee recalled that this aspect of the problem was not unknown to Nehru, who himself had said in Parliament that 'the basic difficulty of the situation is that the policy of a religious and communal State followed by the Pakistan Government inevitably produces a sense of lack of full citizenship and a continuous insecurity among those who do not belong to the majority community'. He claimed that at least a million people had left East Bengal since January, moving to West Bengal, and several lakhs had gone to Tripura and Assam. 'The test of any Agreement is not its reaction within India or in foreign lands, but on the minds of the unfortunate minorities living in Pakistan or those who have been forced to come away already,' he pointed out.[60]

The memoirs of B.N. Mullik showed that Mookerjee was not off the mark. Intelligence gathered by Mullik's men, who stood at the entry points of the border between East and West Bengal interviewing refugees, showed that 'even three weeks after the Pact had come into force, individual oppressions were still being committed on the Hindus in East Pakistan and they were still living in fear and anxiety though the Pakistan Government was assuring the Indian Government that everything was quiet in that country'. Mullik was shocked to find that Nehru refused to believe the intelligence reports and insinuated communal bias against the officers. 'We had been charged with fabricating false reports about oppression on the minority in East Pakistan. Howe could we be expected at the same time to fabricate reports to prove that everything was normal in East Pakistan when it was not?' Mullik wondered.[61]

The exodus of refugees and the question of rehabilitating them would remain problem areas which the government struggled to resolve over the next several decades.

5

Recasting the Civil Service and the Armed Forces

At the dawn of Independence, the leaders of the interim government raced to replace the colonial administrative structure which provided the pivotal support to the British colonial power to rule the country. Complete replacement being beyond any possibility, both due to lack of time and any previous planning, the focus fell on restructuring.

The strength of the Indian Army on 1 January 1921, including both combatant and administrative posts, was about 3.4 lakh, of which 2.8 lakh were Indian soldiers. While the Indian government bore the expenditure for about 2.3 lakh soldiers, the expenditures on about half a lakh Indian soldiers were paid directly by the British government. In addition, there were around 10,000 British soldiers serving in the Royal Air Force. Nearly 20,000 Gurkhas were employed in the Indian Army.[1] The strength of the Indian Army was gradually reduced during the following years of peace, and in September 1939, as the Second World War began, the total strength of regular army in India stood at about 2,37,000.[2]

The slow recruitment during the initial months of the war, which increased the strength of the army to 2,77,648 in April 1940, was followed by a phase of rapid expansion.[3] After the end of the war, on 1 October 1945, the strength of the Indian Army was approximately 1.99 million, including 1.92 Indian and 74,461 British officers and soldiers of other ranks. Following demobilization, the number of Indian soldiers stood at 4.15 lakh, British officers at 6032 and British soldiers of other ranks at 4929 in April 1947. In addition, 1124 officers and 20,017 soldiers of the British Army were still in India in July 1947.[4]

Along with demobilization, the government of the day focused on addressing the issue of Indianization of the army. Field Marshal Claude Auchinleck, the commander-in-chief of the Indian Army, announced in

April the government's plans to create a completely national army officered and manned by Indians in the shortest possible time without lowering the high standards of efficiency.[5] A Committee on Nationalisation of Indian Armed Forces was set up in November 1946 under the chairmanship of N. Gopalaswamy Ayyangar, to report within six months on the ways and means of replacing non-Indian personnel by Indians within the shortest period of time, and also to recommend measures to retain non-Indians as advisers and experts if necessary.[6] In its February 1947 meeting, the committee aimed to complete the Indianization of the army by July 1949.[7] Towards the end of June 1947, however, Mountbatten informed a Special Committee of the Indian cabinet that the British government wanted the withdrawal of British units to commence on 15 August and be completed by the end of February 1948.[8]

The first batch of British troops to leave from Bombay on 17 August 1947 by the troopship *Georgic* was the second battalion of the Royal Norfolk Regiment and a contingent of the Royal Air Force.[9] The first battalion of the Somerset Light Infantry was the last British unit to leave India on 28 February 1948, on the liner *Empress of Australia*.[10]

One of the key areas of concern for Auchinleck, however, was the standard of men attempting admission into the Indian Military Academy in Dehradun was 'very poor', resulting in a very high percentage of rejections.[11] On 26 February 1947, Field Marshal Archibald Wavel, the then viceroy, wrote to the secretary of state for India, Frederick Pethick-Lawrence, that he had learnt that '[K.M.] Cariappa, the Indian Brigadier now at the Imperial Defence College, has been saying in London that he is authorised by Nehru to let it be known (a) that Congress expect to have all British officers of the Indian Army out of it between 5 and 8 years, and (b) that after Indian independence is accomplished India will want a close alliance with Britain'.[12] Other leaders, like the premier of United Provinces, Govind Ballabh Pant, too wanted the British officers to remain in India after the transfer of power. Pant was reported by F. Wylie, the governor of UP, to have said in April 1946 that the British officers 'must in no circumstances be encouraged to go', as they had 'valuable experience acquired as the result of hard and honest work and their departure would be a serious loss to India'.[13]

There were strategic imperatives for the British government in favour of continued association with the armies of the two new dominions. Mountbatten expressed his hope to the governors of the provinces on

31 May 1947 that although the British troops were to be withdrawn after the transfer of power, it was likely that with both Pakistan and Hindustan joining the Commonwealth arrangements, they would be made to allow British officers to serve on in the Indian Army and Navy if they are wanted.[14] The British government also wanted to be associated with any defence agreement between the two new dominions, as it was keen to prevent a situation where either dominion, having British officers and equipment, might allow other nations to establish bases on their territories.[15]

As these matters progressed, the issue that emerged at the top very quickly was the division of the Indian Army for India and Pakistan. Meeting on 18 March 1947 in London, the British Chiefs of Staff Committee wanted to shake the problem off its shoulders, deciding, 'If a division of the Indian armed forces becomes inevitable it is important that it should not be made while we are responsible for the defence of India.'[16] In another meeting chaired by the British defence minister A.V. Alexander on the same day to deliberate on the recommendations of the Chiefs of Staff Committee, Mountbatten expressed his view that at some stage the question would have to be examined by a committee, but secretly so that the armed forces got no hint of it so long as the British were responsible for maintaining law and order in India.[17] Around the same time, Auchinleck told Mountbatten that it would take five to ten years to satisfactorily divide the Indian Army.[18]

Emphasizing the fact that a division of the Indian Army would be a 'most complicated and delicate operation', Auchinleck highlighted the numerous problems involved in such an exercise, in a note he produced at the end of May. Among other things, the note highlighted:

> It is not merely a matter of saying Muslims to the left, Hindus to the right. In all three Forces there are many officers and men whose homes are in parts of India which must inevitably come under the rule of the opposite community or party. In dividing the forces, each such case will have to be decided individually as no officer or man could be compelled to serve a government of which he does not approve. In many cases no such decision will be possible until the boundaries between the two States have been definitely and finally fixed.
>
> In the Navy and the Air Force there are no 'Muslim' units or 'Hindu' units. All classes and creeds are inextricably mixed in all units,

occupations, trades and establishments and the complete breaking down and rebuilding of all units and establishments will be necessary before separate new and efficient forces can be made out of the existing 'all-India' forces. Moreover, the installations necessary for the maintenance of new separate forces will have to be created in each State where they do not now exist.

. . . The administrative units and installations of the Army, on which it depends entirely for its continued existence, such as Ordnance, Supply, Pay and Medical units, are completely 'non-Class' that is they are manned without regard to race, religion or creed similarly to the Navy and Air Force. It would be quite impossible to divide these units as they stand to-day between the new armies of the two States. They, like the Navy and the Air Force, must be gradually broken down and rebuilt. The process must be gradual and centrally controlled, otherwise the Army will cease to be fed, paid, clothed, moved or medically attended and will cease to exist as an organised force.[19]

The Muslim League, however, insisted on a division of the army before the transfer of power. In June, Liaquat Ali Khan told Hastings Ismay, chief of viceroy's staff, that the League would not take charge of the government unless Pakistan had its own army under its own commander-in-chief by 15 August.[20] 'Why are two armies being created? Are they to defend the country against foreign aggression or are they to fight against each other?' Gandhi asked in a prayer meeting on 7 July.[21]

It was estimated that after the division of the armed forces, the strength of the Indian Army would be around 2,60,000 and that of Pakistan 1,50,000.[22] Nehru, however, wanted that the strength of the army should preferably be 1,50,000 and not exceed 1,75,000.[23]

The setting up of Armed Forces Reconstitution Committee was announced in mid-June, and Mountbatten told the Special Committee of the Indian cabinet, overseeing the partition of the country, that although Auchinleck had 'at first been gloomy about the probable effects of the division of the Army on the discipline and morale of troops', as a result of assurances from the leaders, 'he was now optimistic and confident that he could produce at the earliest reasonable moment two Armies each of which would be as efficient as the existing one, provided the advice of the experts on the question of division was given due consideration'.[24] It was decided at the meeting of the Partition Council on 30 June that Auchinleck would be designated henceforth as the supreme commander, since each dominion was going to have their own commander-in-chief.[25]

Nehru had expressed his preference for Field Marshal William Slim as India's commander-in-chief of the Indian Army,[26] but accepted Mountbatten's recommendation for General William Lockhart for the post when Slim declined.[27] Towards the end of July, Nehru met both Air Marshal Thomal Elmhirst and Captain John Talbot Hall on the recommendation of Mountbatten, and informed Baldev Singh of his approval for their appointment as the commander-in-chief of the air force and the navy. Nehru also happily agreed to Elmhirst's condition that he should not be made subordinate to the commander-in-chief of the army, and to enable fast development, the air force should be given independent status.[28]

On 9 July, Ismay informed the Chiefs of Staff Committee that the division of the Indian Army was being carried out in two phases. The first phase, to be completed by 15 August, involved the transfer of units down to the company and squadron level between the two dominions on a communal basis. The second phase, which was expected to take much longer, involved the redistribution of individuals to their preferred dominion. The commanders-in-chief of each dominion were to be British officers, but the administration of the armies of the two dominions would continue to be the responsibility of Auchinleck until the two dominions were in a position to provide for the administration of their own forces. The operational control of the two armies, however, would be with the respective dominions.[29] The final decisions of the Armed Forces Reconstitution Committee were announced by the Partition Council on 12 July.[30] The Special Committee of the Indian cabinet had already decided in late June to set up a Joint Defence Council, comprising the governors-general and the defence ministers of the two dominions, and the commander-in-chief, among others, to administer the defence establishments until the dominions were ready to take charge of their administration.[31]

A month before transfer of power, Mountbatten wrote in his personal report to the king and the British prime minister that the 'need for many British officers and other ranks, including technical personnel, to stay on at least for the transition period of about eight months, and preferably longer' was accepted by the Partition Council, which had as its members Jinnah, Liaquat Ali Khan, Patel, Rajendra Prasad and Baldev Singh, among others. Mountbatten had issued an appeal to these officers, with support from Jinnah and Nehru, when he was told by Auchinleck that very few of them were likely to remain 'in view of the calumny and abuse, particularly in the press', which they had suffered in recent years.[32]

The defence minister confirmed in the Constituent Assembly on 19 November 1947 that the Indian government had decided to continue to employ British officers in non-operational commands, advisory roles, and in technical and training establishments. They would, however, be employed in operational commands only in the Royal Indian Navy.[33] A communiqué on this matter, issued by the government on 20 November, clarified that while British officers would hold His Majesty's Commissions, other ranks would serve on British attestations. The majority of the appointments were to be for one year, from 1 January 1948 for the army, two years in the case of the air force and three years for the navy. The British soldiers would be regulated by the British Pay Code and subject to British income tax.[34]

Although 2714 British officers had volunteered to serve after 15 August, in early November the actual number of serving officers was 1204.[35] By early March 1949, the number was less than 200, with almost all the officers being in technical or advisory roles.[36]

Gandhi's views, which counted for little at this time, were very different. Speaking at a prayer meeting on 22 July 1947, he said that a reporter wanted to know

> . . . if the proposal to retain British officers in the army and the partition
> of the army has my approval. The correspondent should rather ask me if
> I approve of the retention of the army itself. Keeping an army, whatever
> its nature or size, can have no support from me.[37]

A few days later, he sent out a message to army officers:

> You have got your guns and sten-guns and you are proficient in killing
> men and all living things. Instead of that you should learn the art of using
> the sickle, ploughing the land and producing the food necessary for men
> and other living beings. Forget violence and gain proficiency in non-
> violence . . . You note down in your diary that the world will curse the
> scientist who has made the atom bomb.[38]

On 27 November 1947, one of the staunchest Gandhians, Pattabhi Sitaramayya, moved a resolution in the Constituent Assembly, seeking immediately the establishment of a 'national militia' and provisions 'on a country-wide basis facilities for training in the use of arms and the arts of self-defence'. In Sitaramayya's view, the militia was necessary to perform a wide sweep of functions ranging from 'effective defence of the country' to assisting the provincial governments in maintaining law and order in emergencies. The training would also enable law-abiding citizens to defend themselves against anti-social elements and remove the fear of helplessness produced by the policy of emasculation followed by the colonial regime. Sitaramayya argued that the money saved by the exit of the British soldiers could be used for the programme.[39]

The resolution drew wide range of support from members such as Shibban Lal Saksena, N.B. Khare, Gopi Krishna Vijayvargiya, Gammididala Durgabai Deshmukh, Tajamul Hussain, Balkrishna Sharma, Thakur Das Bhargava, M.S. Aney, Lakshmi Kanta Maitra, Govind Malaviya and Naziruddin Ahmed. Not a single member rose to oppose it. The defence minister Baldev Singh, however, in a rather defensive and timid reply, presented a number of difficulties in executing such a resolution, while admitting the need for a national militia or territorial army. Funds were a problem because the number of troops were higher than envisaged in the demobilization and partition plan; appointing home guards was not a central but provincial responsibility; not enough arms were being manufactured in the country; the government was not able to find adequate number of officers for the armed forces. Assuring the assembly that the government, which in principle was in agreement with the need for a national militia, would seriously consider the matter once the peacetime strength of the armed forces was stabilized, Singh requested Sitaramayya not to press the resolution.[40] Just over a year later, Congress president Sitaramayya would explain, 'A non-violent army can only be trained in a non-violent order of society.'[41]

This could not have sat well with Gandhi. On 5 November, he told a prayer meeting:

I have never abandoned my non-violence. I have been training myself in non-violence and it was acceptable till we attained independence. Now they wonder how they can rule with non-violence. And then there is the army and they have taken the help of the army. Now I am of no value at all . . . if I could have my way of non-violence and everybody listened to me, we would not send our army [to Kashmir] as we are doing now. And if we did send, it would be a non-violent army.[42]

When Maj. Gen. Cariappa told Gandhi that 'Non-violence is of no use under the present circumstances in India and only a strong army can make India one of the greatest nations in the world', Gandhi retorted, 'I fear, like many experts, General Cariappa has gone beyond his depth and has been unwittingly betrayed into a serious misconception of ahimsa, of whose working in the nature of things, he can only have a very superficial knowledge.'[43]

The legislative side of the Constituent Assembly passed the legislations establishing a National Cadet Corps in April 1948 and a Territorial Army in September 1948. The first unit of the Territorial Army was raised in August 1949 and formally inaugurated in October.[44] The government announced the expansion of the Territorial Army, the National Cadet Corps (NCC) and the Auxiliary Cadet Corps (ACC) in August 1953, following a discussion in Parliament on a resolution moved by Ram Subhag Singh of the Congress seeking compulsory military training of all high-school and college students.[45] A year later, however, Nehru was not satisfied with the progress of the new institutions. 'It bears no relation with the problem we have to face or to the population of India,' he wrote to the defence minister on 12 August 1954, adding, 'I do not think it is at all in line with modern thinking.' Although the number of people envisaged in these programmes was 'totally inadequate', expanding them further would make the financial burden 'far too great'.[46]

General Lockhart retired on 1 January 1948 due to ill health and was succeeded by Lieutenant General F.R.R. Bucher, who continued for little over a year until 14 January 1949. Lt Gen. Bucher's designation was changed in May 1948 to chief of the army staff and commander-in-chief, and subsequent to India becoming a republic, the post was redesignated as chief of the army staff from 1955.[47] Following his retirement, Gen. Bucher was appointed as an officer on special duty in the defence ministry and tasked with compiling a report on the state of the Indian Army.[48]

Nehru was still not happy with the thought of British officers withdrawing completely from India. He wrote to Baldev Singh on 5 August 1948 that 'the withdrawal of the British officers from the Indian Armed Forces would be unfortunate at the present moment and would result in deterioration in our standards'.[49] Baldev Singh announced in the Constituent Assembly that the nationalization of the army was complete with the appointment of General Cariappa as the commander-in-chief on 15 January 1949.[50]

As Cariappa's tenure came to an end on 15 January 1953, he was succeeded by Lt Gen. Rajendrasinhji, who was then GOC-in-C, Southern Command. Rajendrasinhji was in turn succeeded by Gen. S.M. Srinagesh in May 1955, who served until May 1957.

The air force and the navy, however, continued to be headed by British chiefs. Elmhirst was succeeded by Air Marshal Ronald Ivelaw-Chapman in February 1950, who was followed by Air Marshall Gerald Ernest Gibbs in December 1951. The first Indian to become the chief of the air staff and commander-in-chief, Indian Air Force, was Air Marshal Subroto Mukerjee, who took charge in April 1954 and continued in office until his untimely death in November 1960. It took longer in the navy for an Indian chief to take charge. Vice-Admiral Ram Das Katari became the chief of naval staff in April 1958. The contribution of the British chiefs of the army, navy and the air force was highly appreciated by Nehru. He explained in the Lok Sabha on 25 March 1954:

We have had in the Air Force and in the Navy senior British officers in command because both the Air Force and the Navy, frankly speaking, require expert and experienced guidance. I should like to say—and I say so from personal experience, not only of these two years, but of the last six or seven years—that these senior officers that we have had in the Army, Navy and the Air Force have done us exceedingly well, and I should like to express my high appreciation of the loyal way and the efficient way in which they have worked for us.[51]

Occasional demands for the formation of provincial units in the regular Indian Army were resisted by Nehru. To a request from Ravi Shankar Shukla, the premier of the Central Provinces, along similar lines, Nehru responded that to 'give provincial names to Army units would be to come in the way slightly of a homogeneous Indian Army which thinks in terms of India rather than in terms of a province'.[52]

Although Nehru differed from Gandhi's ideas regarding the need for an armed force, he nonetheless tried to introduce prohibition in the military institution. A controversy over the consumption of alcohol in the defence forces in the context of prohibition in Bombay erupted around a Supreme Court order exempting defence personnel. The controversy was further stoked with allegations of V.K. Krishna Menon, India's high commissioner in the UK, having procured scotch whisky at rates higher than market rates for the defence services canteens. The government, however, exonerated Menon, informing the Constituent Assembly in February 1949 that he had, in fact, succeeded in reducing the procurement rates, leading to savings.[53]

With reference to the government's 'general policy' to encourage prohibition, he wrote to Bucher in September 1948, 'I have little doubt that this general policy will gradually have to be introduced in the Defence Forces also.' He felt that 'our officers indulge far too frequently and far too much in alcoholic drinks'.[54] When Bucher wrote back that alcohol consumption was strictly rationed in the army, Nehru shifted the ground of his objection from prohibition to 'efficient work and secrecy', since there was 'far too much loose talk and alcohol no doubt adds to this'. He, however, agreed that prohibition need not be enforced in the messes. Bucher shared his views on the effect of alcohol on Indians in contrast to other nationalities: 'Indian officers and specially those of certain classes, who consume fairly large quantities of alcohol become prolix and garrulous in speech, whereas similarly addicted Scots and Irishmen resort to pugnacity, Germans to self-pity and Englishmen to gloom.'[55]

As the defence establishments progressed on the path towards stabilization, one aspect that bothered Nehru was the rising defence expenditures. The first full budget of independent India, the one for 1948–49, had estimated the expenditure on defence services at 47 per cent of the total expenditure budget. Although the budget estimates for the next year put the defence expenditure at 48.8 per cent of total expenditure, the revised estimates showed that it was higher, at nearly 51 per cent. A worried Nehru held a number of discussions with the defence minister, the defence secretary and the commander-in-chief of the army, stressing the need to curtail this expenditure. On 28 December 1949, a very worried Nehru wrote to Cariappa:

> We are starving everything, health, education, development schemes, industrial growth. We are retrenching people and creating unemployment. We are reducing salaries . . . We are in fact sacrificing tomorrow for today. And yet in spite of all these tremendous sacrifices all round, the expenditure on the defence services grows and grows and there is no realisation whatever of the seriousness of the situation that faces us.
>
> . . . We are stopping industrial progress and even production for the army. The economic situation is deteriorating, resulting in grave

dissatisfaction among the people. All this means endangering security in a basic sense. If the people generally are miserable and unhappy, the country becomes weak internally.

. . . I remember your telling me that we have not even got full equipment for all the people in the army. What then is the use of that army and how are you going to give it ammunitions etc., in time of need. You will have to rely on other countries and that is not a safe or happy position. Our immediate duty is to increase the productive capacity of the country which will not only increase the standards of the people but also produce ammunitions of war. Ultimately war is carried on more by this productive capacity than by men in the field. More and more modern war depends upon scientific research and industrialisation. Minus these two, no army machine can function for long.[56]

Nehru prescribed limiting the defence expenditure at Rs 150 crore for 1950–51. In order to achieve this target, he suggested reducing the strength of the army. The revised estimates for defence expenditure, however, went up to Rs 181.2 crore in 1951–52 and Rs 202.95 crore in 1956–57, although its share in total expenditure reduced to 44 per cent and 38 per cent, respectively.[57]

The plan for reducing the strength of the army, however, was pulled back by Nehru after a decision on the matter was taken by the ministry. In the existing environment of instability, which almost threatened a war, he felt that the decision to disband temporary as well as regular battalions would be strongly opposed in Parliament and by the general public, apart from creating a sense of insecurity among the armed forces.[58]

Things were not well with the armed forces. The reports which were reaching Nehru from various sources about systemic corruption seriously worried him. He brought it to Cariappa's notice that bribery, corruption and embezzlement of funds were 'rampant', appointments were tarred by favouritism and that senior officers were being kept at the headquarters in Delhi for too long when they should be sent back to active service after a certain period.[59]

Speaking in the Lok Sabha in a debate on demand for grants for the defence ministry on 25 March 1954, Nehru reviewed the progress of the armed forces and explained his ideas for the future. He found the growth of defence industries 'particularly satisfactory' as modern warfare increasingly depended on technological improvements. It was not India's intention to build capabilities for long-range offensive wars, but rather to have a defensive force. With self-reliance, to the extent possible, as a goal, India's approach was to produce what was necessary as soon as possible and to rely on what could be manufactured in the country and 'not on something even better' that might be available from other countries. In other words, 'it is better, in the final analysis, that you should think of . . . very much second-rate in the normal sense, of course, on which we can rely and which we can produce ourselves rather than something for which we have to depend upon others and which we may not get in time of need.' India's navy was small, and without the equipment and training received from the British Royal Navy and without joining their manoeuvres 'we would have been far more backward than we are'.

Since there was yet no Indian pattern of modern warfare, it was natural to adopt the British pattern and not those of America or Russia, because India had so far adopted it in its army organization. According to Nehru it was good enough and could be tinkered with, but 'to upset it completely would have meant really upsetting our defence apparatus completely and that would have been foolish'.[60]

A few weeks later, he wrote to the defence secretary about India's naval policy, the way he saw it. According to Nehru, 'Our Navy will at no time be charged with protecting the sea routes for us or to bring in food supplies etc.' It was completely beyond India's capacity. Therefore, the Indian Navy had to 'perform the smaller but very important task of protecting our ports and making it hard for any enemy ships which seek to attack us'. It followed that 'we do not normally require big ships', aircraft carriers or 'long distance submarines', and having 'a number of small but swiftly moving ships, well-armed' was far more important.[61]

Nehru's views on aircraft carriers and large vessels changed significantly within six months after being briefed by P.M.S. Blackett, the British defence scientific adviser, and Mountbatten. He was now convinced of the usefulness of aircraft carriers which, Mountbatten explained to him, was important for protection of coasts (they could carry aircrafts, and it was not possible to build airfields all over the coast), relief work and evacuation. The carriers also carried helicopters, which could neutralize submarines in the neighbourhood. Nehru was in favour of Mountbatten's suggestion to substitute the Indian Navy's flagship INS *Delhi* (formerly HMS *Achilles*) with HMS *Nigeria* (a cruiser acquired from the UK in 1954 and renamed INS *Mysore* after being modernized in 1957), and also to his proposal to acquire one of the older British aircraft carriers on loan instead of a new one, which would be 'terribly expensive'.[62]

The entire philosophical basis on maintaining a standing army was called into question in 1955 by the President, Rajendra Prasad, the supreme commander of India's armed forces. In a letter to Nehru written in August 1955, Prasad highlighted how India's foreign policy, based on the principle of peaceful negotiations and appeal to 'the conscience of mankind' as opposed to the strength of arms, had been successful in stabilizing peace and was being appreciated globally. The 'big nations' had begun to listen to the voice of peace. India should, therefore, Prasad argued, 'consider to what extent it is necessary for us to continue the incongruity which is inevitable when we profess non-violence' and yet not only maintain but strengthen its armed forces and manufacture arms within the country. His suggestion to the government was 'to consider whether the time has not come when we should reduce, if not abolish, armed forces':

> Mahatma Gandhi was in favour of disarmament. So are we and we are suggesting disarmament to other nations when at the same time we are not prepared to practice it ourselves . . . Not only has it [military expenditure] increased proportionately but it has increased absolutely very largely. That naturally raises a question whether in our profession of non-violence we are genuine and whether we do not attach one meaning to non-violence when we talk of armed Defence Forces of other nations and we mean something else when we come to our own Defence Forces . . . If the Government is prepared to consider it, it should be possible to work out some feasible plan which without causing a sudden break with the present conditions and involving heavy unbearable risks, would give an indication that there is a turn in our policy and in future we are going to move not towards armament but towards disarmament . . . A turn like this will furnish the beautiful *Kalash* to the temple of peace in the world which is being built under your great leadership.[63]

Kailash Nath Katju, the then defence minister, to whom Prasad had marked a copy of his letter, responded that although Gandhi held that 'nonviolence cannot make further headway without the Congress making it a creed', since Independence 'no influential voice has ever been raised towards the changing of this policy into a creed'. On the contrary, 'the movement has been the other way'. Pointing out to Prasad that 'Military training makes very strong appeal to the people, and the success of the NCC and ACC has been phenomenal', Katju argued that whereas the 'adoption of non-violence-cum-non-cooperation, as a method of defence, requires very long training and an intense belief in its efficacy', such a belief 'is wholly non-existent'.[64]

Nehru was more blunt in telling Prasad that

> . . . in present circumstances this did not seem to me very feasible. We could, of course, reduce it somewhat and indeed I believe we have decided to bring about some reductions at the rate of about ten thousand a year. I do not think they have been fully given effect to. But conditions being what they are, I confess that I do not feel like recommending that the Army should be substantially reduced.[65]

Gandhi's disciples in the government officially acknowledged, for the first and probably the only time, having dissociated themselves from their mentor's creed of non-violence.

~

In the early decades of the Congress movement, the Indian Civil Service (ICS) was seen as a great career option for the educated elite. Adopting the civil service as a career was not seen to be in conflict with the national liberation movement until after the first three decades of formation of the Congress in 1885. In fact, ironic as it might appear, three of the most influential leaders who shaped the Congress movement had appeared and been unsuccessful at the civil service exams—Surendranath Banerjee, Chittaranjan Das and Aurobindo Ghosh.

The hardening of the perception of conflict began with Subhas Chandra Bose setting an example by refusing to join the service after being ranked fourth among the successful candidates in 1921. Bose's example did not lead to further resignations, but it did pose the question of how to justify joining the colonial bureaucracy, much reviled by the nationalists, in front of the aspirants. The most common answer formulated to resolve the dilemma was that one could serve the country equally, if not better, by joining the civil service. M.C. Chagla, who was at Oxford and later went on to become the chief justice of the Bombay High Court, India's ambassador to the US, high commissioner in the UK and then the education and foreign minister, claimed that Jinnah too had advised Bose not to leave the ICS, because if people like him left the service, 'the future of the country would be dark, since we would not have patriotic men serving the country'.[66]

One of the persons who witnessed the impact of Bose's resignation from the ICS was G.D. Khosla, who later became the chief justice of the Punjab High Court. Khosla recalled in his biography of Bose:

It was the day he had decided to resign from the Indian Civil Service . . .
I had come upon him in a street near Parker's Piece, where he was the
centre of a group of Indian students, hotly discussing the pros and cons
of joining the ICS and working for alien exploiters and tyrants. I said I
had come up to Cambridge with the firm intention of preparing for the
Civil Service examination, and saw nothing unpatriotic or degrading in
keeping out at least one Englishman from the privileged band of 'heaven
borns' who tyrannised our countrymen. Bose gave me a withering look of
contempt, and continued the exposition of his argument.[67]

A curious feature of the Indian students in England who joined the civil service was that many of them were politically active in favour of the nationalist movement in India. How, then, did they reconcile the conflict between serving the colonial government while supporting the nationalist movement?

The leaders of the new government acquiesced to the claims made by Uma Shanker Bajpai, an ICS officer, who said, 'If I could serve so well a foreign power, how much better will I serve my own countrymen?' The dilemma probably has been articulated most honestly by K.P.S. Menon, India's first foreign secretary, who topped the civil service in 1922. In his autobiography, Menon was forthright:

In the [Oxford] Majlis, we made vehement speeches which we thought
patriotic and which the British thought seditious. At the same time, we
went on studiously preparing for the ICS. The inconsistency between the
making of anti-British speeches and the attempt to enter the ICS, which
was the mainstay of the British Government in India, did not strike us.
Honesty as well as modesty forbids me to plead, in the light of after
events, the foreknowledge that by entering the ICS some of us would
become better qualified to serve independent India than those who,
carried off their feet by the noble call of patriotism, forsook their studies
and entered the serious business of life without adequate preparation.[68]

Menon got into trouble even after passing the examination as he continued with his 'vehement speeches against British rule'. He was summoned by the India Office and questioned by members of the Secretary of State's Council to explain a statement attributed to him, to the effect that India could not long remain in the British empire. Menon explained to them that he meant 'India could not remain in her present position in the Empire but might remain as an equal member of the Commonwealth'.[69]

Bose's example, however, continued to influence later ICS aspirants for a considerable period of time. K.B. Lall, who went on to become India's ambassador to Belgium, Luxembourg and the European Economic Community and also held the posts of defence and commerce secretary in the 1960s and 1970s, passed the ICS examination in 1937. He later recalled, 'When in family circles I was pressed to appear for the competitive examination of the Indian Civil Service I thought I would follow the example of Subhas Basu [sic], try to get through the examination and, if I succeed, would turn my back on it.' But, 'when success came, it was difficult not to proceed ahead'.[70] Hari Vishnu Kamath, a member of the Constituent Assembly and member of Parliament for many terms, was, in fact, the only other Indian to resign from the ICS and join the national movement, which he did in 1938.

Yet another striking aspect of those who went to England to appear for the ICS or to obtain higher qualifications was their interconnectedness and the important roles many of them played after returning to India. Some of the key names from the first few years of the 1920s alone are enough to demonstrate the point: K.P.S. Menon, M.C. Chagla, G.D. Khosla, P.N. Sapru (son of Tej Bahadur Sapru and later judge of the Allahabad High Court and member of Parliament), T.C. Goswami (one of the 'big five' of Bengal politics and member of Central Legislative Assembly), Liaquat Ali Khan, S.W.R.D. Bandarnaike (prime minister of Sri Lanka), B.R. Sen (later director general of UN Food and Agricultural Organization and India's ambassador to Japan), Sukumar Sen (India's first chief election commissioner), R.K. Nehru (India's foreign secretary and ambassador to China), Tara Chand (well-known historian and vice chancellor of Allahabad University) and Purushottam Tricumdas (Socialist Party leader), among others.

It is unlikely that when nationalist leaders vilified the bureaucracy, these highly networked elite group felt threatened or alienated. The more likely targets of such bitter criticism were the British bureaucrats and the

Indian officials at low or middle level in the provinces, in addition to those in the police service. In fact, the series of discussions between the viceroy, the secretary of state and the governors of the provinces regarding safeguards for the civil service seemed to revolve almost entirely around British officers. Gradually, the criticism and the demands for punishment disappeared as the Congress moved from an agitational role to being the party in power. For instance, Nehru was vehement in his demand for punishing those responsible for suppressing the 1942 movement, but by the middle of July 1946 he took 'a more reasonable line', after Wavell 'left him in no doubt that the Services would have to be protected'. V.P. Menon, who had very recently been conferred the title of Rao Bahadur, believed that the Congress did not have any well-thought-out plan on the issue, and once it formed the interim government the political pressure would ease.[71] Menon's observation proved prescient. The interim government functioned wholly on the basis of the existing Constitution, that is, the Government of India Act of 1935, and agreeing to work within that framework, the Congress had practically no other option than to work closely with and depend on the bureaucracy that it had been attacking for decades.

The countrywide mass agitation that was triggered by the government's decision to hold the public trial of the INA soldiers at the Red Fort and the subsequent series of upheavals across the country introduced a serious attitudinal shift among the members of the civil service. Wavell noted in early November 1945, 'The British members of the ICS and IP [Indian police] are dispirited and discontented; the Indian members of these services are uneasy about the future and under strong political and social pressure; while the Indian subordinates on whom the administration so largely depends are naturally reluctant to make enemies of the future masters of India.'[72] The Intelligence Bureau also reported instances from the provinces where some of the 'Indian IP officers are intent on ingratiating themselves with the [provincial] Ministry'.[73]

In April 1946, the home member in the Viceroy's Executive Council was reporting that although the situation in the police was not as bad as in the armed forces, they had economic grievances which could be turned into an issue by the Congress and the communists, leading to a mutiny if the Cabinet Mission talks failed. He anticipated strikes by the staff in the railways, posts and telegraphs too, which materialized before long.[74]

A piece of information greatly agitated Wavell once the Congress started forming provincial governments after the elections of 1946. Wavell was told that some of the provincial governments were planning to recruit the former soldiers of the Indian National Army (INA) into their police force. He immediately took the matter to Nehru in mid-May to have the Congress Working Committee (CWC) stop any such measure. A hesitant Nehru admitted to Wavell that organizational elections within the Congress showed a definite tendency towards extremism, and he was not sure whether the existing CWC 'would retain their influence over the more extreme elements'. He also told Wavell that 'while most people now realised that they had gone too far in their glorification of the INA, and the tendency was now swinging the other way', the Congress couldn't afford to be indifferent to the INA soldiers because 'all parties were now angling to use them'. If they were not provided with employment, they would play into the hands of 'the more extreme elements'. Moreover, the police forces being long considered 'instruments of oppression', Nehru was concerned that 'it was necessary to put something more "popular" in their place'. Wavell, however, reassured him that just like the other services, the police 'would loyally serve' the Congress government, 'provided that their morale was not upset by purges or witch-hunts'.[75]

The recruitment of INA soldiers into the police force became a matter of contention between Govind Ballabh Pant and the governor of UP, with the latter overruling the decision. Pant dropped the proposal after discussing it with Nehru.[76] 'Nehru seems to have taken a reasonable attitude,' observed a satisfied Pethick-Lawrence.[77] A conflict between UP's home minister and the inspector general of police, however, reached a critical state where the Congress ministry was ready to resign. The matter ended due to intervention by the viceroy and the secretary of state with the resignation of the police officer.[78]

In spite of strong concerns expressed by the viceroy and the governors that holding inquiries by the provincial governments on the role of the officers in suppressing the 1942 movement would break the morale of the civil and the police services, Attlee and Pethick-Lawrence took a very flexible stand. If a gentleman's agreement with the Congress didn't work, Pethick-Lawrence informed Wavell after a discussion with Attlee, the governors of the provinces should not invoke their special powers to prevent such an inquiry. The British prime minister and the secretary of state took this decision because they understood 'that there were actions taken by individuals in 1942 which were clearly unjustifiable'. They went to the extent of suggesting that Wavell set up a 'properly constituted commission of enquiry' presided over by a high court judge. The governors in the provinces could follow the same path.[79] Matters cooled down before reaching that stage, as none of the Congress governments in the provinces pushed hard for the inquiry. Nehru himself told Wavell on 22 July that he was against a general inquiry, but in view of strong public sentiments, he asked the viceroy whether certain individuals could be retired.[80] The India and Burma Committee of the British Cabinet decided that the viceroy should discuss the cases of officers unacceptable to the Congress with the governors of the provinces, and in 'extreme cases' to let them leave at once.[81] The secretary of state had more reasons to be happy, which he shared with the Viceroy:

> Fact that Nehru took reasonable line with regard to enquiry into Services cases connected with 1942 disturbances leads us to hope that he is not disposed to be altogether unreasonable. From evidence of views expressed by several Congress spokesmen there seems moreover to us to be considerable ground for hope that the representative men and women who have been elected to the Constituent Assembly will not pursue extreme courses there.[82]

The India and Burma Committee also took up the matter of future of the secretary of state's services (ICS and IP) at its meeting on 31 July 1946. A critical issue was that of compensation to the officers of secretary of state's service. The Government of India Act of 1935 assured compensation to any officer appointed by the secretary of state whose condition of service was adversely affected by anything done under the act. The secretary of state asked the committee for its opinion on whether the officers who stayed back should receive the same compensation as those who left the service. The committee was divided in its opinion. It was decided that the chancellor of the exchequer, who felt this obligation should be met by the Indian government from its own revenues, should further discuss this issue with the secretary of state and thereafter, if necessary, it would be deliberated by the cabinet.[83] Fresh recruitments to the ICS, both British and Indian, were to stop, except for a special Central Service, to which ninety-five candidates would be recruited on special terms.[84] The scheme of compensation, developed after consultation between the treasury, the India Office and the representatives of the viceroy, was presented in a memorandum by the secretary of state in September. The compensation scheme, which was estimated to cost around GBP 15.5 million, was forwarded to the viceroy for sharing with the interim government.[85]

A cabinet meeting of the interim government on 9 October 1946 approved Vallabhbhai Patel's proposal to create a new all-India administrative service on the lines of the ICS, and also cleared an earlier proposal for setting up an Indian Foreign Service (IFS), which had been put on hold until a popular government took charge at the centre.[86] Towards the end of October 1946, Patel's home department informed the secretary of state that a provincial premier's conference a few days ago had unanimously agreed that the secretary of state's services should be terminated at the earliest, even if the framework for the proposed all-India service was not ready by then.[87] The conference agreed on setting up an Indian Administrative Service (IAS) and an Indian Police Service (IPS). The stumbling block for progress on the new plan was that until the date for the termination of the secretary of state's services and the associated financial implications became known, the central or the provincial governments were unable to formulate the terms for the new services.

The India and Burma Committee endorsed a revised scheme of compensation submitted by the secretary of state at its meeting on 13 November 1946 and passed it on to the British cabinet for final approval. The new scheme brought down the cost of the scheme to GBP 10 million, and the British Treasury agreed to the plan only on the condition that the cost would be borne by the Indian and not the British government. The committee argued that the Indian government could utilize its sterling assets with the British government for the payout.[88] The British cabinet approved the proposed scales of compensation for the secretary of state's services and asked the viceroy to place the scheme in front of the interim government. All officers in the ICS, the IP, the Indian Political Service, the Indian Ecclesiastical Establishments, and those appointed by the secretary of state in the railway, engineering, forest, veterinary, educational and agricultural services were given the option of taking the compensation, in addition to the accrued pension, and cease to be employed by the Indian government.[89]

The idea of compensation was acceptable to Patel neither on political nor on administrative grounds. He argued that the British government had known since 1919 that transfer of power was inevitable and was just a matter of time. The constitutional changes, therefore, could not be called sudden or unexpected and did not warrant a deviation from the conventional practice of right to retire on proportionate pension. From the administrative point of view, Patel pointed out, the constitutional change would only mean a 'transference of control from the Secretary of State to the Government of India'.[90]

According to Patel, the constitutional change would result in three categories of officers—those who would like to continue under the new Indian government under existing conditions and scale of service, and would either be retained or relieved from service by the Indian government, and those who would like to retire. While services of the first category of officers would be transferred to the Indian government under a new contract with pension and leave rights, there were precedents for the second category not being compensated. The third category of officers, as had been the past practice, would be given the right to retire with proportionate pension. He pointed out that by quitting en bloc, the European officers would invite the charge of being a mercenary body, and the Indian government would be 'seriously embarrassed by their departure'. In such a scenario, it was not the officers but the Indian government which deserved to be compensated for the embarrassment.[91] Nehru, too, expressed his desire for the officers of the secretary of state's services to continue after transfer of power and felt that the compensation terms devised by the British government provided incentive for the officers to leave the service.

In sum, Patel concluded:

> In my view, therefore, there is no claim for compensation whatsoever for the Services, whether European or Indian. Even if the Secretary of State feels himself bound to honour the pledge given in 1945, it cannot be done by imposing a liability on Indian revenues, but the cost must be met by His Majesty's Government. There is no case whatsoever for the Indian element of the service to be compensated by an Indian Government for the transfer of their services to the latter. If an Indian member of the service is so unpatriotic as to seek compensation for such transfer, he deserves to be discharged without any compensation.[92]

Patel chalked out a timeline for the subsequent steps. After the announcement of the terms of service by the secretary of state, the Central and provincial governments should have the full information by the end of January 1947 on all the officers who would prefer to continue or to retire. In February, the governments should decide on the officers they would like to retain and make arrangements for the replacement of those who would opt to retire. The secretary of state should therefore declare 1 March 1947 as the date for severing his connection with the services.[93]

With the British government unwilling to accept Patel's arguments, the stalemate continued. On 13 March 1947, the India and Burma Committee decided to adhere to its earlier scheme and reiterated that if India refused to pay for the compensation, the amount would be adjusted with India's sterling balance with the UK.[94] The secretary of state also communicated that the transfer of control of the services would not be possible before the transfer of power.

Things changed with the arrival of Mountbatten. When Mountbatten discussed the compensation scheme, which had undergone some modification, with the full cabinet of the interim government, he obtained their agreement on the principle of compensation. However, the Indian ministers suggested that the compensation should be paid to only British officers and not to Indians, except in certain circumstances.[95]

The final scheme was announced by Attlee in the House of Commons, the secretary of state in the House of Lords and by Mountbatten in Delhi on 30 April 1947. It had been agreed that the members of the secretary of state's service would have the option to serve under the Indian government at the existing pay scale, leave, pension rights and safeguards. Compensation would be available to the officers who chose to retire after the transfer of power but not before, thus encouraging them to continue. Provincial governments had been asked to provide the same assurance to the officers serving their respective provinces. Compensation would also be provided to those officers not invited by the government to continue in the service and also those who were unable to continue due to specific circumstances. While the British government would take responsibility for the compensation to be paid, the Government of India would be responsible for paying the pension of the officers in the service.[96]

In the meantime, the IAS, which the premiers' conference of October 1946 had agreed to set up, was making gradual progress. The immediate focus was to meet the shortage of skilled officers in the services. As Nehru noted:

It seems to me that the present arrangements for recruiting men or women to the Indian Administrative Services might prove inadequate . . . I should personally imagine that the number of persons recruited will be totally inadequate in future and something in a much bigger scale must be thought of and arranged for.[97]

The provincial governments informed the Central government about the number and nature of posts that needed to be filled up by the provincial cadres of the IAS. The same process was being followed for setting up the Indian Police Service (IPS) November 1946 onwards. The IAS training school was opened in Delhi in March 1947, followed by the first combined competitive examination for IAS, IPS and IFS in July 1947. Recommendations for recruitment and training were provided by a committee headed by A.D. Gorwala. The government also accepted the Gorwala Committee's recommendation to send officers to the UK for training in order to set up the Directorate of Operations and Methods. Applications were invited from retired officers who were willing to be re-employed, and also from those who had ranked above 40th in the ICS examinations between 1938–45.[98] [99]

In December 1946, the cabinet of the interim government decided to remove the ban on employing ex-INA personnel to civil posts, and all ministries were informed of the decision.[100]

Based on the recommendations of the Committee on Reorganization, headed by G.S. Bajpai, the departments of the Government of India were reorganized and their officer strength refixed to make optimum use of manpower. It was on the recommendation of the Bajpai Committee that the Gorwala Committee, set up in September 1947, was asked to explore the option of recruiting officers from the 'open market' and then train them. The Gorwala Committee's recommendation to implement an Emergency Recruitment Scheme for filling up the gap created in the civil service by the exit of the British officers was accepted by the government, and a Special Recruitment Board was set up in the home ministry.[101]

Nehru informed the Central Legislative Assembly on 1 November 1946 that the interim government had decided to set up a separate Indian Foreign Service (IFS) for diplomatic, consular and commercial representation abroad.[102] The recruitment of new officers was going to be through a common competitive examination for the IAS and IFS, but, he clarified, it was not going to suffice to recruit only new members. Therefore, the new service would have to be staffed by a number of people of various age groups from the existing Indian Political Service (which was going to cease), Emergency Commissioned Officers (ECOs) from the army and other Central and provincial services who had experience in representing India in foreign countries, as also by people from outside any of the services.[103]

Subimal Dutt, later to become India's foreign secretary, was transferred from the post of agriculture secretary in the Bengal government to join as the secretary in the Commonwealth Relations Department at Nehru's behest. Arriving in Delhi in about a month before transfer of power, Dutt noticed how the official environment had changed:

> I had been away from the Central secretariat for six and half years. The first thing that struck me when I entered the department was a complete change in the surroundings. Gone was the placid atmosphere in the spacious corridors of the massive building. The whole place was humming with activity. Officials were flitting from one room to another with an air of suspense and anxiety. Khadi clad persons were walking about with supreme unconcern, and here and there, could be seen a few Jinnah caps . . .
>
> The British civil servants were departing and there was a scramble amongst Indian officials for the places falling vacant. Appointments to senior secretariat and administrative posts were within the special responsibility of the powerful Home Minister, Vallabhbhai Patel. He was anxious to secure the loyalty of the senior civil servants by guaranteeing them rights and privileges they had enjoyed under the old regime. But one heard of court being held in his house from day to day. I found myself out of place in such an atmosphere.[104]

A pertinent but uncomfortable question was thrown by Sri Prakasa directly at Nehru when he talked about the IFS in the assembly. Would he consider not applying the rule of possessing a first-class university degree to qualify for the service to the large number of bright men who had boycotted universities under the advice of Nehru and his comrades in the Congress? 'I am afraid if really competent persons are allowed to come to Service it is a little difficult to make vague rules and the Honourable Member will remember that the choice lies with the Federal Public Services Commission,' Nehru replied. Thus, the problem was difficult, but there was nothing that the Congress leaders now in government could do for those who had given up their career for the sake of the national movement.[105]

When N. Sivaraj complained that the minimum qualifications for recruitment to the IFS had been set so high that it would 'really result in shutting out the members of the Scheduled Castes', Patel responded:

> So far as the standard of qualifications is concerned, it is alleged that the standard for foreign service is kept very high. I am afraid that the standard for foreign service cannot easily be lowered without detriment to our cause, but with the progress of education and the number of scholarships that have been given to the Scheduled Caste students to go outside and the scholarships that may be liberally provided in this country for their education, I do not see any reason why we would not be able to train young men from the Scheduled Castes who may be able to discharge their duties efficiently and with credit in foreign countries. Therefore, I have every sympathy for the suggestions that Mr. Siva Raj has made, and we shall do our utmost to see that all impediments or handicaps in their way are removed.[106]

Pressed by N.G. Ranga, Nehru agreed with Patel's statement: 'It would be a dangerous precedent' to reduce the qualification standards. The IFS required even higher standards than any internal service, he explained, and therefore the best way was to promote training facilities for the disadvantaged groups and communities.[107] Yet, Nehru later informed the Constituent Assembly that 'some people who do not even hold University Degrees, not to say anything about First Class Degrees, have been recruited to foreign service'.[108]

The interim government, however, reserved 12.5 per cent post in the Central services (including IAS and IFS), where recruitment was done through competitive examinations for the scheduled castes.[109]

Nehru's insistence on maintaining a high standard for the IFS officers is understandable in view of the challenges a nascent country had to face in a world of volatile geopolitics. Inheriting the legal identity from the colonial state, India had to put in place her own representatives not only for multilateral forums like the United Nations (UN), but also to establish fresh connections with countries in a divided world. The need for people who knew the tricks of the trade, backed up by capable officers, could not have been overemphasized.

The first task Nehru faced as India's foreign minister was to select a delegation for the first session of the General Assembly of the UN in

New York. Nehru merged the two departments of external affairs and commonwealth relations under him into a single one in July 1947.

Girija Shankar Bajpai, India's envoy to the US during the British Raj, who was described by Nehru as 'a tower of strength' to him,[110] remained a dominant figure who called the shots. The Department of Commonwealth Relations largely maintained a separate entity. The external affairs ministry had no additional secretary, but it had three senior officers at the joint-secretary (JS) level: P.A. Menon, who had been in the Washington Supply Mission during the war, became the new JS (external); R.R. Saxena, who had earlier been in the Customs Service and had served in Canada, was now the JS (protocol) and also in charge of the consular and passport division; S. Ratnam of the Indian Audit and Accounts Service became the JS (administration), who supervised personnel, accounts, supplies and the entire administrative infrastructure. Y.D. Gundevia, who had been counsellor in the Indian mission in Rangoon, also joined as a JS. Subimal Dutt remained the commonwealth secretary. Although Bajpai wanted K.P.S. Menon to take the post of India's first foreign secretary, Menon expressed his reluctance, but finally agreed and joined in April 1948 when sought out by Nehru himself. N.R. Pillai was sent as commissioner general and chargé d'affaires to Paris.[111]

Politicians also doubled up as diplomats. Asaf Ali was nominated in February 1947 as India's ambassador to the US; Vijaya Lakshmi Pandit, Nehru's sister, was sent to Moscow in April; and K.P.S. Menon was appointed India's high commissioner in the UK. Dhirubhai Desai, the son of Bhulabhai Desai, was posted in the legation in Bern in March 1948.

~

One of the earliest institutions for which the British in India started preparing for a possible transfer of power to Indians was the Intelligence Bureau. A note titled 'The Future of the Intelligence Bureau' was prepared in September 1943 by the Indian Political Intelligence (IPI), a secret organization within the India Office in London, which kept a watch on the activities of India's extremist politicians and revolutionaries who worked outside India. The IPI reported to the secretary of state for India through the India Office's public and judicial department, and to the Government of India through the Intelligence Bureau. The IPI recommended that in the event of the Central government being formed by Indians, 'Before any transfer of the records of the Intelligence Bureau to the new Government could take place, they would undoubtedly have to be thoroughly sifted and a large portion of them either sent home or destroyed.'

Wavell asked the secretary of state Leo Amery towards the end of 1944, 'What would happen to the Intelligence Bureau, which is now under the Home Department, if we were called upon to form a "political" government at the Centre of the kind suggested in the Cripps offer?' Reginald Maxwell, former home member in the viceroy's executive council and then an adviser to Amery, noted his suggested methods by which intelligence could be kept away from an Indian home member:

> . . . I am inclined to think that, so long as matters go no further than a political Executive Council under the present Constitution, it would be best to leave the IB under the control of the Home Department of the Government of India and to be careful to appoint a Home Member who was reasonably reliable. But there may be a section of intelligence which could not be exposed to such risks as there would be; and, if so, it might be necessary to have small separate office for this purpose in the Governor-General's Secretariat with corresponding branches in the Governors' Secretariat, not forming part of the official intelligence organizations but keeping in touch with them, so far as necessary, by personal contact in the same way as Central Intelligence Officers now work in the Provinces.

Maxwell's idea found great resonance with the IPI. P.J. Patrick, assistant undersecretary of state, informed David Monteath, permanent undersecretary of state for India and Burma in January 1945, that the IPI 'attached great importance to the removal to the Governor-General's Secretariat of compromising past records, e.g. on the activities of individuals who might become members of the Executive Council or even Home Member'. This, in effect, meant that as the home member, Patel wouldn't even know about the existence of intelligence collected on him or his comrades if the IB so decided.

In February 1945, the director of the IB (DIB), Denys Pilditch, in consultation with the home member in the Viceroy's Executive Council, Francis Mudie, proposed two options. Firstly, the introduction of a convention backed by the viceroy's overriding powers to provide immunity to the DIB from curiosity and inquisitiveness of the Indian home member about his records and sources of information. The second suggestion was to create an 'external' section of the IB, as a separate entity, in the governor-general's secretariat, 'to deal with matters of imperial significance' and at the same time remain closely connected with intelligence work in the UK and other dominions. The IB believed this to be the most effective way of protecting the information which it had obtained from other organizations solely on the understanding that such information would be kept protected. It would allow an arrangement where, instead of destroying them 'on a fairly comprehensive scale', records up to the transfer of power could be transferred out of its corresponding organizations, including those abroad, to 'form a pool of information available on request in the interests of the Government of India through necessary close contact and liaison between the head of the section and the Director of the Intelligence Bureau'. Although the note did not make any specific mention of information flowing out of India, the idea was implied, clarified Pilditch.[112]

After much discussion and debate between MI5, MI6, IPI, IB, the secretary of state for India, the viceroy and Mudie, an agreement was reached that a rule of business would be made whereby the viceroy would authorize the DIB to share or withhold any information under his control and to decide the form in which information is shared. Moreover, records in the IB would be split into an internal and an external section, the external records being accorded greater security.[113]

When the DIB pointed out that it would be difficult to conceal the existence and the 'general character' of the IPI from the Indian ministers, the IPI suggested that the ministers should be told in confidence only for their personal information about the IB having a 'link in London for liaison with certain departments of H.M.G.' without revealing the names of those departments.[114]

The focus of the ongoing deliberation gradually shifted to the eventuality of the post of the DIB being occupied by an Indian. An undated and unsigned top-secret note, probably issued by the IPI, noted, 'British authorities might be prepared to continue their present degree of co-operation so long as the DIB remained a European: but it is very unlikely that they would be prepared to co-operate if DIB as well as the Home Member were to be an Indian—in which event IPI would have to close down.' It was also possible that the home member would himself shut down the IPI realizing that its continued existence was dependent on the goodwill of the British security authorities. In such an eventuality, the note recommended an exchange of liaison officers to be located in London and Delhi.

When Norman Smith, the then DIB, had his first meeting on 4 September 1946 with Vallabhbhai Patel, the home minister in the interim government, Patel told him that instead of continuing to focus on extremist political parties, such as the Socialist Party, Forward Bloc and other similar ones, the IB should turn their attention to 'particularly dangerous individuals' in these organizations. At the same time, according to information available to P.J. Patrick, Patel also approved Smith's proposal to 'discontinue the collection of intelligence on orthodox Congress and Muslim League activity'. Sensing that Patel wanted an Indian to become the next DIB, Smith, who was to retire in March 1947, saw in it the opportunity to set up the liaison mechanism with the British security establishment. He felt that 'India with an Indian DIB will have more confidence in him and therefore the more readily accept any arrangement of liaison officers at either end'.[115] Patrick noted the dilemma regarding the Indian government's natural inclination not to gather intelligence on Congress and League supporters vis-à-vis the British government's need for such information in case the interim government resigned or followed a markedly different policy. Patel, while agreeing to the continuance of the IPI, indicated that he would not like 'information reaching DIB and his agents which would be prejudicial to India's interests' to be passed on to the British authorities. One way to circumvent this handicap, Patrick noted, was intelligence collected on the anti-British activities of the interim government's supporters would not be shared with the interim government to avoid embarrassment. On the whole, Patrick was hopeful: 'There is nothing to show that the Interim Government or at any rate the experienced Mr. Patel undervalues the importance of political intelligence.'[116]

Patrick referred to a directive issued by Clement Attlee placing responsibility on MI5 for covering 'subversive activities conducted by Indians whether in India or in this country [UK] so long as India remains a part of the British Commonwealth'. Accordingly, both MI5 and MI6 were asked to 'examine the means of obtaining covert intelligence in India and the adjacent countries'.[117]

On 15 March 1947, Monteath informed George Abell, the viceroy's private secretary, that the IPI would have to be replaced by 'some kind of Liaison Office on reciprocal basis if that is acceptable to Patel'. A meeting between Patel and Guy Liddell, deputy director general of MI5, who was scheduled to be in Delhi on 24 March, was suggested to discuss the liaison arrangements.[118] What happened subsequently remained a secret until the authorized history of MI5 by Christopher Andrew was published in 2009; Andrew was given virtually unrestricted access to the agency's files.

After meeting Liddell, the interim government agreed to have an MI5 security liaison officer (SLO) stationed in New Delhi after the transfer of power. Accordingly, Lieutenant Colonel Kenneth Bourne, who had served in India with the Intelligence Corps during the Second World War, was appointed the first SLO. According to Andrew, relations between the MI5 and the IB 'were closer and more confident than those between any other departments of the British and Indian governments' for over the next two decades.[119]

With Smith scheduled to retire in April 1947, Rao Bahadur T.G. Sanjevi Pillai, the then deputy inspector general of the police of Madras city, was selected to replace him. On 25 March, Patel wrote to Madras premier Ramaswami Reddiar, 'After great deal of search we have been able to find in him a suitable person.'[120] Pillai was joined in September 1948 by B.N. Mullik as the deputy director of IB.

Mullik took charge as the DIB when Sanjevi went on a prolonged leave in July 1950, with S. Balakrishna Shetty, who had joined IB as an assistant director in March 1947, being promoted as the deputy director. Before the expiry of the leave, however, Sanjevi rejoined the Madras government as the inspector-general of police in November 1950.[121] According to Mullik, Nehru was not at all happy with Sanjevi's 'sudden demotion' under Patel's orders, for which 'some misunderstanding between the two leaders' was responsible.[122]

When Mullik joined as the deputy director, he held some old grudge against Nehru and felt that neither did the prime minister have a high opinion of intelligence nor did he have a proper understanding of how intelligence functioned. He met the prime minister for the first time only after taking over as the director nearly two years later:

I came back from this interview with all my previous resentment, diffidence, inferiority complex, anger, grievance and everything adverse washed away. I was won over by Pandit Nehru's personality, charm, courtesy, learning and humanity. I came back with the conviction that I had met the man whom I could serve without the slightest strain

on my loyalty and whose word would be enough for me to undertake
the most serious responsibilities and hazardous tasks which might
confront me.[123]

His opinion that Nehru did not have a proper understanding of intelligence
gathering also changed completely. According to Mullik, 'From Pandit
Nehru, Intelligence got the support and appreciation which it needed to
develop almost from scratch to a position where it could measure itself
against the Intelligence Organisations of other countries with abundant
resources at their disposal.'[124] Mullik went on to serve as the DIB for the
next fourteen years. The time he spent with Nehru 'were the greatest
moments of my life and I used to drink deep at his feet'.[125]

In all these years, Mullik also continued the practice of leaving the
Congress party out of IB's scope of intelligence gathering. When Nehru
noticed that the political intelligence brought to him by Mullik covered
only non-Congress organizations, he asked the IB chief for the reason.
Mullik told him that the IB 'studiously avoided the Congress because it
was one of the principles of Intelligence not to meddle in the internal
affairs of the ruling party'. Strangely, Mullik tried to convince himself
that the 'avoidance by the IB of meddling in the affairs of the Congress
Party convinced the Prime Minister as well as the Home Minister of our
impartial approach in political matters'.[126]

In spite of his devotion to Nehru, Mullik later wrote that he was
untruthful to him about the arrangements regarding the SLO. He recalled
that the prime minister 'enquired if we maintained any connections with
the British Intelligence and I replied in the negative'.[127] The MI5, on the
other hand, noted the enthusiasm with which both Sanjevi and Mullik
welcomed the arrangement. Mullik requested the MI5 for help on training
in counter-espionage and transcription. The then SLO, John Allen, noted
in 1955 that Mullik was very careful in avoiding the attention of the
Ministry of External Affairs (headed by Nehru) in terms of the intelligence-
sharing arrangement and that he did not have 'sufficient confidence in the
Prime Minister's continuing approval of the liaison willingly'. While a
number of officers attended training courses by the MI5 in London,[128] the
British intelligence also sent an officer to review IB's counterintelligence
operations against the Soviet Union and propose improvements. An MI5
expert on the Communist Party of Great Britain (CPGB) was brought in
to examine the IB records on the finances of the Communist Party of India

(CPI), which confirmed that the CPI received regular secret subsidies from Moscow.[129]

The SLO continued to function until 1968, when he was recalled as a consequence of the findings of the Committee on Overseas Representation on British intelligence, a decision that was resented by the IB. The MI5 recorded that the then DIB, S.P. Verma, regarded the step as a 'disaster' and that he did not know how the IB would manage without the arrangement.[130]

6

Nehru's Supremacy

Wavell's selection of the invitees to the Simla Conference in June–July 1945 indicated how the British viewed the Indian political landscape. The purported objective of the conference, which was to form a new Executive Council 'more representative of organised political opinion', was transformed into the requirement for a council that 'would represent the main communities and would include equal proportions of Caste Hindus and Moslems'.[1] The line separating the political and the communal was obliterated. Apart from Gandhi and Jinnah, as the recognized leaders of the two main political parties, the conference would have representatives of the scheduled castes, the Sikhs and the Europeans, and also the leader of the Nationalist Party in the Central Assembly. Wavell thus adopted a queer mix of political and communal approaches to resolve a political problem. For him Congress represented Hindu India and the Muslim League Muslim India. He felt that other political parties weren't reasonable enough to be brought to the conference table. In October 1944, Wavell had written to Churchill that there was 'every reason to mistrust and dislike Gandhi and Jinnah, and their followers' but 'I can see no prospect of our having more reasonable people to deal with'.[2] He informed the secretary of state for India that he 'had no intention of handing over Executive Council to . . . those who would not support the war'.[3] When the existing council suggested the inclusion of Syama Prasad Mookerjee of the Hindu Mahasabha among the invitees to the conference, Wavell accepted the suggestion, only to drop him within the next few days. On 9 June he informed the secretary of state:

> [Governor of Bengal, Richard] Casey has just brought to my notice consistently anti-British and anti-Allies character of articles in Shyama

[*sic*] Prasad Mookerjee's paper *Nationalist* which was founded at end of 1944. Mookerjee is bitterly communal as well and would clearly refuse to co-operate with me or with other leaders. I have therefore decided to drop him.[4]

The absence of the leftist and radical leaders, most of whom were still in prison, left the political arena open to the Gandhian camp. Jayaprakash Narayan and Ram Manohar Lohia, the socialist leaders, were released on 11 April 1946, ten months after the release of the Congress Working Committee members. The ban on Forward Bloc, which was imposed on 22 June 1942, continued until June 1946 'in the interests of public safety and maintenance of public order'.[5] The key leaders of the Bloc who were not in prison, such as Sheel Bhadra Yajee and R.S. Ruikar, opposed the Congress policy of office acceptance following the elections to the Central Assembly and the provincial legislatures.[6] The party was, however, too weak and too dispersed to influence decisions by the Congress leadership. Systematic release of the several hundred political prisoners began only after Congress ministries were formed in the provinces.

Soon after his release in June 1945, Nehru took up the cudgels against the Communist Party of India (CPI) for its activities during the war. In several speeches and press conferences, Nehru accused the party of acting against the national movement. On 12 August, Nehru wrote to the British Communist leader Rajani Palme Dutt:

> . . . at a time when there was bitter conflict between nationalism and the imperialist structure, they [the CPI] appeared before the people as acting on the side of the latter . . . Politically the fact that has gone most against them and aroused the greatest resentment is their attitude on the communal question. They have become full-blooded supporters of Jinnah's demands (unspecified and vague as they are) and in the name of Congress-League unity they demand a complete surrender by Congress to Jinnah.[7]

Taking formal cognizance of the complaints received against the politics of the Communists June 1942 onwards, the Congress Working Committee appointed a sub-committee in September 1945 comprising Nehru, Vallabhbhai Patel and Govind Ballabh Pant to investigate into the matter. The sub-committee, in its report of 21 September 1945, came to the conclusion that 'there is ample evidence on record before us to establish a strong prima facie case against the members of the Communist Party in the Congress'. The CPI was asked to respond to the charges within two weeks. Protesting against this move, P.C. Joshi, the general secretary of the CPI, asked all Communist members of the Congress to resign, except those who were members of the All India Congress Committee (AICC), so that they could respond to the charges. Joshi complained that although the CPI had consistently demanded the release of the Congress leaders for the past three years, the Congress leadership was now demonstrating 'sectarian arrogance', which, instead of winning India her freedom and building democracy, would 'only divide and disrupt the freedom forces themselves'. Joshi further argued:

> Their [Congress's] declaration of fight against the Muslim League will only unleash forces of civil war, not forge the future Indian Union. To glorify the strength of the Congress and deny that of the League is to be blind. To demand self-determination from the British and to deny it to a section of our own countrymen is plain injustice. We do not think it is good patriotism to seek British intervention in our internal affairs, for it will lead not to Indian freedom, but to a British-planned imposed constitution.

Accusing the CPI of mounting 'a tirade against the Congress' in the tone of 'self-righteous arrogance' instead of answering the specific charges, Nehru, Patel and Pant recommended the expulsion of all the Communist members of the AICC and instructed the Provincial Congress Committees to remove all Communist members from elective offices in December 1945.[8] The clash between the Congress and the Communists soon became public over the mutiny of the ratings in the Royal Indian Navy in February 1946. Speaking at a public meeting in Bombay on 26 February 1946, Patel accused the Communists of misleading the people and exploiting their patriotism for resurrecting the prestige of the party. He asked: Who would take the anti-imperialist stance of the CPI seriously after they whole-heartedly cooperated with British imperialism during the Quit India movement?[9]

The CPI faced more virulent criticism by Congress leaders during the provincial elections, particularly in Madras province, where they were organizationally strong. Asserting that India did not want the Moscow brand of communism, Kamraj Nadar, the president of the Tamil Nadu Pradesh Congress Committee, said that although the CPI was claiming to fight British imperialism, it would not hesitate to betray the country, as it did in 1942, if Russia and Britain settled their feud.[10] Referring to attempts to disrupt his meetings, Kamraj said, 'We fight for Swaraj to secure first and foremost freedom of expression. If Communists deny that freedom to their own comrades, I wonder whether they are fighting for Swaraj or Moscow Raj.'[11] 'If Russians should decide on invading India,' asked Pattabhi Sitaramayya, 'will Communists fight them?'[12] Jayaprakash Narayan was blunter. Talking to the press in Delhi in April 1946, he declared, 'I consider the Communists to be Russian fifth columnists and as such a perpetual danger to the country, irrespective of what policy they may be following at a particular moment.'[13]

The election results clearly demonstrated that neither the communists nor the Hindu Mahasabha were in a position to influence the Gandhian wing or to beat them in elections. Wavell's assessment of the political situation of the previous year still held good. 'There is generally speaking no organised opposition to Congress amongst Hindus in British India (except possibly in the Punjab),' he had written to the secretary of state for India in December 1945, 'and nothing to put in its place if we suppress it. Neither the Communist Party nor M.N Roy's Social Democrats have any influence.'[14]

Yet, the Congress was gradually entering a phase of transition itself. Elections to the Central and provincial legislatures being held after nearly a decade and reorganization of party structures created new opportunities, unleashing a whole new level of political ambitions leading to contests for reaping rewards.

The scramble for power was most visible during and after the provincial elections. 'The forthcoming session of the Congress will be called upon to decide whether the spirit of sacrifice or scramble for power is to prevail within the Congress,' Patel had to remind a meeting of the Gujarat Provincial Congress Committee in January 1946.[15] 'There should be no race for Congress tickets,' he warned the Congress workers in another meeting.[16] There was, however, little impact of such exhortations. The Orissa Congress received 240 applications for fifty-six seats.[17] In the Central Provinces there were 152 applications for sixteen seats.[18] Other provinces too showed similar patterns.

Some of the provinces were going through a churn in the leadership too. The efforts of the Gandhian high command to reinstate C. Rajagopalachari

(Gandhi kept praising him in his articles and speeches while Patel worked the Congress machinery in his favour),[19] as premier of Madras were snubbed by the provincial leadership. In August 1940, Rajagopalachari had suggested forming a national government led by the Muslim League. Under his leadership, the Madras Congress Legislature Party in April 1942 passed resolutions recommending to the AICC the acceptance of Muslim League's demand for Pakistan, and inclusion of League members in the Madras ministry. While he received support from the Communists, Rajagopalachari reciprocated by defending the removal of the ban on the CPI. Soon, he also opposed Gandhi's Quit India resolution. Asked by Nadar, the then president of the Tamil Nadu Congress, to show cause why action should not be taken against him, Rajagopalachari resigned from the Congress.[20] At the close of the war, however, he became a regular invitee to the CWC meetings and was formally inducted back by Nehru in July 1946.

Rajagopalachari's stand on the Quit India movement and the Pakistan issue had become so unpopular that Gandhi's continued defence of him also failed to have any impact. In fact, Gandhi's visit to Tamil Nadu in February 1946 was widely construed in the Congress circles to be an effort to reinstate Rajagopalachari as the premier of the province. Gandhi refuted the allegations, but at the same time made it clear that if he had the power, he would have put his old comrade in office.[21] Gandhi's article in *Harijan* alleging that it was 'a clique that evidently counts in the official Congress in Madras' which ran the campaign against Rajagopalachari, although he was popular among the masses,[22] led to the resignation of the president of the Tamil Nadu Provincial Congress Committee, Kamraj Nadar, which he later withdrew at the request of Gandhi.[23] Rajagopalachari in turn wrote to Gandhi, expressing his desire not to contest the assembly elections.[24] Following the provincial elections, Azad, Gandhi and Patel's proposal to elect Rajagopalachari as the leader of the Madras Congress Legislature Party was defeated by 148 to thirty-eight votes at a party meeting.[25] 'This is the first instance in Congress history where responsible Congressmen have failed to respond to a reasonable appeal from the leaders,' an angry Patel wrote to V.V. Giri.[26] T. Prakasam, president of the Andhra Provincial Congress Committee, was elected the leader instead, contrary to Gandhi's explicit advice to select Pattabhi Sitaramayya over Prakasam,[27] and subsequently became the premier of Madras. Rajagopalachari was moved to the central politics first as a member of the CWC and next as a member of the interim government. Although the provincial leaders successfully prevented the central high command from imposing Rajagopalachari's leadership on them, they failed to agree on a consensus candidate. Prakasam won the contest by a narrow margin, obtaining eighty-two votes against sixty-nine by C.N. Muthuranga Mudaliar, with twenty-three abstaining. As soon as the election was over, the clash between the Congress committees of Andhra, Tamil Nadu and Kerala was brought out in the open when Mudaliar announced that he had been compelled to contest. Admitting that it was he who had compelled Mudaliar, Nadar made it clear that he was not happy with the results. He warned Prakasam not to antagonize the Tamil Nadu Congress, without whose cooperation he would not be able to govern. Madhava Menon, the chief of the Kerala Congress, divulged that he had reluctantly supported the candidature of Mudaliar, but was happy that Prakasam had won.[28]

During elections to the United Provinces Congress Committee in May 1946, Nehru asked one of the presidential contenders, Shibbanlal Saxena, to step down not on the question of merit or ideology, but because 'I am afraid you are very irresponsible'. Saxena, who had been awarded a ten-year rigorous imprisonment for his role in the Quit India movement, had recently been released from prison by the newly elected Congress government. When Saxena refused to oblige, Nehru told him bluntly that he would not serve in the committee if Saxena was elected president. With such a strong stand taken by Nehru, it was of little surprise that Saxena lost the contest to the socialist leader Seth Damodar Swarup.[29] Although Gopinath Bardoloi was elected the premier of Assam, he lost in the organizational elections held to elect AICC delegates from the province.[30]

The principles underlying the organization and its central leadership were also undergoing a churn. In May 1946, amid the scramble for power, Gandhi suggested some radical changes to the constitution of the Congress:

> The supreme change that is desirable for the sake of avoiding untruth and hypocrisy is to remove the words 'legitimate and peaceful' from the first article of the Congress Constitution as also the clause about khadi. Experience shows that the people who form the bulk of Congressmen are not wedded either to truth and non-violence or to khadi. As an ardent lover of truth and non-violence and khadi as their symbol, I make bold to suggest that these clauses should go. It will be open to anyone to be truthful and non-violent and to wear khadi if he or she chooses to. Only there will be no deception practised on India or the world.[31]

A rearrangement of the Congress leadership started with the presidential election in the middle of 1946, as the formation of an interim government became the burning issue. It was well understood the next president of the Congress would lead the party in the interim government. The selection of the president, however, began a process that would continue to influence the politics in independent India. Gandhi was still the most powerful voice in the organization and the cementing force, but his influence had started showing signs of waning. It was evident during the negotiations with the Cabinet Mission and the central and provincial elections.

On 9 May 1946, J.B. Kripalani, the Congress general secretary, issued a communiqué announcing Nehru as the next president of the Congress, for the fourth time. The voting for electing the president was to take place in the provinces a week later, but it became unnecessary due to the withdrawal of the other two candidates—Patel and Kripalani himself.[32]

As early as 20 April, Gandhi had made it clear to the outgoing president of Congress who had been in that post for the past six years, Maulana Azad, that it was not proper for him to continue as president any more and that he preferred Nehru as the next president.[33] Azad accordingly issued a statement a few days later recommending Nehru as the next Congress president.[34] Patel, however, was the preferred candidate of the provincial Congress committees, twelve of which out of fifteen nominated him.[35] According to Kripalani, he got a few members of the working committee and some Delhi leaders to propose Nehru's name, in deference to Gandhi's wishes, since none of the provinces had nominated him.[36]

Gandhi had made his choice known unambiguously when he had selected Nehru over Patel for the Congress presidentship in 1929. In January 1942 he had declared, 'I have always said that not Rajaji, nor Sardar Vallabhbhai, but Jawaharlal will be my successor.' He predicted, 'When I am gone he will do what I am doing now.'[37] A few months later Gandhi clarified:

He [Nehru] has never accepted my method in its entirety. He has frankly criticized it, and yet he has faithfully carried out the Congress policy largely influenced . . . by me. Those like Sardar Vallabhbhai who have followed me without question cannot be called heirs. And everybody admits that Jawaharlal has the drive that no one else has in the same measure.[38]

Both Azad and Kripalani were aware of Patel's willingness to become the next president when they canvassed support for Nehru and later came to regret it, Azad more bitterly than Kripalani. 'Patel never forgave me for that,' Kripalani later told journalist Durga Das.[39] Azad called his support to Nehru over Patel 'the greatest blunder' of his political life. He claimed that Patel 'would have never committed the mistake of Jawaharlal which gave Mr Jinnah the opportunity of sabotaging the [Cabinet Mission] plan'. 'I can never forgive myself when I think that if I had not committed these mistakes, perhaps the history of the last ten years would have been different,' Azad lamented in his memoirs compiled during 1956–57.[40] Nehru took charge as president on 6 July 1946 at the AICC meeting in Bombay.

The Congress had to elect a new president again with Nehru set to take charge as the vice-president in the interim government as announced by the viceroy on 24 August. At the annual session of the Congress held in Meerut on 22–24 November 1946, J.B. Kripalani was announced to be the new Congress president.

Immediately upon joining the interim government, Nehru presented a broad outline of the government's objectives. In his first broadcast from the All India Radio on 7 September and in an informal meeting with reporters, Nehru talked about reaching out to villagers and factory workers, feeding, clothing, housing, educating, providing sanitary and health conditions to the millions of Indians and raising their standard of living. As far as global politics was concerned, India was not to align with any power blocs but focus on the emancipation of colonial and dependent countries and peoples, and have friendly relations with the British Commonwealth. He sent out good wishes to the United States, to the Soviet Union and hoped that a united and democratic China would emerge out the turbulence she was going through.[41]

Gandhi viewed the priorities for the interim government differently. The immediate tasks for 'our uncrowned king Pandit Jawaharlal Nehru and his colleagues' in the government were to abolish salt tax, bring together Hindus and Muslims, remove untouchability and adopt khadi.[42]

Both Nehru and Patel were aggressive and bitter towards the Muslim League in their speeches at the Meerut session of the Congress. Nehru complained that the entry of the Muslim League had broken the cabinet system of government as the party was working as a separate bloc. He divulged that as a result of the League's attitude, the Congress was on the verge of resigning from the government twice. He was 'fed up with' the delay in dealing with the government officials 'who were guilty of acts of brutality and savagery against our people', as a result of which 'all those who thought that they would be punished for their brutal deeds have become reassured and are now obsequiously salaaming us'.[43] The Calcutta killings of August were not the work of 'goondas' but 'was a game played to achieve political ends', said Patel. With reference to Muslim League's Direct Action Day slogan of '*Ladke Lenge Pakistan*' (We shall fight and get Pakistan), Patel thundered, 'the sword must be met by the sword.' He warned the League that Pakistan could not be achieved by the sword or bloodshed and wanted people to take recourse to violence, even if only in self-defence. Patel was unsparing towards the leftists in the Congress too. Some people deceived themselves, he said:

> . . . by imagining that they were bringing about revolution. This was like the dog in the fable, which while walking under a heavily-loaded cart imagined that the cart would not move if it stopped.[44]

Pyrarelal Nayyar, Gandhi's personal secretary, has hinted that Nehru voiced his complaints against Patel during his visit to Gandhi, who was then staying at Srirampur in Bengal, in the last days of 1946. On 30 December, just as Nehru was to take his leave, Gandhi wrote to Patel:

> I have heard many complaints against you . . . Your speeches tend to be inflammatory and play to the gallery. You have lost sight of all distinction between violence and non-violence. You are teaching people to meet violence with violence. You miss no opportunity to insult the Muslim League in season and out of season. If all this is true, it is very harmful. They say you talk about holding on to office. This also is disturbing, if true.[45]

Patel defended himself strongly in his reply, arguing that the complaints 'are not only false but some of them are beyond my imagination'. He guessed that 'these accusations must have been dinned into your ears by Mridula [Sarabhai, the new general secretary of the Congress] for she has made it her pastime to heap abuses upon me'. Patel accused Sarabhai of 'indulging in a nauseating propaganda that I want to get rid of Jawahar and also found a new party'.[46]

Clement Attlee's statement of 20 February, the arrival of Mountbatten on 22 March and the escalation of the communal violence were the three strands that determined the course of politics in the subcontinent in 1947.

The interim government had reached a deadlock because of the determined obstructionist policy of the Muslim League. It was, however, a decision of the Congress that empowered the League to play such a role. Despite his non-acceptance of the Cabinet Mission plan, Jinnah agreed to join the interim government because he feared that if the League stayed away, firstly the administration of the country would go into Congress's hands, and secondly, the viceroy would nominate non-League Muslims that would take the wind out of the League's sail.[47] When the matter for allocating portfolios came up, Wavell suggested to Nehru that out of the four main portfolios—defence, external affairs, home and finance—home department be handed over Muslim League. Nehru's objection was that 'it would be very difficult to shift Patel'.[48] With Patel being reluctant to release the home department, during the negotiations that followed Rafi Ahmed Kidwai suggested handing over the finance portfolio to the Muslim League. The suggestion was made under the assumption that no League representative was competent to deal with the subject. The League, however, accepted the offer and Liaquat Ali Khan, who took charge of the department, ran it with the help of capable and experienced Muslim bureaucrats in the government. Since the finance department controlled the expenditures of every other department with a power of veto, Patel came to realize that 'he could not create the post of a chaprasi' without Khan's approval, and that the proposals of the Congress members were 'either rejected or modified beyond recognition' by the department. Azad later described the handing over of the finance department as 'our own foolish action'. The icing on the cake was Khan's March 1947 budget that proposed very high taxes on profits of industrialists, a measure calculated to hit the financial support base of the Congress.[49] 'We strongly feel that these Budget proposals will put back economic progress and we cannot be parties to them unless they are very greatly altered and amended,' Patel protested to Wavell.[50] The tax rates were later brought down through Mountbatten's intervention.[51]

Morarji Desai, however, strongly contested Azad's interpretation of Patel's reluctance to let go of the home department, describing it as 'Maulana Saheb's prejudice against Sardar Saheb'. According to Desai, later events proved the correctness of Patel's view that if the Home Department was handed over to Muslim League, 'there would be no safety in India at all', whereas letting the League have the finance department 'did not endanger the safety of India and whatever harm was done could be rectified'.[52]

As Nehru wrote to Gandhi, there were probable grey areas in Attlee's statement, but 'the real thing is that they have finally decided and announced that they are quitting', and 'everything that happens from now onwards must be governed by it'.[53] Only Nehru and Patel could carry the organization with them, and they did. On the contrary, Gandhi, having failed to convince the Congress Working Committee of the practicality of his desire to let Jinnah form a new interim government and transfer power to it, told Mountbatten that then onwards the Congress point of view would be represented by the members of the interim government, and he 'represented none but himself'.[54] Mountbatten, however, could not trust Gandhi's acceptance of partition of India and remained wary of the possibility that he might exert his influence to undo the 3 June Plan. He noted in his personal report of 8 August 1947:

Gandhi's absence from the celebrations in Delhi on the 15th August is, of course, intentional. He has never given the 3rd June plan his unqualified blessing and his position might be difficult. He also realises that it would not be possible to fit him into the programme in the way to which he would feel himself entitled.[55]

When Gandhi expressed his wish to spend the rest of his life in Pakistan, Mountbatten noted, 'This will infuriate Jinnah, but will be a great relief to Congress for, as I have said before, his influence is largely negative or even destructive and directed against the only man who has his feet firmly on the ground, Vallabhbhai Patel.'[56]

Partition became a reality, but most Congress leaders believed it to be a temporary measure. Gandhi told a prayer meeting on 4 June 1947 that 'the wonderful thing about it is that we can undo it anytime we want'.[57] The AICC resolution of 13 June 1947 accepting the 3 June plan declared that the 'AICC earnestly trusts that when present passions have subsided. . . the false doctrine of two nations in India will be discredited and discarded by all'.[58] Kripalani wrote to Mountbatten in a similar strain on 2 June that 'when the present passions have subsided our problems will be viewed in their proper perspective and a will union of all parts of India will result therefrom'.[59]

On 3 November, Govind Ballabh Pant announced in the United Provinces (UP) state legislative assembly, 'Khwaja Nazimuddin, the Premier of East Bengal, has declared it high treason to strive for the unification of the country. Whatever may be the law in Pakistan the people in this country would always strive for the unification of India.'[60] Speaking at a reception organized by the Sikh Seva Dal in Delhi on 28 November, Nehru predicted, 'Anyone who is not carried away by momentary passions will easily realise that ultimately both the dominions will unite into one country. The unity, I am confident, will be brought about not by force but by the march of events all over the world and consideration for mutual interests.'[61]

With the transfer of power approaching fast, it became necessary to decide upon the governors for the provinces and ministers in the interim government. On 2 July 1947, Nehru intimated Mountbatten that he would like John Colville and Archibald Nye to continue after the transfer of power as governors of Bombay and Madras, respectively. He also wanted Chandulal Trivedi, who was then the governor of Orissa, and Akbar Hydari, the then governor of Assam to continue.[62] The final list of governors was shared by Nehru with Mountbatten on 29 July, which included Rajagopalachari (West Bengal), Jairamdas Doulatram (Bihar), Mangaldas Pakvasa (Central Provinces), Chandulal Trivedi (East Punjab), Kailas Nath Katju (Orissa), Dr Bidhan Chandra Roy (United Provinces). Nye, Colville and Hydari were to continue as mentioned in his earlier letter.[63]

Mountbatten took great interest in the formation of the new ministry. He had gathered from press reports and private sources that Nehru's cabinet was going to be an 'unimaginative' one comprising of 'old-time Congressites', which he felt 'would be disastrous'. At the viceroy's staff meeting on 28 July, V.P. Menon raised the concern that Nehru 'was having a great difficulty in forgetting his loyalties', whereas it was an opportunity to select a 'Ministry of talents' comprising 'a number of young men'.[64] Mountbatten told Nehru the next day that 'unless he got rid of a lot of top-weight like Rajagopalachari and Maulana Azad, he would find himself greatly hampered'. Although he was not sure whether he had been able to convince Nehru, Mountbatten claimed to have received information that after meeting him Nehru tore up the list of ministers that he was planning to submit and with Patel's support had started working on a new list. Mountbatten also claimed that Nehru wanted to induct Jayaprakash

Narayan in the cabinet, but dropped the idea after Narayan demanded the portfolios of finance, home and states departments for the Socialist Party.[65]

Mountbatten was initially not in favour of Baldev Singh continuing as the defence minister but changed his mind when he was informed the Syama Prasad Mookerjee was being considered for the position. He noted:

> It is of course admirable that they should have got an important member of the Hindu Mahasabha to join the Government, and Mukerji [sic] is an intelligent man (whom they wanted to remove from Bengal); but [Bengal governor] Burrows, who knows him well, described him to me recently as being so low that a snake could not crawl under his belly.[66]

On 30 July, Nehru informed Patel that he had spoken to B.R. Ambedkar and Rafi Ahmed Kidwai, and they had agreed to join the new government. He was going to talk to N.V. Gadgil and Amrit Kaur, and asked Patel to approach Syama Prasad Mookerjee, Rajagopalachari and Shanmukham Chetty.[67]

The next day, he sent a formal invitation to Patel to join the cabinet since 'formalities have to be observed to some extent', although the writing was 'somewhat superfluous because you are the strongest pillar of the Cabinet'. Patel responded with great warmth:

> Our attachment and affection for each other and our comradeship for an unbroken period of nearly 30 years admit of no formalities. My services will be at your disposal, I hope, for the rest of my life and you will have unquestioned loyalty and devotion from me in the cause for which no man in India has sacrificed as much as you have done. Our combination is unbreakable and therein lies our strength. I thank you for the sentiments expressed in your letter.[68]

Nehru sent the list of thirteen ministers of his cabinet to Mountbatten on 4 August. All Congress members of the interim government (except Rajagopalachari, who was to become the governor of Bengal) would continue and six new ministers were appointed. Although Gandhi, Patel and Amrit Kaur were against Azad being made a minister,[69] the latter continued in the cabinet. 'Gandhi has written to Maulana Azad asking him as a gesture to Congress to make way for a younger man,' Mountbatten observed, 'but the old Maulana has not yet taken the hint and they cannot drop him until he does.'[70]

With the transfer of power, the Constituent Assembly was scheduled to act as the new central legislature until a new parliament was elected after the promulgation of the Constitution. The Constituent Assembly had its first sitting as the central legislature on 17 November, where G.V. Mavalankar, president of the previous Central Assembly, was elected as the Speaker.[71]

~

In his broadcast on the occasion of transfer of power, Nehru, calling himself the 'first servant of the Indian people', shared the priorities of the first national government. These included putting 'an end to all internal strife and violence', a focus on large-scale industrialisation, rapid increase in production and reform of the antiquated land tenure system to address the problems of acute shortage of food and clothing, and spiral of inflation. Nehru had a special mention for the large river valley projects which were already under way and would lead to increase in food production, growth of industry and all-round development.[72]

While the momentous events around transfer of power moved at lightning speed, questions were raised whether it was necessary to disband the Congress, since it had achieved its goal of winning freedom for India. In Nehru's opinion, the Congress had two options ahead of it—either to continue as an organization encompassing all anti-imperialist forces or to become a party based on certain political and economic principles. He argued that it was important for the Congress to continue as it was, although later on it would have to transform into a party, because its dissolution would strengthen various disruptive forces which had already started showing signs of growth.[73] The AICC appointed a committee in November 1947 to revise the Congress constitution to reflect the changed circumstances.

The central leadership of the Congress, however, was anyway in the midst of another crisis. The difficult times for Kripalani started almost immediately after taking over as the Congress president in November 1946, beginning with problems in forming the working committee. Both Patel and Nehru refused to join the working committee initially, which Kripalani thought was 'because they were annoyed with each other', and agreed after much persuasion. Although Jayaprakash Narayan joined the committee, 'he never attended any of its meetings and soon resigned'.[74]

The AICC session of June 1939 had adopted a resolution defining the relationship between the provincial congress committees (PCCs) and the provincial Congress ministries. The resolution had called for cooperation between the two but stipulated that the PCCs would draw the attention of the ministries to important issues, but not interfere in matters of administration. In the event of differences over policy matters, the disputes were to be arbitrated by the parliamentary sub-committee of the Congress. This resolution was reaffirmed by the Working Committee in August 1946.[75] It was the lack of such clarity in the relation between the Congress Working Committee and the interim government that precipitated the crisis. Kripalani was aggrieved that decisions were taken by the Congress members of the interim government without consulting him or the Working Committee.

He wrote to Gandhi on 8 April 1947 that the Congress was 'marred by factions and divisions, based more on personal rivalries than on any discoverable principles'. He complained that the policies of the Congress appeared to be not applicable to the interim and the provincial governments, and that some of the Congress members in the government 'may even feel that the organisation stands in the way of their freedom of action'. He also wondered whether he didn't command their confidence. 'On several occasions I have felt that I have received rebuffs which have pained me but which I have quietly borne in the interest of the organisation,' Kripalani wrote. The two options in such a situation, according to him, were either to let those in the government take charge of the organisation, or else 'to put the Congress organisation in cold storage for the time being'. He offered his resignation along with the resignation of the two general secretaries, but the matter remained unresolved until the transfer of power was completed.[76]

In a note circulated to the working committee, Kripalani pointed out that with the transfer of power from the British to a popular and responsible government

> . . . the main function of the Congress as a political organisation will be to lay down the policy of the government and to serve as a link between it and the people . . . the leadership in the government and in the Congress must either be identical or must work in the closest harmony. Or else, the result is misunderstanding and confusion . . . If this confusion is not checked in time, I am afraid the Congress as an organisation will speedily disintegrate and its place in the national life will be captured by either the

Hindu Mahasabha or some organisation of militant communalism or by
the Communist Party.[77]

'None of you have a high opinion of him, Gandhi wrote about Kripalani to
Patel on 26 August 1947, advising him, 'If he does not enjoy the confidence
of his seniors, it is best to let him go.'[78]

Kripalani submitted his resignation formally at the AICC session
held in Delhi on 15 November 1947. On Gandhi's recommendation his
resignation was accepted, but the issues raised by him were not taken up for
discussion. Kripalani continued outside the government despite attempts
to co-opt him, first by offering him the posts of the governor of Bihar and
subsequently that of the food minister.[79]

Rajendra Prasad was unanimously elected the new president of Congress
on 17 November, with Patel proposing his name and Nehru seconding the
proposal.[80] A relatively greater focus on running the government than on
strengthening the organization can be inferred from the fact that it took
Prasad nearly two months to nominate his working committee.[81]

The power play and conflicts within the leadership didn't escape
the notice of observant commentators. Krishnalal Sridharani, a regular
commentator in Indian newspapers observed:

Behind the purdah, a palace revolution has taken place . . . It has been
a home spun, quiet revolution *a la* Gandhi. From the springboard of
the All-India Congress Committee session, Mahatma Gandhi has once
again jumped into the nations' saddle. According to his own confessions
he was not enjoying the same influence over his top colleagues during
their office-holding as he did during their struggle for power. But now
he is supreme once more . . . Acharya Kripalani's contention sounded
plausible on another count. The austerity policy of the Congress kept the
front-rank leaders out of office while it sent second-line leaders to hold
official position. Thus the Parliamentary Board was able to control its
puppets. But now the top leaders themselves are sitting on the gadi and
the second-line leaders who are left out are asking for hegemony on the
strength of past practices. It simply cannot be done. Politics are politics
even in Gandhiji's India.

The choice of Babu Rajendra Prasad was the easiest way out of
this dilemma. His position is fourth in the Congress Party hierarchy
whether he is the Food Minister or the Congress President. He forms

the foursome with Gandhiji, Panditji and the Sardar, He is in the sanctorum in his own right, but now the illusion will be created that it is the Congress President who is being consulted and taken into confidence. Politics are politics even In Gandhiji's India. On the eve of the A.I.C.C. meeting a great fuss was made over the necessity of defining the economic programme of the Congress Party. If invoking vague and nebulous concepts means defining a thing, the economic creed of the Congress should now be regarded as duly defined. The Congress is against the acquisitive oligarchy which results from capitalism. The Congress is also opposed to the raj of the bureaucrat which results from socialism. Then what is the Congress for? It is for something that lies in between these two extremes and which is tendentiously described as decentralised economy. The economists of the world are eagerly awaiting a blueprint for this hodgepodge.[82]

A few months after Kripalani's resignation, Nehru spoke to Congress workers at Nagpur on the topic. 'The Government cannot place every item of its activity before Congress committees. But it is very necessary that all major items and all policies should be jointly discussed,' he told the gathering.[83] It is a matter of wonder why Nehru failed to state his position so clearly to Kripalani and to implement the policy, which could have avoided the conflict at the top-leadership level.

A resolution adopted at the AICC session on 17 November 1947 laid down the objectives of the Congress, which aimed at extending democracy from the political to the social and the economic spheres, empowering popularly elected panchayats, large-scale and centralized industrialization organized on a basis so that workers not only had a share in the profits but were also increasingly associated with the management and administration, and regulation of land with its mineral resources by the community. Although the economic structure should aim to maximize production, it should not create private monopolies and the concentration of wealth. To achieve these goals, an eight-member committee comprising Nehru, Azad, Jayaprakash Narayan, Achyut Patwardhan and others was set up for drawing up the economic programme for the Congress.[84] Increasing production as rapidly as possible was the consensus decision of the cabinet. Speaking at the Southern India Chamber of Commerce in Madras in November 1947, Syama Prasad Mookerjee declared, 'We should make this our immediate task—India must produce and produce all she can without delay.'[85] Finance minister Shanmukham Chetty explained to the central legislators, 'I am clear in my mind that the inflation today is not so much due to monetary causes but really to the very rapid fall in production.'[86] The US ambassador in India, Henry Grady, too, joined the issue when he opined that India needed to increase production in order to increase wages, but 'I am afraid economically India is going down as far as production is concerned'.[87]

The food situation in the country was grim. 'For some time past I have been gravely disturbed by certain aspects of the economic situation in India, particularly by the food situation,' Mountbatten wrote in a long letter to Nehru on 23 August. He listed three fundamental factors that stared the country in its face: (a) a breakdown of urban food rationing; (b) a coal crisis; and (c) a severe inflationary spiral that will turn urban wage levels grossly inadequate even for subsistence. Mountbatten warned that the food stocks which support rationing systems in the country (particularly in south India), were likely to be depleted before the kharif crop would become available in late October or early November. To make things worse, parts of India were facing complete crop failure, and procurement from the previous crop harvest (rabi) had already come to an end. Mountbatten informed Nehru that since imports too couldn't fill the supply gap, 'rationing systems in many urban areas will be in grave danger of breaking down' early September onwards despite severe cuts. India was looking at another famine situation averting which required immediate and vigorous efforts by both the central and the state governments at procurement and distribution, 'backed by the whole weight of the Congress party machine'.[88]

The idea of importing food grains did not sit well with Gandhi. At a prayer meeting, two days after Mountbatten's note, he lamented to his audience:

> I don't feel that we have won freedom. Should Hindustan known as the land of gold beg food from abroad? I feel very much pained about all this. If I had my way I would tell the people to die of hunger or else work hard [to produce food] but not a single grain should be imported from outside.[89]

Towards the end of September, Gandhi sent a message to Rajendra Prasad through Amrit Kaur asking him to give up the food portfolio, retaining that of agriculture. Gandhi felt that Prasad wasn't being able to do enough to improve the food situation. Prasad agreed to relinquish the post, provided it did not embarrass the government, and informed both Patel and Nehru accordingly.[90]

Announcing the new food policy of the government in the central legislature on 10 December, Rajendra Prasad gave a clear picture of the dismal situation in the country. The population covered by the rationing system increased nearly six-fold, from 26 million in 1944, the year in which the system was introduced, to 148 million after Partition. In comparison, the total grain available to the government from domestic procurement and imports increased from 5.69 million tonnes in 1944 to 7.15 million tonnes in 1946, and stood at 6.18 million tonnes in the first half of 1947. The share of imported food grains had increased from 13.3 per cent in 1944 to 3.5 per cent in 1947, resulting in sharply increasing food subsidy. Lack of growth in grain availability as compared to number of people availing the rationing system led to a drastic reduction in per capita availability: the allocation of one pound per adult (approximately 453.6 grams) and half a pound per child in 1944 declined to twelve ounces (approximately 340 grams) for adults and six ounces for children in 1946, further declining in many provinces in 1947.[91]

The rationing system, Prasad argued, had resulted in several problems, like corruption among government staff, unauthorized agents, black marketing and ghost ration cards. In order to address these problems, the new food policy instructed the provincial and state governments to gradually reduce their commitments under rationing and controlled movement of grains. The procurement price of food grains was left at the discretion of the provincial and state governments, and the power to import was restricted to the Central government only. The government hoped that with these decontrol measures, hoarding and profiteering would stop, making more stocks available and therefore reduce dependence on imports.[92]

Responding to the criticism by some members of the assembly that decontrol would lead to a spiral of inflation, Prasad made it clear that the government had adopted the policy with full awareness of the risks, because 'it was better to take those risks rather than to take the greater risk of a complete breakdown.' He advised that 'if there is a rise in prices we should be prepared for that; only it should not be allowed to go to such heights that it may upset our whole economy'.[93]

The question of food policy was politically the most sensitive, but it was clear to the Nehru government that to stabilize the overall economy and set it on a growth path, framing policies in all economic sectors was critical. Nehru outlined the political approach towards industrialization while speaking at the annual general meeting of the Associated Chambers of Commerce in Calcutta on 15 December 1947. The government's approach was not of adopting one 'ism' or another but would involve 'a large measure of socialism', that is, state control with regard to certain basic industries. Yet, a large field would be left open to private enterprise. Even foreign capital would be welcomed when available in favourable terms to India.[94]

Notwithstanding the utterance of the political framework for economic policymaking, the specifics were yet to come. The problem was articulated by G.D. Birla in an industries conference in December when he emphasized the need to lay down a definite policy to be able to create confidence among investors and attract private capital. The government, he complained, was speaking in two voices, and the industrialists did not know where they stood.[95]

The government's immediate focus was on the sectors that concerned the daily lives of the people. For instance, in early November it had announced its textile policy which laid down the continuation of control on cloth and yarn, a target for the increase in production by 800 million yards, setting up a tariff board to advise on the question of prices and guidelines for labour.[96]

There was much back and forth on the issue of decontrol. It was only in September 1950 that Nehru informed the chief ministers of the provinces: 'After a long debate and much argument, Congress has definitely declared in favour of controls for essential articles so long as they are in short supply. This must put an end to all argument on this question.'[97]

This policy was another deviation from Gandhi's professed views. At his prayer meeting on 17 October 1947, Gandhi had directed his scathing criticism at the bureaucrats and the policy of control of food and cloth:

Mill-owners say they have piles of cloth stocked with them. But how can they release it when there is control on it? . . . How terrible it is that there is enough stock of grains in the country but it does not reach the people it should. It seems to me that there is something basically wrong about it. Our bureaucrats wish to work sitting at their desks. They have in front of them their tables and red tape and wax. All that they have to do is to put red tape and make the file. Have they ever lived among the peasants? Have they ever acquainted themselves with the peasants? Very respectfully, I wish to tell them that they should not take it for granted that people will die. With open eyes we see that people are dying because of controls . . . I would say that both these controls should be removed as early as possible . . . The soaring prices of cloth, foodstuffs and other things will come down. Now there is no war and nothing is going out of the country. But the prices are still going up. I feel it is most disgraceful and our heads should hang in shame. The Government should trust the people and have courage. It should act boldly and remove controls as early as possible. This is my firm belief which is increasing day by day.[98]

Another area of reform that drew early attention as soon as the provincial governments were formed after the 1946 elections was the abolition of zamindari, an issue that was a component of Congress's election manifesto. With several provinces moving ahead with their own legislation, the Congress leadership took particular interest in the matter. In November 1947, Shanker Rao Deo, the general secretary of the Congress, issued a circular to the premiers and revenue ministers of the provinces asking them to introduce uniformity in their respective schemes, particularly in method and quantum of compensation, and to state clearly the financial and administrative mechanism being contemplated to improve agricultural production.[99]

A two-day conference of the provinces' revenue ministers held in December, however, agreed that due to the differing circumstances in each province, it was not possible to frame a uniform scheme. In a remarkable example of coordination between the Congress organization and the provincial governments, the ministers' conference decided to submit memoranda on the financial implications of the abolition of zamindari to the office of the AICC as well as to the central finance ministry. Moreover, the Congress president was requested to appoint a committee of experts which would tour the provinces and recommend agrarian reforms to be carried out after the abolition. Apart from the revenue ministers or their representatives from the provinces, the conference was attended by Rajendra Prasad, Azad, Kripalani and Deo.[100]

The Bihar legislative assembly passed the Bihar Abolition of Zamindaris Act in 1948, but the law had to be repealed in 1950 as it was successfully challenged in the law courts.[101] The province passed the Bihar

Land Reforms Act in 1950. Zamindari abolition and land reforms laws were passed by the Madras legislative assembly in 1948 and by the Uttar Pradesh assembly in 1950.

The government was trying to put in place several other measures to provide a boost to the industrial economy. In November, the finance minister Shanmukham Chetty introduced a bill in the central legislature to set up an Industrial Finance Corporation, industries and supplies minister Syama Prasad Mookherjee initiated a review process to further develop the Hindustan Aircraft factory in Bangalore, and C.H. Bhabha, the commerce minister, announced a six-point programme for the rapid expansion of Indian-owned ships, including the establishment of 2–3 government-controlled shipping corporations.[102] Surveys and investigations on multipurpose river valley projects, such as the Damodar valley, Ramapada Sagar and Machkund, had also commenced.[103] In December, N.V. Gadgil, minister for works. mines and power, introduced the bills for setting up the Damodar Valley Corporation and for the nationalization of production and supply of electricity. Being particularly interested in these multipurpose projects, Nehru wrote to Gopi Chand Bhargava, the premier of Punjab, 'We want to consider all these river valley schemes with targets in view which have to be checked frequently so as to avoid delay.'[104] In Orissa to inaugurate the construction of the Hirakud dam, Nehru declared on 12 April 1948, 'I am vastly interested in these river valley schemes—the Mahanadi, Damodar Valley, Kosi, Bhakra and others, for I feel that they will be the foundation of all future developments in India.'[105] The river valley projects, he had told the Constituent Assembly while speaking on the government's Industrial Policy before arriving in Orissa, 'are far more important than all your existing industries.'

The resolution on the Industrial Policy was presented by Syama Prasad Mookherjee in the central legislature on 6 April 1948. The policy announced the setting up of a National Planning Commission to steer the country's development. Industries were put into three categories—industries which were state monopolies (manufacture of arms and ammunitions, production and control of atomic energy, and railways); those industries where only the state could start new ventures (allowing existing private ones to exist for the next ten years) and were to be under state control (such as, coal, iron and steel, aircraft manufacture, ship-building, manufacture of telephone, telegraph and wireless apparatus including radio sets, and mineral oils); all remaining industries, which were open to private enterprises. At around the same time, a bill to reorganize the Port Trusts in order to achieve representation from labour as well as commercial interests was introduced in the Constituent Assembly by Dr John Matthai, the transport minister.[106]

Nehru focused a major part of his speech on the policy, the next day, championing river valley projects over other industry sectors, but also explained the fundamental reason for the policy being essentially non-disruptive in nature, not in line with his radical ideas of the previous decades:

> . . . after all that has happened in the course of the last seven or eight months, one has to be very careful of what step one might take which might not injure the existing structure too much. There has been destruction and injury enough, and certainly I confess to this House that I am not brave and gallant enough to go about destroying much more . . . It seems to me that in the state of affairs in the world today and in India, any attempt to have what might be called a clean slate, that is to say a sweeping away of all that we have got, would certainly not bring progress nearer but might delay it tremendously, which far from bringing economic progress may put us politically so far back that the economic aspect itself may be delayed tremendously.[107]

There was plenty of socialism, but also enough to calm the jittery nerves of the industrial investors. Ensuring inflow of capital was critical to stimulate economic growth. yet, the speech wasn't without a dig at the 'profit motive' of the private industry which, Nehru predicted, 'will come more and more into conflict with the new sense of the social state'. He made it clear that:

> There are going to be greater burdens on industry because the state itself if burdened so much with its social problems; it has to solve them or cease to be a social state . . .[108]

On 28 October 1947, Nehru had written to V.K. Krishna Menon, 'We seem to live here from crisis to crisis.'[109] As the government was stabilizing and gathering momentum in an environment marred by the invasion of Kashmir, influx of refugees and widespread communal riots and labour unrest, two developments threatened to pull it back.

One of these was the increasing schism between Patel and Nehru. The conflict between the two most powerful leaders of the government crystallized over the riot-stricken Ajmer and the negotiations in Kashmir in December 1947.

Upon receiving the news of the communal outburst in Ajmer, Nehru wrote to Patel on 16 December, inquiring about the steps taken to contain the riots, in response to which Patel sent him a detailed statement on the situation in Ajmer which he had issued on 19 December. When, shortly after sharing his statement with Nehru, Patel came to know that H.V.R. Iengar, Nehru's principal private secretary, had visited Ajmer, he found it inappropriate on at least two counts: firstly, he felt that Iengar's visit would be construed as the prime minister's dissatisfaction with Patel's report or with the handling of the situation by the chief commissioner in charge of Ajmer; and secondly, since the chief commissioner reported directly to the Central government, any investigative visit by anyone other than a minister or a secretary of the relevant ministry was bound to generate a sense of resentment in him. Being 'shocked' by the incident, Patel wrote to Nehru on the same day to let him know that 'the whole proceeding is such as fills me with considerable distress', ending his letter with, 'the hope that we have seen the last of such "visits of inspection"'.[110]

On his part, Nehru too reacted quite sharply, writing back to Patel on the same day. After explaining the rationale behind Iengar's visit, he asked Patel, 'Am I to be constrained in taking any action in regard to inspection or visit or like matters, which I consider necessary?' That would make him a prisoner, he claimed, 'without freedom to act in accordance with what I might consider the needs of the situation'. Then he dropped the bombshell: 'If I am to continue as Prime Minister I cannot have my freedom restricted . . . Otherwise, it is better for me to retire.' Nehru couldn't have not known the repercussion of his outburst, and with that understanding he advised that they should take a decision only after giving 'full thought to the situation' instead of taking action in haste. 'If unfortunately you or I have to leave the Government of India, let this be done with dignity and goodwill,' was his view. He was ready to go: 'On my part I would gladly resign and hand over the reigns to you.'[111] Patel responded with his characteristic bluntness, making it clear that questioning the propriety of his ministerial jurisdiction being encroached by the prime minister did not amount to restricting the prime minister's liberty. 'I shall maintain that your sending Iengar to Ajmer was not right,' he reiterated. Both the leaders had disagreed on many occasions in the past but the significance of this instance was quite different. Patel explained:

... when it is clear to us that on the fundamental question of our respective spheres of responsibility, authority and action there is such vital difference of opinion between us, it would not be in the interest of the cause which we both wish to serve to continue to pull on longer.[112]

But instead of Nehru he himself should go since it would be impossible for him to function in an arrangement where encroachment of another minister's area of responsibility was viewed as legitimate. Surely, Nehru would not want him to 'continue as an ineffective colleague'? Therefore, the 'question of your resignation or your abdicating your functions does not arise', Patel wrote.[113]

This letter of 24 December was Patel's second letter of resignation. He had sent another letter of resignation to Nehru on the previous day because of a similar situation that arose in Kashmir. Nehru had appointed N. Gopalaswami Ayyangar, a former Dewan of Kashmir and a member of the Constituent Assembly, as a minister without portfolio. When Ayyangar issued certain instructions relating to the Kashmir affair, Patel took it as another instance of encroaching upon what he considered the administrative jurisdiction of the states ministry under him. Patel raised the matter with Nehru, but the prime minister told Patel that the states ministry should not intervene and come in the way of arrangements being made by Ayyangar under his direction. 'I do not propose to abdicate my functions in regard to matters for which I consider myself responsible,' Nehru wrote to Patel. 'Your letter . . . has caused me considerable pain,' Patel replied, adding:

In any case, your letter makes it clear to me that I must not or at least cannot continue as a Member of Government and hence I am hereby tendering my resignation. I am grateful to you for the courtesy and kindness shown to me during the period of office which was a period of considerable strain.[114]

Remarkably, both chose to correspond through letters over matters that do not appear as much more than a battle for territorial supremacy, something that could have been resolved face to face if they chose. That they did not, is a clear pointer to the lack of a camaraderie.

As one of their cabinet colleagues noted the extent of differences that had cropped up between Patel and Nehru:

. . . the schism between the viewpoint of Vallabhbhai and Nehru began to come to surface gradually . . . The differences between them became sharper as time went on. Nehru was not pleased by the action taken in Junagarh by Vallabhbhai. He was equally displeased at the firmness displayed by Vallabhbhai in the Hyderabad affair . . . The differences between Nehru and Patel on how to deal with Muslims continued to grow.[115]

As in the earlier decades before transfer of power, the conflict was taken to Gandhi for resolution with both the prime minister and the deputy prime minister holding discussions with him on 24 December afternoon. Patel had already resigned, and both waited for Gandhi's verdict. Towards the end of the month, Gandhi told Patel, 'Either you should run things or Jawaharlal should,' in response to which Patel expressed his desire to move out due to his age but promising to assist Nehru to the extent possible from the outside. There was yet no verdict from Gandhi, who continued to ponder over their written notes submitted to him.[116] Nehru and Patel also shared their notes submitted to Gandhi with each other and tried to fix a mutually convenient date to meet Gandhi together, but that did not materialize.

In the meantime, another development took place that presented an unexpected challenge in front of Patel. On 12 December 1947, Patel had announced in the central legislature the details of the financial settlement between the governments of India and Pakistan according to which Pakistan was to receive Rs 75 crore out of undivided India's cash balance of Rs 400 crore. With Rs 20 crore of this amount being already paid on 15 August 1947, the outstanding due was Rs 55 crore. While speaking on this occasion, Patel mentioned that successful implementation of the settlement 'obviously depends on the continuation of the spirit of accommodation and conciliation on both sides', and discord on any 'vital issue' was 'bound to place the good work which we have achieved in jeopardy'.[117] In a cabinet meeting in early January 1948, however, Patel forcefully argued that if the money was given to Pakistan it would certainly be used to build its war capabilities against India and therefore it should be withheld. He received strong support from Mookerjee, Gadgil and Ambedkar, Nehru too agreed and the cabinet decided to withhold the Rs 55 crore.[118] Along with the finance minister Shanmukham Chetty, Patel announced in a press conference on 12 January, 'India cannot reasonably be asked to make a payment of cash balances to Pakistan when an armed conflict with its forces is in progress and threatens to assume an even more dangerous character.' Pakistan's role in the invasion of Kashmir was likely to destroy the whole financial settlement, he warned.[119]

That evening, Gandhi sprung a surprise by announcing that he was going to undertake an indefinite fast from the next day, declaring that he would end the fast 'when and if I am satisfied that there is a reunion of hearts of all communities'.[120] He had not shared his plan with anyone, not even Patel who had visited him earlier that day after the press conference.

Not paying Pakistan the Rs 55 crore was immoral, Gandhi told Patel when he came to meet him on 13 January morning. Gandhi had apparently formed this opinion as a result of his talks with Mountbatten who had opined that withholding the payment was 'unstatesmanlike and unwise' and that it would be India's 'first dishonourable act'. On being confronted by Patel soon afterwards, Mountbatten revised his opinion by agreeing to withdraw the word 'dishonourable' and communicated it to Gandhi. On being asked by Patel, Gandhi informed him that Nehru admitted to him that it was a cabinet decision, but added that 'we don't have a case. It is legal quibbling.'[121]

Another meeting on the next day where apart from Patel, Nehru, Chetty and Matthai were also present, turned out to be an intense one. Gandhi wept and Patel spoke some 'extremely bitter words'. Patel 'reeled under the blow and was considerably embittered'. He broke down and wept when later in the day the cabinet reversed its earlier decision to release the money.[122]

Before leaving for Bhavnagar to deal with the Kathiawar states integration issue, Patel wrote to 'Poojya Bapu' in an emotional letter:

> The sight of your anguish yesterday has made me disconsolate. It has set me furiously thinking.
>
> The burden of work has become so heavy that I feel crushed under it. I now see that it would do no good to the country or to myself to carry on like this anymore. It might even do harm.
>
> Jawahar is even more burdened than I. His heart is heavy with grief. Maybe I have deteriorated with age and am no more any good as a comrade to stand by him, and lighten his burden. The Maulana (Azad) too is displeased with what I am doing and you have again and again to take up cudgels on my behalf. This also is intolerable to me.

In the circumstances, it will perhaps be good for me and for the country if you now let me go. I cannot do otherwise than I am doing. And if thereby I become burdensome to my lifelong colleagues and a source of distress to you and still I stick to office, it would mean—at least that is how I would feel—that I let the lust of power blind my eyes and so was unwilling to quit. You should quickly deliver me from this intolerable situation.[123]

According to Manibehn Patel, Gandhi had by this time made up his mind that both Nehru and Patel should continue in the government. Although Mountbatten had criticized the decision to stop the payment to Pakistan, he too had argued in favour of retaining Patel in the cabinet. In his discourses during the fast too, Gandhi didn't speak a single critical sentence against Patel; rather, he kept defending Patel's speeches and actions which were criticized by some as anti-Muslim.[124] However, he complained that Patel was no more his 'yes-man as he was once popularly and affectionately nick-named'.[125] Soon he clarified:

When he was my 'yes-man', he permitted himself to be so named, because whatever I said instinctively appealed to him . . . When power descended on him, he saw that he could no longer successfully apply the method of non-violence which he used to wield with signal success.[126]

On his return, Patel met Gandhi on 23 January and then again on 30 January, on which occasions the two had a heart-to-heart talk. It was critically important that Patel and Nehru worked together, Gandhi made it clear. He was scheduled to meet Gandhi again the next morning, along with Nehru, but it turned out to be his last time he saw his mentor. Minutes after Patel left, Gandhi was brought down by an assassin's bullets.

It was an irreparable loss to both, and as in life so in death, Gandhi brought them back together. 'In this crisis that we have to face now after Bapu's death I think it is my duty and, if I may venture to say, yours also for us to face it together as friends and colleagues,' Nehru wrote to Patel on 3 February 1948. 'Not merely superficially, but in full loyalty to and with confidence in each other.' He was aware of the now widely held perception about his differences with Patel:

I have been greatly distressed by the persistence of whispers and rumours about you and me, magnifying out of all proportion any differences we may have. This has spread to foreign ambassadors and foreign correspondents; mischief makers take advantage of this and add to it. Even the Services are affected and this is bad. We must put an end to this mischief.[127]

Patel reciprocated by writing to Nehru on 5 February, 'I am deeply touched, indeed overwhelmed, by the affection and warmth of your letter . . . I fully and heartily reciprocate the sentiments you have so feelingly expressed.' Recalling their decades-long comradeship, he wrote:

Recent events had made me very unhappy and I had written to Bapu when I was going to Bombay appealing to him to relieve me, but his death changes everything and the crisis that has overtaken us must awaken in us a fresh realisation of how much we have achieved together and the need for further joint efforts in our grief-stricken country's interests.[128]

Both agreed that they should meet and talk more often.

Although at the spur of the moment Nehru liked to dismiss all talks about his differences with Patel as 'whispers and rumours', it would be pertinent to ask whether baseless rumours could gain such currency in the corridors of power.

A contemporary analyst observed that 'the tragedy is that Nehru is obliged to hunt for compromises because he is a great man but a poor organizer. Without the support of the conservative leaders of the Congress party he would still be able to fire the people with enthusiasm but would fail to organize them for action.'[129]

In the weeks before his assassination, Gandhi came down heavily on the Congress organization and its leaders for the way they had turned out after assuming power. On 12 January, at the prayer meeting where he announced his plan to commence his fast, Gandhi was bitterly critical about the state of the Congress:

The one great problem, apart from many other political and economic issues of very complicated nature, is the moral degradation into which the men in Congress circles have fallen . . . The taste of political power has turned their heads. Several of the MLAs [members of legislative assembly] and MLCs [members of legislative council] are following the policy of make hay while the sun shines. Making money by the use of influence, even to the extent of obstructing the administration of justice in the criminal courts presided over by magistrates. Even the District Collectors and other revenue officials do not feel free in the discharge of their duties on account of the frequent interference by the MLAs and MLCs on behalf of their partisans. A strict and honest officer cannot hold his position, for, false reports are carried against him to the Ministers who easily lend their ears to these unprincipled self-seekers.

Swaraj was the only all-absorbing passion, which had goaded men and women to follow your leadership. But now that the goal has been reached, all moral restrictions have lost their power on most of the fighters in the great struggle, who are joining hands even with those who were sworn opponents of the national movement and who now, for their personal ends, enlist themselves as Congress members. The situation is growing intolerable every day with the result that the Congress, as well as the Congress Government, have come into disrepute . . . The people have begun to say that the British Government was much better and they are even cursing the Congress.[130]

Those 'who have perfect faith in ahimsa [non-violence] should not hold any office in the Government', Gandhi wrote to one of his followers.[131]

As Sampurnanand, one of the key leaders from Uttar Pradesh who went on to become the chief minister of the province, noted:

The Congress of 1947 was not, however, the Congress of 1921. The old Congress had nothing to offer but hard work and tears, jail, financial ruin, self-suppression, humiliation and death . . . The new Congress, however, offered seats in local bodies and the legislatures, places of profit and honour, and participation in the Government. Such work does not necessarily involve high ethical values. The result was that new men, with no record of national service, began gradually to infiltrate into the Congress and, by dubious methods, to drive out genuine Congressmen whose life-long training under Mahatmaji made them singularly unable to defend themselves against such attack. Bossism began to raise its sinister head . . . Members of legislatures are selected by a wide electorate and the ministers have heavy constitutional responsibilities. On the other hand, members of the various Congress Committees are drawn from one particular party and chosen by very small groups. The office-bearers of such committees have absolutely no responsibilities and an increasing number of them have no roots in the Congress, which they want to use as a jumping off platform to high office. It is these committees which indirectly control the selection of candidates to legislatures. The result of such a state of affairs can easily be foreseen. There is frequent friction between what, for want of better names, are generally known as the legislative and organisational wings.[132]

In a draft constitution for the Congress that he prepared a day before his assassination, Gandhi proposed disbanding the organization and forming a Lok Sevak Sangh instead, which would be organized on the basis of village panchayats. It was a sketchy outline that focused on the method of raising the organization and the qualification of its members, but did not dwell upon the question of its relation to the governance of the country.[133]

A curious event to take place during Gandhi's fast was a change of guard in West Bengal, an event that demonstrated the inner workings of Congress politics. On 15 February 1948, Prafulla Chandra Ghosh, the premier of West Bengal, resigned and Dr Bidhan Chandra Roy was elected as the new leader of the Congress legislature party. In a statement issued that day, Ghosh said that he had received a note signed by twenty-five members of the party asking the Bengal ministry to be reconstituted under Roy, who was elected to the assembly a few weeks ago on 5 January. Ghosh stated that on receiving the note he met Roy and communicated his decision to resign.[134] Roy was sworn in as the new premier on 23 January.[135]

The inside story of what was apparently a simple process of change in leadership was divulged by Ghosh during the general elections of 1957. Speaking at an election rally, Ghosh claimed that he was removed from the post of the premier of West Bengal because he refused to accept recommendations from Patel and Gandhi to include either D.P. Khaitan (a member of the Constituent Assembly) or Badridas Goenka (then chairman of the Imperial Bank of India) in his cabinet as the finance minister.[136] On being accused by the Bengal Congress leadership that he was distorting facts, Ghosh released a letter which Gandhi had written to him on 30 June 1947 at a press conference in Delhi and Calcutta. Gandhi had written to Ghosh, 'Sardar [Patel] has conveyed to me that you should have a Marwari in your cabinet—either Badridas Goenka or [D.P.] Khaitan. I think your doing this will be the proper course and not doing it will be improper.' Ghosh alleged that business community of Calcutta worked with his political opponents to bring down his government after he refused to accept Gandhi's advice. He claimed that he had communicated his unwillingness to comply with Gandhi's request to Kripalani and after consulting Gandhi, Kripalani informed him that in view of his refusal it was Gandhi's wish to consider that the letter was never written. 'Gandhiji was undoubtedly a great man but I don't think either Patel or [G.D.] Birla were. The whole conspiracy was hatched in Birla House,' Ghosh stated at the press conference.[137]

The intra-party squabbles in the provinces were played out in public, giving credence to Gandhi's pessimism. In some cases, such as in Bengal, it led to the fall of the government. Another such instance was the Madras provincial government where group conflicts led to the resignation of the province's premier, T. Prakasam.

When a group of Congress assembly party members expressed lack of confidence in Prakasam in February 1947, Prakasam blamed the groups present in the assembly (the provincial committees of Tamil Nadu and Kerala) of conspiring against him. Both Nehru and Patel when approached by Prakasam, advised him to act according to the wishes of the majority party members. On 28 February a large number of Congress legislators voted in favour of a no-confidence motion against him, but Prakasam ruled out the verdict on the grounds of rules specified in the Congress constitution. Patel suggested that he should resign 'now that it is clear that a large number of Congress members of the Madras Assembly Party are against your continuing to be the leader of the party and the Premier'. Finally, after being defeated at an election of leader of the party in the assembly by seventy-three to 116 votes, Prakasam resigned office with Omandur Ramaswamy Reddiar becoming the new premier of Madras.[138] Within two years, however, Ramaswamy was unseated by another power struggle in the Madras Assembly resulting in the election of Kumaraswami Raja as the new premier on 31 March 1949.[139]

In view of the clashes within the Congress, Nehru issued an appeal on 13 March 1948 while speaking in Nagpur to party members for a two years' truce among various groups within the Congress to allow the government to settle down.[140]

The national political dynamics too were undergoing several changes as efforts to consolidate the opposition to the Congress gathered momentum.

Although many socialist leaders, like Jayaprakash Narayan and Achyut Patwardhan, shared a cordial relationship with Nehru and Gandhi, with the two Congress leaders being sympathetic towards their politics, Patel on the other hand was a stringent critic, often viewing them, along with the communists as disruptors to the national movement.

To counteract the influence of the communists in the trade union movement, which they did by dominating the All India Trade Union Congress (AITUC), Patel encouraged the setting up of a new organization—Indian National Trade Union Congress (INTUC). He was, however, annoyed by the attitude of the socialists who decided to stay out of both the unions.[141] In 1947, Patel was still trying to get the socialists to work together with the Congress. On 18 June, he wrote to Ram Manohar Lohia, that 'unless we consolidate our forces and act with one voice, there are grave dangers ahead and the future is dark'.[142]

By early 1948, his outlook towards the leftists had hardened. On 20 January 1948, Patel issued a stern warning to the socialists and the Communists when striking Port Trust workers attempted to break up a public meeting where he spoke against strikes. The socialists were still within the Congress, he said, but working against the organization. On the other hand, Patel pointed out, the Communists who had helped the British government during the war years were engineering labour unrest when the Congress was running the government of the country. Since the socialists were talking about leaving the Congress, the door is open for them to go out, Patel was blunt in his message.[143]

The members of the CPI having already being expelled from the Congress, the socialists remained the only organized leftist force within the organization. However, with their ideological and strategic differences becoming increasingly prominent, the socialist leaders started considering whether to completely break away from the Congress and form a new party.

Addressing the issue in an article published in mid-January, Jayaprakash Narayan wrote that the key question in front of them was: 'can we build up a socialist India by remaining within the Congress or by working outside it?' Criticizing Patel's statements disparaging political 'isms', Narayan wrote, 'When Sardar Patel decries socialism, he is defending the status quo and is saying that his ism, namely, status-quo-ism is superior to all others.' He believed that it was possible to steer the Congress towards socialism by the socialists within the Congress, working along with the other smaller groups of leftists, the constructive Gandhians and with leaders like Nehru, Azad and Gandhi himself. Although other leftists who were disenchanted with the Congress were growing impatient, it was not easy for the socialist leaders to hastily leave Congress particularly because they had given the best years of their lives to the organization and also because their 'love and admiration' for Gandhi and Nehru were 'not circumscribed by Marxian dogma or the Party line'. With the new constitution of the Congress likely to disallow membership to any other political party workers, it would not be possible for the socialists to continue as a parallel and independent party within the Congress. Instead, they would have to revert to the arrangement of the pre-Independence years when they worked within the Congress as an ideological group. Yet, without being fully convinced that it would be possible to convert Congress into socialism, the socialist party couldn't risk dissolving itself.[144]

The Congress, according to Narayan, was undergoing a rapid and significant change by transforming into a parliamentary party, and those like Gandhi who struggled to build Congress as 'a body of voluntary servants of the people' were losing the battle. Having become a source of power and personal advancement, the Congress was fast becoming a centre for vested interests resulting in corruption and jobbery. The moral edifice of the Congress had collapsed, he claimed.[145]

Although on paper Congress policies and programmes were never reactionary, 'the social interests that are at present working within the Congress will, in their pursuit of self-interest, bypass this programme without openly opposing it'. In the given scenario, it wasn't possible for Congress to change structurally from being dominated by middle-class interests to a labour or proletarian party based on trade unions and organized peasantry. Under these circumstances, Narayan concluded, it was 'futile for the socialists to continue longer within the Congress.'[146]

The national executive of the Socialist Party decided to break away from the Congress on 17 March 1948. The decision was approved by the national convention the party held at Nasik a few days later.[147]

'I have all along been of the view that if the future of India is in the hands of men like Jai Prakash [sic], it would probably be a most unfortunate circumstance,' Patel wrote to Nehru on 15 June, adding, 'I sincerely feel that it is time he was pulled up.'[148]

Communism, he believed, didn't have much chance in India. The main reason was that 'they did not help the struggle for freedom', thus creating 'a considerable resentment against them'. Moreover, Patel claimed, 'the general tendency (in India) is against any foreign element in the body-politic of India'.[149] These were undoubtedly oversimplified views about the communist movement which was gaining strength in different parts of the country, but are at the same time a useful indicator of the extent of Patel's antagonism with the Communists.

The Communists were the 'biggest enemies of the working class', Patel declared at the second session of the INTUC held in Indore in May 1949. Outlining the positions of the INTUC and the AITUC, Patel said:

> There was a time when the All India Trade Union Congress was regarded as the most representative organization of workers in the country and their representatives used to go abroad to represent us. They [the communists] utilised the platform afforded by the international conference to abuse us as gents of the capitalists. Within two years of the formation of the INTUC, with the affiliation of over 800 trade unions comprising 12 lakhs of workers, the INTUC has stolen the winds out the sails of the AITUC and no representative of AITUC can now represent India abroad.[150]

In Nehru's view the opposition to the Congress governments were of two kinds, as he explained to B.G. Kher, the premier of Bombay, in a letter written on 30 January 1949:

> One kind is which aims at complete disruption and chaotic conditions regardless of the consequences. This is chiefly represented by the Communists and some minor groups. The other kind does not want this disruption or chaos, but nevertheless wants to create trouble for the Government and to exercise continuous pressure. This is chiefly represented by the Socialists. To put it differently the Communists are completely anti-national and do not attach any importance to national interests . . .
>
> The Socialists, on the other hand . . . have got a nationalist background and do not wish to disrupt everything even if they could. Because of this difference between these two types of opponents, I think that we should also distinguish in our dealings between them.[151]

Organized leftist unity was still far away, but on occasions smaller parties got together to pose formidable challenge to the Congress. The Congress faced one such situation in a provincial bye-election for the South Calcutta constituency in June 1949. The West Bengal government faced a strong opposition challenge on the grounds of a piece of legislation giving extraordinary powers to the government for dealing with emergency situations, police firing on political processions and its handling of the refugee influx from East Bengal. Sarat Chandra Bose, elder brother of Subhas Chandra Bose, who had served in the interim government for two months before being dropped on account of the Muslim League members joining the government, emerged as a key figure around whom the various leftist parties rallied. Bose had resigned from the CWC in January 1947 and formed his own political party a few months later.

Nehru kept a keen watch on the developing situation and wrote to V.K. Krishna Menon in a disdainful tone in February 1949:

> In Calcutta especially there are dozens of small groups of so-called revolutionaries, Trotskyites, the Revolutionary Socialist Party, and the like and they have been giving any amount of trouble. Sarat Bose having lost all the influence he possessed, now seeks to regain part of it by encouraging and inciting these people.
>
> Sarat Bose is bent on mischief and is now trying to organize the refugees from East Bengal with the deliberate intention to give as much trouble as possible.[152]

While the CPI, the Revolutionary Socialist Party, the Forward Bloc and other smaller parties, apart from his own Republican Socialist Party, supported Bose, Nehru got involved issuing two personal appeals to the voters to vote for the Congress candidate. With the province's premier and the country's prime minister throwing their weight behind the Congress candidate for a legislative assembly seat, the contest became a prestige issue for both sides. In the election preceded by widespread violence, Bose handed an overwhelming defeat to the Congress candidate receiving 19,030 votes and 5780 votes against.[153]

Sucheta Kripalani, who was sent by Nehru as an observer, reported back 'a complete bankruptcy of the Congress'. 'There was so much feeling against the Congress generally and the local government that it was hardly possible for prominent Congressmen to show their faces,' a perturbed Nehru wrote to Patel.[154] In view of the high profile nature of the election, it was a clear message of the kind of challenge that the Congress was likely to face in the near future, at least in some areas of the country. The potential for damage to the Congress arising out of this election didn't escape Nehru's attention. Speaking at the Delhi Provincial Political Conference a few days later, he mentioned, 'To minimise the importance of this election is to close one's eyes to the realities.' He spoke at length on the need and ways to revitalize the Congress.[155]

Sarat Bose took up the opportunity to build a bigger platform for uniting the leftist parties, holding discussions with several national and regional leaders across the country, but his untimely death in February 1950 brought the initiative to a premature halt.

The factionalism of the provincial Congress committees was to reflect over the next few months at the highest level of the party's leadership in the form of clashes among the leaders.

The first occasion was the selection of the first President of the Republic of India. Both Durga Das and V. Shankar (Patel's private secretary) have described how Nehru and Patel differed on the matter of selection. While Nehru came to favour Rajagopalachari because of his experience as the governor of West Bengal and subsequently as India's governor general (his secular outlook was an additional factor for Nehru), Patel, based on the feedback he received from party sources, came to believe that Rajendra Prasad was the more favoured candidate. Although Patel as such was not against Rajagopalachari's candidature, he was too sharp an organization man to ignore how Rajagopalachari's role during the Quit India movement and his attitude towards the Muslim League still rankled the Congress workers, which was seen as late as during the election of the Madras premier in 1946.

Nehru decided to put his choice in the form of a resolution in front of the Constituent Assembly members, acting against Patel's advice. His speech was rudely interrupted multiple times by the members who denounced Rajagopalachari for opposing Quit India and giving respectability to the demand for Pakistan. To make things worse, Patel declined to support the resolution when asked by Nehru. Most speakers opposed the resolution. Patel stepped in to stop the acrimony, appealing for calm and dignity and assuring the members that the prime minister would take their views into account. Hurt by the show of vociferous opposition by his own party members, Nehru wrote to Patel that he intended to resign on his return from the US, for which he was leaving shortly, something that neither Patel nor Nehru felt the need to act upon once the tempers calmed down.[156]

The prime minister and his deputy failed to reach an agreement yet again on the person who should be elected Congress president in August 1950, again dividing the party into two camps of followers. According to V. Shankar, Nehru and Patel discussed the matter in Dehradun in June

1950, whereby both ruled out Kripalani as a possible candidate. While Patel disagreed with Nehru's suggestion in favour of Shankar Rao Deo, the general secretary of the Congress, Nehru raised objections on Patel's choice of Purushottam Das Tandon, the president of United Provinces Congress Committee. The discussion remained inconclusive. Towards the end of July, Nehru convened a meeting of those working committee members who were in Delhi and decided upon Kripalani as the next presidential candidate, after his initial suggestion for Deo found no takers. Although invited, Patel declined to attend the meeting both because he found it improper not to have a meeting of the full working committee to decide on such an important issue, and also because he was unwell. It transpired that Nehru had settled on Kripalani at the suggestion of Rafi Ahmed Kidwai. Patel reacted by announcing his support for Tandon. Deo too entered the contest, making it triangular.

Nehru was dismissive of all the candidates in his private correspondence. To V.K. Krishna Menon he wrote:

> Not one of them is suitable. Shankerrao Deo is negatively good. Kripalani is cantankerous and frustrated. When he was President last, he did not function well and the Congress went down . . . Tandon has some virtues, but . . . has become tied up with communal and revivalist tendencies and has become a symbol for some of the most reactionary forces in India . . . Tandon is being supported fully by Vallabhbhai Patel. This in spite of the fact that I informed him and others that if Tandon is elected, I could not be in the Congress Working Committee and very probably I would resign from the Prime Ministership. Perhaps Sardar Patel thinks that I was not serious enough or that I would adapt myself to new developments. He is mistaken if he thinks so and I have tried to make that clear to him.[157]

Not one to mince words with his colleagues, Nehru wrote to Tandon, elder to him by seven years and whom he had known for the past fifty years, directly and bluntly about his objections regarding his candidature:

> Unfortunately, you have become, to large numbers of people in India, some kind of a symbol of this communal and revivalist outlook and the question rises in my mind: Is the Congress going that way also? . . .
>
> I would have gladly welcomed your election to the Congress Presidentship. But when I look at this matter impersonally and from

DREAMING OF THEE!

Mr. H. N. Brailsford, the British Socialist writer, thinks that Mr. Jinnah, League President, is banking on the return of Mr. Churchill to power in Great Britain.

Amrita Bazar Patrika, 4 February 1947

Mountbatten addressing the Chamber of Princes on 25 July 1947
(Source: *Amrita Bazar Patrika*, 29 July 1947)

Gandhi addressing a Hindu–Muslim Unity meeting in Calcutta on the occasion of Eid,
19 August 1947
(Source: *Amrita Bazar Patrika*, 20 August 1947)

Peace procession in Calcutta on 26 August 1947, led by Maj. Gen. Shah Nawaz Khan and
H.S. Suhrawardy
(Source: *Jugantar*, 27 August 1947)

The new flag of India being shown to the
members of the Constituent Assembly
(Source: *Amrita Bazar Patrika*, 28 July 1947)

Nehru bidding farewell to Asaf Ali,
India's ambassador designate to the
United States, at the Palam aerodrome
(Source: *Amrita Bazar Patrika*,
11 February 1947)

Mohammad Ismail, Pakistani high
commissioner in India, with finance ministers
of India and Pakistan, Shanmukham Chetty
and Gulam Mohammad (*right*), at the
Inter-Dominion Conference in Delhi
(Source: *Amrita Bazar Patrika*, 6 May 1948)

Vijayalakshmi Pandit, India's ambassador to the Soviet Union, and her daughter seen off
at the Willingdon airport by Nehru, Sarojini Naidu and the Chinese ambassador to India
(Source: *Amrita Bazar Patrika*, 6 August 1947)

Indian delegation to the UN General Assembly in Paris: (*Sitting from left to right*) B. Shiva Rao,
A. Ramaswami Mudaliar, Vijayalakshmi Pandit, B.N. Rau and Jam Saheb of Nawanagar
(Source: *Amrita Bazar Patrika*, 5 October 1948)

Refugees from East Pakistan at the Sealdah railway station
(Source: *Amrita Bazar Patrika*, 8 October 1948)

Nehru with the Commonwealth prime ministers at 10 Downing Street
(Source: *Amrita Bazar Patrika*, 17 October 1948)

Demonstration against the Hindu Code Bill outside Parliament
(Source: *Amrita Bazar Patrika*, 14 December 1949)

G.V. Mavalankar, speaker of Lok Sabha, congratulating Rajendra Prasad
(Source: *Jugantar*, 1 February 1950)

Refugees arriving in Calcutta from Chittagong
(Source: *Jugantar*, 3 March 1950)

Refugees from East Pakistan crossing over to West Bengal
(Source: *Jugantar*, 23 March 1950)

Pakistan's prime minister Liaquat Ali Khan discussing the refugee problem with
Jawaharlal Nehru and Vallabhbhai Patel in Delhi
(Source: *Jugantar*, 7 April 1950)

Syama Prasad Mookerjee's funeral procession in Calcutta
(Source: *Jugantar*, 25 June 1953)

Russian prime minister Nikolai Bulganin and first secretary of the Communist Party
of the Soviet Union Nikita Khrushchev, received at the Delhi airport by Nehru
(Source: *Jugantar*, 20 November 1955)

the larger point of view, I feel that this election would mean great
encouragement to certain forces in India which I consider harmful.
Hence my difficulty and my distress.[158]

Tandon refuted Nehru's charges, arguing that he was not dogmatic about
the Vedas or the Koran, which he did not consider to be last word in
human thought, but he was indeed in favour of reviving some of the past
spiritual values of India. As far as communalism was concerned, he had
openly advocated marriages between Hindus and Muslims.[159]

In response to Nehru's agitated letters, Patel tried to explain to him
patiently that although he supported Tandon, his success would finally depend
on whether he could adjust to the decisions taken by the forthcoming Congress
session at Nasik. Tandon's victory did not imply a defeat of Nehru's policies.[160]

Tandon had also contested the presidential elections in October 1948
but lost out to Pattabhi Sitaramayya by a narrow margin of 114 votes.
Although Nehru and Patel had expressed neutrality in that contest, Tandon
was widely perceived as Patel's candidate and Sitaramayya being backed by
Nehru. In the ensuing contest, Tandon, who received 1306 votes, defeated
Kripalani by a margin of 214 votes. [161]

In just over three months, an ailing Patel passed away on 15 December
1950.

~

On 28 February 1950, presenting the annual budget in the provisional
parliament, John Matthai announced that the government had decided to
set up a six-member Planning Commission with Nehru as its chairman
and Gulzarilal Nanda, labour minister in the Bombay government, as the
deputy chairman. C.D. Deshmukh (former governor of the Reserve Bank),
G.L. Mehta (president of the Indian Tariff Board) and R.K. Patil (food
commissioner) were the other three members. The sixth member would be
announced later. N.R. Pillai, the cabinet secretary, would function as the
secretary to the commission, assisted by Tarlok Singh, deputy secretary in
the finance ministry.[162]

Among others who served at various points of time during the first
five years of the commission were V.T. Krishnamachari, J.C. Ghosh, K.C.
Neogy and as an unofficial member, the director of the Indian Statistical
Institute, P.C. Mahalanobis.[163]

The functions and the terms and conditions of the commission were published on 15 March 1950 in the Gazette of India Extraordinary. The commission was mainly tasked with assessing India's material, capital and human resources and investigate the possibilities of augmenting them, formulating a plan for their utilization and propose the allocation of resources for the execution of the plan in stages.[164]

From 15 October 1947 onwards, Nehru had put in place a practice of writing detailed letters to the premiers of all the provinces every fortnight, sharing with them the developments across the world and the country and his views on them. The premiers, in turn, wrote back to him on issues that were of concern to them.

Nehru dwelt at some length on the topic of planning in his letter of 1 December 1949. He recalled that he was appointed the chairperson of the planning committee set up by the then Congress president Subhas Chandra Bose and that on joining the interim government in September 1946, he had appointed an Advisory Planning Board, chaired by K.C. Neogy. Although the board submitted its report within the stipulated three months, it could not be implemented because of the chain of events that followed. Several other measures, such as setting up an economic as well as statistical unit attached to the Cabinet Secretariat, in addition to appointing an economic committee for the Cabinet, were taken, but an all-encompassing approach to planning was yet to materialize. In the letter Nehru outlined the roles the provincial governments would be required to play if a planning authority was set up, starting with establishing a counterpart to the central authority in the provinces.[165]

One of the immediate triggers for setting up the Planning Commission was a report produced by an American engineer Solomon Trone, who spent about three and a half months in India as Nehru's adviser. Trone travelled to several industrial areas and river valley schemes, identified some of the problem areas and accordingly made some suggestions for improvement.[166]

A National Development Council, comprising the prime minister and the chief ministers of the states, was set up in 1952 to periodically review the working of the plan and to promote common economic policies. A standing committee of the council was set up in 1954, comprising nine chief ministers and a few key cabinet ministers.[167]

The final version of the first plan was approved and signed by Nehru on 9 November 1952, about fifteen months after the preparation of the first draft which went through several rounds of scrutiny and discussions among the several layers of government.

The results were encouraging. At the end of the plan period, that is 1955–56, national income had increased by 17.5 per cent (against an increase in population of 6 per cent), and production in key items such as food grain by 29.6 cent, cotton 37.5 per cent, jute 28 per cent, steel 30.5 per cent, bicycles 407.9 per cent, automobiles 53 per cent, etc. Food grain production, in fact, was more than the target laid down in the plan. Industrial production increased by about 40 per cent. Prices at the end of the plan period were 13 per cent lower than at the beginning. Total public expenditure by the Centre and the states increased by about 75 per cent, the bulk of which was developmental expenditure.[168]

Announcing an eight-point scheme for self-sufficiency in food, cotton and jute on 22 May 1950, K.M. Munshi, the food minister, declared, 'We are not going to import food after 1951, and we should make a vigorous and calculated drive to redeem the pledge.'[169]

~

The Congress presidential elections set off a chain of events that altered the political environment substantially. The process, however, did not begin immediately. At the Nasik Congress held in the middle of September 1950, the major resolutions passed, such as those on foreign policy, economic policy and communalism, were drafted by Nehru, proving Patel right that Tandon's victory did not imply a defeat for Nehru's policies. Nehru was quite pleased with his performance. The atmosphere at Nasik was 'one of an attempt to please me because of the fear that I might keep out', he wrote to V.K. Krishna Menon.[170]

A parallel course of events was shaping up at Nasik around Kripalani. Unhappy with the corrupt practices within the organization and the general inefficiencies in the provincial administrations some Congress members, who did not belong to the dominant groups in the provinces, decided to form a reformist group within the Congress. Kripalani agreed to lead this group, which was named the Congress Democratic Front (CDF), and included leaders like Prafulla Chandra Ghosh, Kidwai and Prakasam. According to Kripalani, the idea was approved by Nehru, who, however, changed his mind later. Tandon, however, expressed his reservations about the move arguing that it would have a disruptive influence on the organization. He suggested that the members of the group, who were old colleagues, should raise their concerns at the relevant platforms, which would be given full consideration. Based on a report by the Election Disputes Committee appointed by the working committee, which had found widespread irregularities and corrupt practices in the organizational elections, the CDF demanded the institution of a general inquiry. Tandon agreed to look into specific complaints but declined to set up an overarching general inquiry.[171]

Kripalani informed both Tandon and Nehru that if the general inquiry was not instituted and if pressure from senior leaders to dissolve the CDF continued, many Congress members would leave the party. Several senior leaders in Bengal, led by Prafulla Chandra Ghosh, had already moved out of the Congress and formed a new party called the Krishak Mazdoor Praja Party (KMPP) in November 1950.[172]

Kripalani announced his resignation from the Congress on 17 May 1951, followed by the other members of the CDF, except Kidwai. A month later, on 16 June, they met at a convention in Patna and joined the KMPP. The party's constitution was approved, a manifesto prepared and a national executive was formed with Kripalani as the president, also including Ghosh, Kidwai, Prakasam and K. Kelappan.[173]

A confusion following the resignations of Kidwai and Ajit Prasad Jain precipitated the showdown between Nehru and Tandon, which both had been cautiously avoiding for so long. After resigning from the Congress as well as from the cabinet in mid-July, Kidwai and Jain announced a few days later their decision to withdraw the resignation from the cabinet, repeating their virulent criticism of the Congress president. They claimed that they were withdrawing their resignation from the cabinet on the basis of an assurance given by Nehru that they were free to join a political party that opposed the Congress. Jain, however, clarified to Nehru that he did not wish to join any other political party.

Tandon issued a stern rejoinder that being responsible to the Congress, the prime minister and his cabinet were supposed to carry out the policies enunciated by the party. If Nehru really allowed his ministers the liberty to work against Congress policies, that would create an impossible situation. Nehru wrote to Tandon accepting his fault in not taking Kidwai's explicit statement about joining a political party opposed to the Congress, after advising Kidwai not to join any other party and await further developments. Taking a corrective step, Nehru accepted Kidwai's resignation towards the end of July, but asked Jain to continue since he didn't intend to join any other party.

Early in August, Nehru intimated Tandon about his decision to resign from the working committee and the central election board. He was unhappy with the composition of the committee from the very beginning, being compelled to join it due to circumstances but that too nearly two months after the Nasik Congress. Since then, his multiple attempts to reconstitute the committee bore no result. 'I am convinced that I do not fit into the Working Committee and am not in tune with it,' he wrote to Tandon. Tandon offered to give up the presidentship of the Congress if that helped change Nehru's mind, because he had no doubt Nehru's resignation would divide the Congress and further weaken it. Nehru himself was acutely aware of the repercussions. A few days ago, he had written to Vijayalakshmi Pandit that his resignation would 'create another major crisis, for whatever my failings, I still hold the crowd'. It wasn't only the crowd; the leaders too were solidly behind Nehru. It was clear to everyone that after Patel passed away there was no one who could match Nehru's stature. Thus, a meeting of the Congress Parliamentary Party expressed its confidence in his leadership, with 234 of the 279 members of Parliament present voting for him.

The same working committee with which Nehru had repeatedly expressed his inability to work, accepted Tandon's resignation on 8 September and requested Nehru to take over the presidentship. Nehru agreed, but asked the AICC members to think the matter over and express their opinion the next day. On 9 September, when Nehru asked the AICC delegates 'to indicate their final decision by raising a full-throated cry of Jai Hind', the response left no one in doubt about the verdict.[174]

Nehru's triumph had far-reaching consequences. It consolidated his hold on both the organization and the government, successfully transitioning from a phase where the responsibilities were divided between him and Patel. There were critics and irritants, but no serious challenger who could threaten his position. He reached the spot where, from now onwards, in his own words, 'Nehru will implement Nehru's programme'.[175]

Opposition to Nehru in the cabinet too was on the way of disappearing. A few ministers had dropped out in the current and the previous years because of their differences with the prime minister. Syama Prasad Mookerjee (industry and supply) and K.C. Neogy (commerce) resigned in April 1950, protesting against Nehru's agreement with the Pakistani prime minister Liaquat Ali Khan on the treatment of refugees and minorities by their respective governments. John Matthai, the finance minister, went towards the end of May.

When asked by reporters the reason for his resignation, Matthai mentioned it was due to his differences with the prime minister, but 'it will not be in the interests of the country to embarrass the Government by making these differences public'.[176] So far as Nehru was concerned, there was no question of embarrassment. Speaking at a public meeting in Trivandrum the next day, he gave it out that Matthai believed that the Planning Commission was neither necessary nor desirable at that point of time, because resources were limited and should not be wasted on big plans.[177]

The Planning Commission was just one of the reasons, and there was more to his resignation than what was said by Nehru. Matthai issued another statement the next day. 'I consider the Planning Commission not only ill-timed but in its working and general set up ill-conceived,' he said. The commission, Matthai felt, was tending to become a parallel cabinet, weakening the finance ministry and the cabinet system. The Planning Commission, however, was only one of the many disagreements between him and the prime minister. Matthai was seriously concerned about the control of expenditure in the government. He found 'a general tendency' among the ministries to disregard the authority of the Standing Finance Committee, with some of the biggest offenders being ministers directly under the control of the prime minister, working with his approval. Yet another reason, Matthai said, was his strong reservations against the Nehru–Liaquat agreement.[178] Matthai's statement drew a rejoinder from Azad, defending Nehru and the government, the next day.[179]

The next resignation of a cabinet minister created a more bitter and a bigger public controversy weeks within Nehru's triumphant takeover of the Congress presidency. On 27 September 1951, law minister B.R. Ambedkar requested Nehru to relieve him of his ministerial responsibilities with immediate effect. Ambedkar had written to Nehru on 11 August that his physicians were pressing him for a period of continuous treatment which could take about a month, but before starting the treatment he was keen to see the Hindu Code Bill passed, if possible, by 1 September. 'You know I attach the greatest importance to this measure and would be prepared to undergo any strain on my health to get the Bill through,' Ambedkar wrote. Nehru pointed out to Ambedkar that the cabinet had already decided that the bill should be taken up in early September, since the government needed to proceed with some tact in view of 'a good deal of opposition' within and outside Parliament.[180]

Ambedkar sent his letter of resignation to Nehru once it was clear that discussion on the Hindu Code Bill was going to be adjourned. Nehru announced the adjournment in Parliament on 26 September, and Ambedkar's letter reached him the next day. He had been thinking of resigning from the cabinet for a long time, Ambedkar wrote, but the hope of having the Hindu Code Bill passed before the current Parliament came to an end stopped him. Now that there was no hope, 'I see no purpose in my continuing to be a member of your cabinet'. Ambedkar wanted to make a statement in Parliament as a retiring minister on 11 October.

Ambedkar, however, was stopped by the deputy speaker Ananthasayanam Ayyangar from making his statement at the scheduled time for not providing a written copy of the statement in advance, although a copy was provided to the prime minister. Ayyangar rescheduled the statement at 6 p.m. Pointing out that the deputy speaker had previously not asked for a copy and protesting this sudden imposition of a new condition, Ambedkar walked out. Thereafter, Nehru, who was present while the argument was going on between Ambedkar and the deputy speaker, read out to the house the correspondence between him and Ambedkar.[181]

The statement, which was released to the press by Ambedkar received not only national but international coverage. The *Manchester Guardian* noted in its editorial:

The ruling by the Speaker in the Parliament which prevented Dr Ambedkar from making his resignation speech must appear to the outside world as ungracious. The text of the speech, which he has now issued direct to the public as a manifesto, strikes the Cabinet at Delhi in its weakest places.[182]

In his statement, Ambedkar dilated on the four reasons that made him resign from the cabinet. The first, and according to him the least important reason, was a story of his disappointment with the way he was underutilized in the government. He complained of neither being allotted an additional administrative portfolio, in spite of his express wish, nor being made a member of the main committees of the cabinet, although some other ministers were given multiple portfolios and were overworked.

Another reason for his dissatisfaction with the government was the inadequacy of measures taken to safeguard and uplift the backward classes and the scheduled castes. Declaring that 'the same old tyranny, the same old oppression, the same old discrimination which existed before, exists now, and perhaps in a worst form', Ambedkar posed the question: 'And yet why is no relief granted to the Scheduled Castes?' He drew attention to the contrasting attitude of the government towards Muslims:

> The Prime Minister's whole time and attention is devoted for the protection of the Muslims. I yield to none, not even to the Prime Minister, in my desire to give the Muslims of India the utmost protection wherever and whenever they stand in need of it. But what I want to know is, are the Muslims the only people who need protection? Are the Scheduled Castes, the Scheduled Tribes and the Indian Christians not in need of protection? What concern has he shown for these communities? So far as I know, none and yet these are the communities which need far more care and attention than the Muslims . . . You can therefore, well imagine what pain it has caused me to see that the cause of the Scheduled Castes has been relegated to the limbo of nothing.

Ambedkar came down equally heavily on Nehru's much publicized foreign policy, which was a cause 'not merely for dissatisfaction but for actual anxiety and even worry'. In his view, India had been alienated because of this policy. 'We are pursuing a lonely furrow with no one even to second our resolutions in the UNO [United Nations],' he claimed. Nehru's foreign policy had resulted in a disproportionately large allocation of resources on India's military expenditure and difficulties in getting aid for the food and industrialization. Of the two main issues between India and Pakistan, Ambedkar believed that 'we should be more deeply concerned with East Bengal where the condition of our people seems from all the newspapers intolerable than with Kashmir'. For Kashmir, his solution was partition according to the same principle applied to Punjab and Bengal: 'Give the Hindu and Buddhist part to India and the Muslim part to Pakistan.' Alternatively, his suggestion was to divide the state into three parts—the cease-fire zone, the valley and Jammu–Ladakh—and hold a plebiscite only in the valley.

The fourth and probably the most immediate reason for Ambedkar's resignation was the death of the Hindu Code Bill.

The efforts towards the codification of Hindu laws came up in the legislative assembly on 26 March 1921, when K.G. Bagde moved a resolution recommending the appointment of a committee to deliberate on the issue and then submit a draft code for consideration by the legislature. The resolution was, however, withdrawn after an assurance given by the law member Tej Bahadur Sapru that the government would consult the high courts, bar libraries, legal associations and other relevant organizations to determine whether the time had arrived to make a serious and organized effort and if the response was positive, they would be further consulted on the next steps.[183] The debate was revived with the passage in 1937 of the Hindu Women's Right to Property Act. The government appointed a Hindu Law Committee headed by B.N. Rau in January 1941 to advise it on the best way to deal with the several 'anomalies and uncertainties' resulting from the act.[184]

The Hindu Law Committee, in its report submitted in June 1941, recommended 'a codification of the Hindu Law by stages beginning with the law of succession and the law of marriage'. Accordingly, the committee submitted two draft bills in March 1942, one on the law of intestate succession and the second on the law of marriage. The Intestate Succession Bill was thereafter referred to a Joint Select Committee of both chambers of the Indian legislature, and the Legislative Assembly adopted a resolution in November 1943 to circulate the amended bill for eliciting public opinion. In accordance with the recommendation of the joint committee and the Council of State, the Hindu Law Committee, under Rau, was revived on 20 January 1944 to consider the remaining aspects of Hindu law, and it submitted its report to the government on 21 January 1947.[185]

A rough draft code dealing with all the topics of Hindu law on which the government could legislate was prepared and circulated in May 1944 to a few lawyers, and 6000 copies of the subsequent draft revised on the basis of their feedback was published in August to elicit public opinion. The draft was also translated into twelve languages for circulation in the provinces. From the end of January 1945, the committee travelled to the major cities and recorded evidence of 121 individuals and 102 associations represented by 257 people. The conclusions arrived at by the committee in September 1945, however, were opposed by one of its members, Dwaraka Nath Mitter, who submitted a dissenting note.[186]

Making the observation that 'at the present day there is no means of making changes in the Hindu Law except by legislation', and unless the

Hindu society was 'to remain static and stagnant' the periodic changes were necessary, the committee's report, submitted on 21 February 1947 by B.N. Rau, J.R. Gharpure and T.R. Venkatarama Sastri, concluded that 'the proposal to codify Hindu Law is a sound one' and that 'it will be a boon to Hindu society'.[187]

The bill 'to amend and codify certain branches of the Hindu Law' was introduced in the Legislative Assembly on 11 April 1947 by the then law member of the interim government Jogendra Nath Mandal.[188] The bill was discussed in the Constituent Assembly's legislative arm on 9 April 1948, when Ambedkar moved for referring it to a Select Committee. He explained that the bill sought to codify the rules relating to different aspects of Hindu law which were scattered across 'innumerable decisions of the High Courts and of the Privy Council, which form a bewildering motley to the common man and give rise to constant litigation'. The issues it aimed to address included the rights of inheritance, the order of succession among the different heirs, and the law of maintenance, marriage, divorce, adoption, minority and guardianship.[189]

The report of the Select Committee, also known as Ambedkar Committee because of his instrumental role in finalizing the draft code, was presented to the central legislature on 12 August 1948.[190] A disagreement between President Rajendra Prasad and Prime Minister Nehru had erupted by then. Immediately after meeting a deputation of eight members of the Select Committee on 21 July 1948, Rajendra Prasad wrote a letter to Nehru. In the exchange of letters that followed, Prasad set out his list of problems: the merit of the bill was irrelevant at that point of time as more fundamental principles of democratic politics needed to be resolved first. The bill had never been discussed at the meetings of the Congress and a majority of the Committee members who met him advised not to rush the bill. The Constituent Assembly sitting as a legislature was only a temporary arrangement, he argued, and not competent to pass a legislation of such far-reaching consequences, to which most people were opposed. Dwaraka Nath Mitter's note of dissent had demonstrated, the president recalled, that the bill was totally at variance with the evidence recorded by the Hindu Law Committee. Moreover, neither had the issue been placed before the electorate nor had any programme been taken up to build public opinion in favour of the legislation.[191]

Prasad was apprehensive that forcing the bill was bound to adversely impact Congress's performance in the next elections. It would mean 'riding roughshod on the cherished sentiments of the vast bulk of our people and that without having any warrant or sanction from them simply because we consider certain things to be right'.[192]

According to Nehru, however, 'Few contemplated pieces of legislation have been so thoroughly thrashed out and publicly discussed than this Bill.' He was worried that the Congress was being called 'a reactionary and a very conservative body now, which dares not face any radical change', and shelving the bill would not only confirm that image, but the Congress 'would also go down in the mind of foreigners outside India'. After extending their support to the bill, how could both Nehru and the cabinet now 'give up something that we consider right and on which so much labour has been spent, because some people object?' In any case, the bill was 'before the Assembly and it is for the Assembly to consider it and decide this way or that way'.[193]

Prasad had so far not commented on the content of the bill, but he laid it out in no uncertain terms in a formal note to Nehru, which he also shared with Patel, for placing in front of the party members when they met to consider the legislation:

> The matter is of fundamental importance to everyone who is governed by the Hindu Law. It substitutes for the concepts and the reasons underlying that law, new concepts and new ideas, which are not only foreign to Hindu Law but may cause disruption in every family.[194]

His suggestion to the party was to wait until the Constitution came into effect and then take it to the electorate in the next elections.

Ambedkar made the motion for the consideration of the bill as suggested by the Select Committee on 31 August 1948, but the discussion on that motion commenced on 17 February 1949, and the assembly adopted the motion on 19 December after debating it for eight days in the intervening months. Rajendra Prasad took up the matter again on 4 December when he sent another note to Patel arguing against the Hindu Code Bill, largely repeating his previous arguments with some additions, and asking for his opinion whether he should send it to Nehru and to the press. Patel himself did not come across as someone enthused by the bill. When the debate on the bill was dropped in April 1949 after two days of discussion in that month Patel justified any further debate during that session by calling it 'unnecessary waste of time'.[195] Patel, however, strongly advised Prasad against taking such a step.[196]

Although Nehru was hopeful that the bill would be passed in 1950, it was not taken up for discussion during the year. A few days after Patel's death, he wrote to Ambedkar that he was anxious to have the bill passed, but some 'very urgent problems of governmental reconstruction' arising out of Patel passing away needed to be taken care of. When the clause-by-clause debate took place only for three days in February 1951 and then dropped again, Ambedkar bitterly complained in a letter to Nehru about a 'vociferous and obstructive minority' in Parliament, also criticizing him for declining to issue a whip to the Congress members. 'I have been much troubled myself about the obstructionist tactics of some Members and the inordinate delay caused by them,' Nehru agreed, repeating that he wished to have the law being passed in the current session of Parliament.[197] The President, however, was still unwilling; he wanted the reference to the Hindu Code Bill taken out from his address to Parliament at the beginning of its fourth session on 6 August 1951. Not only the President, but the speaker and the deputy speaker of the provisional parliament were also against the bill, Nehru informed Sri Prakasa. Refusing to oblige Prasad, Nehru informed Ambedkar at the same time that the Congress parliamentary party had agreed to pass the bill during that session, with even those who had earlier opposed the bill having coming around. There was, however, a demand from them that the bill be passed after dropping the controversial clauses.[198]

By mid-September it was clear to Nehru that passing the entire bill would not be possible in the current Parliament, which would soon be dissolved. The Congress parliamentary party, therefore, decided only to take up Part II of the Hindu Code Bill, which dealt with marriage, and aim to pass it as a standalone piece of legislation.[199] Rebuffed by Nehru, Prasad in the meantime decided to use the discretionary powers accorded to the President by the Indian Constitution. On 15 September, he informed Nehru that since he held that the provisional parliament did not have the authority to enact a major legislation like the Hindu Code (since it was indirectly elected and did not have the people's mandate), he would use the power of his office to shelve the bill or veto it, going against the advice of the cabinet if necessary. Nehru told him that in the cabinet's view, the President had no power or authority to go against the will of Parliament in regard to a bill that has been well considered by it and passed, but at the same time, on the advice of Rajagopalachari, sought written opinions from the attorney general M.C. Setalvad and former member of the Constituent Assembly Alladi Krishnaswami Aiyar on this constitutional problem.[200]

As the debate resumed on 17 September, Nehru announced that the government had decided to take up only Parts I and II of the bill and consider the rest of it only if time permits.[201] After only two clauses of the bill were passed in the week following the resumption of debate on the Hindu Code on 17 September, Nehru announced the adjournment of the bill on 26 September. The 'rate of progress is so remarkably slow that so far as this session is concerned, after very careful calculation it seemed to us obvious' that it was not possible to have even the two parts of the bill passed.[202]

In his resignation statement, Ambedkar claimed that he had agreed to go ahead with Nehru's plan to go through with the truncated bill keeping in mind the proverb 'it is better to save a part when the whole is likely to be lost'. Nehru's subsequent decision to drop the whole bill 'came to me as a great shock—a bolt from the blue. I was stunned and could not say anything'. That was the last straw for Ambedkar:

The Hindu Code was the greatest social reform measure ever undertaken by the Legislature in this country. No law passed by the Indian Legislature in the past or likely to be passed in the future can be compared to it in point of its significance. To leave inequality between class and class, between sex and sex which is the soul of Hindu Society untouched and to go on passing legislation relating to economic problems is to make a farce of our Constitution and to build a palace on a dung heap. This is the significance I attached to the Hindu Code. It is for its sake that I stayed on notwithstanding my differences.[203]

'Mr Nehru Starts a Controversy' ran a headline in the 17 May 1951 edition of the *Manchester Guardian*,[204] reporting Nehru's motion in the provisional parliament on the previous day to refer a bill to amend the Constitution, which he had introduced on 12 May, to a Select Committee. The move was triggered by a number of setbacks that the Central and some provincial governments had faced in the high courts and the Supreme Court based on the judiciary's interpretation of the Constitutional provisions, especially those relating to some of the fundamental rights.

That he was considering the amendment of the Constitution, was given out by Nehru as early as in March. When asked at a press conference whether he would amend the Constitution to deal with the unfavourable court rulings, Nehru answered in the affirmative and then explained the premise of such an action:

> . . . Naturally, Government must respect the decision of the High Court or the Supreme Court. If the Constitution is interpreted by the Courts in a way which comes in the way of the wishes of the legislature in regard to basic social matters, then it is for the legislatures to consider how to amend the Constitution, so that the will of the people as represented in legislature should prevail . . .[205]

The statement of objects and reasons gave the brief background to the bill and what it wanted to achieve. Referring to the adverse judicial decisions, it said that the 'citizen's right to freedom of speech and expression guaranteed by article 19(1)(a) has been held by some courts to be so comprehensive as not to render a person culpable even if he advocates murder and other crimes of violence'. While the existing article 19(1)(g) states that a citizen's right to practise any profession or to carry on any occupation, trade or business is subject to reasonable restrictions which the laws of the State may impose 'in the interests of general public', the government felt that it was important 'to place the matter beyond doubt by a clarificatory addition to article 19(6)'. The bill also wanted to address the problem of 'dilatory litigation' faced by the provinces in the implementation of zamindari abolition and land reforms measures due to article 31.[206]

The Supreme Court had recently annulled a policy of the Madras government providing for community-based reservations in educational institutions and as a result limiting the opportunity for upper-caste students. The bill argued that since one of the directive principles of state policy contained in article 46 stipulated that the State should promote the educational and economic interests of the weaker sections of the people and protect them from social injustice, it became necessary to amend article 15(3) so that such measures 'may not be challenged on the ground of being discriminatory'. Apart from these major amendments, the bill sought to amend the articles dealing with the convening and proroguing of the sessions of Parliament.[207]

While moving to refer the bill to the Select Committee, Nehru addressed some of the criticisms first. Answering the charge that he was hurrying the passage of the bill, he retorted that he did not understand how prolonging the consideration of 'a relatively simple Bill' by the Committee and the parliament would allow for 'greater thought'. To the objection that the provisional parliament was not based on universal adult franchise and therefore it was improper to amend the Constitution, Nehru reminded the members that 'it is we after all, who were the Constituent Assembly and who drafted this Constitution'.[208]

Asserting that the bill did not intend to curtail any right but proposed enabling measures only meant to 'clarify the authority of Parliament', Nehru speculated that it was 'highly unlikely that this Government or this Parliament will take advantage of them by passing laws to that effect, unless some very severe crisis, national or international, arises'. Regarding the amendment of article 19 related to freedom of speech, he claimed, 'I do not think there is any country in the world at the present moment where there is so much freedom—if I may use the word for the moment—in regard to Press publications as in India.' 'The vulgarity and indecency and falsehood, day after day,' propagated by the 'less responsible news-sheets' was not 'for me a political problem but a moral problem'. On the issue of community-based reservation, Nehru clarified:

> I want to make it perfectly clear that so far as Government are concerned, they do not wish to have any truck with communalism in any form. But you have to distinguish between backward classes which are specially mentioned in the Constitution that have to be helped to be made to grow and not think of them in terms of this community or that. Only if you think of them in terms of the community you bring in communalism.'[209]

The most stringent criticism of the bill came from Syama Prasad Mookerjee, Nehru's former cabinet colleague: 'To my mind, the explanation which he gave was weak and halting and not acceptable, nor was it satisfactory.' Mookerjee was not convinced by the justification of the bill provided by Nehru. He pointed out that his and other members' suggestion to have the bill circulated to elicit public opinion was not intended to delay the process. If the prime minister was not in a hurry, Mookerjee wondered, why was he not agreeable to wait for a few more weeks to receive public opinion on a proposed change in the Constitution; and more so since the prime minister seemed to claim that the changes were not for immediate use by the government but for future parliaments.[210]

Claiming that Nehru knew 'it in his heart of hearts . . . that what he is going to do is nothing short of cutting at the very root of the fundamental principles of the Constitution', Mookerjee asked whether Nehru was 'incapable today to carry on the administration of the country unless he is clothed with more and more powers to be arbitrarily utilised so that his will may be the last word on the subject'. He emphasized that the current Constitution gave adequate powers to parliament and state legislatures to deal with the abuse of press freedom described by the prime minister.[211]

Pointing out to the fact that although the land reforms legislation of Bihar was turned down by the judiciary but not similar laws enacted by other provinces, Mookerjee asked the government whether it wanted to change the Constitution if certain laws, even if 'nonsensical' were found to infringe upon the Constitutional goals. 'They why have the Constitution?' he asked. Mookerjee warned that 'here is a beginning of the encroachment of the liberty of the people in Free India'.[212]

After the Select Committee submitted its report on 25 May, the modified bill was passed on 2 June.

~

As India became a republic, the Constituent Assembly, which functioned as the combined chambers of the central legislature, was transformed into a provisional parliament until the first general elections were held.

Holding elections to the central and the provincial legislatures based on adult suffrage for an estimated population of 348 million, however, required massive preparatory work and time. The ball was set rolling in November 1947 by the secretariat of the Constituent Assembly asking the provincial governments to assess the magnitude of the administrative effort required to prepare the voters' list. On 8 January 1949, the Assembly adopted Nehru's motion to issue instructions for the preparation of electoral rolls for holding the elections 'as early as possible in 1950'. The provisions of the Constitution relating to citizenship and the Election Commission came into force on 26 November 1949, before the rest of the Constitution. The office of the Election Commission was set up in January 1950, and the chief election commissioner (CEC) took office on 21 March 1950.[213] The person in Nehru's mind for the post was B.N. Rau, due to his unavailability Sukumar Sen, then chief secretary to the West Bengal government, was selected as India's first CEC.[214]

The big hurdles to holding the elections at that moment were that the laws governing the election were not yet ready, the population of the scheduled castes and scheduled tribes had not been determined, the exercise concerning delimitation of constituencies had not been taken up and the preparedness of conducting the elections varied considerably across the states.[215] It was obvious that the elections could not be held in 1950. Informing the chief ministers of the states about the CEC's appointment, Nehru wrote in his fortnightly letter of 1 April 1950 that 'we must have this election at all costs early next year', latest by April 1951.[216]

The electoral laws were passed in two phases to expedite the electoral process. On 20 April 1950, Parliament passed the Representation of the People Act, 1950, which dealt with the preparation and publication of electoral rolls and delimitation of constituencies. The Representation of the People Act, 1951, was passed more than a year later, on 17 July 1951, setting up the electoral machinery. The Scheduled Castes Order and the Scheduled Tribes Order were issued on 10 August and 6 September 1950, respectively. It was clear by the end of the year that the elections had to be postponed again. Addressing the third session of the provisional parliament on 14 November 1950, the President announced that the elections would be held in the second half of November or in early December 1951.[217]

While the majority of the polling to the Lok Sabha and the state legislatures took place during December 1951 and January 1952, some places in Himachal Pradesh and Uttar Pradesh, where accessibility was a problem, went to the polls in October 1951 and February 1952. Elections to the upper houses of the legislatures took place in March, and the presidential elections were held in May 1952.[218]

With the talk about the elections floating in the air from 1950, most political activities then needed to be seen as calculated to maximize electoral benefits.

Immediately after taking up the Congress presidentship, Nehru focused on putting together the new working committee, strengthening the party organization and rejuvenating its morale. He reached out to Kripalani, Prafulla Ghosh and others who had left asking them to return to the party. He was going to do something that he had always turned away from: run both the government and the party, and that needed some explanation to the party members as well as to himself. Nehru's address to the Congress parliamentary party on 21 August 1951 provides a glimpse of how he saw the developments.

On the whole Nehru had stayed away from organizational affairs as long as Patel carried the responsibility on his shoulders, his involvement largely being restricted to discussing major policy matters. However, he felt that 'the situation slipping away from us' and 'this feeling of isolation grew within me—the isolation of the Congress from the people'. The increasing conflicts within the party emerged as a 'weakening factor' that became an obstacle for him to talk about a broader unity in the country. He had 'a powerful feeling that we are losing touch with the larger masses, that we are too busy with our work in Parliament and assemblies, in Congress committees, or are too slack'. The obvious and only solution was 'to get going with the public', but to do that effectively, the first requirement was to have a strong organization. It was this situation that 'drove me back to the organisation'.[219]

His first approach, Nehru explained, was to infuse new ideas through resolutions, but it soon became clear that although his resolutions were being accepted without much opposition, they were not being adhered to. This led him to conclude that he was wrong in his approach, and while those arrayed against him 'did not go against them [the resolutions] but they did not attach any importance to them'. 'They lacked warmth, they lacked imagination', and although many showed themselves to be interested in Nehru's ideas, they did things that created problems in executing those plans.[220]

But he knew, Nehru said, that a 'very large number of people could be influenced by me' not just because he was the prime minister. It placed a great responsibility on him, and 'one cannot run away from the responsibilities which come from the faith of the people'. That would be treason. Even with this realization Nehru resigned from the working committee, because he felt he would become more ineffective if the rift in the party continued. He was clear that the 'sensation and shock' resulting from his resignation would be good for the country. His resignation had forced the Congress to decide which way it was going and what it stood for, 'without a shadow of doubt'.[221] Nehru's arguments clearly laid out that once the decision was made, it could only be him who could and should lead the Congress into the future. 'I have realised that having created the hiatus . . . I cannot run away from responsibility.'[222]

At once, Nehru started reaching out to the leadership of the Pradesh Congress Committees (PCCs), sharing his advice and broad guidelines to strengthen the party as well as to select the right candidates for the general elections.[223] His earlier policy of maintaining distance from the functioning of the PCCs obviously had to change. Now he tried to unite the different factions in the states together; for instance, in Bihar, where he tried to bring together the PCC president Anugrah Narayan Sinha and the chief minister Sri Krishna Sinha.[224] He actively involved himself, with the help of senior leaders in the Centre and in the provinces, in the process of selection of candidates.

Nehru told the leaders of the PCCs, 'Our chief opponents in our work and in the elections are the communal organisations.' Although he was not worried about parties like the Hindu Mahasabha and the Ram Rajya Parishad, since he believed that they wouldn't get much support, he was concerned that the recently founded 'Jan Sangh', which had a broader appeal, 'is likely to prove a stronger antagonist'. The party, which, 'whatever they may say, is an intensely communal organisation', would undoubtedly get the support of the Rashtriya Swayamsevak Sangh (RSS). Nehru was worried that while 'some members of the Congress have functioned almost as if they were members of the Hindu Mahasabha', some others had actually gone over to the Jan Sangh.[225]

The Bharatiya Jana Sangh (BJS), referred to by Nehru, was the party formed on 27 May 1951 in Jalandhar. It aimed to work in Punjab, Patiala and East Punjab States Union (PEPSU), Himachal Pradesh and Delhi. Balraj Bhalla, a former revolutionary, was elected the president of the new party and Balraj Madhok the general secretary.[226] About a month prior to this, on 28 April 1951, Syama Prasad Mookerjee announced in Calcutta his decision to form a new political party which he called the People's Party. An eight-point programme adopted at a meeting of over a hundred eminent citizens set the core focus areas of the party. Some of the key areas of focus were a reunited and undivided India (Akhand Bharat), reciprocal dealing with Pakistan instead of appeasement, independent and practical foreign policy based on national interest, planned resettlement of refugees, demanding compensation from Pakistan, increased production and equitable distribution of essential goods like food and cloth, decentralization of industries, regional self-sufficiency, administrative reforms, nurturing a common Indian (Bharatiya) culture, ethos and dignity, and redrawing West Bengal's boundaries based on administrative and economic considerations. Mookerjee declared that although the party started in Bengal, it would either set up branches in the other provinces of the country or align with parties with similar political goals.[227]

When a national convention of the BJS met in Delhi on 21 October to declare itself a national party, it had expanded to almost all the provinces. Mookerjee was elected the first president of the BJS. Mookerjee chose the twenty-five-year-old Atal Bihari Vajpayee as his private secretary.[228] Mookerjee, Nehru declared in a press conference in November, 'happens to represent, at the present moment, everything that I consider wrong and objectionable in this country'.[229] The Sangh's first experience in an election before Mookerjee took charge, however, was not a happy one. In the Delhi municipal elections held on 15 October, the Jana Sangh managed to win in only five out of fifty seats, with forty-two going to the Congress.[230]

At the time of the general elections, Mookerjee's former party, the Hindu Mahasabha, had weakened considerably in the aftermath of Gandhi's assassination. Mookerjee gradually dissociated himself from the Mahasabha, resigning from its working committee in November 1948, continuing only as an ordinary member.[231]

Among the other Hindu nationalist parties in the electoral fray, probably the most orthodox was the Akhil Bharatiya Ram Rajya Parishad (RRP), founded by Swami Hariharananda Saraswati, better known as Swami Karpatri, in 1948. The stated objective of the RRP was to establish a society devoid of oppression, governed by the rules of dharma, which reflected the golden days of the rule of Ram. The party aimed to reunite India through peaceful and legitimate means, and advocated fraternity among all beings with the understanding that all were parts of a supreme divine being. It wanted a state with an Indian ethos that would work for the political and economic upliftment of citizens irrespective of their caste, community or religion; provide food, clothing and shelter; ban cow slaughter; promote barter system by limiting the system of legal tender; protect the country from the negative impacts of Western industrialization; make the villages the basic unit of administration with the help of the traditional panchayat system; declare Hindi as the national language; and improve the social status of the backward and scheduled castes by providing special facilities and appointing them to the highest posts 'suitable for them'.[232] For Swami Karpatri, attaining a Hindu state was not enough, it had to be based on dharma to become Ram Rajya. As a contrast, he cited the rule of Ravana and Indra, where the common citizens suffered because they deviated from the path of dharma. The RRP was, in Swami Karpatri's view, a united front of Hindus, Muslims, Christians, Parsis, Sikhs, Jains and Harijans, and in his perceived Ram Rajya people would be able to follow their respective religions without interfering in the religious practices of others.[233]

Staunchly against the Hindu Code Bill and zamindari's abolition, Swami Karpatri criticized the Nehru government for trying to establish a socialist and secular state based on a materialist philosophy, which he claimed was delinking both the education system and the larger society from dharma. He accused the government of destroying the fabric of Hindu traditions at a greater scale than the British did, for instance, by taking over the management of temples in the name of secularism. While some of the grudges of the RRP reflected the views of a wider segment of Hindu traditionalists, in many instances the party advocated an extreme form of social conservatism. In fact, Swami Karpatri accused the Jana Sangh, the Hindu Mahasabha and the RSS of not following the path of dharma and a lack of understanding of Hindu scriptures.[234]

On the other end of the political spectrum were the leftist parties, among which those with some influence and organizational strength were the CPI, the Socialist Party, the Revolutionary Socialist Party (RSP), the Forward Bloc (FB) and the Revolutionary Communist Party of India (RCPI).

The Socialist Party 'is the only secular Indian party of nation-wide significance which appears capable of becoming a serious competitor to the Congress', observed Werner Levi, associate professor of political science at the University of Minnesota, after his India visit during the winter of 1950–51.[235]

The KMPP, in the meantime, went through some changes in the party leadership. In October 1951, after Nehru had taken up the presidentship of the Congress and reconstituted the working committee, Kidwai declared his intention to return to the Congress.

An analysis of the results of the by-elections in the provincial legislatures held between January 1950 and March 1951 by the general secretary of the Socialist Party led the party to conclude that it was the second-largest party in India and that the split in the Opposition votes across smaller parties was an important contributing factor to Congress's victory in these elections. Following this conclusion, the Socialist Party entered into electoral arrangements with the Jharkhand Party in Bihar, the RCPI in West Bengal, the Scheduled Caste Federation of Ambedkar and a faction of the Forward Bloc led by R.S. Ruikar. Jayaprakash Narayan also appealed to Kripalani to join the Socialist Party with the other members of the Congress Democratic Front, instead of forming a new party.[236]

Kripalani refused a merger with the Sociality Party, arguing that the party's programme expressed in intellectual jargon was not intelligible to the common Indians, and in any case, Gandhian philosophy and programme, rather than socialism, had emerged as the key determinants in Indian politics. Although the top leadership of the two parties agreed for an electoral alliance, it could not be executed at the local level in many districts and provinces. Myron Weiner has argued that the failure in effectively implementing the electoral alliance was because of an overestimation of their respective strength by each party and did not stem from ideological differences, since the Socialist Party too had endorsed the Sarvodaya plan developed by the Gandhians, and leaders like Narayan had over a period of time grown closer to the Gandhian ideals: 'The influence of Gandhism on Jayaprakash grew after Gandhi's death, until by 1952 he spoke in Gandhian terms as frequently as he did in socialist terms.' Concomitant with his increasing scepticism about the concept of material progress in an industrial society was a growing inclination for the religious values and constructive work of Gandhi and, subsequently, Vinoba Bhave.[237] Narayan 'wishes an infusion of Gandhism in Indian socialism as the best way of making Socialists respect the ordinary moral law', noted an editorial in the *Guardian*.[238]

Nehru was now in charge of both the party and the government, but his influence in selecting candidates was limited, with the state-level party bosses calling the shots. On 13 October 1951, Nehru complained to Vijayalakshmi Pandit, 'I am fed up with the kind of things going on and the kind of persons selected.'[239] 'My experience in recent days in scrutinising candidates' lists has been one of the most depressing that I have ever had . . . Many of them are third rate from any point of view,' he wrote to Morarji Desai.[240] Against certain Opposition candidates, such as Kamala Devi Chattopadhyaya and Narendra Deva, Nehru strongly recommended not putting up any Congress candidates. Morarji Desai, then home minister of Bombay province and a member of the Congress Parliamentary Board, however, didn't agree, and Chattopadhyaya lost to the Congress candidate.[241]

In the 1951–52 general elections, over 60 per cent of the nearly 106 million registered voters cast their votes to elect 489 members of the Lok Sabha, the lower house of Parliament, and over 3000 members of the state legislatures. The results reflected an overwhelming mandate for Nehru and the Congress, which won 364 seats, securing 45 per cent of the total votes polled. The second-largest party with sixteen seats was the CPI, followed by the Socialist Party and the KMPP, which won twelve and nine seats, respectively. The CPI won more seats with a lower vote share than the Socialist Party and the KMPP, as it focused in the areas where it was strong. It won a third of the seats it contested, which came from the Kerala region in Madras province, West Bengal, Tripura and Orissa. In contrast, the results were a blow to the aspiration of the Socialist Party and the KMPP—which won just 5 and 6 per cent of the contested seats, respectively—to establish themselves as the national opposition to the Congress. The three right-wing parties, Hindu Mahasabha, BJS and the RRP, won a total of ten seats. Compared to the Hindu Mahasabha and the RRP, however, the BJS performed better, despite being a new party. The BJS could put up more candidates and secure more votes than the other two combined.[242]

A notable feature of the election results was the strong performance of the independent candidates, who secured thirty-seven seats with a 16 per cent vote share in the Lok Sabha, and a total of 335 seats with about 22 per cent vote share in the state legislatures. In the Lok Sabha as well as in most of the state legislatures (for instance, Assam, Bhopal, Bombay, Himachal Pradesh, Hyderabad, Madhya Pradesh, Madras, Mysore, Rajasthan, etc.), the independent members formed the second-largest bloc. In four legislative assemblies, the Congress failed to achieve the majority, although emerging as the single largest party—Orissa, Patiala and East Punjab States Union (PEPSU), Travancore–Cochin and Madras. While the Congress won 70 per cent of the seats it contested, the BJS won only 4 per cent, the Socialist Party 7 per cent, the KMPP 8 per cent, the Hindu Mahasabha 9 per cent and the CPI nearly a quarter.[243]

Nehru started sharing his reflection on the electoral process and the results as the election neared the final stages. To the Congress general secretary U.S. Malliah, he wrote, 'One fact appears clear to me that our organisation, as it exists at present, is not very suitable for elections or indeed for any solid work among the people. We have not developed leadership at the lower levels and we have relied too much on top committees.'[244] He identified several issues that worked in favour and against the party, was scathing in his remarks about the 'defeat of Congress Ministers in bulk', but above all he had no doubt about his own impact on the results. 'My tours all over the country had undoubtedly a powerful effect,' he wrote to the Congress Working Committee. 'I am inclined to think that but for these tours, we would have suffered far greater defeats.'[245]

According to Nehru's prognosis, parties like the KMPP, who 'are just dissidents angry with the world and more specifically with the Congress', did not count and would 'fade away'. The socialists suffered because their leadership was 'feeble in the extreme' and were not likely to make much progress 'unless some great change comes over them'. He anticipated that 'part of their membership will drift to other parties'. The 'purely communal' parties like the BJS, RRP, the Hindu Mahasabha and the Akali Dal were 'not likely to grow in strength', Nehru wrote, but 'flourish in a limited way'. The 'caste complex', in contrast, 'will no doubt continue to affect elections and our politics generally'. The emergence of the leftist fronts indicated 'a strong demand for economic change and progress'. 'No party that ignores this can have much of a future,' he noted.[246] This assertion became a recurring theme in his speeches and interactions. For instance, while speaking to the Congress legislators and workers of Madras in October, he repeated: 'The Communists or the Socialists represent, in a measure, certain ideas which are progressive in the domain of economic theory, and a certain change which is gradually coming all over the world.'[247] The elections had clarified, at least for Nehru, the path forward. Economic change was set to take the centre of the political programme for the next few years.

In view of the election results, a common reaction among the political groups was an attempt to consolidate their strength by bringing together the various parties with similar ideologies and programmes. While the Congress sought to further strengthen its lead, the right-wing parties and the socialists strove to bring together several small parties in order to put up an effective opposition to the government.

Due to the efforts of Mookerjee, thirty-four members of Parliament, belonging to the BJS, the Hindu Mahasabha, the Common Weal Party and the Tamil Nadu Toilers Party of Madras, the Akali Dal, the Orissa-based All India Ganatantra Parishad and several independent members, formed an opposition parliamentary front called National Democratic Party in June 1952. Outside Parliament, talks started from early 1952 between the BJS, the Hindu Mahasabha and the RRP for a merger as the parties found common ground over Jammu and Kashmir and the demand for a ban on cow slaughter. Mookerjee's sudden death on 23 June 1953 after he was arrested for his attempt to enter Jammu, however, removed the biggest unifying figure from the scene. The effort to execute a merger fell apart by the end of the year, as the parties were not ready to give up their core identities. While the RRP refused to forsake its principles with respect to religion, the BJS's criticism of the Hindu Mahasabha for allowing only Hindus in its fold created an unbridgeable gulf. L.B. Bhopatkar and V.D. Savarkar reportedly opposed the idea of a merger with the Jana Sangh so long as it insisted on admitting non-Hindus in the new party.[248] The fallout of this failed effort was more bitterness among the parties, completely opposite of what it was supposed to achieve.

Apart from its efforts to build an alliance with the KMPP, the Socialist Party also tried to bring together the smaller leftist parties prior to the general elections. The effort, however, failed primarily due to the insistence of the smaller parties on including the CPI in such an alliance, to which the socialists were vehemently opposed. The only alliance that the Socialist Party was able to put together was with the Peasant and Workers' Party in Hyderabad, the Jharkhand Party in Bihar and the Scheduled Castes Federation. These alliances, however, came in for stringent criticism from both within the party and its political opponents as being opportunists as well as a deviation from the party's principles.[249]

Soon after the elections, the national executive of the Socialist Party issued an appeal in February 1952 to all parties committed to nationalism, liberties and rights of the people and social change to come together. The appeal was reiterated in May, at a special convention in Panchmarhi.

In the meantime, in February 1952, the KMPP had joined the United Democratic Front (UDF), a non-Congress coalition in Madras that also included the CPI, the Forward Bloc (Marxist), the Scheduled Caste Federation and a host of state parties, in an attempt to form the government as the Congress party was in a minority in the province. When KMPP's alliance with the CPI became a thorny issue in the face of stringent criticism by the Socialist Party, the Congress managed to cobble together a coalition government, and the UDF came to an end.[250]

On 1 June, Kripalani, Narayan and Asoka Mehta announced the merger of the KMPP and the Socialist Party into a single parliamentary party. A common programme evolved to provide the foundation to the merger, included egalitarian social order, land to the tiller, decentralization of industry, nationalization of key industries, swadeshi and a spirit of neutrality in foreign policy. The decision to completely merge the two parties and name it the Praja Socialist Party (PSP) was taken at a meeting in Bombay on 26 and 27 September.[251] Welcoming the formation of the PSP, Nehru expressed hope of having 'as much cooperation as possible with them'.[252]

Nehru took the initiative to transform his wish to a more concrete form. He began a series of talks from the autumn of 1952 with Narayan, Narendra Deva and Kripalani to give a formal shape to his desire for cooperation at all levels with the PSP. It only helped him to become the uncontested Congress president in December; S. Nijalingappa and Lal Bahadur Shastri, who had also been nominated, withdrew from the contest. The desire to meet Narayan was not hinged on any particular event, Nehru explained to him in a letter, but because he wanted a joint effort to hasten the progress towards the 'big things to do in this country', for which 'the next five or ten years are crucial in our existence'.[253]

In March 1953, Narayan shared with Nehru a fourteen-point programme for five years to be adopted by the government in order to make a collaboration with the PSP possible. Some of the points included were land reforms, abolition of the upper houses of Central and state legislatures, organization of village industries on cooperative basis, nationalization of industry and development of state trading, etc.

After considering the proposed programme and meeting Narayan on 16 March, Nehru wrote that although 'To each one of these, considered separately, I have little objection', it wouldn't be possible for him as the prime minister and the Congress president to commit to specific points of action. What he had in mind was cooperation as a matter of general approach and not in terms of precise and specific programmes. Therefore, 'I feel it is better for us not in any way to tie each other down, but rather to try, to the best of our ability, to develop both the spirit and the practice of cooperation'.[254]

The question of collaboration with the Congress was hotly debated at a special convention in Betul from 14–18 June. On this question the PSP was a divided house. While leaders such as Asoka Mehta appeared to lean towards an agreement with the Congress, both Narendra Deva and Lohia were opposed to it. Lohia opposed Mehta's thesis of 'compulsions of a backward economy', which advocated the broad-basing of the government as well as the fourteen-point programme presented by Narayan.[255] The PSP at this time was further strengthened by the joining of the Ruikar faction of the Forward Bloc.[256]

The strengths of the political groups were tested in some of the provinces before the second general elections of 1957. Elections became necessary in PEPSU and in Travancore–Cochin, where the Congress had failed to win majority, as no stable ministries could be formed. A United Front led by the Akali Dal and supported by the independent candidates and the CPI formed the government in PEPSU after a minority Congress government had to resign in April 1952 within a month of forming the government.[257] The first non-Congress government also proved unstable and as a result President's rule was imposed in PEPSU on 12 March 1953.[258]

A coalition government of the Congress, with the Travancore Tamilnad Congress Party, the Kerala Socialist Party and one nominated Anglo–Indian member formed government. The assembly was dissolved by the rajpramukh as the government led by A.J. John lost a motion of confidence on 23 September 1953, and fresh elections were announced.[259]

The elections held in the two provinces in 1954 produced significantly different results. While the Congress achieved a clear majority in PEPSU, winning thirty-seven out of sixty seats, in Travancore–Cochin it won in forty-five out of 117 seats, with the CPI and the PSP making significant gains, winning in twenty-three and nineteen seats, respectively. The PSP formed the government with support from the Congress, which fell in February 1955, when the Congress withdrew support. The Congress itself formed a coalition government, but that too lasted just over a year. The government resigned on 10 March 1956, after six Congress members decided not to support it, and President's rule was announced on 23 March 1956. A.K. Gopalan of the CPI, however, launched a scathing attack on the Central government when the home minister Govind Ballabh Pant introduced the motion on President's rule in Lok Sabha. He alleged that the rajpramukh of Travancore–Cochin did not give P. Thanu Pillai, leader of the PSP in the assembly, a chance to form another government, although he had secured the support of sixty-one legislators, which gave him the majority. Asoka Mehta of the PSP also accused the Central government of conspiracy, alleging that the rajpramukh acted in the interests of the Congress party.[260]

The third province which had to elect a new government was the newly formed Andhra Pradesh, which demonstrated several curious characteristics of Indian politics. At the time of its formation in 1953, being carved out of the province of Madras, the Congress and the CPI formed the two largest blocs in the Andhra legislative assembly. Despite the breakdown in the Nehru–Jayaprakash talks, Neelam Sanjiva Reddy, the leader of the Congress legislature party, and T. Prakasam, the leader of the Andhra PSP, announced on 28 May that their parties had agreed upon a minimum programme on the basis of which they would cooperate in the legislature.[261] The two parties continued to collaborate on various matters, including the selection of Kurnool as the capital of the new state. Prakasam announced towards the end of August that 'We of the Praja Socialist Party, have been pledged to a coalition', and that it would be 'utter childishness to think of going back upon the idea of coalition' with the Congress.[262] Nehru informed Chandulal Trivedi, the governor-designate of Andhra Pradesh in early September, two possible courses of action regarding government formation in the state that had emerged from his discussion with this party colleagues. The first option was to appoint Prakasam as the chief minister if he resigned from the PSP to become an independent member in the legislature and join the Congress legislature party as a member or an associate member. In the event of that option failing to materialize, Sanjiva Reddy should form 'a purely Congress Government', even though it might not be a stable one. Nehru had already discussed the matter with Prakasam, who 'seemed to be very happy about it'. Clear instructions for Trivedi were then laid out by the prime minister: Trivedi should deal with Reddy to begin with and 'Prakasam comes in not by direct invitation from you, but on the invitation of the Congress Party conveyed to him through Sanjeeva Reddi [sic], who then informs you of this. Subsequently you deal with Prakasam and Sanjeeva Reddi together.' Nehru also pointed out that it would be 'of course, be desirable for Sanjeeva Reddi to be Deputy Chief Minister'.[263]

The PSP national executive was willing to allow the Andhra unit of the party to form a coalition, but probably did not expect the way matters would develop. Kripalani strongly criticized the Congress move when on 25 September Prakasam resigned from the PSP and joined the Congress legislature party as an associate member. 'This is not done,' he remarked. The national executive of the party held that Prakasam 'has set a deplorable standard of political conduct'. Jayaprakash Narayan lamented that the Congress had 'degraded party politics in the country'.[264] Nehru presented a feeble defence of his decision while inaugurating India's first linguistic province on 1 October by claiming that the move should not be seen as a manoeuvre against any party, since his approach was one of seeking the cooperation of other parties and not of harming them.[265]

In thirteen months, however, the Prakasam ministry had to resign, as a no-confidence motion was passed by the assembly for its failure to scrap the prohibition programme in the state as recommended by the S.V. Ramamurthy Committee in May 1954. The committee had suggested using the excise on liquor for economic betterment, but the recommendation was against one of the fundamental Gandhian principles staunchly adhered to by the Congress. Even the report of Justice K.N. Wanchoo, which studied the financial aspects of the formation of the new state, had recommended abandoning the prohibition programme to improve the revenue position of the state.[266] Andhra Pradesh probably became the only state in India where a government had to resign for not withdrawing its prohibition programme.

The Congress, however, succeeded spectacularly in the February 1955 elections. An alliance of the Congress, the Krishikar Lok Party and a splinter group of the PSP won in 146 out of the total 196 seats.[267] Bezwada Gopala Reddy was elected to be Andhra Pradesh's new chief minister. A more than 50 per cent reduction in the strength of the CPI in the assembly made Nehru gleeful at least on one count. Just prior to the elections, the British journalist Kingsley Martin had remarked, 'If I happen to be a voter of Andhra today, I would certainly vote for the Communist Party.' Nehru believed that coming from someone of Kingsley's public position, the statement was 'not at all proper'. After the declaration of the results he wrote to Vijayalakshmi Pandit, 'The best answer that could be given to Kingsley Martin has been given by the peasantry of Andhra.'[268]

Otherwise too, Nehru was very glad with the Communists' defeat. 'There could be no more smashing defeat for the communists in an areas which they had nursed for years and where their organisation was far the best,' he wrote to Pandit.[269]

In the meantime, Nehru relinquished the post of Congress president, with U.N. Dhebar taking over in January 1955 at the 60th session of the Congress at Avadi in Madras. Dhebar would continue as the party president until 1959.

On 14 September 1948, Nehru had complained to John Matthai that India's capitalist class had 'proved totally inadequate to face things as they are today in the country. They have no vision, no grit, no capacity to do anything big.' 'The only alternative,' Nehru wrote, 'is to try to put forward some big thing ourselves and rope in not only these classes but the people as a whole.'[270]

It was in the Avadi session that Nehru had the Congress commit itself formally to socialism. The resolution that he drafted for the approval of the AICC read:

> In order to realise the object of the Congress as laid down in Article I of the Congress Constitution and to further the objectives stated in the Preamble and Directive Principles of State Policy of the Constitution of India, planning should take place with a view to the establishment of a socialist pattern of society, where the principal means of production are under social ownership or control, production is progressively speeded up and there is equitable distribution of the national wealth.[271]

Although Nehru had used the word socialist in his original draft, it was changed to 'socialistic' to remove any hint of the party appearing dogmatic. When he stood at the open session on 21 January to move the resolution, Nehru carefully avoided defining or describing what he meant by socialistic pattern of society that he had presented as the goal. It was not just a Western concept with its associated history and connotation: 'Whatever it is going to be, it has to be in keeping with the Indian genius.' The socialistic order in India would have to be achieved through peaceful means, just as the British imperialism was met with effectively by peaceful means, and similarly the subsequent problems of princely states and land reforms. While similar problems in other countries were solved by civil war and bloodshed, India solved her problems, inspired by Gandhian ideals, peacefully. India was going to get her socialism not by revolution or by a decree but 'by hard work, by increasing our production and by distributing it equally'. An 'economics of scarcity' had no relevance any more because the 'world is producing a lot', the only problem being 'it is not distributed properly'.[272] A related resolution on economic policy aimed at establishing a welfare state and a socialist economy set the aim of ending unemployment within ten years.[273] Nehru, however, told his biographer Michael Brecher a year later that the driving force behind the socialistic pattern resolution was not him, but the new Congress president Dhebar.[274]

The second general elections were held in the spring of 1957. The number of national parties were down to only four—the Congress, the BJS, the CPI and the PSP—because of the criteria on vote share laid down by the Election Commission. Parties such as the Hindu Mahasabha,

Forward Bloc, the RSP and the Scheduled Caste Federation were given the status of state parties.

In the elections to the Lok Sabha, the Congress increased both its vote share (by about three percentage points) and number of seats (by seven seats). In the state elections, however, its influence declined with the share of votes declining from 42.2 per cent in 1951 to 39.5 per cent in 1957 and the share of total seats going down from 68 per cent to 65 per cent. The BJS and CPI, too, increased their vote share and number of seats both at the national and the state levels, whereas the PSP suffered a decline in both when compared the combined statistics of the Socialist Party and the KMPP in 1951.

7

Foreign Relations

The two Congress leaders who were most prolific in their activities and words—both spoken and written—on India's foreign relations were Subhas Chandra Bose and Jawaharlal Nehru. Although there were some common elements in the framework envisioned by them, Nehru's thoughts were more grounded in Gandhian moral outlook compared to Bose's views, which can be loosely said to be based more on realism. At the end of the war, however, Bose went missing and there was practically no challenge to the dominance of the Nehruvian policy that came to define India in the global power play. India's foreign policy barely had any independent existence other than Nehru's foreign policy. Bose's stinging admonition of Nehru in 1939—'Frothy sentiments and pious platitudes do not make foreign policy. It is no use championing lost causes all the time'—however, would come back to haunt India on a number of occasions.[1]

Set to form the interim government on 2 September, Nehru was asked late in August by Wavell to recommend delegates for some of the most important global conferences which were about to be held soon. The International Labour Organization was scheduled to meet in Montreal from 19 September, the Paris peace talks had already begun in July and the UN General Assembly was to meet in New York from 23 October 1946. While Nehru did not recommend any change in the Indian delegation for the ILO conference and the Paris peace talks, he suggested to Wavell that the Indian delegation should be led by Vijaya Lakshmi Pandit. He also agreed to the British government's suggestion that A. Ramaswami Mudaliar should continue as the president of the UN Economic and Social Council.[2]

The Indian delegation to the UN led by Pandit also included M.C. Chagla, V.K. Krishna Menon and P.N. Sapru. K.P.S. Menon functioned as an adviser to the delegation. The Indian delegation's main issue was to lodge a protest on the South African government's racial discrimination against Indians. India's resolution, presented jointly by France and Mexico and supported by the Soviet Union, asking the South African government to ensure that the treatment of the Indians was in conformity with international obligations and the UN Charter, was adopted by the General Assembly on 8 December 1946 despite opposition from the British and the Americans.[3]

In the meantime, food shortage in India had reached a critical state, to alleviate which Nehru reached out to several countries. He requested the acting secretary of state of the US to arrange urgent dispatch of the wheat allotted to India which had got delayed due to shipping strike in the US.[4] Nehru also wrote to the Pethick-Lawrence to facilitate the transport of 7,00,000 tonnes of rice from Indonesia which its prime minister Sutan Sjahrir had offered in exchange for consumer goods, primarily textile, but was held up due to objections by the Allied military forces.[5]

Not receiving an encouraging response from the trade agent of the Soviet Union in India to a request for supply of wheat, Nehru wrote directly to Vyacheslav Molotov, the Soviet foreign minister, on 21 and 23 September 1946. Nor did the Russian delegation to the first session of the UN General Assembly, held in January in London, respond to a direct appeal by Ramaswami Mudaliar to send food to India.[6] Nehru faced a dilemma. 'Is it desirable to approach Russia directly on a high level and ask the Soviet Government to send us foodgrain?' he wondered. There was the possibility of receiving a delayed or even no response, which would not be in keeping with India's dignity. 'I do not see why another party's lack of courtesy should prevent us from taking a step which might yield possible results,' he finally decided. He felt India should make a friendly approach to the Soviet Union politically too. Keeping it confined to the food-grain issue would not commit India to other political issues, but at the same time it would show the Soviet government that India was ready to interact with it in a friendly manner.[7] Nehru took the opportunity to propose a proper diplomatic relation between the two countries: 'It is our earnest desire to develop friendly relations with the USSR and to exchange diplomatic and other representatives with your country.'[8]

Nehru asked V.K. Krishna Menon, who was then in Paris as his personal emissary, to meet Molotov. Menon met Molotov on 28 September, whose initial response was not quite promising. However, in a meeting that lasted nearly a couple of hours, they discussed the development of social, cultural and diplomatic ties and India's views on international affairs. Menon suggested getting Soviet military experts to India for the military training schools. Nehru appreciated that Krishna Menon had 'laid a good foundation for our future relations with the Soviet'.[910]

Molotov sent a personal message to Nehru about a week later, explaining that he was unable to send food grains due to drought in a number of agricultural districts, but that the Soviet Union was ready to develop friendly relations with India and exchange diplomatic representatives.[11] Nehru was keen that Krishna Menon accept Molotov's invitation to visit Moscow for further talks.[12]

Nehru also wanted Krishna Menon to establish contact with other European countries but had to drop the idea as Wavell opposed the personal approach, sidestepping the official route.[13] To work around Wavell's objection, the interim government formally appointed Krishna Menon as its special representative in November 1946 to hold exploratory talks with governments of certain European countries for establishment of diplomatic relations.[14] Accordingly, Nehru wrote to the foreign ministers of France, Belgium, the Netherlands, Switzerland, Czechoslovakia, Denmark, Norway and Sweden, requesting them to receive Krishna Menon.[15] Krishna Menon submitted his report to Nehru on his visits in April 1947. Pointing out to the desire of these countries to establish diplomatic and cultural relations with India, the report recommended that in view of shortage in qualified diplomatic staff to head missions in these countries, certain number of missions should be grouped under an ambassador in London. After discussing the report with the cabinet, Nehru asked Girija S. Bajpai, the officer on special duty, and H. Weightman, the foreign secretary, to study the report and make their recommendations.[16] He also sent Krishna Menon to meet the British foreign secretary Ernest Bevin in London and discuss the report with him.[17]

Matters were progressing faster with the countries with which India already had some kind of formal diplomatic relations. After announcing on 21 October that the diplomatic missions between India and China would be raised to the status of embassies,[18] the Indian government announced on 30 November the appointment of K.P.S. Menon as agent-general and ambassador-designate for India in China. Menon was also appointed as a special representative who would visit Moscow to make preliminary arrangements for exchange of diplomatic representatives.[19] The appointment of Asaf Ali, the railway minister in the interim government, as India's ambassador to the US was announced on 6 December.[20] 'I hope you do not think that this is in anyway a slight on you,' Nehru wrote to Girija S. Bajpai, who, as the mouthpiece of British policy in India, was stationed in Washington from 1941. Although Nehru was keen that 'every effort will have to be made to get rid of this ICS outlook in India', he wanted Bajpai, who he believed was 'quite capable of adapting yourself to the new India that is taking shape' to continue as Asaf Ali's second-in-command. Bajpai was later called back to be appointed first as officer on special duty and in June 1947 as the secretary general in the external affairs department.[21]

In laying down the general guideline on Indo–US relations to Asaf Ali, Nehru wrote:

> The United States are a great Power and we want to be friendly with them for many reasons. Nevertheless, I should like it to be made clear that we do not propose to be subservient to anybody and we do not welcome any kind of patronage. Our approach, while being exceedingly friendly, may become tough if necessity arises, both in regard to political and economic matters. We hold plenty of good cards in our hands and there is no need whatever for us to appear as suppliants before any country.[22]

Aung San, the deputy chairman of the Burma Executive Council, was received by Nehru at the airport when he arrived in India on 2 January 1947, on his way to London for talks on Burma's independence. 'There is no question of Dominion Status for Burma. We want complete independence,' Aung San declared, also calling for a united front against imperialism in Asia.

The Indian government had appointed Dr Abdul Rauf as India's representative in Burma in October 1946. Nehru commended Rauf highly to Y.D. Gundevia, who was then serving as the secretary to the Indian representative in Burma, for his 'deep knowledge of Burma and the present Burmese leaders', and his friendship with Aung San was an additional advantage. This was an important factor as Nehru was particularly keen on developing closer ties with Aung San, who was friendly towards India and had an outlook that was 'definitely advanced, politically and economically'.[23]

As Aung San left on 7 January after meeting a number of leaders and broadcasting a speech on All India Radio, Nehru issued a statement wishing him success. There was 'a great deal in common in our respective viewpoints and we look forward to close cooperation in many fields for the mutual advantage of Burma and India and the development of Inter-Asian relations', he said.[24]

In the same statement, Nehru expressed his views on the intensifying war in Vietnam. India had always had a high regard for France and hoped to draw closer to the country in 'political and cultural domains', but France's 'attempt to crush the spirit of freedom in Indo–China' had put the goodwill for France under 'severe strain'. 'I earnestly trust,' Nehru said, 'that the French Republic will revert to peaceful methods in Indo–China and show by its own example that it stands for freedom everywhere.'[25] When the French government proposed to extend by ten years the existing agreement with India permitting military air ferries across India, Nehru agreed to a six-month extension, after which the agreement would be reviewed. The arrangement was to be restricted to the transport of official passengers only and passage across India of military aircraft which might be used for war purposes would not be allowed. 'In no event must we appear to be aiding the French in their hostilities against the Indo–China,' he wrote in a note to the external affairs department.[26] However, Nehru highlighted that India should not forget the support India received from France at the UN General Assembly on the South African issue. Towards the end of January 1947, India accepted the French proposal for exchanging embassies.[27]

India had signed a bilateral air transport agreement with the US in November 1946, fixing the routes and rates for civil aviation.[28] In January 1947, the Dutch government also approached the interim government to revive the agreement, which had lapsed during the war years, on Dutch airlines flying over India to Indonesia. Observing that since for some time to come Indonesia would not be in a position to start its own air service and therefore the agreement would facilitate intercourse between India and Indonesia, Nehru wrote to Sjahrir asking for his government's views.[29] India entered into the agreement with the Government of the Netherlands as Sjahrir informed Nehru that Indonesia had no objection as long as certain conditions were met.

The showpiece in Nehru's efforts to hoist India into prominence in global geopolitics was the ten-day Asian Relations Conference that began on 23 March 1947 at the Red Fort in Delhi. By one estimate, the opening session of the conference was attended by more than 200 delegates from thirty-three countries and a crowd of 8000.[30] 'Whatever it may achieve the mere fact of its taking place is of historic significance,' Nehru declared while opening the conference. 'Asia, after a long period of quiescence, has suddenly become important again in world affairs.' The 'dynamic Asia from which great streams of culture flowed in all directions' had gradually stagnated, but a 'change is coming over the scene now and Asia is again finding herself'. The isolation of the Asian countries from one another, which had resulted from Western imperialism, was coming to an end with the fading away of colonialism. It was significant that India, the 'natural centre and the focal point of the many forces at work in Asia', was playing her part in this resurgence.[31]

The hype generated by the conference notwithstanding, several incidents underscored the divisions that characterized the real situation. Delhi was rocked by communal riots as the conference began, with curfew being declared in parts of the old city. The Chinese delegation demanded that the issue of Tibet's political status should not be discussed and protested against the independent representation of the Tibetan delegation. An altercation erupted between the Jewish and the Palestinian delegates.[32][33]

At the end of the conference on 2 April, an Asian Relations Organization was set up 'to promote the study and understanding of the Asian problems and relations' as well as to 'foster friendly relations and cooperation among the peoples of Asia'. Nehru was elected the president of the thirty-member Provisional General Council tasked with setting up the organization.[34] The next conference was planned to be held after two years, in China.

India was represented at the Special Committee of the UN on Palestine in New York, which began its deliberations on 26 May 1947, by Abdur Rahman. In providing an overall guidance to Rahman, Nehru wrote that India's sympathies were naturally with the Arabs, as Palestine was essentially an Arab country and to 'try to change it forcibly into something else is not only wrong, but not possible'. At the same time, India's sympathies were also with the Jews, who had 'done very fine work in Palestine and have reclaimed land from the desert'. Factories and orchards existed at places which were desert some time ago, and 'the standards of the people have risen higher than anywhere in the Middle East'. The question for India was how to reconcile the attitudes towards the Arabs and the Jews with regard to the Palestinian problem. Nehru claimed that he had no definitive solution to the problem except to suggest 'an autonomous Jewish area within an independent Palestine'. He instructed Rahman that the 'general attitude of India must necessarily be friendly to both parties but clearly indicating that an agreement must have Arab approval'.[35]

When the majority report of the Special Committee, which recommended that Palestine be divided into two independent states—Arab and Jewish, with a separate City of Jerusalem district under a governor appointed by the UN—came up for vote at the General Assembly on 29 November 1947, India voted against the proposal.[36] The Indian government finally decided to recognize the state of Israel at its cabinet meeting of 5 August 1950 after Nehru observed that only a few countries of the 'Arab group', Afghanistan and India had not recognized Israel till then.[37]

The External Affairs and Commonwealth Relations Department issued a press communiqué on 25 June 1947 that 'His Majesty the King' had approved the appointment of Vijayalakshmi Pandit as 'His Majesty's Ambassador for India' in the Soviet Union. After his meeting with Molotov in September, Krishna Menon approached the Russian ambassador in Washington during the UN General Assembly session to discuss the possible visit by Nehru and K.P.S. Menon to Moscow, but the response was not favourable. Nehru was not happy. 'I wish you had not pressed the matter of an invitation being sent to me from the Soviet Union,' Nehru wrote to Krishna Menon in January 1947. 'We cannot make ourselves too cheap or too eager,' Nehru told him.[38] Extending a friendly gesture on his part, Molotov hosted a luncheon in early December for the Indian delegation to the UN session in New York, which gave Pandit an opportunity to discuss the matter of diplomatic exchange with him.[39] She informed the foreign office in Delhi that according to Molotov they could directly proceed to setting up embassies, and hence there was no need to send Krishna Menon for any preliminary talk.[40] The Indian government had already decided and informed K.P.S. Menon in November 1946 that he was being sent to Moscow to continue the talks regarding exchange of diplomatic representation. Instead of accompanying him, Krishna Menon would then continue his informal talks in other European countries. H. Weightman, the foreign secretary, suggested on 11 December that in view of Molotov's discussion with Pandit there was also no need to send an official representative to hold talks in Moscow. Thus, the plan to send K.P.S. Menon to Moscow for preliminary talks was dropped. Instead, Menon, upon joining as India's ambassador to China, was asked to take up the matter with his Soviet counterpart in Nanking, which Menon did on 2 April 1947 and received a written confirmation from the Soviet government five days later. Pointing to the fact that while India took five months after the Krishna Menon–Molotov talks to formally approach the Soviet government, the latter responded favourably in just five days, K.P.S. Menon urged the Indian government to expedite the process. Supporting Menon, Girija Shankar Bajpai wrote on 11 April:

> In the present state of strained relations between the USA and the USSR, and Russia's extreme sensitiveness, indefinite delay in making a start with our representation in Moscow while we maintain a full-fledged Embassy in Washington is likely to be misunderstood by the Soviet Government.[41]

The decision to exchange diplomatic missions was announced jointly by the Indian and the Soviet governments on 13 April 1947. Nehru's decision to appoint Pandit as India's ambassador to Russia was communicated to the secretary of state and thereafter to the king in mid-May.[42] The advance team from India, which arrived in Moscow on 21 July to make arrangements for setting up the Indian embassy, included T.N. Kaul (appointed as private secretary to the ambassador), A.V. Pai (counsellor-minister), Prem Kishen (first secretary) and H. Ghoshal (cultural officer and chief interpreter).[43] Pandit, accompanied by her daughter Chandralekha, arrived in Moscow on 6 August.[44]

The Indian embassy in Moscow intimated Delhi on 30 September that Kiril Vasilevitch Novikov had been appointed as the Soviet ambassador in India. The appointment was approved by the king on 16 October.[45]

As Partition became a reality, Nehru had to clarify to India's representatives abroad the position of India in its international relations as there was much confusing talk going on about the status of India and Pakistan. On 18 June 1947, he wrote to Asaf Ali:

> The first thing to bear in mind is that the proposed so-called division of India is in fact a secession of some parts of India. That is to say, India and the Government of India continue as international persons and all our treaties and engagements with other countries also continue. Our membership of the U.N.O. continues. In fact there is no change in our external relations whatever because we are a continuing entity. On the other hand the seceding provinces form a new State which has to begin from scratch.[46]

South-East Asia continued to be in a turmoil. On 19 July, Aung San, the vice president of the transitional government of Burma, was gunned down along with six other ministers while a meeting of the executive council was under way in Rangoon.[47] As hundreds were arrested, including Burma's former premier U. Saw and other political leaders, and curfew was imposed in Rangoon,[48] Nehru allowed the Indian troops still in Burma to be used by the Burmese government, if required, to maintain law and order, a decision that drew criticism, particularly from Congress president J.B. Kripalani.[49][50] Burma became an independent republic on 4 January 1948 with Thakin Nu as its first prime minister.

When armed conflict flared up again in Indonesia between the Dutch and Indonesian troops in July 1947, Nehru pushed for a peaceful settlement through arbitration. Even before the hostilities escalated, he cautioned the secretary of state for India on the basis of information received from an Indonesian food delegation visiting India that 'the Dutch now having collected a large army in Java will try to overwhelm the Indonesians by military force'. He kept writing regularly not only to the secretary of state but also to Krishna Menon in London to convince the British government to intervene.[51] When the Dutch forces mounted an attack on the Indonesian troops, Nehru issued a public statement warning that the 'sudden attack by the Dutch in Indonesia is an astounding thing which the new spirit of Asia will not tolerate', assuring the people of Indonesia that 'so far as India is concerned, we will give every possible help'.[52]

India and Australia referred the Indonesian crisis to the UN Security Council on 30 July. The British government offered to mediate in the crisis apart from suspending all military supplies and facilities to the Dutch authorities in the Far East.[53] The Security Council passed a resolution on 1 August calling on the Netherlands and Indonesia to stop the fighting immediately and settle the dispute by arbitration or other peaceful means.[54] It was in October that Nehru sent N. Raghavan, formerly a lawyer in Malaya and a minister in Subhas Chandra Bose's Provisional Government of Free India as India's consul general to Indonesia.[55]

On 20 November 1947, the General Assembly of the UN voted in favour of the resolution moved by India calling for a roundtable conference between India and South Africa on the basis of the resolution passed on 8 December 1946. With the relation between the two countries having deteriorated, India had recalled its high commissioner R.M. Deshmukh and terminated its trade agreement in protest against South Africa passing the discriminatory Asiatic Land Tenure and Indian Representation Act 1946. While Field Marshal J.C. Smuts, the prime minister of the Union of South Africa, insisted that negotiations could not be held until India reversed these decisions, India refused to enter the negotiations until the resolution of December 1946 was complied with. India therefore took the matter back to the UN. Among the countries which supported India's resolution were China, Egypt, France, Iran and the Soviet Union. However, having failed to obtain a two-thirds majority, the resolution was not binding. Thus, although Nehru claimed a moral victory, Smuts held that this failure had nullified the previous resolution, but agreed to hold friendly negotiations.[56]

By mid-July 1947, it had been decided and communicated to the British prime minister by both Nehru and Mountbatten that Krishna Menon was going to take over as the next Indian high commissioner in London. 'I am glad to think that I shall have a personal friend as the first High Commissioner in London,' Mountbatten congratulated him and wrote to Attlee that Krishna Menon 'would be able to provide a good idea of what is in the minds of the present Congress leaders'. Nehru informed Attlee:

> In view of the impending changes the post of the High Commissioner for India in London has an added significance. We attach considerable importance to it as we do to the future relations of India with the UK. We have therefore given a great deal of thought to the choice of a suitable person for this post. In consultation with the Viceroy and my colleagues we have decided to appoint Krishna Menon to this post.[57]

Journalist Durga Das has claimed that Patel confided in him that Attlee preferred John Matthai or Sarvepalli Radhakrishnan as independent India's first high commissioner to UK. He did so, Patel told Das, 'with the aim of hinting broadly to Nehru that Krishna Menon would not fit the bill'. But Krishna Menon 'had already succeeded in working Nehru round to getting Mountbatten to propose him for the post'.[58] Historian Stanley Wolpert too has claimed that 'Krishna Menon was eager to become free India's first high commissioner to London' and that Nehru promised him the job. According to Wolpert, the claim is supported by Krishna Menon's letter of 4 June 1947 to Mountbatten,[59] in which he hinted, 'Jawaharlal also had talks with me about the "hereafter" and wants me to talk them over with you. They involve detail and important issues of principle which are vital to the furtherance of the success you have achieved.'[60]

The secretary of state for India William Francis Hare, the 5th Earl of Listowel, too, was sceptical about Krishna Menon. He shared his opinion with Mountbatten on 18 July:

> It has to be admitted that in the past the impression he has created in home circles has been by no means favourable . . . I am arranging for him to meet some of the Opposition leaders to whom at the moment he is by no means *persona grata*. The great need at India House at the moment is, of course, for someone at the top with real organising and administrative capacity. I rather doubt whether Krishna Menon will supply this need . . .[61]

'I was aware that he is "persona non grata" in many circles at home, and I would not say that he was popular or entirely trusted here,' Mountbatten responded to the secretary of state and went on to explain Krishna Menon's usefulness:

> I have found him a valuable contact between Nehru (whose complete confidence he has) and myself, and through him I have been able to be particularly well informed about the trend of Congress thought and opinion. I need not stress how useful this has been to me since I came out. In fact with V.P. Menon and his close contact with Vallabhbhai Patel I have been able to know all that has been going on in both 'camps' in the Congress Party.[62]

After Krishna Menon's appointment the secretary of state for India informed Mountbatten that 'a certain amount of opposition to Menon's appointment is showing itself here, more particularly in Indian circles in London'.[63] Rather strangely, Nehru 'forgot' to write to M.K. Vellodi, an ICS officer who had been officiating as the high commissioner in London after the resignation of S.E. Runganadhan earlier in the year.[64] In fact, Nehru had informed Krishna Menon about Vellodi, who was then the deputy high commissioner, taking over charge from Runganadhan even before Vellodi himself was told about it.[65] An upset Vellodi's reactions obviously did not please Nehru. He wrote to Krishna Menon that 'the whole episode has left a rather bad taste' and that 'if he works in this office he will have to work under our directions'.[66] In October he wrote to K.P.S. Menon, 'I would rather not have him in the office here for the present.'[67]

Krishna Menon had been under surveillance of the British intelligence from the late 1930s for his communist links.[68] As early as 1 November 1946, the secretary of state Pethick-Lawrence wrote from London to Wavell that 'There seems to be an impression gaining ground here that Krishna Menon aims at succeeding [S.E.] Runganadhan as High Commissioner', a development that he cautioned 'would not be well received here'.[69] Nehru's decision to send Krishna Menon to the European countries, however, came as a relief to the British. The assignment 'disposes of any immediate fear that Krishna Menon might succeed Runganadhan as High Commissioner in London', J. Colville, governor of Bombay, wrote to Pethick-Lawrence on 2 December.[70] Menon's activities in all the countries that he visited were monitored and reported to the British government, the summary of which were passed on to the viceroy in India by the secretary of state. The British surveillance on Krishna Menon continued at least as long as he continued as India's high commissioner.

Mountbatten was an exception to the suspicious and sceptical outlook of the British administrators towards Krishna Menon, who in April 1947, according to Mountbatten, offered his services when they met in Delhi in April 1947:

> . . . [Krishna Menon] reminded me that he was staying out here specially in the hope of being of use to me personally as a friend (or acquaintance) of some four years standing, to help to give me the background of what was going on in Congress circles, and to help me put over any points that I found too delicate to handle directly myself. He offered to stay as long as he was of use, and I have asked him to stay at all events till next week.[71]

Krishna Menon became the principal intermediary between Mountbatten and Nehru in convincing the latter on opting for dominion status and remaining within the British Commonwealth.

Despite the number of statements and interventions in the international forums, India was yet to formally frame its foreign policy. In January 1947, Nehru observed, 'We have not developed such a policy yet and our views on foreign affairs lack precision and definiteness.' What went in the name of foreign policy, according to him, was partly 'a continuation of British foreign policy; to some extent a reaction against it'. At the same time, apart from the Soviet Union, he felt, 'all other countries are pursuing a confused and sometimes contradictory policy'.[72]

The two occasions when India's foreign policy was discussed fairly comprehensively by the legislative arm of the Constituent Assembly were during the presentation of the provisional budget in 1947 and the full budget in 1948. The debate took place when some members of the Assembly moved cut motions against the demand for grants by the Ministry of External Affairs and Commonwealth Relations on 4 December 1947 and 8 March 1948. In fact, an exposition on India's foreign policy during the Budget discussions in Parliament became a regular feature in the subsequent years.

While some members such as N.G. Ranga and Seth Govind Das paid glowing tributes to Nehru's foreign policy measures, there were severe criticism and alternative policy suggestions from members such as N.B. Khare, B. Shiva Rao, Hasrat Mohani, Brajeshwar Prasad, M.A. Muthiah Chettiyar, Hussain Imam, K. Santhanam, Naziruddin Ahmad and H.V. Kamath.

A wide range of issues was brought up by the speakers. Questions were raised regarding India's attitude towards British Commonwealth: whether India was going to continue within it or otherwise. The example of Burma, a country that chose complete independence over dominion status, inevitably came up as a counter-example. Dark clouds of conflict were gathering around the world: while the United States was apprehensive of a confrontation from Soviet Union, Europe was yet to come out of conflict, and movements for freedom of the suppressed nations were escalating in Asia. How was India preparing to face such contingency?

It was argued that if India was following a neutral policy, it should not take part in any power politics or disputes between rival countries. Some members also contended that it was worthwhile to consider whether it would not be beneficial for India to join one of the power blocs? The world has reached such a stage that it is impossible for any country to remain neutral, it was said. A few members suggested that India should be naturally more inclined towards the Russian bloc, which would help ending the occupation of Asian countries by the Anglo–American bloc. Such an alliance would also help guard against the danger of pan-Islamism since imperialist forces were using the bait of pan-Islamism in order to purchase friendship with Muslim states.

One member went to the extent of suggesting a plan of union between India and China on the basis of their shared heritage. The economic resources of such a union, he argued, would be greater than any other political combination of states and would quickly attract in its fold Malaya, Burma, Japan, Siam, Korea, Ceylon, Nepal, Bhutan and Sikkim. Alternatively, Russia, China and India should try to form one bloc.

The government was asked about its plan for developing diplomatic relation with Pakistan. One member suggested common citizenship with neighbouring countries like Burma and Ceylon; another recommended India to take the responsibility of foreign affairs and defence of its neighbours such as Nepal, Bhutan and Sikkim, where penetration of foreign influence would be a source of danger to India. An integrated defence system led by a joint defence council with neighbouring countries like Ceylon, Burma and Malaya was also suggested. There was a need for a Nehru doctrine, a member insisted. Referendum in Kashmir under the UN would mean foreign interference in India's internal affairs and hence should be opposed. Hope was expressed that India would be reunited in the fulness of time. French revolution, it was said, brought in liberty, Russian revolution brought equality and now India must preach the gospel of fraternity.

Responding to the members' speeches, Nehru admitted that the Ministry of External Affairs and Commonwealth Relations Department had not been able to achieve as much it should have, but at the same time, was scathing in the dismissal of all criticism:

> Listening to the debate, to the speeches made by Honourable Members, I find, as was perhaps natural, that there was no immediate issue, no particular question for discussion, but rather pious hopes, vague ideals and sometimes a measure of let us say, denunciation of things that had happened in the world. It has been a vague debate, with nothing pointed about it to which one could attach oneself.

Reducing a deliberation on foreign policy to a matter of joining one power bloc or another, Nehru said, was 'an utter simplification of issues'. Foreign policy, according to him was the outcome of economic policy and until India had properly evolved her economic policy, 'her foreign policy will be rather vague, rather inchoate, and will rather grope about'. 'The unfortunate events that have happened in India since the 15th August 1947,' Nehru explained, 'suddenly brought down our credit in the international domain tremendously.' The result of India trying to avoid joining one bloc or the other had been that they considered India undependable, 'because we cannot be made to vote this way or that way.' In the existing climate of fear and suspicion of each other between the rival groups 'anybody who is not with them is considered as against them'. Yet, 'they respected us much more, because they realised that we had some kind of an independent policy'. Therefore, Nehru claimed, in the course of two or three years 'India will not only be respected by the major protagonists in the struggle for power but a large number of the smaller nations which today are rather helpless'.

In the final analysis, a government functions for the good of the country, whether it is imperialistic or socialist or communist, and its foreign minister acts in the interests of that country. But some think only of the interests of their country regardless of other consequences, while in contrast, a policy with a longer-term view considers the interests of another country equally important, Nehru explained. The interest of peace is more important because in the long-term view 'self-interest may itself demand a policy of co-operation with other nations'. India's foreign policy, therefore, must be seen 'in the context of world co-operation and world peace, in so far as world peace can be preserved'. Nehru announced, 'We intend co-operating with the United States of America and we intend cooperating fully with the Soviet Union.' In the matter of taking economic or other help, 'it is not a wise policy to put all your eggs in one basket'.

Nehru claimed that he was under no illusion as to what the consequences would be in the event of facing one of the great military powers. That, however, need not frighten India because of her past experience in conducting a national movement against one of the greatest military powers 'in a particular way and in a large measure we succeeded in that way'. In the present context, 'if the worst comes to worst, and in a military sense we cannot meet these Great Powers, it is far better for us to fight in those ways than submit ourselves and lose all the ideals which we have'. In other words, fighting a great power through peaceful satyagraha movement was the preferred option in the event of a military defeat.

As far as international disputes were concerned, 'I have more and more come to the conclusion that the less we interfere in international conflicts, the better, unless our own interest is involved.' The premise of this policy was that it was not in consonance with India's dignity to interfere without producing any result. 'Either we should be strong enough to produce some effect or we should not interfere at all,' Nehru explained.[73] [74] At the same time, he held that 'India is a natural leader of South East Asia if not of some other parts of Asia also'.[75]

Nehru refuted the charge of 'immoral neutrality' hurled at India by John Foster Dulles. Non-alignment meant having the freedom to decide each issue on its merits, to weigh what was right or wrong and then take a stand in favour of what was right, he explained. Nehru declared:

> So far as all these evil forces of fascism, colonialism and racialism or the nuclear bomb and aggression and suppression are concerned, we stand most emphatically and unequivocally committed against them . . . We are unaligned only in relation to the cold war with its military pacts. We object to all this business of forcing the new nations of Asia and Africa into their cold war machine. Otherwise, we are free to condemn any development which we consider wrong or harmful to the world or ourselves and we use that freedom every time the occasion arises.

~

Although the Objectives Resolution in the Constituent Assembly had made it amply clear that being a Dominion was a temporary measure and India would become a republic with the inauguration of the Constitution, the question of whether India would continue to be within the British Commonwealth or not was left hanging.

The views of the Constitution-makers varied sharply on this point. While Alladi Krishnaswamy Ayyar held that 'There is nothing to prevent republican India from being a member of the British Commonwealth',[76] Sarvepalli Radhakrishnan argued in favour of going out of the Commonwealth.

> So far as India is concerned, it is not a mere Dominion like Australia, like New Zealand or Canada or South Africa. These latter are bound to Great Britain by ties of race, religion and culture. India has a vast population, immense natural resources, a great cultural heritage and has had an independent career for a very long time, and it is inconceivable that India can be a Dominion like the other Dominions.[77]

Dodging the debate on for versus against continuing within the Commonwealth during the discussion on the Objectives Resolution on 22 January 1947, Nehru stopped by remarking, 'We want to be friendly with the British people and the British Commonwealth of Nations.'[78] His private correspondence, however, clearly shows that he did not entertain the thought of being within the Commonwealth yet. On 8 April 1947, he wrote to defence minister Baldev Singh, an early convert to the idea of Indian remaining within the Commonwealth:

> . . . I am quite clear in my own mind. There can be no weakening of any kind on the subject of India's future connection with the United Kingdom. India must go out of the British Commonwealth. Apart from our own personal views in the matter, there is not the least shadow of a doubt that any other proposition would be rejected completely by the Indian people . . . We shall be in a far safer position as an independent country than as one tied up to Britain in any way.[79]

A week later, he wrote again to Singh, 'Any attempt to remain in the Commonwealth will sweep away those who propose it and might bring about major trouble in India.'[80]

Nehru moved away from his definitive view within the next one year, but he had not yet made the final decision. Responding to a question from Attlee regarding India's objections towards remaining within the Commonwealth, Nehru responded on 18 April 1948, 'It is not easy for me to answer adequately at this stage.' He delayed a firm decision because 'I am myself not clear in my own mind', waiting to see how events shape up before deciding on the question. He admitted that a year earlier the answer would have been a definitive 'no', and credited the Mountbatten couple for bringing in the change in his attitude:

> The mere fact that another opinion is held now by many persons indicates the change that has come over the situation. This change has undoubtedly been due to the change in British policy in regard to India and more particularly to the presence and activities of our present Governor-General. Indeed it is remarkable what Lord Mountbatten, and may I add Lady Mountbatten also, have done to remove many of the old causes of distrust and bitterness between India and England. I have often wondered what the history of India would have been if they had come

a year earlier. I imagine it would have been very different and that we might well have avoided many of the perils and disasters that we have had to face.[81]

The Mountbattens would continue to play a critical role in Nehru's decision-making on a wide range of issues. On his first visit to the UK as the prime minister, Nehru remarked, 'I think it would not be incorrect of me to say that there are few persons in India, Indian or other, who are so beloved as Lady Mountbatten,'[82]

The British high commission in India brought to the Indian government's notice 'a great deal of apprehension' among British commercial interests regarding their future in India. The high commission wanted to be provided with information on policies, which were likely to impact British interests, at the draft stage in order to be able to put forward their points of view. Nehru assured Terence Shone, the British high commissioner, of being consulted by the relevant ministry on policies or legislation that would concern British interests, but at the same time told him that the issue of how to deal with British interests vis-à-vis Indian and foreign interests was being examined by his government.[83]

The close working relation between the Intelligence Bureau (IB) and the MI5 continued on its own track. On some occasions, however, it resulted in unexpected reactions when the administrative arrangement crossed path with the political world. When Krishna Menon learned about a trip of IB director T.G. Sanjevi to the UK in December 1948, he wrote to Nehru apprehensive of whether a part of Sanjevi's brief was to report on him and his staff in the Indian high commission. Nehru informed Krishna Menon that there was already a plan to send Sanjevi to the UK to study the methods of intelligence gathering, when Sanjevi received a personal invitation from Percy Sillitoe, the director general of MI5. 'This was not to link up with British intelligence in any particular way, though some kind of a linking might be there,' he explained to Krishna Menon. Nehru wrote as if he was unaware of the agreement between the intelligence agencies of the two countries: 'I have told Sanjeevi [sic] that in regard to many matters there is no particular secret and he can give him [Sillitoe] such information. But he must not tie himself with him in any way.'[84]

Sanjevi, however, reported to Patel that in conversation with him, Krishna Menon went on a bitter rant criticizing the government of India's policy regarding the Communists in a very strong language, and accused

Sanjevi of opening and reading his letters. 'I gathered that the British Cabinet was fully aware of Mr Krishna Menon's Communist sympathies and that on occasions the communication of secret information to him caused considerable concern, as they were not sure that the secrecy would be maintained,' Sanjevi informed H.V.R. Iengar, the home secretary. On reading Sanjevi's note, Nehru wrote to Patel that he was 'greatly distressed' but 'I can only explain and excuse it to some extent by imagining that he was under some deep mental strain and consequently completely upset'. Krishna Menon claimed that Sanjevi's report was inaccurate and apologized to Patel. Nehru wrote to Krishna Menon that although he was 'shocked and distressed' to read Sanjevi's report, 'since you say you did not say anything of the kind referred to in his report, I must accept your statement'.[85]

Nehru himself arrived in London on 6 October 1948 to attend the conference of prime ministers of the dominion which was held from 11 to 22 October. The conference did not take up the relation between India and the Commonwealth, which was confined to private talks between Nehru and prime ministers of the Commonwealth countries. 'No commitments of any kind were made at the conference on behalf of India,' Nehru informed his cabinet colleagues upon his return.[86] The real position, however, was as Nehru described to Rob Lockhart, former commander-in-chief, Indian Army, upon his return: 'So far as we are concerned, we have expressed our willingness, but the lawyers and jurists at the other end cannot make up their minds.'[87] Nehru told the Constituent Assembly too on 4 March 1949 about not making any commitment, but did not mention that he had expressed willingness on behalf of India to remain within the Commonwealth.[88]

What Nehru referred to in his letter to Lockhart was a top-secret memorandum dated 28 October that he had shared with Attlee. The eleven-point memorandum proposed the basis of India's participation in the Commonwealth. The provisions in the memorandum which had Constitutional relevance included maintaining India's status as a republic, repeal of the Indian Independence Act of 1947, and incorporation of the relevant provisions of the British Nationality Act of 1948 which would make Indian nationals Commonwealth citizens in any Commonwealth country, and in the same way make nationals of any other Commonwealth country Commonwealth citizens when in India. The points that did not need any Constitutional change were accepting the king as the Commonwealth's 'fountain of honour' and not treating Commonwealth countries and their citizens as foreign states or foreign citizens, including in new commercial treaties for the purpose of 'most-favoured nation' clause. The memorandum also provided for the President of India to act on behalf of the king, at the request of the Crown, to fulfil the Crown's obligations towards Commonwealth citizens other than Indian nationals. Moreover, since the king had waived all the functions of sovereignty as far as India was concerned, including his rights of appointment, Indian people and their representatives would exercise all functions of sovereignty. [89]

The secretary of state for Commonwealth Relations, Noel Baker, communicated to Girija Shankar Bajpai in mid-November that although all the member countries of the Commonwealth were very keen about India remaining within the Commonwealth, 'it would be extremely difficult to get their Parliaments and peoples to eliminate King as link of such association'. Therefore, they requested India to consider the permanent delegation by the king to the President of India the authority to appoint heads of missions abroad. Nehru responded that in a scenario in which mentioning the king as the fountain of honour is not liked in India, he doubted whether the authority to appoint heads of mission to be derived from the King would be acceptable. The legal advisers to the British government also highlighted several problem areas in the memorandum regarding the role of the king and citizenship clauses. [90]

Attlee informed Nehru on 12 March 1949 that another conference of the Commonwealth prime ministers had been convened from 20 April. The specific objective of this conference was, Attlee wrote, to find out a way to India's continued membership in the Commonwealth. Nehru announced his participation in the conference in the Constituent Assembly on 29 March, but without giving away its real objective, even when specifically asked by H.V. Kamath.[91] He informed the Assembly that the conference was convened to discuss 'future constitutional arrangements' and 'certain constitutional questions relating to the commonwealth'.[92]

At the conference, while Britain and Canada were sympathetic to India's position, Australia and New Zealand insisted that India's status of being a republic must in no way weaken the issue of allegiance to the king for those member countries who wished to retain it. To get around the differences, it was initially agreed that India would issue a declaration separately from those countries which wanted to emphasize their allegiance to the king, an idea that was eventually dropped. Nehru kept Patel informed about each step.[93]

The conference reached its final agreement on 27 April:

> The Governments of the United Kingdom, Canada, Australia, New Zealand, South Africa, India, Pakistan and Ceylon, whose countries arc united as Members of the British Commonwealth of Nations and owe a common allegiance to the Crown, which is also the symbol of their free association, have considered the impending constitutional changes in India.
>
> The Government of India have informed the other Governments of the Commonwealth of the intention of the Indian people that under the new constitution which is about to be adopted India shall become a sovereign independent Republic. The Government of India have however declared and affirmed India's desire to continue her full membership of the Commonwealth of Nations and her acceptance of the King as the symbol of the free association of its independent member nations and as such as the Head of the Commonwealth.
>
> The Governments of other countries of the Commonwealth, the basis of whose membership of the Commonwealth is not hereby changed, accept and recognise India's continuing membership in accordance with the terms of this Declaration.
>
> Accordingly the United Kingdom, Canada, Australia, New Zealand, South Africa, India, Pakistan and Ceylon hereby declare that they remain united as free and equal members of the Commonwealth of Nations, freely co-operating in the pursuit of peace, liberty and progress.[94]

Since Nehru didn't like the phrase 'Head of Commonwealth', a separate minute was put on record to explain that the phrase did not imply that the king discharged any constitutional function by virtue of headship. Nehru also explained to Patel that the phrase 'British Commonwealth' was used only in the first paragraph of the declaration to denote the existing status of the Commonwealth, but thereafter the word 'British' was not used anywhere else.[95]

Vallabhbhai Patel announced and explained the implications of the agreement at a press conference in India on 28 April.[96]

Presenting the agreement in the Constituent Assembly for ratification on 16 May 1949, Nehru explained it was only 'an agreement by free will, to be terminated by free will', and that there was 'hardly any obligation in the nature of commitments'. Regarding the constitutional position of the King, he reiterated that the 'binding link' of allegiance to the king 'ends when we become a Republic'. Answering the question of how India could associate herself with the Commonwealth 'in which there is racial discrimination, in which there are other things to which we object', Nehru said:

> So far as we are concerned, we could not bring their domestic policies in dispute there; nor can we say in regard to any country that we are not going to associate ourselves with that country because we disapprove of certain policies of that country.
>
> I am afraid if we adopted that attitude, then, there would be hardly any association for us with any country, because we have disapproved of some thing or other that that country does.
>
> . . . take any great country or a small country; you do not agree with every thing that the Soviet Union does; therefore, why should we have representation there or why should we have a treaty of alliance in regard to commercial or trade matters with them? You may not agree with some policies of the United States of America; therefore, you cannot have a treaty with them. That is not the way nations carry on their foreign work or any work.[97]

Arguing that India could not remain isolated as a country, Nehru pointed out:

> If we are completely dissociated from the Commonwealth, for the moment we are completely isolated. We cannot remain completely isolated, and so inevitably by stress of circumstances, we have to incline in some direction or other.[98]

The Constituent Assembly ratified the agreement on 17 May 1949.

~

In the international arena, two major new developments that concerned India directly were the proclamation of the People's Republic of China (PRC) under the Communist Party of China on 1 October 1949, replacing the Republic of China (ROC) under Kuomintang, and the formal transfer of sovereignty from the Dutch colonial government to the Republic of Indonesia on 27 December 1949.

As the conflict in Indonesia continued, on 24 December 1948 India and Pakistan suspended the rights of the Dutch airlines KLM to operate in the two countries. Sri Lanka had already closed their ports and airfields to Dutch ships and flights, and the Australian dockers had boycotted the ships sailing to Indonesia.[99] On the same day, the UN Security Council also adopted a resolution asking both the Dutch and the Indonesians to cease hostilities. Asking the Dutch government to release all Indonesian leaders arrested on 18 December, the resolution instructed the UN Good Offices Committee to report on the compliance of the resolution.[100]

Nehru felt that the Dutch would continue to ignore the UN resolutions and therefore to build up greater international pressure, he convened a conference of Asian countries on Indonesia in Delhi from 20–23 January 1949. The conference, attended by delegates from fifteen countries, recommended an eight-point plan to the Security Council which included immediate release of the Indonesian leaders, restoration to the republican government of the areas held by them before 18 December 1948, setting up of an interim government with full powers by 15 March 1949, elections to a Constituent Assembly before 1 October, and complete transfer of power by 1 January 1950.[101]

Immediately after the conference, on 28 January the Security Council laid down a timetable for the Dutch authorities in Indonesia, which differed a little from the one agreed in the Delhi conference: interim government by 15 March, elections to the Constituent Assembly by 1 October and transfer of power over the whole of Indonesia as soon as practicable but not later than 15 July 1950. The Good Offices Committee was transformed into a Special Commission on Indonesia for supervising the implementation of the timetable.[102] The commission, however, informed the Security Council on 1 March that the Dutch authorities had not acted in accordance to the timetable adopted on 28 January.[103] The Netherlands, on 14 March, agreed to a Canadian proposal at the Security Council for a roundtable conference in The Hague. The roundtable conference that started 23 August reached an agreement on 2 November for a complete transfer of power to the Republic of Indonesia by 30 December.[104] Apart from the fact that an Indian delegate was present at the signing of the agreement, what stood out in the whole process leading to the transfer of sovereignty to the Indonesians was Nehru's untiring support, not only in terms of organizing global opinion, establishing formal diplomatic relations and India's interventions at the UN regularly, but his continuous moral support through his regular direct communications with the leaders of Indonesia.

In a guideline to India's diplomats for the upcoming sessions of the UN General Assembly, Nehru wrote in September 1948 that in view of the turbulent state of affairs in China due to its civil war, 'We should not attach ourselves too closely to any party in China so as to make the other party hostile to us'.[105] He had started detaching from the nationalist regime gradually. Towards the end of 1948, Nehru shared with K.P.S. Menon his prognosis about how things were going to shape up in China, with some guidance on how to prepare for it:

> It is clear that any kind of Government that may be established by the Communists in China will be outwardly a coalition government, though it will be dominated by the Communists . . . To begin with this coalition government will try not to follow what might be called a Communist policy. It will adopt moderate policies in order to win over the other elements in China. It will be anxious to develop relations with neighbour countries, notably India . . .
>
> . . . we have to be wide awake and not merely hang on to Chiang Kai-shek and his fading authority. Nor should we just follow what the U.K. or U.S.A. might do in China. All this means that our Embassy should be alive to these considerations, and secondly, if possible, we should develop some informal contacts with the Communist side.[106]

K.P.S. Menon had returned to India by then, being appointed as foreign secretary, as the new ambassador to China K.M. Panikkar took charge in April 1948.

When Madame Chiang Kai-Shek reached out to Nehru through Vijayalakshmi Pandit for help, Nehru told Pandit, 'I am quite convinced that if we stood up for the bankrupt Government in China now, we would be condemned in India and this would give a fillip to communism in India, strange as that sounds.'[107]

As the Chinese communists continued to gain ground, India's external affairs ministry started deliberating on the possible scenarios in Tibet. On 15 June, H.E. Richardson, the Indian trade agent at Gyantse and officer-in-charge of the Indian Mission in Lhasa alerted the ministry that the Tibetan officials would resist the Chinese communists and recommended to the Indian government to continue the Mission in Lhasa and provide arms and material help to Tibet. While K.P.S. Menon agreed with Richardson and emphasized India's support to Tibet in terms of arms and ammunitions as well as moral support, Bajpai cautioned that India's support should not be considered provocative by the Chinese communists. He stressed on social and economic reforms in Tibet as well as precautionary military measures to strengthen India's northern frontier.[108]

Nehru suggested the continuation of the Mission as well as the aid that was being already given to Tibet, with the warning that India 'should be very careful in taking any measures which might be considered a challenge to the Chinese Communist Government'. In this planning exercise for the possible future scenarios, Nehru believed, there was no need for defence preparedness:

> Whatever may be the ultimate fate of Tibet in relation to China, I think there is practically no chance of any military danger to India arising from any possible change in Tibet. Geographically, this is very difficult and practically it would be a foolish adventure. If India is to be influenced or an attempt made to bring pressure on her, Tibet is not the route for it.
>
> I do not think there is any necessity at present for our Defence Ministry, or any part of it, to consider possible military repercussions on the Indo–Tibetan frontier. The event is remote and may not arise at all. Any present thought being given to it will affect the balance we are trying to create in India. It may also not remain a secret and that would be unfortunate.[109]

Nehru wrote in the same tenor to Thakin Nu in January 1950. 'There is not much danger of Chinese aggression across the Indian border,' he wrote, while clarifying that in the event of such a possibility 'the slightest attempt at such aggression whether in India or Nepal would be stoutly resisted by us'. Nehru also turned down Nu's proposal for a defence pact between India, Burma, Sri Lanka and Pakistan as he thought such a step would make China think 'it is aimed against her and cold war will begin and there might be trouble at the frontiers'.[110]

Defence might not have been the priority in Nehru's understanding at the time, but the importance of infrastructure was not lost on him. In September 1949, he wrote to finance minister John Matthai that an attack on Tibet by the Chinese communists would bring the Chinese or the Tibetans to the Assam, Bhutan or Sikkim border, and therefore those areas would need a good road development programme to proceed slowly.[111] However, chairing a meeting of the Standing Committee of the Central Legislature on External Affairs in December, Nehru assured that there was no danger of invasion of Assam or Nepal.[112]

Nehru was keen on India's election to the Security Council as a non-permanent member in 1949. Having failed twice, in November 1946 and September 1947, to be elected to one of the three non-permanent seats, India was finally elected in 1949.[113]

Following the formation of the PRC on 1 October 1949 with General Chou En-lai as the prime minister as well as foreign minister of the Central People's Government, and Mao Tse-tung as chairman of the People's Revolutionary Military Council, the first recognition of the government came from Soviet Union on 2 October.[114] 'We are in no way opposed to such recognition,' Nehru wrote to the premiers of the provinces on 16 September, 'but we shall have to wait and watch developments before we take any such step.'[115] Panikkar was called back to Delhi to discuss the issue of recognition soon after the formation of the PRC. Nehru communicated to Chou En-lai India's recognition of the PRC on 30 December and the desire to establish diplomatic relations. On the same day the Government of India also withdrew recognition from the Chinese nationalist government. The nationalist government, in response, recalled its diplomatic mission in Delhi. The new government conveyed its formal agreement for the appointment of Panikkar as India's ambassador in March 1950.[116]

Ten days after the formation of the new Chinese government, on 11 October, Nehru arrived in Washington on his first ever visit to the US that lasted till 7 November (he also visited Canada in between). The US ambassador to India had approached him a number of times in 1948 and in early 1949 too. His sister Vijayalakshmi Pandit had been appointed India's ambassador to the US in March, succeeding B. Rama Rau, and assumed charge in May.[117]

Nehru wrote to the members of the economic committee of the cabinet:

America is the most powerful and the richest country in the world and can certainly help India a great deal. There is no reason why we should not get that help and remove causes of friction between us. But it is also true that America represents a reactionary policy in world affairs, and I think, a policy which will not succeed . . . The safest policy, therefore, appears to be is to be friendly to America, to give them fair terms, to invite their help on such terms, and at the same time not to tie ourselves up too much with their world or their economic policy. Keeping a free hand we will ultimately get more from them and at the same time get the friendship and cooperation of other countries also . . .[118]

An India which was isolated completely from the Commonwealth would inevitably have had to slope in some direction. Practically speaking, that is in terms of capital goods and money or credit required, that sloping could only have been in the direction of the U.S. America wants very much to tie ourselves with her foreign policy and in a sense relies a little more on us in regard to her Asian policy. All this suffers a slight setback because we are associated with the Commonwealth . . . It would have been dangerous for us to isolate ourselves and risky for us to slope too much towards the U.S. in the present context. That would have made it more difficult for us at any time to play the role of a friendly neutral to any of the parties concerned. It must be remembered also that with all the expressions of goodwill that are showered upon us from America, the State Department has been far from friendly . . . In regard to Kashmir, you will remember the kind of hint or threat that was held out by some official of the State Department, when B.R. Sen went to discuss the U.N. Commission s proposals. That is a sort of thing which does not make us teel very friendly towards the U.S.[119]

The *Los Angeles Times* reported:

Prime Minister Nehru of India, currently visiting the United States, calls his visit a good-will tour. But like that of other foreign visitors, the main object of his visit is wheat and dollars—wheat to prevent one of the recurrent Indian famines, dollars for the industrialization of his country.

Nehru has not said so publicly, but others have guessed that a million tons of wheat is approximately his goal. He wants to borrow it on long-term loan and perhaps pay for it if, as and when the British government settles its billion-pound debt. And he wants funds to build a huge hydroelectric development on the Damodar River.

One of Nehru's talking points is that the present Indian government is strongly opposed to Communism. But Nehru is a Marxian Socialist and the eventual intent of his government is nationalization of all important industry, a situation not very attractive to American capital. He is said to be willing to pledge there will be no nationalization for 10 years, if ever, but 10 years is a short period in the life of an investment. Nor could Nehru guarantee that his government will be in power that long.

While the people of the United States have nothing but good will for the people of India, it does not follow that we can or should solve all the Indian problems, particularly since some of them are so difficult as to seem unsolvable. A wheat loan, even though the security seems pretty sketchy, might be generally approved, since we have a big surplus and no one in Washington seems to have any intelligent ideas on how to dispose of it. But a dollar loan, of a size likely to do India much good, looks risky.[120]

According to a record of the talks between Dean Acheson, secretary of state, on 12 October 1949,[121] Acheson's impression of Nehru wasn't quite favourable. 'He talked to me,' Acheson recalled, 'as Queen Victoria said of Mr Gladstone, as though I were a public meeting.' Acheson hoped to develop a personal relationship with Nehru through a private meeting that lasted for two-and-a-half hours, but at the end of it he came to the conclusion that 'I was convinced that Nehru and I were not destined to have a pleasant personal relationship', and 'he was one of the most difficult men with whom I have ever had to deal'.[122]

In fact, Nehru's visit did not result in any immediate significant gain for India, and by the end of 1950, all that India received was only $4.5 million in economic aid, which compared unfavourably with $35.3 million granted to Formosa and $6.2 million sanctioned for Indochina.[123]

Patel wasn't too impressed either. He is reported to have said, 'We have to get on with the job here. Of what use is the fanfare of a trip through America with speeches and all?'[124]

In a letter to C. Rajagopalachari, Nehru wrote:

I must say that I am continually being surprised at the type of popular welcome I am getting here. I am not referring so much to the organizations that welcome me and fix up functions although even this is impressive enough. 1 am referring rather to the crowds gathering in the streets. It reminds me somewhat of India. In fact, an American friend who had been to India mentioned to me today, after seeing the crowds in Chicago streets, that he was surprised to find the darshan habit spreading to the United States.[125]

And in his letter to Vijayalakshmi Pandit, Nehru said:

> Recently we have seen that American help is often associated with political pressure, as in the case of Greece and Korea. Anything savouring of political conditions or pressure or the possibility of such pressure being exercised in the future would of course be totally unacceptable to us. We have therefore to be a little careful in considering proposals of financial help. Even in the case of the U.K. this political pressure, though not so obvious, becomes apparent occasionally. There is a tendency in the U.S. to treat the countries they help as some kind of clients to it, which are expected to toe their general policy. This is a warning to us and has to be borne in mind.[126]

The UN Security Council, in the meantime, had run into a deadlock over the question of which China should get representation in the UN. Early in January 1950, the PRC sent a telegram to the president of the General Assembly demanding the expulsion of the nationalist delegate from the Security Council.[127] The Soviet delegate Jacob Malik walked out of the Security Council after his resolution to expel the Chinese nationalist delegate was defeated. While India voted in favour of the Soviet motion, it was opposed by the US, with Britain abstaining. Malik announced that he would not attend the council until the Chinese nationalist delegate was expelled.[128] In his efforts to bring in the PRC into the Security Council, Nehru wrote to Ernest Bevin, seeking his support. Bevin agreed with Nehru, assuring him that he would issue relevant instructions to the British delegation at the UN. However, before any progress could be made in this direction, the UN was overtaken by the Korean crisis.[129]

As the stalemate in the Security Council continued, the US state department initiated a move to have India elected as a permanent member in the council in place of ROC. Vijayalakshmi Pandit wrote to Nehru on 24 August 1950 that John Foster Dulles, special adviser to US President Harry Truman and Philip Jessup, US ambassador-at-large, who had met with her, insisted on the plan. Marquis Childs, an influential columnist in Washington, told her that he had been asked by Dulles to build public opinion in favour of the idea. Pandit discouraged them on the grounds that it would not be received well in India. Nehru refused to even consider the plan as 'It would be a clear affront to China and it would mean some kind of a break between us and China'. He wanted to adhere to the position taken by India, which was to have the PRC replace ROC as a permanent member. He feared that Soviet Union might permanently quit the UN if the full delegation which the PRC was planning to send to the next session of the General Assembly failed to get it in, which 'would mean the end of the UN as we have known it'.[130]

A new crisis erupted when, on 25 June 1950, North Korea invaded South Korea, crossing the River Imjin with ninety tanks. The Security Council passed a resolution moved by the US on the same day describing the North Korean move as an act of aggression and asking the aggressors to withdraw behind the 38th parallel—the frontier between North Korea and South Korea. The resolution asked all members of the UN to refrain from giving any assistance to North Korea.[131] B.N. Rau, India's delegate who presided over the session, voted in favour of the resolution on his own initiative as there was no time to refer the issue to the government at home. Nehru supported Rau's action, as 'information we possess indicates clearly that North Korea has committed aggression and has done so after full preparation'. However, he instructed Rau not to commit India further without consulting the ministry of external affairs.[132]

Rau therefore abstained from voting in the next resolution that came up at the Security Council on 27 June, recommending to UN member countries to provide to South Korea the assistance necessary to repel the aggression and restore peace. The resolution, moved by the US and supported by Britain and France, was based upon information provided by the UN Commission for Korea that North Korea had neither ceased hostilities nor withdrawn its forces behind the 38th parallel, and in response to appeal from South Korea immediate help. Truman ordered US air and sea forces to provide cover and support to South Korean troops, also asking its Seventh Fleet to prevent any attack on Formosa, the headquarters of the Chinese nationalist government, in addition to strengthening US forces in the Philippines and French forces in Indochina. General Douglas MacArthur, supreme commander of the Allied forces based in Japan, was given the responsibility to lead the operation.[133] Attlee announced on 28 June Britain's decision to put British naval fleet in Japanese waters at the disposal of the American forces.[134]

When Loy Henderson, US ambassador in India, met Nehru on 28 June, the Indian prime minister expressed his displeasure about the US linking Formosa, Philippines and Indochina with the Korean issue. At a time when India was trying to develop friendly relations with the PRC, she couldn't appear to be supporting the US decision on Formosa. Moreover, there was little sympathy for the French in Indochina. Nehru and his colleagues were already being criticized within the country as tools of Anglo–American imperialists, he told Henderson.[135] The Indian cabinet issued a statement on 29 June, accepting the Security Council's second resolution too, pointing out that it did not involve any departure from its policy of staying aloof from rival and hostile group of nations.

India's decision to go with the US resolutions worried Radhakrishnan, who had succeeded Vijayalakshmi Pandit. He argued that had the Soviet Union been present in the Security Council, it would have vetoed the resolutions. The absence of the Russians practically converted the council into one bloc, and India's support to the resolutions strengthened that bloc, which was bound to impact India's relations with China.[136] Nehru's thoughts ran along the same course. 'We are not in as strong a position as we were to approach China and the USSR now,' he wrote to B.N. Rau, hoping, 'Still we have not quite lost our old position and there is some hope that we might be able to play a useful role in preventing the conflict from spreading or in bringing the warring factions nearer to one another.'[137] Nehru's cabinet had the opposite point of view too. K.M. Munshi, the agriculture minister, wrote, 'USSR never has been a friend and never will be. Why should we lose the goodwill of friends without whom we cannot face Russian expansion?'[138]

Nehru told a press conference that the admission of the People's Government of China to the Security Council and ensuring the return of Soviet Union, which had withdrawn from all UN bodies, were necessary conditions to enable the council to discharge its functions and end the Korean conflict.[139] He sent identical messages to both Stalin and Acheson on 12 July, explaining India's position and seeking their cooperation:

India's purpose is to localize the conflict and to facilitate early peaceful settlement by breaking the present deadlock in the Security Council, so that representatives of the People's Government of China can take seat in the Council, the U.S.S.R. can return to it, and whether within or through informal contacts outside the Council, the U.S.S.R., the U.S.A. and China, with the help and cooperation of other peace-loving nations, can find a basis for terminating the conflict and for a permanent solution of the Korean problem.[140]

In response, while Stalin agreed with Nehru's approach, Acheson held that the Korean issue should not be linked with the PRC's admission to the Security Council. Nehru wrote again a few days later to Attlee and Acheson on the need to bring back the Soviet Union and admit the PRC into the Security Council. On 18 July, he wrote to Vijayalakshmi Pandit, 'Our efforts to do something to tone down the war fever, resulting from the Korean affair, appear to be doomed to failure.'[141]

The Soviet Union returned to the Security Council on 1 August after staying away for nearly seven months, with a dramatic plan. According to the rule of rotating presidency at the Security Council between its eleven members, it was Jacob Malik's turn to preside over its meetings in August. Based on the two-point agenda—that of Chinese representation and peaceful settlement of the Korean conflict—circulated by Malik a day before the session, B.N. Rau alerted Nehru about the possibility of a ruling by Malik disqualifying the nationalist Chinese delegate and the ruling being challenged by other members. Nehru asked Rau to vote in favour of Malik's resolution. By his estimate, the UK and Norway would also do the same since they had already accorded recognition to the PRC; not doing so would be illogical and would negatively impact the chances of their diplomatic relation with the communist regime in China, apart from pointing out complete subordination to the US.[142]

On 1 August Malik ruled that the representative of the Kuomintang group was not the true representative of the Chinese people. Contrary to Nehru's expectation, the British delegate challenged Malik's ruling along with the US delegates. Drawing support only from India and Yugoslavia, Malik's motion lost by eight to three votes.[143]

On the motion on Korea, reading the full text of Stalin's reply to Nehru's appeal, Malik said that while the Russian premier had promptly welcomed Nehru's 'noble initiative', the US had rejected it outright. 'The reply of Premier Stalin and the appeal of Pandit Nehru,' Malik asserted, 'are like litmus paper—they show up those who stand for peace and those who stand for the continuance of aggression.' He argued that Truman's action amounted to an act of armed intervention in the domestic affairs of the Korean people.[144]

'It seems to me that the greatest danger that we have to face today is probably the hysterical state of mind of the Americans,' Nehru told B.N.

Rau. Criticizing the widespread bombing of North Korea, he wondered that even if the US won the war, 'how can they deal with any part of Asia afterwards?'[145] The military situation being entirely in favour of the North Koreans, Nehru did not see any chance for progress towards cease fire, without which a new constitution was not possible, for at least the next eight months. The North Koreans were fighting, he observed, not only 'with ability and courage, but also with a faith in their cause, which gives them tremendous driving power'. The South Koreans, in contrast, 'have shown an equally amazing capacity for not fighting and for running away'.[146]

While Nehru kept pressing the US and the UK for a declaration to the effect that they had no intention to attack Chinese mainland, he also believed that the UN should make a categorical statement reiterating previous declarations—the Cairo declaration reaffirmed at Potsdam towards the close of the Second World War that all Chinese territories captured by Japan should be reverted to China—that Formosa should be returned to China.[147]

On 11 September, India voted in favour of a Soviet resolution in the Security Council inviting a Chinese communist representative to attend the council's debate on the PRC's complaint that American planes had bombed Manchuria. Although the resolution received six votes, with the UK and France voting in favour and the US opposing it, it could not be adopted as it fell short of the mandatory seven votes.[148] India's motion to replace the Chinese nationalist member with a delegate from the PRC, introduced by B.N. Rau on the opening day of the General Assembly on 19 September was also defeated by sixteen to thirty-three votes, with ten abstaining.[149] Despite the defeat, Nehru was glad that India took the lead in proposing China's admission to the UN.[150]

On 20 September 1950, Dean Acheson presented before the General Assembly a plan for prevention of war. It provided for (1) an emergency session of the Assembly on twenty-four hours' notice if the Security Council should be prevented from acting; (2) the setting up of a Peace Observation Commission for immediate and independent observation in any area where international tension might exist threatening peace and security; (3) designation by each member of units of its armed forces for U.N. service; and (4) the establishment of a special committee to develop further means of collective action.[151] The resolution was adopted by the General Assembly on 3 November and came to be known as the 'Uniting for Peace' resolution.[152]

On 17 September, the US embassy in India requested the Indian government to convey a warning to the Chinese that they should not intervene in the Korean conflict. India's Ministry of External Affairs told the US embassy that it cannot convey a warning, but would instruct its ambassador in China to request the Chinese to be patient. However, apprehensive that such a request might be misunderstood by the Chinese, it was dropped.[153] Nehru anyway pleaded with Chou En-lai to continue to exercise patience and restraint, as 'By waiting a little longer China will, I feel sure, achieve all that she desires, peacefully and thus earn the gratitude of mankind'.[154] Panikkar shared his assessment with Nehru that there was very little chance of China getting involved in the Korean war, unless a large-scale war started because of the UN forces crossing the 38th parallel and a consequent intervention by the Soviet Union.

On 27 September, Nehru received a draft resolution from Bevin, proposing a Commission for the Unification and Rehabilitation of Korea (UNCURK) to be set up by the General Assembly. The resolution recommended necessary steps to ensure peace throughout Korea, elections under the auspices of the UN and establishment of a unified, free and democratic government of Korea.[155] The resolution was eventually adopted by the General Assembly on 7 October, India having abstained.[156] Although Rau informed that the British and other delegations believed that India could influence the working of the UNCURK from within by joining it, India decided against joining as Nehru argued that she was more likely to helpful by staying out of the Commission.[157]

The UN forces crossed the 38th parallel on 8 October, making rapid progress initially but soon faced strong resistance about fifty miles south of the Manchurian border. On 5 November, General MacArthur issued a statement alleging that Chinese communist military units had been moved from Manchuria into North Korea.[158]

Nehru argued that even if condemnation of the PRC by the UN was legally justifiable, the only chance of bringing in peace was by a meeting of the US, the UK, the USSR and the PRC.[159] Panikkar informed Nehru that China could not be expected to join discussions if termed an aggressor and the only possibility now was direct negotiations between the big powers on an equal basis in which China's right to participate in all matters concerning the Pacific was unequivocally recognized.[160]

Panikkar met the senior vice foreign minister Chang Han-fu on 7 December and told him that India had been assured that the question of

Formosa would also be settled at the conference on the basis of the Cairo and Potsdam Declarations and China's membership of the UN would follow.[161] Chou En-lai, however, refused to commit to India's proposals unless the US accepted them. Nehru forwarded the information to Attlee requesting him to persuade the US to soften its position regarding Formosa. Otherwise, it would not be possible to obtain a ceasefire or hold broader negotiations.[162]

On 14 December, the General Assembly constituted a Ceasefire Group comprising Nasrollah Entezam, president of the Assembly, B.N. Rau and Lester Pearson, foreign minister of Canada. The group's offer to discuss ceasefire was, however, rejected by the Chinese authorities who claimed that the 'ceasefire first' proposal a trap designed to tie the hands of the Chinese and the North Koreans to enable the US to occupy Formosa.[163] The Chinese agreed to advise its volunteer forces to withdraw from Korea only if the UN forces were withdrawn, the American occupation of Formosa was terminated and the PRC was admitted into the UN.[164]

The Commonwealth Prime Ministers' Conference, held in London in January 1951, decided upon a new resolution for the General Assembly proposing a conference of the US, the UK, the USSR with the Chinese Government on all outstanding questions relating to East Asia in conformity with existing international obligations and the provisions of the United Nations Charter.[165] Nehru had intervened to modify the original resolution proposed by Bevin so that it remained restricted to holding the conference. He explained to B.N. Rau that the resolution was drafted in a manner to meet the Chinese demand for including the issue of Formosa in the discussions on the basis of the Cairo and Potsdam Declarations.[166]

On 13 January, the First Committee at the UN adopted the Ceasefire Group's revised proposals calling for an immediate ceasefire in Korea, followed by a conference of representatives including those of the UK, the USA, the USSR and China to arrive at a settlement in conformity with existing obligations and provisions of the UN Charter, including those of Formosa and of the Chinese representation in the UN. The proposals were forwarded to the Chinese government to ascertain their acceptability as a basis for consultations. When the US privately stated that their acceptance of the group's proposals was contingent upon India's acceptance, Rau confirmed it explaining that the phrase 'existing international obligations' meant for India the Cairo and Potsdam Declarations, stipulating that the resolution should provide for the conference simultaneously with a ceasefire as without a ceasefire implementation of proposals was not possible.[167]

China refused to accept a ceasefire before the negotiations as that would give the US troops an opportunity to strengthen themselves and pointed out that the phrase 'existing international obligations' did not clearly specify the Cairo and Potsdam Declarations. It proposed a seven-power conference to be held in China on the basis of agreement on withdrawal of foreign troops from Korea and self-determination by the Koreans of their internal affairs. China also demanded the inclusion of the withdrawal of US forces from Formosa and the legitimate status of China in the UN for discussion in the conference. While Acheson considered China's reply as a total rejection, Nehru held that it was 'partly accepted, partly request for elucidation, partly counter proposal, and leaves room for further negotiation'. He requested Attlee 'to urge Washington not to precipitate matters'.[168]

Despite Nehru's incessant efforts to keep the possibility of a negotiated peace alive, the negotiations broke down as the Political Committee of the UN adopted a US resolution, supported by the UK, declaring China an aggressor in January 1951.[169] After a prolonged stalemate and intense negotiations, the Korean Armistice Agreement was signed on 27 July 1953. India played an important role in return of prisoners of war at the end of hostilities, whereby Major General K.S. Thimayya headed the Neutral Nations Repatriation Committee.

~

Independent India's relations with the Soviet Union, even after their embassies were established and ambassadors exchanged, were strained. According to T.N. Kaul, who went to Moscow before Vijayalakshmi Pandit to set up the embassy, although Pandit went there with high expectations to make an impression, she was soon disappointed. In fact, during her entire tenure in Moscow neither did she receive any invitation, nor did she show any keenness to meet Stalin. What shocked the embassy officials most was that there was no condolence message from the Russian government after Gandhi's assassination. Governed by an atmosphere of fear and suspicion, movements of foreign diplomats were restricted to a radius of twenty-five kilometres around Moscow, with very few exceptions. Kaul explained in his memoirs that India's relation with the Soviet Union was at a low not because of lack of effort on India's part, but because of the 'failure of the Soviet leaders to understand the new India', and their preoccupation with Europe and America. Moreover, India was considered a British satellite, not fully independent.[170] Expectations has declined so much that Nehru was pleasantly surprised to receive a message of congratulation from Stalin on the occasion of India's Independence Day in 1948,[171] although Stalin wished him on his birthday too.

There has been a progressive deterioration in Indo–Soviet relations, an unhappy Nehru wrote to Krishna Menon on 26 June 1948. 'The Russian attitude towards India has become progressively one of condemning and running down the Government of India and all its works,' he complained. Moreover, in Russian periodicals, 'we are continually being referred to as some kind of a stooge of the Anglo-American bloc'.[172] 'We are very anxious to have friendly relations with the USSR. But . . . we have had very little encouragement from them.'[173]

Nehru, along with Vijayalakshmi Pandit, met the Russian ambassador in India over dinner to set things right, when it turned out that the ambassador had almost as much complaint regarding India as the Indian embassy in Moscow had about Soviet Union.[174] He thought that although most of India's contacts were with the UK and the USA, India should make an effort to develop such contacts with the Soviet Union too, for which a good starting point was through trade and small cultural missions, particularly films and art.[175]

Efforts to explain India's standpoint on international affairs appear to have gathered pace after Radhakrishnan was appointed at India's ambassador in Soviet Union in May 1949. He met high officials such as K.A. Mikhailov, head of the South-East Asia Division of the Soviet Union's Ministry of Foreign Affairs, to explain how India followed an independent foreign policy and did not belong to any power bloc. This approach irritated Nehru to some extent. 'From your report it almost appears that we were somewhat apologetic about what we had done or that it required some explanation,' he wrote to Radhakrishnan. 'If any explanation is needed, it is by us from the Soviet Government for the continued and deliberate falsehoods propagated in the press there,' an annoyed Nehru observed. Yet, his foreign-policy approach meant 'we shall try to continue functioning according to our own lines and to the best of our ability, and not be diverted by these outbursts in the Soviet press'.[176]

Nehru's persistence on admitting the PRC into the Security Council and her support to Jacob Malik's ruling seemed to him to be turning things around. On 6 August 1950, he wrote to Radhakrishnan, 'For the present, we are in the good books of the Russians, because of the attitude we have taken up in the Security Council.' The relations with the PRC were also good at that moment.[177]

The apparent improvements in the relations notwithstanding, they were not as good as India expected. Nehru complained in a letter at the end of 1951 that there was still no trade treaty with Soviet Union, and the individual deals such as that of procuring wheat in exchange for materials like jute, rubber and shellac were largely unfavourable to India. Yet, India had to accept the unfavourable terms because of her need for foodgrains.[178]

The Indo–Soviet relations of this period has been aptly summarized by K.P.S. Menon, who after serving as foreign secretary was sent to Moscow in September 1952 as India's ambassador:

> For the first six or seven years, the Soviet Government regarded India as a State which was nominally independent but really subservient to the West, especially in the economic sphere. They received the appointment of Mrs Pandit as Ambassador in Moscow with great satisfaction . . . yet she made no headway in the Soviet Union. Her successor, Dr Radhakrishnan, was better liked and had the rare distinction of being received by Stalin. Nevertheless, India and the Soviet Union behaved towards each other like two embarrassed acquaintances who had to be polite and could not be friendly. There were hardly any cultural exchanges, nor was there any trade except an occasional barter deal.[179]

Menon described in his memoirs how his efforts to remove the disparaging comments on Gandhi in the Great Soviet Encyclopaedia remained unsuccessful, although the head of the department dealing with India in the Soviet foreign office was the former Soviet ambassador to India, Novikov. 'I had hoped that Novikov, having been in India for five years, would show some appreciation of the sentiments of our people, but I found him cold and unsympathetic,' Menon remembered.[180] Stalin's death on 5 March 1953, however, according to Menon, brought in significant changes. Noticeably, in his lengthy obituaries to Stalin in the Lok Sabha and Rajya Sabha, Nehru did not have more than a few vague sentences to connect Stalin with India.

Within a couple of days after India officially recognized the PRC, the Chinese government declared its intention of liberating Tibet. The Tibetan government sent out delegations to India, Nepal, the UK and the US seeking support. China declared these delegations illegal. The delegation to India met Nehru on 8 September 1950, and sought India's help to proceed to Hong Kong for holding the negotiations, since they had been directed not to go to Peking. Nehru advised them not refuse an invitation to Peking when they met the Chinese ambassador in India but should ask for some preliminary talks to be held in Delhi. Accordingly, while they waited for the British to issue visas, the members of the delegation started preliminary negotiations with the Chinese ambassador in Delhi. At the same time, the Indian government advised the Chinese not to take any step which could prejudice her case at the UN.[181]

'What happens in the future I do not know, but we do wish Tibetan autonomy to continue under some kind of Chinese suzerainty,' Nehru wrote to Krishna Menon on 18 August 1950.[182] The Peking Radio announced on 25 October 1950 that the process of liberating Tibet had begun as the People's Liberation Army (PLA) crossed the Sino–Tibetan border and progressed towards Lhasa. It worried Nehru that the military action 'will put an end to our efforts to bring her [China] into the United Nations'. India registered her protest with China the next day, reminding it of its assurance to Panikkar to solve the issue peacefully. In response, China sent a stern message emphasizing that it would not tolerate any outside interference on the matter of Tibet, which was its domestic issue. China accused that India's views had been affected by foreign influence hostile to China.[183]

Asserting that India had no territorial ambition on Tibet, India communicated to China that her only interest was in a peaceful solution and hoped that China would accommodate the legitimate Tibetan claim of autonomy within the framework of Chinese suzerainty.[184]

When the Tibetan government approached India to sponsor a resolution on Tibet's case at the UN, Nehru refused, advising the Tibetan government to put up the resolution directly in the UN, and informing B.N. Rau at the same time, that if such a resolution came up, India might decide to support it 'generally'. The Political Committee of the UN took up a resolution sponsored by El Salvador asking for the establishment of a committee to study the appropriate measures that the UNGA could take against the unprovoked aggression by China. Consideration of the issue, however, was postponed at the intervention of the UK, with strong support from India. 'Draft resolution of El Salvador completely ignores realities of situation and overlooks fact that only result of passing such a resolution will be to precipitate conquest of Tibet,' Nehru wrote to Rau.[185]

On 23 May 1951, the Chinese announced that it had arrived at an agreement with Tibet by which China would take control of Tibet's external affairs but would not interfere with Tibet's autonomy on its internal matters.[186]

The decision to accept the Chinese accession of Tibet, however, was not unanimous in Nehru's cabinet. N.V. Gadgil, a cabinet member, later recounted how the process developed:

> The question of Tibet came up in 1950. Rajaji [Rajagopalachari] was then in the Cabinet and he opposed Nehru's Tibet policy. I said that the Chinese would not be satisfied with the occupation of Tibet. Our Ambassador in China at the time, Dr Pannikar [*sic*], analysed the situation as inevitable, just and proper. Our military officers were opposed to the developments m Tibet. Nehru asked Pannikar to persuade them. The Army officers asked him only one question, 'What purpose has China in coming over to the Himalayas in spite of so many difficulties?' Instead of giving a straight answer, this learned doctor accused them of thinking like British military officers. What could they do in the face of such logic, except to keep silent?[187]

Apart from some of his cabinet colleagues, President Rajendra Prasad too was unhappy with Nehru's China and Tibet policy, which he felt was 'riddled with weaknesses and a proneness to wishful thinking'. According to journalist Durga Das, Prasad was very upset at India's impassivity when the PLA occupied Tibet and believed Nehru had been misled by Panikkar. Prasad told Das, 'I hope I am not seeing ghosts and phantoms, but I see the murder of Tibet recoiling on India.'[188]

India's continued support for China's admission to the UN helped her tide over the disagreements over Tibet. At a reception given by Panikkar on the Indian Republic Day in 1951, Mao Tse-tung himself raised a toast for India, hoping to see Nehru soon in China. Early in 1951, China also offered a million tonne of foodgrains to India to tide over her food shortage in exchange for other commodities. Nehru announced in parliament on 7 April that China had accepted India's request for immediate supply of

50,000 tonnes of foodgrains. On 4 June, India announced an import of 80,000 tonne of rice and 1,50,000 tonnes of wheat from China.[189]

The question of India's interests in Tibet was informally taken up by Panikkar with Chou En-lai in September 1951 and then again in February 1952 with the Chinese vice foreign minister. In September 1952, India renamed the Indian Political Agency in Lhasa as Consulate General, thereby emphasizing that India had no political ambition in Tibet.[190] With an overall favourable environment, the Indian foreign office started considering whether the areas of disagreement regarding the Indo-Tibetan frontier should be raised at this time. Nehru decided against raising the issue in negotiations with China: 'About Tibet, our position is first of all that our frontiers with Tibet, that is, the McMahon Line, must stand as they are. There is no room for controversy over that issue.'[191]

Disagreeing with a note prepared by S. Sinha, officer on special duty in the Ministry of External Affairs, which described the 'Chinese Designs on the North East Frontier of India', Panikkar opined that the problem was not Chinese military adventures against Indian borders but one of strengthening administration within India's border. Agreeing with Panikkar's assessment, Nehru noted on 25 October 1953 that Sinha did not take an objective view of the situation 'but has started with certain presumptions'.[192]

N. Raghavan, who had been posted as India's ambassador in Czechoslovakia, had succeeded Panikkar when the negotiations with Tibet commenced in December 1953 in Peking, in the presence of Chou En-lai. Signing the agreement between the two countries in Peking on 29 April 1954, Chou En-lai said the questions that between the two countries regarding the Tibetan region 'which were ripe for settlement' had been settled. The agreement allowed India to retain her trade agencies at Gyantse, Yatun and Gartok, while allowing China to establish trade agencies New Delhi, Calcutta and Kalimpong. The agreement also specified six mountain passes which could be used by traders and pilgrims across both countries. India agreed to withdraw the small military contingent at Gyantse which had been posted there since 1904 for protection of the trade routes and to hand over to the Chinese government her posts and telegraphs installations.[193]

The agreement was based on five principles of (1) mutual respect for each other's territorial integrity and sovereignty; (2) mutual non-aggression; (3) mutual non-interference in each other's internal affairs; (4) equality and mutual benefit; and (5) peaceful coexistence. While India wanted the duration of the agreement to be twenty-five years, China negotiated for five years and ultimately both sides settled for eight years. According to T.N. Kaul, this raised his suspicion: 'I reported to Nehru that the Chinese would consolidate their hold over Tibet in 5 to 8 years and recommended strengthening our border before that.' By Kaul's account, Nehru issued the orders, but those were not followed by the defence or the home ministry.[194] At that time, Kaul was joint secretary in the ministry of external affairs and a member of the delegation that negotiated the agreement.

The five principles, named 'Panch Shila' by Nehru, also featured in the joint statement issued in Delhi on 28 June 1954 at the conclusion of Chou En-lai's three-day India trip. The prime ministers claimed in the joint statement that Indo–China friendship would help the cause of world peace and these principles should be applied in their relation with other countries in Asia as well as in other parts of the world.[195]

On invitation from the Chinese premier, Nehru visited China from 18–30 October 1954. Just over a month before Nehru's trip to China, eight countries, including Pakistan, came together at Manila, Philippines, to sign the US-sponsored 'South-East Asia Collective Defence Treaty', also known as the Manila Pact. The other countries that signed the collective security treaty directed against 'communist aggression and subversion' in the region were the UK, France, Australia, New Zealand, the Philippines and Thailand. These countries formed the 'South-East Asia Treaty Organization' or SEATO in 1955.[196] In May 1954, Pakistan had signed a bilateral defence agreement with the US and in 1955 it joined another collective security and defence organization of the western bloc—the Middle East Treaty Organization, also known as the Baghdad Pact. The day Nehru reached Peking, Mohammad Ali, the Pakistani prime minister was in New York, where he strongly criticized the principle of neutrality in foreign policy and championed Pakistan's alliance with the US.

A couple of days before his trip, a journalist in Calcutta asked Nehru if his China visit was in any way connected with the developments around the Manila Pact. Nehru was downright derisive:

Numerous conferences like the SEATO are being held here, there and everywhere. But these two great nations—India and China have lived for 10,000 years and want to do it another 10,000 years or more. The meeting, therefore, between the Prime Ministers of India and China is a very big thing itself and a world event.[197]

Mao and Chou had their first meeting with Nehru and Raghavan on 19 October. Nehru also met the Dalai Lama and the Panchen Lama. Mao told him that India was 'industrially somewhat more advanced' than China and given peace, China would need about twenty years to become 'an industrial country with foundations laid for a socialist economy'.[198] On his way back from China, Nehru visited Rangoon, Vientiane, Hanoi, Saigon and Phnom Penh. To the leaders of the countries he visited, he impressed that China had no aggressive intentions against them and was interested in peaceful co-existence.[199] On his return, Nehru shared his happy experience at a number of public meetings and press conferences, and also wrote in detail to Edwina Mountbatten. The death of Rafi Ahmed Kidwai, while he was away in China, deeply affected him.

Towards the end of the year, Nehru occupied himself in planning for an Afro–Asian conference that had been proposed by the Indonesian prime minister Ali Sastroamidjojo at the sixth Colombo Conference of the prime ministers of India, Burma, Indonesia, Pakistan and Ceylon in April 1954. The five prime ministers met in Bogor on 28 December 1954 to have a preliminary discussion on the agenda and composition of the conference. While China's participation was insisted upon by U Nu, the Burmese premier, and supported by Nehru, Pakistan and Ceylon opposed the proposal. China's participation was finally agreed upon on condition that participation of any country in the conference would not imply its recognition.[200]

The Conference held from 18–24 April 1955 in Bandung was attended by twenty-nine Asian and African countries and was presided over by Sastromidjojo. Nehru dominated the proceedings throughout. Amid Nehru and Chou En-lai's bonhomie, the conference was marked by undercurrents of tension between the participants. While Chou used the opportunity to assure the South-East Asian countries of China's policy of non-interference in their domestic issues, and declared that China did not want a war with the US and was willing to negotiate on Formosa, Ceylon and Pakistan, on the other hand, were suspicious of the closeness between Nehru and Chou, and felt that the conference was taking an anti-West attitude. Durga Das, who attended the conference, observed the beginning of some developments that would shape the relations in Asia over the coming years. From being the high point of India's relation with Indonesia, the Bandung conference tilted Indonesia's balance towards China, Jakarta's relation with Delhi deteriorating subsequently. Das also noted that 'the seeds of Chinas subsequent friendship with Pakistan were also sown at Bandung'.[201]

The Indo–China relations continued to strengthen with the second visit by Chou in November 1956 and then again towards the end of December and again in January 1957. The issue of Indo–China border came up between the two prime ministers during these visits. Chou told Nehru that he had examined the McMahon Line in connection with border disputes with Burma and although devised by the British, it should be given recognition since it was an accomplished fact and China was keen to have peaceful relations with both India and Burma. The recognition, however, would be given after consulting the Tibetans.[202] In 1957, the Indo–China friendship had reached its peak.

~

After Stalin's death in 1953, K.P.S. Menon, India's ambassador in Moscow, noted:

> . . . there was an almost magical change in the atmosphere of the Soviet Union . . . In Stalin's time, India was regarded as a State which was ostensibly independent but was bound hand and foot to the chariot of predatory Western imperialism . . . Now the newspapers began to describe the progress which India had been making after she attained independence . . . In Stalin's time, Jawaharlal Nehru's name hardly ever appeared in the newspapers . . . Now his name became almost a household word in the Soviet Union . . . Soviet policy towards the neutral and non-aligned States and especially India, entered a new phase.[203]

The Soviet Union signed an agreement with India in February 1955 for setting up a modern iron and steel plant at Bhilai, the first major project of economic assistance by the Soviet Union to a non-socialist country. It was in this atmosphere that Nehru visited Moscow, accepting a Soviet invitation, in June 1955 amid tumultuous welcome from the Soviet leaders and the people. During the two weeks that Nehru spent in Russia, he had a series of meetings with Premier Nikolai Bulganin, first secretary of the Communist Party of Soviet Union (CPSU), Nikita Khruschev, foreign minister V.M. Molotov and other leaders. He was shown their secret atomic power station, and Bulganin offered Nehru Soviet Union's support for India's inclusion in the UN Security Council as the sixth permanent member. Nehru, however, replied, 'I feel that we should first concentrate on getting China admitted [to the UN].'[204] Bulganin and Khrushchev returned their visit to India in November 1955.

The epoch-making twentieth Congress of the Communist Party of the Soviet Union was held in February 1956, a few weeks after the return of Khrushchev and Bulganin from India, which became famous for Khrushchev's condemnation of Stalin and his policies.[205]

~

Towards the end of 1956, Nehru went on his second trip to the US. He returned from his visit to the US and Canada on 28 December 1956. Nehru was well acquainted with President Dwight Eisenhower, Vice President Nixon and the secretary of state John Foster Dulles. Both Nixon and Dulles had visited India more than once but by the time of Nehru's visit, the relations between India and the US were on the decline. The primary reason was the sceptical, if not negative, attitude of both Nixon and Dulles. While Dulles had strongly criticized India's non-alignment policy as evil and considered Indian stand on China, the negotiations on Korean war and the Japanese peace treaty as anti-American and pro-communist, Nixon, who had visited India in late 1952, had complained that his meetings with Nehru were a long lecture on world affairs, as if he was an ignorant novice.[206]

Moreover, Nehru's refusal to associate himself with the United States' efforts to raise the issue of the Soviet Union's suppression of the revolt in Hungary had created more distance between the two countries. In fact, Nehru did not have a high opinion of Dulles either. During his meeting with Mao in Peking, Nehru told him:

A man like Dulles is a great menace. He is a Methodist or a Baptist preacher who religiously goes to Church and he is narrow-minded and bigoted. He thinks everyone must agree with him and a man like him might take any move.[207]

Apart from discussing economic and trade issues of interest to India, Nehru tried to soften the adversarial attitude of the US leaders towards the Communist Bloc, but noted that Eisenhower 'did not appear to disagree with much that I said, although . . . he laboured continuously under the fear of the Soviet Government extending its field of activities and more especially, getting a grip of the Middle East'.[208]

As the first decade came to an end, India appeared as a peacemaker with formidable clout. The network of friends and foes would, however, change drastically over the next decades.

8

Seeds of Disruption

After the announcement of the 3 June plan, Mountbatten went up to Kashmir on 18 June and spent the next four days holding preliminary talks with the ruler of Jammu and Kashmir, Lt Gen. Maharaja Hari Singh and his prime minister, Ramchandra Kak, to urge him to make up his mind on joining one of the two dominions.[1] According to V.P. Menon, Mountbatten cited Vallabhbhai Patel's assurance to Singh that India wouldn't mind even if he decided to join Pakistan.[2] Patel, however, wrote to Kak on 3 July that 'I realise the peculiar difficulties of Kashmir, but looking to its history and its traditions, it has, in my opinion, no other choice' than to join India.[3] Patel also wrote to assuage Hari Singh's apprehensions about Congress and Sheikh Abdullah:

> I am sorry to find that there is considerable misapprehension in your mind about the Congress. Allow me to assure Your Highness that the Congress is not only not your enemy, as you happen to believe, but there are in the Congress many strong supporters of your State. As an organisation, the Congress is not opposed to any Prince in India. It has no quarrel with the States. It is true that recent events resulting in the arrest of Pandit Jawaharlal Nehru and the continued detention of Sheikh Abdullah have created a feeling of great dissatisfaction amongst many Congressmen who wish well of your State. Pandit Jawaharlal Nehru belongs to Kashmir. He is proud of it, and rest assured he can never be your enemy.
>
> . . . I fully appreciate the difficult and delicate situation in which your State has been placed, but as a sincere friend and well-wisher of the State, I wish to assure you that the interest of Kashmir lies in joining the Indian Union and its Constituent Assembly without any delay. Its past history

and traditions demand it, and all India looks up to you and expects you to take that decision.[4]

Having failed to get a commitment, Mountbatten sent Hastings Ismay, his chief of staff, to Kashmir immediately after the transfer of power, but Ismay too returned without a decision from Singh. Unable to make up his mind, Singh tried to sign the Standstill Agreement with both India and Pakistan, but India decided to wait while Singh signed the agreement with Pakistan, but not the Instrument of Accession.

Towards the end of September, Nehru alerted Patel about the developing situation in Kashmir. On 27 September, he wrote:

> It is obvious to me from the many reports I have received that the situation there is a dangerous and deteriorating one. The Muslim League in the Punjab and the N.W.F.P. are making preparations to enter Kashmir in considerable numbers. The approach of winter is going to cut off Kashmir from the rest of India. The only normal route then is via the Jhelum valley. The Jammu route can hardly be used during winter and air traffic is also suspended . . .
>
> I understand that the Pakistan strategy is to infiltrate into Kashmir now and to take some big action as soon as Kashmir is more or less isolated because of the coming winter.
>
> . . . I rather doubt if the Maharaja and his State forces can meet the situation by themselves and without some popular help. They will be isolated from the rest of India and if their own people go against them, it will be very difficult to meet the situation. Obviously the only major group that can side with them is the National Conference under Sheikh Abdullah's leadership . . .
>
> It becomes important, therefore, that the Maharaja should make friends with the National Conference so that there might be this popular support against Pakistan. Indeed, it seems to me that there is no other course open to the Maharaja but this . . .
>
> . . . It seems to me urgently necessary, therefore, that the accession to the Indian Union should take place early.[5]

Sheikh Abdullah, whose National Conference was staunchly against the Muslim League and in favour of joining the Indian Union and who was sentenced to three years in prison for launching the Quit Kashmir movement in May 1946 against Hari Singh, was released on 29 September 1947, following the pressure being put by Patel and Nehru. Soon after his release, Abdullah declared, 'I never believed in the Pakistan slogan. It has been my firm conviction that this slogan will bring misery for all. I did not believe in the two-nation theory but in spite of it Pakistan is a reality . . . Pandit Jawaharlal Nehru is my best friend and I hold Gandhiji in real reverence . . . Our choice for joining India or Pakistan would be based on the welfare of the forty lakhs of people living in Jammu and Kashmir State.'[6]

In mid-October, Meherchand Mahajan, the new prime minister of Jammu and Kashmir who had taken charge in early October, complained to British prime minister Clement Attlee that Pakistan had broken the Standstill Agreement by cutting of essential supplies to the state and by stopping the railway service from Sialkot to Jammu. Mahajan also expressed apprehension that the entire Western border of the state from Gurdaspur to Gilgit was under threat of invasion from Pakistan, as raids had already begun in Poonch.[7] Receiving similar complaint, Jinnah expressed his displeasure over the tone and the language of Mahajan's letter, and explained that the delay in supplies and the disruption in railways was due to widespread disturbances in East Punjab and shortage of coal.[8]

For Nehru, on the other hand, the Kashmir issue was, in his own words, 'both a personal and public matter'. He wrote again to Mahajan on 21 October, 'Pakistan are terribly anxious to get Kashmir', but 'It would be a tragedy, so far as I am concerned, if Kashmir went to Pakistan'.[9]

On 22 October 1947, around 200–300 lorries containing about 5000 frontier tribesmen and Pakistani soldiers, led by some army officers who were well acquainted with Kashmir, advanced along the Jhelum valley road and captured Garhi and Domel, reaching Muzaffarabad. All the Muslim soldiers and officers of the state battalion joined the invaders, acting as advance guard, and shot the commanding officer Lt Col Narain Singh dead. As the invaders progressed towards Uri, Brigadier Rajinder Singh, the chief of staff of the state forces confronted them with about 150 men, succeeding in destroying the Uri bridge. All of them, however, lost their lives, being hacked to pieces. The invaders captured the Mathura Power House on 24 October, leading to a total blackout of Srinagar, the city which the invaders had planned to take over by 26 October for celebrating Eid.[10]

Singh sent out a desperate plea for help to the Indian government on the evening of 24 October. On 25 October, Mahajan wrote to Patel:

> . . . We are practically working on a war basis and every minute of our time is taken up with the border situation which is worsening every day. Practically the whole of our Muslim military and police has either deserted or has not behaved in the proper manner. The help that you kindly promised has not arrived and we are surrounded on all sides. You will agree with me that it is hardly the time to think of any constitutional issues.[11]

Nehru's initial reaction was an urge to send help to Kashmir. He wrote to Attlee on 25 October:

> We have received urgent appeal for assistance from the Kashmir Government. We would be disposed to give favourable consideration to such request from any friendly State . . . Security of Kashmir, which must depend upon its internal tranquillity and existence of stable government, is vital to security of India, especially since part of southern boundary of Kashmir and that of India are common. Helping Kashmir, therefore, is an obligation of national interest to India. We are giving urgent consideration to the question as to what assistance we can give to the State to defend itself.
>
> I should like to make it clear that question of aiding Kashmir in this emergency is not designed in any way to influence the State to accede to India. Our view which we have repeatedly made public is that the question of accession in any disputed territory of State must be decided in accordance with wishes of the people and we adhere to this view. It is quite clear, however, that no free expression of the will of the people of Kashmir is possible if external aggression succeeds in imperilling the integrity of its territory.[12]

Meeting on the same day, the Defence Committee of the cabinet, presided over by Mountbatten, decided to fly Menon immediately to Srinagar to assess the situation on ground and report back. When Menon reported back to the Defence Committee on the morning of 26 October about the dire situation in Srinagar, Mountbatten opined that India could intervene only if Kashmir, which was now an independent country, became a part of India. He also stipulated that since the state was a Muslim-majority one with a Hindu ruler, its accession to India will be provisional, subject to the will of the people being ascertained after restoration of law and order, through a plebiscite. Menon, along with Mahajan, again flew to Jammu, where Singh had transferred himself from Srinagar and got his signature on the Instrument of Accession. Singh also agreed to set up an interim government and put Sheikh Abdullah, the leader of the National Conference, in charge of administration of the state.[13]

The government of India accepted the Instrument of Accession on the condition that a plebiscite would be held in the state only when law-and-order conditions permitted. Early from 27 October morning and over the subsequent days troops were airlifted to Srinagar by over a hundred civilian Royal Indian Air Force (RIAF) planes. Nehru wrote to Liaquat Ali Khan on 28 October seeking the Pakistan government's cooperation 'in stopping these raiders entering Kashmir territory from Pakistan'.[14]

Nehru later informed Mahajan that

. . . a whole brigade of Pakistan Army was kept on the Jammu border and another brigade was kept at Kohala. They were expected to march into State territory as soon as Srinagar fell. This manoeuvre was foiled by Kashmir's accession to the Indian Union and our sending troops by air. As a matter of fact it was touch-and-go on the 27th morning as to whether Pakistan brigades should march into Kashmir territory or not. Final orders stopping them were passed on the 27th morning.[15]

In view of the invasion, Abdullah announced that his first priority was setting up of a responsible government and then decide on the question of accession. Now, after invasion, question of accession had become secondary, and the first duty of every Kashmiri was to defend the motherland.[16]

Hearing about the accession of Kashmir to India and the presence of the Indian troops in Srinagar, Jinnah issued order to General Gracey, the acting commander-in-chief of the Pakistan Army, to proceed to Kashmir. Gracey told Jinnah that he couldn't move troops without approval from Field Marshal Claude Auchinleck, the supreme commander. Auchinleck flew to Lahore on 28 October and explained to Jinnah that if the Pakistan Army invaded Kashmir, which was now part of India, every British soldier would be automatically withdrawn. Compelled to cancel his order to the army, Jinnah then invited Mountbatten and Nehru to Lahore, to discuss the Kashmir situation.[17]

While both Mountbatten and Nehru were keen to go to Lahore, Patel raised strong objections on the grounds that Pakistan was the aggressor and appeasing Jinnah would be inappropriate. Due to the differences of opinion, the matter was referred to Gandhi. Since Nehru was unwell, it was decided that Mountbatten would go to Lahore alone. However, before he could leave, Pakistan issued a statement on 30 October rejecting the accession of Kashmir as it was 'based on fraud and violence and as such cannot be recognized'. The statement alleged that the state troops had attacked the Muslims in the state first and its attack on the Muslim villages in Pakistan had triggered the raid by the tribesmen. By this time Sheikh Abdullah had formed the interim government in Kashmir, and three more battalions and a brigade headquarters had reached Srinagar.[18]

Nehru sought Patel's advice on what he perceived to be a developing communal situation. He informed Patel on 30 October:

Information has reached me that RSS [Rashtriya Swayamsevak Sangh] volunteers have been organised in East Punjab to be sent to Jammu for a campaign against the Muslims. It is stated that 500 were sent via Pathankot some days ago in special trucks. Further that a Special Recruiting Officer has been appointed by the Kashmir Government to go to Gurdaspur District and Kangra to recruit Sikhs, Dogras, etc. This officer is especially in touch with the RSS.

I do not know what we can do about all this, but we should at least try to stop in so far as we can the activities of the R.S.S. and the Hindu and Sikh refugees in this direction. Probably the Akali Dal is also functioning in the same way. The whole Kashmir position will crack up if in Jammu Province an anti-Muslim drive takes place now.

... You may have seen in the paper today a resolution of the Hindu Mahasabha disapproving of our action in appointing Sheikh Abdullah as head of the administration as well as in laying down that there should be a plebiscite after the troubles are over. A resolution does not much matter, but if the RSS carry on agitation on these lines and are supported by other elements, this would seriously hamper our work and would give a handle to the Pakistanis.[19]

On 31 October, Abdullah sworn in as prime minister of Jammu and Kashmir. A few days later, hosting some reporters for a dinner, he said, 'There may not be a referendum at all after the disaster at Baramulla,

Uri, Pattan and Muzaffarabad and other places. After what has happened in these places, the people of Kashmir may not bother about a referendum.'[20]

Accompanied by Ismay, Mountbatten reached Lahore on 1 November. Absolutely unwilling to discuss the withdrawal of the raiders, Jinnah rejected the offer of plebiscite, which he argued would be a futile exercise with Indian soldiers being stationed in Srinagar and an interim government having been established under Sheikh Abdullah. He also shot down Mountbatten's proposal to conduct the plebiscite under the supervision of the United Nations, asking instead a plebiscite under the joint control of the governors-general of India and Pakistan, that is, Jinnah himself and Mountbatten. This plan was not acceptable to Mountbatten. The talks remained inconclusive.

After a visit by Patel and Baldev Singh to Srinagar on 2 November where they consulted Brigadier L.P. Sen, the commander of the Indian troops, it was decided to establish a new divisional headquarters in Kashmir. Maj. Gen. Kalwant Singh was selected to take charge of the new Jammu and Kashmir Division. The Indian troops under Maj. Gen. Singh captured Baramulla on 8 November. As the Indian forces entered Baramulla, it found the town devastated, with no women or wealth left. Only a thousand out of the 14,000 population had managed to survive.[21]

On 9 November, Mountbatten travelled to the UK to attend the wedding of Princess Elizabeth and would return on 14 November. In his absence, Maj. Gen. Singh, who had prepared a plan to clear out the invaders along the Pakistan border (a plan that was opposed by Mountbatten for being too risky), retook the towns of Koti, Jhangar and Naoshera from the invaders and reinforced the troops in Poonch.[22] By 11 November, the Indian forces had taken Uri, forcing the invading tribesmen to give up Tangmang and Gulmarg without any resistance. The Jammu and Kashmir force was subsequently divided into a Srinagar Division which had General K.S. Thimayya as its general officer commanding (GOC) and the Jammu Division, whose GOC was Maj. Gen. Atma Singh.[23]

Nehru kept urging the Maharaja of Kashmir to work along with Sheikh Abdullah. 'But the real point is that no satisfactory way can be found in Kashmir except through Sheikh Abdullah,' he wrote to Hari Singh on 13 November 1947, who was 'the only person who can deliver the goods in Kashmir'. Nehru portrayed a very bright picture of Abdullah for Singh:

The way he has risen to grapple with the crisis has shown the nature of the man. I have a high opinion of his integrity and his general balance of mind. He has striven hard and succeeded very largely in keeping communal peace. He may make any number of mistakes in minor matters, but I think he is likely to be right in regard to major decisions.[24]

The people of Kashmir are more likely to be asked to ratify the provisional decision to accede to India at the general elections than to vote in a referendum to decide the future of the State in the light of the atrocities committed by the raiders, said Ghulam Mohammad Bakshi, deputy chief of the emergency administration of Kashmir. Bakshi revealed that in September he and Ghulam Mohammad Sadiq, vice president of NC, went to Lahore and met Liaquat. They found that the Pakistan leaders were unwilling to let the Kashmir issue be decided by a referendum and told the NC leaders that unless Abdullah privately pledged to Pakistan that the party would solidly vote for the state's accession to Pakistan, they could not agree to a referendum.[25]

The presence of RSS in the state continued to bother Nehru. He wrote in a letter on 21 November:

. . . [the] RSS is an injurious and dangerous organization and fascist in the strictly technical sense of the word. We have known about it for many years and some of our colleagues have been up against it for a long time. It is bad enough in Maharashtra where it originated. But the combination of RSS and Punjab has produced something worse. I have little doubt that we have to stand up against this . . . They are very well organised but extraordinarily narrow in their outlook and completely lacking in the appreciation of any basic problem.[26]

At Mountbatten's insistence, Nehru met Liaquat Ali Khan in Delhi on 26 November, who had come to Delhi for a Joint Defence Council meeting. The two prime ministers, in the presence of Mountbatten considered options such as Pakistan using its influence to persuade the invaders to stop fighting and withdraw from Kashmir at the earliest, withdrawal of the bulk of Indian troops, leaving behind a small contingent for securing the frontier, and the Indian and Pakistani governments jointly approaching the UN for holding a plebiscite in Kashmir under its supervision. No decision, however, was reached.[27]

After another visit to Srinagar, Patel and Baldev Singh reported to the Defence Committee that soon after returning from India, Liaquat Ali made speeches encouraging tribesmen who had gathered in large numbers in certain places across the border to invade Kashmir and that Pakistan would never give up Kashmir. Despite the impact of these reports on the Indian leaders, Mountbatten persuaded them not to give up negotiation with their Pakistani counterparts.

Nehru met Liaquat again on 8 December in Lahore, accompanied by Mountbatten. Liaquat agreed to Mountbatten's suggestion of asking UN observers to help India and Pakistan solve the impasse, but Nehru rejected it outright, arguing that he would agree to have UN observers to help with plebiscite only after the cessation of hostilities.[28]

Faced with a situation where on the one hand a negotiated settlement looked impossible and a serious risk of the situation developing into a full-scale war if no solution was found, Mountbatten pressed Gandhi and Nehru to take the help of the UN. By mid-December Nehru had come around the idea of approaching the UN. He sounded out M.C. Setalvad, who would become India's attorney general from 1950, on 20 December, that his services might be required if India approached the UN:

> Conditions for carrying on military operations in Kashmir State are not favourable to us chiefly because our lines of communications are bad and limited, while Pakistan can just walk in whenever it likes. We cannot enter Pakistan territory because that would involve aggression on Pakistan. This is a highly unsatisfactory position because while they commit aggression all the time we have to be on the defensive in Kashmir State.
>
> We are therefore thinking now of making an approach to the Security Council of U.N.O. charging Pakistan as an aggressor country, encouraging raids and invasions on Indian Union territory and pointing out that while we have scrupulously avoided entering Pakistan territory, we cannot afford to allow Pakistan being used as a base for invasion and we may have to take necessary steps to prevent this. The issue before U.N.O. would thus be whether Pakistan has committed an act of aggression or not. Other issues may also arise but so far we are concerned we should like to limit it to that.[29]

When Nehru met Liaquat Ali again on 21 December, he found the Pakistani prime minister 'toned down and chastened'. He told Liaquat that India intended to approach the UN with a formal complaint charging Pakistan as an aggressor. Liaquat Ali 'did not say much in reply to this except that he would welcome UNO's intervention as he was anxious that a third party should come into the picture'.[30]

Nehru personally handed over a copy of the letter of complaint to Liaquat Ali when they met again on 22 December 1947. He pointed to the help the raiders were getting from Pakistan and therefore to stop all such help. The Government of India formally appealed to the UN on 31 December when no response came from Pakistan.[31] The Pakistan government's reply, accusing India of trying to destroy Pakistan, arrived on the next day.

Announcing India's complaint to the UN at a press conference in Delhi on 2 January 1948, Nehru claimed that 50,000 raiders were still in the state and another 1,00,000 were being trained and armed at the border for the invasion of Kashmir.[32]

In January 1948, T.G. Sanjevi, the director of the Intelligence Bureau, shared with Patel a report from one of his sources 'operating for the Bureau at Lahore', who also visited Sialkot, Gujranwala, Wazirabad, Hafizabad, Pattoki Kasur and other places. The report claimed:

> There is an all out dive for enrolment of the National Guards, and all the District Officers are vigorously engaged in surpassing one another in the number of enrolling able-bodied men . . .
>
> . . . As for Kashmir and Jammu, the Pakistan Government and every Muslim is keen to fight to the finish and conquer it at all costs and sacrifice. Their morale is very high. At Sialkot Cantt., I learnt that almost half the troops stationed there had gone to fight on Jammu front. They are sent in plain clothes and there have been a good many casualties amongst them. The same is the case at other places where troops are stationed.[33]

The Indian delegation to the UN Security Council session held at Lake Success in February 1948, led by N. Gopalaswami Ayyangar, had a disappointing experience. Gopalaswami and Sheikh Abdullah returned from New York 'thoroughly fed up with the Security Council', Nehru wrote to Vijayalakshmi Pandit on 16 February. 'I could not imagine that the Security Council could possibly behave in the trivial and partisan manner in which it functioned,' wrote an annoyed Nehru, furious with the UK and the USA whom he charged with having 'played a dirty role'. The British and the American delegates had tried to turn India's specific complaint to a broader issue of Indo–Pak relations, insisting on withdrawal of the Indian army from Kashmir. While Noel Baker, the Commonwealth Relations Secretary of the British government, told Sheikh Abdullah that India's charges were not true and that the Pakistan government was not to be blamed, the US delegate insisted that India should first hold plebiscite in Kashmir.[34] [35]

On 18 March 1948, the Chinese delegate at the Security Council introduced a draft resolution asking Pakistan to withdraw the invaders, following which India should progressively withdraw her troops. Thereafter, India should set up a plebiscite administration officiated by international personalities. Six other member countries, including the UK and the US, however, presented an amended draft that proposed a five-member commission for the restoration of peace and holding a plebiscite, stoppage of incursions and withdrawal of tribesmen by Pakistan, maintaining minimum troops in Kashmir by India and formation of a coalition cabinet in the state involving all major parties. In addition, it proposed appointment by the Kashmir government of a plebiscite administrator nominated by the UN secretary general.[36]

The amended resolution was passed by the Security Council on 21 April 1948 despite India's strong protests by nine votes against zero, with the Soviet Union and Ukraine abstaining. A supplementary resolution moved by the Syrian delegate in the Council was adopted on 3 June, directing the UN Commission to further study and report to the council on matters raised by the foreign minister of Pakistan. Besides Pakistan, these matters included Junagadh, genocide and agreements between India and Pakistan. When Nehru protested against this resolution, the president of the Security Council explained that the commission had only been asked to collect information and that the merit of Pakistan's complaints had not yet been decided.[37]

The UN Commission on India and Pakistan (UNCIP) arrived in Karachi on 7 July and reached Delhi on 12 July 1948.[38]

The commission publicly announced its proposals to the Indian and Pakistani governments, which were drafted on 13 August and on 7 September 1948. The proposals had three components: a ceasefire and a truce agreement, followed by consultations for a plebiscite. The ceasefire agreement stipulated the high commands of the Indian and Pakistani forces to issue separate and simultaneous cease fire orders, not augment the armed forces and appointment of military observers by the commission to supervise the observance of ceasefire. Under the truce agreement, Pakistan was required to withdraw its troops and tribesmen from Kashmir, and once that process was completed, India would start withdrawing bulk of its forces in phases and maintain only those forces considered necessary within the lines existing at the time of cease fire. Plebiscite would follow the successful completion of these two steps. While Nehru accepted the resolutions, Pakistan argued that it was only the Azad Kashmir government in areas under occupation which could issue ceasefire order.[39]

On 18 November, Attlee asked Nehru whether he had received a communication saying that the Indian Army and Indian Air Force in Kashmir had been 'considerably reinforced'. 'I sincerely trust that you will be able to assure me that this is not the case,' Attlee wrote to Nehru.

An infuriated Nehru mentioned to V.K. Krishna Menon that Pakistan had been collecting large forces in various parts of Kashmir and convoys of 200–300 military trucks travel from Pakistan to Kashmir daily transporting troops and material supplies. In such a scenario:

> It is not clear to me what Attlee expects us to do. Are we to sit tight and watch all this happening, are we just to remain where we are and resist when attacked and not attack ourselves, or are we to take all necessary measures to protect ourselves and to push back the invaders? There is either a ceasefire and truce or there is not. There is no middle stage except in so far as various circumstances may lead to a moderation of military operations. Consequently it is incumbent on us to protect our possessions and where we find ourselves weak, to add to our strength.[40]

Dr Alfred Lozano and Dr Erik Colban of the UNCIP and representing the UN secretary general arrived in Delhi in late December 1948 to discuss the plebiscite proposals of the commission which had not been detailed out in their 13 August plan. As negotiations proceeded and Nehru explained his reservations, events took a new turn quite abruptly: India and Pakistan arrived at an agreement on ceasefire. In his letter of 31 December to Sheikh Abdullah, Nehru described to him how the decision was arrived at:

> . . . In view of political developments and taking into consideration all relevant circumstances we decided to suggest to Pakistan to ceasefire on

all Kashmir and Jammu fronts. Our Commander-in-Chief [Roy Bucher] sent message accordingly to Pakistan Commander-in-Chief [Douglas] Gracey suggesting ceasefire and our troops remaining in present positions pending further developments, subject to reciprocal and effective action on behalf of Pakistan. Gracey has replied that his Government agree to proposal and have authorised him to implement action on lines suggested.[41]

A ceasefire on both sides came into effect from midnight of 1 January 1949. According to V.P. Menon, 'The initiative was definitely in our favour along the entire front.'[42]

The UNCIP announced the terms for the implementation of the second phase of its plan, that is truce, on 28 April 1949, prescribing a line of demarcation to be fixed according to the factual positions of the Indian and Pakistani troops on 1 January. The plan also recommended a schedule for withdrawal of the invaders and troops.[43] India insisted that the question of Azad Kashmir should not be left in a state of uncertainty, that the phasing out of her troops should be linked to the disbanding of these forces, and claimed the right to garrison important strategic points in the northern region. Pakistan, on the other hand, claimed that the withdrawal of tribesmen and Pakistani nationals had been completed, wanted synchronization of its troop withdrawal with that of India and objected to Indian troops garrisoned in the northern region.[44]

As disputes and negotiations on the two phases after ceasefire, that is, truce and plebiscite went on, the political atmosphere of Kashmir also started evolving. The relation between Hari Singh and Sheikh Abdullah continued to be volatile although not as openly adversarial as before accession to India. Yet, both Nehru and Patel had to intervene on occasions to cover for Abdullah's outbursts against Singh. On 14 April, for instance, the *Scotsman* quoted Abdullah saying that an independent Kashmir was preferred to accession to either India or Pakistan.[45] On vehement reaction from Patel, Gopalaswami Ayyangar and Nehru, Abdullah clarified that independence 'may be and is a charming idea but on consideration meaningless'. Kashmir, he said, thought of no other alternative than accession to India.[46]

By early 1949 the clashes between Singh and Abdullah had reached such a level that Nehru and Patel decided to move the maharaja and the maharani out of Kashmir.[47] The maharaja and maharani moved to

Delhi towards the end of April 1949. Patel wrote to Nehru about how he explained the situation to them:

> I had a talk with him [Hari Singh] on 29 April and 1 May, when I explained to him the whole position and commended to him my view that, in the circumstances of his relations with the Ministry and the situation created by the reference to UNO and the plebiscite issue, it would be best for him to absent himself from the State for some time and to make the Yuvraj Regent. Both of them [Her Highness was also present] were visibly taken aback by this proposal, and I could notice that there was a sense of shock and bewilderment at the end of my discussion with them on 29 April.[48]

At the same time, discussions on the future constitution of Jammu and Kashmir were also making progress. Abdullah and Nehru, meeting at Patel's house in mid-May 1949, agreed upon some broad features of the future constitution of the state. It was agreed that the Government of India would not object to a constitutional monarchy in the state, that Jammu and Kashmir stood acceded to India only in terms of defence, foreign affairs and communications, and that it was up to the Constituent Assembly of the state to decide what other subjects the state might accede to the Union government. It was also agreed that the state armed forces would be under the operational and administrative control would be with the Indian Army.[49]

The Constituent Assembly of India deliberated upon and adopted Article 306 A (Article 370 in the final form of the Indian Constitution) on 17 October 1949, that accorded special status to Jammu and Kashmir incorporating the provisions agreed upon between Abdullah, Nehru and Patel. Introducing the Article, N. Gopalaswami Ayyangar explained the reason behind providing the special status:

> . . . the Government of India have committed themselves to the people of Kashmir in certain respects. They have committed themselves to the position that an opportunity would be given to the people of the State to decide for themselves whether they will remain with the Republic or wish to go out of it. We are also committed to ascertaining this will of the people by means of a plebiscite provided that peaceful and normal conditions are restored and the impartiality of the plebiscite could be

guaranteed. We have also agreed that the will of the people, through the instrument of a constituent assembly, will determine the constitution of the State as well as the sphere of Union jurisdiction over the State.

At present, the legislature which was known as the Praja Sabha in the State is dead. Neither that legislature nor a constituent assembly can be convoked or can function until complete peace comes to prevail in that State . . . Till a constituent assembly comes into being, only an interim arrangement is possible and not an arrangement which could at once be brought into line with the arrangement that exists in the case of the other States.[50]

Yuvaraj Karan Singh, the head of the Jammu and Kashmir state, announced the formation of the state's Constituent Assembly on the basis of adult franchise on 1 May 1951. The National Conference won all seventy-five seats in the state's Constituent Assembly, which opened on 31 October. After the Constituent Assembly of Jammu and Kashmir framed the key principles of its constitution, representatives of the Indian government and Jammu and Kashmir met to discuss their implications. The agreement emerging out of this deliberation was signed by Abdullah and Nehru in July 1952 and came to be known as the Delhi Agreement.

The relation between Nehru and Abdullah began to be marked by growing tension from this time. Frequent intemperate speeches by Abdullah, often hinting at threats of seceding from India and at other times being overly critical of his opponents, annoyed Nehru. 'I have been reading Shaikh Abdullah's speech reported in this morning's papers. I confess that I do not like it—neither the tone nor the content of it. His lumping India and Pakistan, more or less together, and his attack on the Indian press as a whole are, to say the least of it, most unwise,' Nehru wrote to Gopalaswami Ayyangar on 12 April 1952.[51] A few days later, he wrote to Maulana Azad, 'It seems to me that Shaikh Abdullah has become very angry and, as a consequence, he has delivered and goes on delivering speeches which are most unfortunate.'[52]

The trend continued as Abdullah got embroiled in controversies within the state and also with his cabinet colleagues. On 9 August 1953, Nehru wrote to Indira Gandhi:

In Kashmir, after a continuing crisis, things have boiled over. The Cabinet there split up and Shaikh Saheb carried on a bitter campaign against India and to some extent against me. Last night the Sadar-i-Riyasat [Karan Singh] dismissed his ministry and called upon Bakshi [Ghulam Mohammad] to form a new Government.[53]

Issuing a statement containing a long list of charges which included acute differences of opinion between ministers on basic issues expressed publicly, majority of the cabinet members being opposed to Abdullah, increasing economic distress of the people, corrupt administration, etc., Karan Singh, the head of the state, dismissed the Abdullah ministry and had him arrested on the night of 8 August 1953. Bakshi Ghulam Mohammad, the new prime minister, accused Abdullah of harbouring the ambition of 'carving out a portion of the state from the wreckage as an independent state'. The charges on which Abdullah and some of his comrades were arrested included disruption, corruption, nepotism, maladministration and establishing foreign contacts which threatened the peace and security of the state.[54]

Clarifying that the Government of India had no role in these developments, Nehru offered full sympathy and support to the people of the state and the new government.[55]

~

In its annual session of December 1920, held in Nagpur, the Congress adopted its new constitution. While submitting the final draft of the amended constitution to the chairperson of the All-India Congress Committee (AICC), Gandhi, on behalf of the drafting committee informed him that a 'noteworthy change we have made is to redistribute the provinces on a linguistic basis'. The reason for doing this, Gandhi explained, was that the existing provincial organization of the British colonial rulers 'is unscientific and is calculated to retard the political and social progress of the respective communities speaking a common vernacular and therefore the growth of India as a whole'. Gandhi's view, which was adopted at the annual session, was clear and emphatic: 'So far as the Congress is concerned, we should re-divide India into provinces on a linguistic basis. This would also strengthen the movement for securing such a redistribution by the Government.'[56]

As correctly estimated by Gandhi, the popular demand for linguistic reorganization of the British Indian provinces kept gathering momentum over the next two decades. The Congress repeated the assurance of reorganizing the provinces along linguistic and cultural lines in its election manifesto in 1945–46. However, it also became clear that simply because the principle was embodied in the constitution of the organization, it would not automatically translate into action when the same organization formed the government in independent India.

A joint meeting of the Union Constitution and the Model Provincial Constitution committees appointed by the Constitution Assembly adopted a resolution recommending that the dominion government should set up a commission to examine the question of creating new provinces based on language and culture, as soon as the Constitution came into force. Responding to a question in the central legislature by N.G. Ranga on the government's view on the problem, Nehru explained that the government accepted the principle of linguistic provinces, but 'if we tackle this problem in a large way at present, there is grave danger of our energies being diverted from some of the more urgent tasks'. The demand for a separate province of Andhra was 'perfectly legitimate' and being relatively less problematic, could be accommodated in the new constitution's list of provinces. The cases for separate Maharashtra and Karnataka were more complicated and required careful consideration.[57]

During further debates on the draft constitution, T. Prakasam, former premier of Madras province, did not spare even Nehru, his party leader and the prime minister of the country. Pressing his demand again for linguistic reorganization of provinces on 19 November 1949, Prakasam said:

> He [Nehru] is a person who could take the Gandhian principles, who could take the other principles, combine them, go to America and give them the peace message and to the other countries also, and, do his best to bring about peace. But he has not been able to give attention to the Gandhian technique . . . of the Organisation of the country or a division of the whole country on a linguistic basis.[58]

The Constitution drafting committee considered mentioning Andhra as a separate province in the first schedule of the Constitution that listed the states and territories of India, but then dropped the idea, because mere mentioning a new province was not enough. Since creating a new province needed a lot of preparatory steps, the committee directed the setting up a commission which would examine the issue and recommend the names of the new provinces to be included in the first schedule.[59]

The president of the Constituent Assembly accordingly set up a commission headed by S.K. Dar, retired judge of the Allahabad High Court, on 17 June 1948 to examine the formation of new provinces of Andhra, Karnataka, Kerala and Maharashtra. Rejecting the idea of forming new linguistic provinces in its report submitted on 10 December 1948 the Commission held that

> . . . in forming the provinces, the emphasis should be primarily on administrative convenience, and homogeneity of language will enter into consideration only as a matter of administrative convenience and not by its own independent force.[60]

The annual session of the Congress held in Jaipur in December 1948 set up its own committee, comprising Nehru, Patel and Sitaramayya, to look into the issue. Arguing that the 'first consideration must be the security, unity and economic prosperity of India and every separatist and disruptive tendency should be rigorously discouraged', the committee recommended postponing the formation of new provinces for a few years. However, it also pointed out that 'if public sentiment is insistent and overwhelming, we as democrats, have to submit to it, but subject to certain limitations'.[61] The report was accepted by both the Congress Working Committee (CWC) and the government.

The recommendations of the commission and the committee, however, failed to reduce the force of the popular demand. The legislative assembly of Bombay passed a resolution in February 1949 recommending the creation of a province of Maharashtra, including Bombay city. Nehru too continued to receive deputations from the Southern states and from East Punjab. He found it curious that Congressmen would 'go on challenging something which has been accepted by the Working Committee after careful consideration'.[62]

Despite a broad agreement between the Telugu- and Tamil-speaking population in the Madras province on the matter of forming a new Andhra province, and a November 1949 recommendation of the CWC favouring it, the creation of the new province was held back because of lack on agreement on the location of the province's capital, the need for a thorough assessment of the financial implications and also upcoming general elections.[63] In the meantime, Rajagopalachari was back in provincial politics, being selected as the chief minister of the government which the Congress had to form with support from the independents. Rajagopalachari was made the chief minister not as an elected member of the legislative assembly, but as a member of the legislative council, and would hold the post until March 1954, when he had to resign due to the unpopularity of his government. As the demands continued to increase, Nehru suggested that the government should take some step. Rajagopalachari, however, was against any move to form the new provinces. He was also apprehensive that accepting the demand for a separate Andhra province would make it appear as giving in to the communists, who had performed exceedingly well in the elections, emerging as the second largest party.[64] The Andhra provincial Congress committee passed a resolution in June 1952 asking the Central government to take immediate steps on the matter.

Although the question of provincial reorganization had been kept restricted to the western and southern parts of the country, demands were coming up from other areas too. In the Lok Sabha, when Syama Prasad Mookerjee pressed for readjusting the boundaries of West Bengal to include some Bengali-speaking areas of Bihar, Nehru said that he found the demand logical. However, pointing out that Mookerjee's demands were not liked by the members from Bihar, he reminded the members of Patel's statement categorically rejecting similar demands made by the Gurkha League for a separate province in North Bengal. On this premise, he argued that if reorganization or redistribution of boundaries is opened for one area, similar demands from other areas will naturally arise. 'Everything comes up in the boiling cauldron of distribution all over India,' Nehru told Parliament.[65] A resolution in favour of a new Andhra province was moved in Rajya Sabha two weeks later. Nehru opposed the resolution, blaming lack of agreement among the parties for the issue not being resolved and again warning about diversion of significant financial resources to effect large-scale reorganization.[66] In mid-June 1952, Nehru had assured N. Sanjiva Reddy that if there was a consensus on leaving Madras city out of the demanded Andhra province, the government could move quickly.[67]

Apart from the popular agitation, some prominent figures began fasting too. In May 1952, Swami Sitaram undertook his second fast in Cuddapah after this thirty-six day fast in August–September 1951. Nehru was not pleased. 'I must say that Swami Sitaram has a peculiar way of doing the wrong thing and thereby exasperating people,' he wrote to V.V. Giri.[68] It was the fast unto death undertaken by fifty-one-year-old Congressman

Potti Sriramulu from 19 October 1952 that stirred the region. The fast, however, did not stir Nehru. 'Some kind of a fast is going on for the Andhra Province,' Nehru wrote to Rajagopalachari, telling him, 'I am totally unmoved by this and I propose to ignore it completely.'[69] 'I realise that his death will be very unfortunate and may have serious consequences,' he wrote to Sri Prakasa, governor of Madras, a few days later. 'But it is impossible for a Government to function under threats of hunger strikes.'[70] 'Bringing pressure of such a kind on very major decisions would, if acceded to, put an end to the authority of Parliament and democratic procedure,' Nehru told the Lok Sabha on 8 December.[71]

Sriramulu died on the night of 15 December after fifty-eight days of fasting. Nehru remained unrelenting, repeating his argument in the Lok Sabha the next day. Syama Prasad Mookerjee stood up to protest Nehru's discussion of the problem rather than focus on Sriramulu and reminded him of Motilal Nehru's speech in the Central Legislative Assembly after the martyrdom of Jatin Das in 1929. Protesting the government's dealing with the whole issue, the Opposition walked out.[72] Angered by the opposition's stand, particularly with Mookerjee, Nehru lampooned them in a letter to Rajagopalachari on the same day:

> The Opposition in the House of the People walked out and, I think, made themselves rather ridiculous. The leader in this business was Dr. Syama Prasad Mookerjee who had been canvassing for it previously. He is of course not interested in the slightest in the Andhra State or, I imagine, in Sriramulu. But everything comes in handy to Dr. Mookerjee now, whether it is Jammu or cow-slaughter or refugees in East Pakistan or the Andhra State.
>
> In a statement issued by the Opposition groups, they say 'We staged a walk-out as a protest.' 'Staged' is of course the right word. Probably the significance of the word is not apparent to the leaders of the Opposition.[73]

Nehru announced the formation of the Andhra State 'consisting of the Telugu-speaking areas of the present Madras State, but not including the city of Madras' a few days later, on 19 December 1952. In a letter to the chief ministers of the states, however, he claimed that this decision was taken as planned and was not influenced by Sriramulu's death. Justice K.N. Wanchoo, chief justice of the Rajasthan High Court, was appointed to study the financial and other implications of this decision and report by

January 1953.[74] The new state of Andhra was inaugurated on 1 October 1953, with Kurnool as its capital.

The demands from other parts of the country obviously could not be suppressed any more after the formation of the Andhra state. The government appointed a States Reorganization Commission (SRC), headed by Sayeed Fazl Ali, then governor of Orissa, H.N. Kunzru and K.M. Panikkar, ambassador to Egypt, in December 1953. The commission was asked to submit its report by 30 June 1955.[75]

The SRC submitted its report on 30 September 1955. Its main recommendations were:

1. There should be sixteen states and three centrally administered territories;
2. UP, Orissa, and Jammu and Kashmir should retain their present boundaries;
3. Andhra, Assam, Bihar, West Bengal and Rajasthan should be subject to minor boundary changes;
4. Bombay, Madhya Pradesh, Madras, Punjab, and Hyderabad should undergo more extensive changes;
5. Three new States of Karnataka, Kerala and Vidarbha should be formed;
6. Madhya Bharat, Mysore, PEPSU, Saurashtra, Travancore-Cochin, Vindhya Pradesh, Ajmer, Bhopal, Coorg, Himachal Pradesh, Kutch and Tripura should be merged with the reorganized states;
7. Delhi, Manipur and Andaman and Nicobar Islands should become centrally administered territories.[76]

The commission also recommended that Bombay should continue as a bilingual province, containing Marathi- and Gujarati-speaking people. The Marathi-speaking districts of Hyderabad were transferred to Bombay, but certain other Marathi-speaking areas were to be part of the separate state of Vidarbha. The Telugu-speaking districts of Hyderabad were also not to be transferred to Andhra till 1961.[77]

The publication of the report produced widespread agitation, Bombay and Punjab being the two major areas of discord. In addition, disputes arose between Orissa and Bengal and between Bengal and Bihar over border districts. To get around the disputes, Srikrishna Sinha proposed a complete merger of Bihar and Bengal. The proposal was accepted and supported by B.C. Roy, the Bengal chief minister, and also by Nehru and the CWC. The proposal, however, could not materialize due to popular protests.[78]

The Sikhs and the Marathi-speaking people wanted a state of their own. While Nehru was able to pacify the demand for a separate state for the Sikhs, large-scale violence began in Bombay. Nehru's refused to consider the demand for Maharashtra as long as it was backed by violent agitation. Although his proposal to convert Bombay into a separate city-state received the support from the CWC, it was severely criticized by the Maharashtrians when publicly announced. This was followed by several alternative proposals subsequently. The rejection of Bombay as a city-state led to a new formulation in March 1956 of two separate states of Maharashtra and Gujarat with Bombay city being a centrally administered territory. The Marathi-speaking areas of the proposed Vidarbha were to be integrated with Maharashtra. This idea, too, failed to garner consensus. In June, Nehru announced that the people of the city of Bombay would decide its fate after five years. The non-acceptance of this proposal too led to a reversal to the idea of Bombay remaining a bilingual state, as sought by a petition signed by majority of the members of parliament from Maharashtra and Gujarat in August 1956. The government accepted their proposal.[79]

Violence now erupted in Ahmedabad and other areas of Gujarat. However, the government stuck to the original proposal of a bilingual state with the proposed Vidarbha integrated into it. The Telugu-, Marathi- and Hindi-speaking areas of Hyderabad were allocated to Andhra, Bombay and Madhya Pradesh respectively. The recommendations of the SRC, amended later, were legislated as the Constitution (Seventh Amendment Act), 1956.

~

A thorny problem on the matter of integration, other than the princely states, was that of the areas marked by the Government of India Act, 1935, as excluded and partially excluded areas. To study the issues around these areas, the Advisory Committee of the Constituent Assembly appointed two subcommittees on 27 February 1947—the 'North East Frontier (Assam) Tribal and Excluded Areas Sub-committee' headed by Gopinath Bardoloi, and the 'Excluded and Partially Excluded Areas (Other than Assam) Sub-committee' headed by A.V. Thakkar. The reports of these subcommittees were submitted to the president of the Assembly by Vallabhbhai Patel on 4 March 1948. The reports were prepared on the basis of extensive tours of the provinces and interactions with representatives of the people and provincial governments by the members of the subcommittees.[80]

The excluded areas of Assam as identified by the Government of India Act, 1935, were the North-East Frontier (Sadiya, Balipara and Lakhimpur), the tracts of the Naga Hills districts, the Lushai Hills district and the North Cachar Hills subdivision of the Cachar district. The partially excluded areas were the Garo Hills district, the Mikir Hills in the Nowgong and Sibsagar districts, and the British portion of the Khasi and Jaintia Hills district, other than Shillong municipality and cantonment. The subcommittee found that 'the Hill people, even of the Excluded Areas, were not found lacking in political consciousness', and 'perhaps not without instigation by certain elements' they sought independence with external relations to be governed by treaty or agreement only. The subcommittee reported on their political aspirations:

> In the Lushai Hills District the idea of the Superintendent who constituted himself the President of the 'District Conference' which he himself had convened . . . was that the District should manage all affairs with the exception of defence in regard to which it should enter into an agreement with the Government of India. A 'Constitution' based on this principle was later drafted by the Conference . . . In the Naga Hills, although the original resolution as passed by the Naga National Council at Wokha contemplated the administration of the area more or less like other parts of Assam, a demand was subsequently put forward for 'an interim Government of the Naga people' under the protection of a benevolent 'guardian power' who would provide funds for development and defence for a period of ten years after which the Naga people would decide what they would do with themselves . . . In the Garo Hills the draft constitution asked for all powers of government including taxation, administration of justice etc. to be vested in the legal council and the only link proposed with the Provincial Government was in respect of a few subjects like higher education, medical aid etc., other than the subjects of defence, external affairs and communications which were not provincial subjects. In the Mikir Hills and in the North Cachar Hills, which are the least vocal and advanced of the areas under consideration, there

would probably be satisfaction if control over land and local customs and administration of justice are left to the local people. The Khasi Hills proposals were for a federation of the States and British portions; otherwise the proposals were similar to those made for the Garo Hills. A feeling common to all of the Hill Districts is that people of the same tribe should be brought together under a common administration. This has led to a demand for rectification of boundaries . . .[81]

The subcommittee, however, stressed their perception that these were the views of only a minority of the tribal people.

The report laid much emphasis on the question of interaction between the tribal population of the hill areas and outsiders. It noted, 'In the Hills of Assam the fact that the hill people have not yet been assimilated with the people of the plains of Assam has to be taken into account though a great proportion of hill people now classed as plains tribals have gone a long way towards such assimilation.' According to the subcommittee, such assimilation was the lowest in the Naga Hills and the Lushai Hills. It observed that 'assimilation cannot take place by the sudden breaking up of tribal institutions' and therefore 'the evolution should come as far as possible from the tribe itself'. Although contact with outside influences was necessary, 'Until there is a change in the way of life brought about by the hill people themselves, it would not be desirable to permit any different system [than the existing traditional ones] to be imposed from outside.'[82]

The subcommittee also drew attention of the Advisory Committee that the 'anxiety of the hill people about their land and their fear of exploitation are undoubtedly matters for making special provisions'. It warned:

> The question has already acquired serious proportions in the plains portions of Assam and the pressure of population from outside has brought it up as a serious problem which in the next few years may be expected to become very much more acute. There seems to be no doubt whatever therefore that the hill people should have the largest possible measure of protection for their land and provisions for the control of immigration into their areas for agricultural or non-agricultural purposes.[83]

The subcommittee on excluded and partially excluded areas in the other parts of India submitted that the 'excluded areas are few in number and consist of the islands of the Laccadive group on the West Coast of Madras, the Chittagong Hill Tracts in Bengal and the Waziris of Spiti and Lahoul in the Punjab'. Regarding the partially excluded areas, the subcommittee noted:

> The main feature of the Partially Excluded Areas is that they are not altogether excluded from the scope of the Provincial Ministries like the excluded areas nor is the expenditure on them outside the scope of the legislature. In fact the administration of the areas notably of the C. P. and Bombay has not been appreciably different from the rest of the province and the Provincial Governments were in greater or less degree opposed to their exclusion. It is in the Agency Tracts of Madras and Orissa and in the Santal Parganas that a different system prevails.[84]

Among the provinces with greatest share of tribal population, apart from Assam, where the tribal population accounted for 24.4 per cent of the total population, were Centra Provinces and Berar (17.5 per cent), Orissa (19.7 per cent) and Bihar (13.9 per cent). Bihar, however, had the largest tribal population of 5.06 million among the provinces, followed by Centra Provinces and Berar (2.9 million), Assam (2.5 million), Bengal (1.9 million), Orissa (1.7 million) and Bombay (1.6 million).[85]

The report of the subcommittee concluded:

> Both exclusion and partial exclusion have not yielded much tangible result in taking the aboriginal areas towards removal of that condition or towards economic and educational betterment. Representation of partially excluded areas in the legislature and in local bodies has been weak and ineffective and is likely to continue to be so for some time to come. Education shows definite signs of being sought after more and more but the poor economic condition of the aboriginal and the difficulty of finding suitable teachers present problems which must be overcome before illiteracy can be properly tackled. The great need of the aboriginal is protection from expropriation from his agricultural land and virtual serfdom under the money-lender.[86]

Article 244 and 244-A of the Constitution stipulated that the scheduled tribes and areas of all provinces other than Assam would be governed by the Fifth Schedule whereas the Sixth Schedule would govern the administration the scheduled tribes and areas in Assam.

The government introduced the Undesirable Immigrants (Expulsion from Assam) Bill on 20 December 1949, and it was taken up for consideration on 8 February 1950. Considering the legislation urgent, the Bill was promulgated as an Ordinance in the interim. Moving for the consideration of the bill in the provisional parliament, N. Gopalaswami Ayyangar explained:

> In the State of Assam, particularly after the Partition, the influx of persons from outside Assam into that State has been assuming proportions which have caused apprehensions to the Government and the people of Assam as to the disturbance that such an influx would cause to their economy . . . attention to this problem was intensively drawn when the Assam Government reported about the middle of 1949. Their information was that only about a lakh and half to two lakhs of persons had migrated into Assam from the neighbouring Pakistan Province of East Bengal.[87]

The bill empowered the Central government to issue directions to remove any non-Indian person whose presence in Assam was considered to be detrimental to the interests of the country or to any scheduled tribe in Assam. The bill was passed on 13 February 1950.

The north-eastern region was reorganized administratively in 1951, by which the Balipara Frontier Tract, the Tirap Frontier Tract, the Abor Hills district, the Mishmi Hills district and the Naga tribal areas were renamed as North-East Frontier Agency (NEFA). NEFA was reconstituted under North-East Frontier Areas (Administration) Regulation of 1954 into Kameng Frontier Division, Subansiri Frontier Division, Siang Frontier Division, Lohit Frontier Division, Tirap frontier Division, and Tuensang Frontier Division.[88]

The political volatility with continued secessionist tendencies in the region that were to some extent highlighted by the Constitution makers concerned the government. On 1 January 1951, A.Z. Phizo wrote to Rajendra Prasad, informing him about a resolution of the Naga National Council to hold a plebiscite in Nagaland to decide on constituting an independent sovereign state. The letter intrigued Nehru. Noting that it had been 'cleverly drafted', he asked the governor of Assam, Jairamdas Doulatram, 'Who is the person who is responsible for this draft or for advising the Nagas?' Clearly, the government lacked adequate information about the region. He rued the fact that the 'British used to have competent and reliable men working in the hilly tribal areas', but 'Indians do not like these out of the way jobs and seldom have the competence to deal with the people like the Nagas'. He was not 'sufficiently acquainted with the position to offer any advice', but surely there could be 'no question of their independence'. 'We should have a friendly approach always as far as possible,' he wrote to Doulatram, and told him to resort to strong action only when unavoidable. He would be ready to meet their representatives if they so desired.[89]

Phizo, who was engaged in business in Burma, had joined the Indian National Army (INA) of Subhas Chandra Bose as a corporal, according to Intelligence Bureau (IB) chief, B.N. Mullik. He was arrested at the end of the war, brought back to India and imprisoned, but let off towards the end of 1946 as all INA soldiers were being released. Thereafter started his campaign along with a few others for the independence of the Nagas.[90]

The Naga Hills District Tribal Council started in 1945 by the then deputy commissioner to unite the different tribes of the Nagas and settle their disputes was transformed to the Naga National Council in 1946. After an initial clash with the moderate leaders of the council and unsuccessful in working up an agitational movement, Phizo, according to Mullik, succeeded in becoming its president. Under his leadership, the council boycotted the district council elections in 1950. Before that, he had met Nehru who took him to be 'a crank' who need not be taken seriously.[91] The Naga National Council also boycotted India's first general election in 1952, with no Naga contesting the elections.[92]

With the aim to press for his demand for independence, Phizo called a conference of the representatives of all the tribes of the Naga Hills district in mid-May 1951 at Kohima. According to Mullik, neither the Assam government nor the central government took the matter seriously, underestimating Phizo and counting on the divisions among the Naga tribes. S.M. Dutt, then deputy director of IB stationed at Shillong, met Phizo and other Naga leaders and was able to extract some concession to the effect that they agreed to leave defence and foreign affairs with the Indian government. By the middle of 1952, Phizo claimed that 99 per cent of the people of Naga Hills had supported the demand for an independent Naga State in the plebiscite, which he communicated to the President of India with the demand that the Government of India should recognize the independence of the Nagas. An assurance from Nehru that the demands raised by him could be met within the framework of the Indian Constitution failed to satisfy Phizo.

When Nehru visited the Naga areas in March 1953, along with Burmese prime minister U Nu, on either side of the Indo–Burma border, his public meeting in Kohima on 30 March turned out to be a disaster. As the deputy commissioner denied permission to a delegation of the Nagas to read out a statement at the public meeting, the entire audience of a few thousand left the ground, leaving behind a few officials and their families.

Naturally, the incident upset Nehru terribly. He instructed Doulatram to admonish the Naga leaders:

> I want you to send for these Naga leaders and tell them yourself that we take a grave view of the discourtesy offered by them to a most distinguished guest of ours, namely the Prime Minister of Burma. Quite apart from political or other questions, it was wholly unpardonable for such a grave affront to be offered to the leader of another nation who was our distinguished guest (I should not like you to lay any stress on the affront offered to me also on this occasion). Tell them further that we had always thought that, with all their failings, the Nagas were a brave people whose word could be relied upon. By the way they have behaved, however, they have shown that no faith or reliance can be placed on their word or assurance . . . We do not wish to punish them for this, because we feel that they are misled by others, but we intend taking a more serious view of any misbehaviour in the future.
>
> Tell them also that by this action, the so-called Naga National Council has put itself outside the pale so far as we are concerned. In future, we shall not recognise it in any way, nor deal with it in any way. We shall accept no letter, representation or communication from it . . .
>
> Further tell them that if the Naga National Council or any individual will offend against the law, immediate action will be taken.[93]

Nehru also asked him to send a strict message to the missionaries working in the area:

> I should like you also to summon, separately of course, two or three prominent missionaries working in the Naga Hills District. Tell them that you and the Government are gravely dissatisfied at the way certain Nagas and. more especially, those associated with the so-called Naga

National Council, have been behaving. Their behaviour at the time of the visit of the Prime Minister of Burma was insulting in the extreme and no Government can tolerate such behaviour which is on the verge of treason.

. . . You should further tell them that the missionaries in these areas have a special responsibility. They have a considerable influence with the people and that influence can be exercised in a healthy way or in an unhealthy way. It is well known that British officials in these areas before India became independent, encouraged separatist and anti-national tendencies among the Nagas. Some missionaries may have done so also. Missionaries are given every freedom for legitimate activity and our Government gives freedom to every religion to function, but if any missionary indulges in any political activity, or any anti-national activity, then he is going beyond his legitimate domain and Government cannot approve of any such person continuing in India.[94]

Towards the end of 1953 or early 1954, Phizo moved to Tuensang Frontier Division, a frontier area with strong resentment against the government, where one political officer was posted along with some units of the Assam Rifles. The geography, history and political conditions provided Phizo an ideal condition for his activities and he set up an independent Naga government there towards the end of 1955 and raised an armed force which he named Naga Home Guards. By early 1956, Phizo expanded his operations to the Naga Hills, district where he formally set up a Naga Central Government (NCG) with Karisanesa Angami as the president and Scato Sema as vice president. The NCG was transformed into a Naga Federal Government, with a governor (Ahang) in charge of each tribal area. An armed force called Naga Safeguards was set up in the Naga Hills district too, under Kaito Sema, a former non-commissioned officer in the Assam Regiment.[95]

A plan by the Intelligence Bureau to mobilize the dissenting segment of the Naga National Council to depose Phizo proved abortive, as he got wind of the plan and wrecked it by kidnapping and torturing key members. This was followed by the moving of the army, one battalion initially and followed by three brigades, and eventually by the setting up of a divisional headquarters in Kohima in April 1956. The IB also set up a CIVINT (civic intelligence) unit comprising the state special branch and IB officers.[96] At a meeting held on 1 May, Phizo had reportedly announced that the Naga National Council did not exist anymore. Nehru told the Lok Sabha that this announcement had not gone down well with a number of Naga leaders, who later passed a resolution to reorganize the Council, asking for general amnesty, the formation of a Naga State within India and a referendum later.[97]

Nehru grappled for the right approach to the Naga problem. He argued that the Naga problem was essentially political and not a military one, but for the present it was necessary to concentrate for the time being on the military aspect. It was also necessary to constantly remember that 'we are not at war with the Nagas, who form an integral element of the entire Indian community', and even the hostile Nagas should be treated 'in a humane and so far as possible friendly way'. He ruled out any constitutional change or a political announcement, lest that be 'regarded as the precursor of approaching surrender to the Phizo group'.[98]

As both sides were strengthening themselves, Phizo prepared an audacious plan of capturing Kohima by launching an armed offensive in June 1956. Although, according to Mullik's claim, the CIVINT succeeded in getting advance intelligence about the attack, Phizo succeeded on capturing the entire Naga village of Kohima and more than half of the civil lines, and retained control in these areas for three days. Only a small part of the district headquarters remained outside their control. The military success, however, fizzled out due to rivalry between the leader of the main striking force Kaito, who belonged to the Sema tribe and Phizo and his commander-in-chief Thungti Chang who belonged to the Angami tribe. As Phizo turned down Kaito's demand for being promoted to the post of C-in-C, he withdrew with the forces under his command from Kohima. Subsequently, the Indian Army and the Assam Rifles cleared the area of the armed insurgents.[99]

About a month before the Kohima debacle, Nehru wrote in a note to G.B. Pant, V.K. Krishna Menon and some others:

> One aspect of this question has intrigued me for a long time. The Nagas were not previously known to be one community. The very name Naga is apparently not indigenous and was coined for these tribes by the British, who lumped up together a large number of tribes under this name. The principal tribes now called Nagas are the Semas, the Angamis and the Aos. It is well known that they have no common language even and that their dialects vary after every ten miles or so. They have blood feuds between different villages and, till fairly recently, they were cutting each other's heads in satisfaction of these blood feuds . . .

How was it that these different tribes, often hostile to each other, came to function more or less as an organized unit? How did they develop this sense of something like common nationality? . . . It might be that the spread of Christianity to some extent brought about this common feeling. Those who became Christians became literate and had a measure of education in the missionary schools. They imposed themselves upon others. It may be also that the common feeling that came into existence was against the government apparatus which came in the way of the principal tribes dominating over the lesser ones and profiting by it.[100]

The attack on Kohima triggered a range of responses from the government that focused on the military preparedness, strengthening the intelligence system to prevent leakage of information, upgrading communications infrastructure in the area, apart from constantly looking for outreach to the tribes for a political resolution. Then there was the administrative approach too. The Naga Hills district along with the Tuensang division, by separating them from the Assam state, was declared as a Union Territory with effect from 1 December. The discontent in the North-east would, however, continue to grow and expand over the next decades.

Notes

Chapter 1: The Transfer of Power

1. 'Power Assumption Ceremony in Durbar Hall', *Amrita Bazar Patrika*, 17 August 1947, p. 1; 'Pageantry in New Delhi', *Manchester Guardian*, 16 August 1947, p. 5.
2. 'Japs Open War on U.S. with Bombing of Hawaii', *Los Angeles Times*, 8 December 1941, p. 1.
3. Milan Hauner, *India in Axis Strategy*, p. 391.
4. Christopher Bayly and Tim Harper, *Forgotten Armies: Britain's Asian Empire and the War with Japan*, Penguin Books, 2005, p. xxix.
5. 'Premier Announces Fall of Singapore', *Daily Telegraph*, 16 February 1942, p. 1.
6. Arun (ed.), *Testament of Subhas Bose*, p. 250.
7. 'War Crisis and India', Congress Working Committee (CWC) Resolution, 8–15 September 1939, *Indian Annual Register (IAR)*, 1939, vol. 2, pp. 211–29.
8. Ibid.
9. *IAR*, 1939, vol. 2, pp. 384–89.
10. CWC Resolutions, 22–23 October 1939, *IAR*, 1939, vol. 2, pp. 236–37.
11. CWC Resolution, 19–23 November 1939, *IAR*, 1939, vol. 2, pp. 237–38.
12. V.P. Menon, *The Transfer of Power in India*, Orient Black Swan, 2017, p. 67.
13. Viceroy's letter to Gandhi and Rajendra Prasad, 2 November 1943; Rajendra Prasad's reply to Viceroy, 3 November 1939, *IAR*, 1939, vol. 2, pp. 242–44.
14. *IAR*, 1940, vol. 1, pp. 57–8.
15. CWC Resolution, 1 March 1940, *IAR*, 1940, Vol. 1, p. 228.
16. 'For Englishmen', *Harijan*, 16 March 1940, *Collected Works of Mahatma Gandhi* (digital) (*CWMG*), vol. 78, pp. 34–40.

17.   'Western Democracy Unsuited for India', *Time and Tide*, 13 February 1940, reproduced in *IAR*, 1940, vol. 1, pp. 302–5.

18.   'Partition Plan for India', *Amrita Bazar Patrika*, 23 March 1940, p. 9.

19.   *IAR*, 1940, vol. 1, p. 312.

20.   *IAR*, 1940, vol. 2, pp. 372–73.

21.   *IAR*, 1940, vol. 2, pp. 373–78.

22.   Menon, *Transfer of Power*, p. 109.

23.   'When?', *Harijan*, 9 March 1940, *CWMG*, vol. 78, pp. 25–26.

24.   'Not Yet', *Harijan*, 1 June 1940, *CWMG*, vol. 78, pp. 256–8.

25.   CWC Resolution, 1–3 October 1940, *IAR*, 1940, vol. 2, p. 222.

26.   Menon, *Transfer of Power*, pp. 110–11.

27.   Hansard (Parliamentary Debates), India (Lord Privy Seal's Mission), Winston Churchill, House of Commons, 11 March 1942, https://hansard. parliament.uk/Commons/1942-03-11/debates/59aa2934-b575-4969-8d2f-09af1d5f0853/India(LordPrivySealSMission)

28.   *Amrita Bazar Patrika*, 24 March 1942, p. 5; R.C. Majumdar (ed.), *The History and Culture of the Indian People: Struggle for Freedom*, vol. 11, pp. 637–8. R.J. Moore, *Churchill, Cripps and India: 1939-1945*, Clarendon Press, 1979, pp. 68–9.

29.   *IAR*, 1942, vol. 1, pp. 224–5.

30.   *IAR*, 1942, vol. 1, p. 225.

31.   *Ananda Bazar Patrika*, 5 April 194, pp. 4, 6.

32.   Broadcast over Azad Hind Radio (Germany), 25 March 1942, Sisir K. Bose and Sugata Bose (eds), *Netaji Collected Works*, vol. 11, pp. 80–3.

33.   Pattabhi Sitaramayya, *The History of the Indian National Congress*, vol. 2, pp. 840–42.

34.   *IAR*, 1942, vol. 2, p. 237.

35.   *Amrita Bazar Patrika*, 9 August 1942, p. 6.

36.   Letter to Wavell, 26 July 1944, *CWMG*, vol. 84, pp. 239–40.

37.   Debate in House of Commons, 28 July 1944, *IAR*, 1944, vol. 2, p. 308.

38.   Letter from Wavell to Gandhi, 15 August 1944, *CWMG*, vol. 84, pp. 454–56.

39.   Nicholas Mansergh (ed.), *Constitutional Relations between Britain and India: The Transfer of Power, 1942–47*, vol. 4, pp. 1158–60.

40.   *Transfer of Power, 1942–47*, vol. 5, pp. 1–6.

41.   *Transfer of Power, 1942–47*, vol. 5, p. 10.

42.   *Transfer of Power, 1942–47*, Vol. 5, pp. 37–41.

43.   *Transfer of Power, 1942–47*, vol. 5, pp. 96–100.

44.   Penderel Moon (ed.), *Wavell: The Viceroy's Journal*, Oxford University Press, 1973, p. 92.

45.   *Transfer of Power, 1942–47*, vol. 5, pp. 126–33.

46. Ibid.
47. *Viceroy's Journal*, p. 120.
48. *Viceroy's Journal*, p. 127.
49. *Transfer of Power, 1942–47*, vol. 5, p. 1118.
50. Ibid., pp. 1122–24.
51. Sumit Sarkar, *Modern India*, Macmillan, 1983, p. 417.
52. Durga Das, *India from Curzon to Nehru and After*, p. 216; V.P. Menon, *The Transfer of Power in India*, Orient Blackswan, 1957, p. 214.
53. H.V. Hodson, *The Great Divide: Britain-India-Pakistan*, Hutchinson of London, 1969, pp. 126–27.
54. Durga Das, *India from Curzon to Nehru and After*, p. 217.
55. Leonard Mosley, *The Last Days of the British Raj*, Jaico Publishing House, 1960, p. 295.
56. *Transfer of Power, 1942–47*, vol. 6, pp. 76–84, 98–9.
57. R.J. Moore, *Escape from Empire*, pp. 33–8.
58. Menon, *The Transfer of Power in India*, pp. 218–9.
59. *IAR*, 1945, vol. 2, p. 93.
60. *IAR*, 1945, vol. 2, pp. 94–112.
61. Menon, *The Transfer of Power in India*, p. 220.
62. Jawaharlal Nehru, *Selected Works of Jawaharlal Nehru*, vol. 14, p. 118.
63. Ibid., p. 121.
64. 'India Demands Speedy Solution, Says Sardar', *Indian Express*, 2 November 1946, p. 3.
65. *Transfer of Power*, vol. 6, pp. 512–5.
66. *Transfer of Power*, vol. 6, pp. 319–20.
67. *Transfer of Power*, vol. 6, pp. 347–49.
68. *Transfer of Power*, vol. 6, pp. 438–39.
69. *Transfer of Power*, vol. 6, pp. 450–54.
70. Ibid.
71. Ibid., pp. 462–63.
72. Ibid., p. 482.
73. Ibid., pp. 501–6.
74. Ibid., p. 516.
75. Ibid., pp. 947–50.
76. Ibid., pp. 597–98.
77. Ibid., p. 602.
78. *IAR*, 1945, vol. 2, p. 100.
79. *Transfer of Power*, vol. 6, pp. 659–60.
80. *Modern India*, p. 426.
81. *Transfer of Power*, vol. 6, pp. 686–91.
82. Ibid.

83. Ibid., p. 786.

84. Announcement by the secretary of state at the House of Lords, 19 February 1946, *IAR*, 1946, vol. 1, p. 129.

85. *Transfer of Power, 1942–47*, vol. 7, pp. 2–5.

86. Prime minister's statement at the House of Commons, 15 March 1946, *IAR*, 1946, vol. 1, pp. 130–32.

87. *Viceroy's Journal*, p. 232.

88. Justice Phani Bhusan Chakravartti described his interaction with Attlee in a letter, dated 30 March 1976, to Sureshchandra Das, publisher of historian Dr R.C. Majumdar. Subsequently, in 1978, a facsimile copy of Chakravartti's letter was published by Dr Majumdar in his autobiographical book in Bengali, *Jibaner Smritideepe*.

89. Barun De, 'Experiments with Truth in a Fractured Land', *Telegraph*, 30 January 2007.

90. 'Appreciation of Internal Situation in India', 24 November 1945, *Transfer of Power*, vol. 6, pp. 577–83.

91. General Auchinleck to Chiefs of Staff, 22 December 1945, *Transfer of Power*, vol. 6, pp. 675–77.

92. General Auchinleck to Chiefs of Staff, 18 January 1946, *Transfer of Power*, vol. 6, p. 813.

93. Field Marshal Viscount Alanbrooke to General Auchinleck, 4 February 1946, *Transfer of Power*, vol. 6, p. 879.

94. General Auchinleck to Field Marshal Viscount Alanbrooke, 14 February 1946, *Transfer of Power*, vol. 6, p. 975.

95. *Transfer of Power, 1942–47*, vol. 7, pp. 582–91.

96. Ibid.

97. Ibid.

98. Ibid.

99. Ibid.

100. Menon, *Transfer of Power in India*, pp. 229–32.

101. *Transfer of Power, 1942–47*, vol. 7, pp. 582–91.

102. Menon, *Transfer of Power in India*, pp. 269–77; *IAR*, 1946, vol. 2, pp. 182–83.

103. Menon, *Transfer of Power in India*, pp. 275–79.

104. *Transfer of Power, 1942–47*, vol. 7, pp. 1044–48.

105. *Modern India*, p. 430; *IAR*, 1946, vol. 2, pp. 131–52, 165–82.

106. *Modern India*, p. 432.

107. Menon, *Transfer of Power in India*, pp. 285–93.

108. Ibid., pp. 295–7.

109. Ibid., pp. 306–17.

110. Ibid., pp. 324–29.

111. *Transfer of Power, 1942–47*, vol. 9, pp. 773–5; R.J. Moore, *Escape from Empire*, Clarendon Press, Oxford, 1983, p. 221.

112. Francis Williams, *A Prime Minister Remembers*, pp. 208–9.

113. *Escape from Empire*, pp. 232–33.

114. *IAR*, 1947, vol. 1, pp. 117–18.

115. *Transfer of Power, 1942–47*, vol. 9, pp. 973–74.

116. Menon, *Transfer of Power in India*, pp. 353–54.

117. *Escape from Empire*, pp. 246–47.

118. Menon, *Transfer of Power in India*, pp. 355, 359.

119. *Escape from Empire*, pp. 248–52.

120. Ibid., pp. 252–53.

121. Menon, *Transfer of Power in India*, p. 357.

122. *Escape from Empire*, pp. 261–64.

123. Menon, *Transfer of Power in India*, pp. 357–65.

Chapter 2: Framing the Constitution

1. *TOP*, vol. 7, pp. 588–90.

2. *Indian Express*, 26 June 1946, p. 1.

3. S. Gopal (ed.), *Selected Works of Jawaharlal Nehru*, first series, vol. 15, Orient Longman, 1982, pp. 248–49.

4. *Amrita Bazar Patrika*, 1 July 1946, p. 1.

5. *Amrita Bazar Patrika*, 10 July 1946, p. 1; 12 July 1946, p. 1.

6. *Amrita Bazar Patrika*, 16 July 1946, p. 1.

7. *Amrita Bazar Patrika*, 20 July 1946, p. 1.

8. *Indian Express*, 25 July 1946, p. 1.

9. Bipan Chandra, Mridula Mukherjee and Aditya Mukherjee, *India After Independence*, Penguin Books.

10. B.N. Rau, *India's Constitution in the Making*, p. lxiii.

11. Penderel Moon (ed.), *Wavell: The Viceroy's Journal*, Oxford University Press, 1973, p. 341.

12. Note to Wavell, 8 September 1946, *TOP*, vol. 8, pp. 450–52.

13. *Viceroy's Journal*, p. 378; V.P. Menon, *The Transfer of Power in India*, Orient Blackswan, 2017, pp. 323–24.

14. Wavell's note on interview with Gandhi, 26 September 1946.

15. Note to Wavell, 8 September 1946, *TOP*, vol. 8, pp. 450–52.

16. *Selected Works of Jawaharlal Nehru*, second series, vol. 1, Jawaharlal Nehru Memorial Fund, 1984, p. 235.

17. 'India's Constituent Assembly Opens Session', *Sun Herald*, 9 December 1946, p. 1.

18. 'India's First Assembly', *Manchester Guardian*, 10 December 1946, p. 5.

19. *Constituent Assembly Debates (CAD)*, official report, vol. 1, 11 December 1946.

20. *CAD*, vol. 1, 13 December 1946, pp. 57–65.

21. *CAD*, vol. 2, 24 January 1947, pp. 347–48.

22. *CAD*, vol. 2, 25 January 1947, pp. 352–58.

23. *CAD*, vol. 3, 28 April 1947, p. 366.

24. V.P. Menon, *Integration of the Indian States*, Orient Blackswan, 2020, p. 72.

25. *CAD*, vol. 3, 28 April 1947, pp. 383–86.

26. *CAD*, vol. 3, 28 April 1947, pp. 380–82.

27. *CAD*, vol. 3, 30 April 1947, p. 470.

28. *CAD*, vol. 3, 29 April 1947, pp. 437–44.

29. *Amrita Bazar Patrika*, 15 July 1947, pp. 1, 8.

30. *CAD*, vol. 4, 14 July 1947, pp. 545–54.

31. *CAD*, vol. 4, 15 July 1947, pp. 577–99.

32. *CAD*, vol. 4, 21 July1947, pp. 710–36.

33. *CAD*, vol. 5, 15 August 1947, pp. 15–23.

34. *CAD*, vol. 5, 20 August 1947, pp. 34–68.

35. *CAD*, vol. 5, 27 August 1947, p. 198.

36. *CAD*, vol. 5, 30 August 1947, pp. 333–34.

37. *CAD*, vol. 5, 29 August 1947, pp. 293–94.

38. *CAD*, vol. 7, 4 November 1948, p. 17.

39. *CAD*, vol. 7, 4 November 1948, pp. 31–44.

40. *CAD*, vol. 7, 4 November 1948, pp. 31–44.

41. *CAD*, vol. 7, 4 November 1948, pp. 31–44.

42. *CAD*, vol. 7, 4 November 1948, pp. 31–44.

43. *CAD*, 17 October 1949.

44. Draft Constitution of India, 21 February 1948, pp. iii–iv.

45. Ibid.

46. *CAD*, vol. 10, 17 October 1949, p. 444.

47. *CAD*, vol. 10, 17 October 1949, p. 447.

48. *CAD*, vol. 7, 15 November 1948, pp. 399–402.

49. *CAD*, vol. 7, 4 November 1948, p. 41.

50. *CAD*, vol. 7, 19 November 1948, p. 476.

51. *CAD*, 15 November 1948.

52. *CAD*, vol. 7, 15 November 1948, p. 402

53. *CAD*, 26 November 1949.

54. *CAD*, vol. 11, 25 November 1949, p. 976.

55. *CAD*, vol. 11, 25 November 1949, p. 975.

56. *CAD*, vol. 7, 4 November 1948, p. 44.

57. *CAD*, 26 November 1949.

Chapter 3: Unification of India

1. White Paper on Indian states, Government of India, July 1948, p. 3.
2. Ibid.
3. White Paper on Indian states, Government of India, July 1948, p. 4.
4. John A.R. Marriott, *The English in India: A Problem of Politics*, Oxford, 1932, p. 280.
5. *Indian Annual Register (IAR)*, vol. 1, 1938, pp. 299–300.
6. Sisir Bose and Sugata Bose (eds), *Collected Works of Netaji*, vol. 8, p. 8.
7. *IAR*, 1939, vol. 1, p. 337.
8. *IAR*, vol. 1, 1939, p. 439.
9. Statement by Cabinet Delegation, *The Transfer of Power: 1942–7*, vol. 7, pp. 586–89.
10. *IAR*, vol. 1, 1946, p. 212.
11. *IAR*, vol. 1, 1947, p. 211.
12. Minutes of the Meeting of the Viceroy with Members of the States, 3 June 1947, *The Transfer of Power: 1942–7*, vol. 11, pp. 84–5.
13. Text of Stafford Cripps' Press Conference on 16 May 1946, *The Transfer of Power: 1942–7*, vol. 7, p. 597.
14. V.P. Menon, *Integration of the Indian States*, pp. 77–83.
15. 'Congress Vote for India Plan', *Daily Telegraph and Morning Post*, 16 June 1947, p. 5.
16. 'Unsolved Problems of the New India', *Daily Telegraph and Morning Post*, 7 July 1947, p. 4.
17. Minutes of Viceroy's Eighteenth Miscellaneous Meeting, 13 June 1947, *The Transfer of Power: 1942–7*, vol. 11, pp. 320–27.
18. 'Unsolved Problems of the New India', *Daily Telegraph and Morning Post*, 7 July 1947, p. 4.
19. *Transfer of Power*, vol. 11, p. 687.
20. V.P. Menon, *Integration of the Indian States*, pp. 85–90.
21. Ibid., p. 99.
22. H.V. Hodson, *The Great Divide: Britan–India–Pakistan*, Hutchinson of London, 1969, pp. 367–68.
23. *Amrita Bazar Patrika*, 7 July 1947, p. 5,
24. Narendra Singh Sarila, *The Shadow of the Great Game: The Untold Story of India's Partition*, HarperCollins, 2005, pp. 300, 314–15.
25. Press Communiqué of an Address by Rear-Admiral Viscount Mountbatten of Burma to a Conference of the Rulers and Representatives of Indian States, 25 July 1947, *Transfer of Power: 1942–7*, vol. 12, pp. 347–52; V.P. Menon, *Integration of the Indian States*, pp. 100–01.
26. *Amrita Bazar Patrika*, 31 July 1947, p. 8.

27. V.P. Menon, *Integration of the Indian States*, p. 103.
28. *Amrita Bazar Patrika*, 31 July 1947, p. 4.
29. V.P. Menon, *Integration of the Indian States*, pp. 105–6.
30. K.M. Panikkar's Undated Letter to Vallabhbhai Patel, P.N. Chopra (ed.), *Collected Works of Sardar Vallabhbhai Patel*, vol. 12, pp. 146–47.
31. V.P. Menon, *Integration of the Indian States*, pp. 106–09.
32. 'Problems for India and Pakistan', *Manchester Guardian*, 19 August 1947, p. 6.
33. Holden Furber, 'The Unification of India', *Pacific Affairs*, vol. 24, no. 4, December 1951, p. 354.
34. V.P. Menon, *Integration of the Indian States*, pp. 138–58.

Chapter 4: The Partition and the Refugees

1. Nicholas Mansergh (ed.), *Constitutional Relations between Britain and India: The Transfer of Power 1942-47*, vol. 11, Her Majesty's Stationery Office, 1982, pp.193–94.
2. *Amrita Bazar Patrika*, 22 July 1947, p. 1.
3. *Amrita Bazar Patrika*, 6 August 1947, p. 5.
4. *Transfer of Power 1942–47*, vol. 11, pp. 194–95.
5. Ibid., Baldev Singh to Mountbatten, 3 June 1947, pp. 69–71.
6. Ibid., p. 204.
7. Ibid., p. 225.
8. Ibid., p. 234.
9. Ibid., p. 331.
10. Ibid., Jenkins to Mountbatten, 15 June 1947, pp. 402–5.
11. Ibid., Nehru to Mountbatten, 22 June 1947, pp. 561–63.
12. Ibid., Mountbatten to Evan Jenkins, 24 June 1947, p. 594.
13. Ibid., Meeting of the Indian Cabinet, 25 June 1947, pp. 621–23.
14. Ibid., Note by Giani Kartar Singh, 30 June 1947, pp. 762–63.
15. Ibid., Viceroy's Personal Report No. 11, 4 July 1947, pp. 896–97.
16. Jenkins to Mountbatten, 10 July 1947, *Transfer of Power: 1942–7*, vol. 12, p. 71.
17. Ibid., pp. 103–4.
18. Ibid., Note by G. Abell, 12 July 1947, p. 119.
19. Ibid., Meeting of the Partition Council, 17 July 1947, pp. 206–7; *Amrita Bazar Patrika*, 24 July 1947, p. 1.
20. *Amrita Bazar Patrika*, 7 July 1947, p. 3.
21. *Amrita Bazar Patrika*, 8 July 1947, p. 5
22. *Amrita Bazar Patrika*, 15 July 1947, p. 4; 26 July 1947, p. 4.
23. *Amrita Bazar Patrika*, 13 July 1947, p. 1.

24. *Amrita Bazar Patrika*, 26 July 1947, p. 5.
25. *Amrita Bazar Patrika*, 3 August 1947, p. 1.
26. *Amrita Bazar Patrika*, 3 August 1947, p. 5.
27. *Amrita Bazar Patrika*, 17 August 1947, p. 1.
28. *Amrita Bazar Patrika*, 11 August 1947, p. 8.
29. Mountbatten to Nehru, 14 August 1947, *Transfer of Power: 1942–7*, vol. 12, pp. 693–94; Ibid., Viceroy's Personal Report No. 17, 16 August 1947, pp. 757–62.
30. *Amrita Bazar Patrika*, 14 September 1947, p. 1.
31. Ibid., Minutes of meeting between Mountbatten and representatives of India and Pakistan, 16 August 1947, pp. 737–40.
32. *Amrita Bazar Patrika*, 20 August 1947, p. 1.
33. *The Constituent Assembly of India (Legislative) Debates (CAID)*, vol. 1, 1947, 18 November 1947, pp. 76–84.
34. *CWMG*, vol. 96, p. 382.
35. *CWMG*, vol. 96, p. 423.
36. *Amrita Bazar Patrika*, 13 September 1947, p. 1.
37. *Amrita Bazar Patrika*, 13 October 1947, p. 1
38. *Amrita Bazar Patrika*, 16 October 1947, p. 1.
39. *Amrita Bazar Patrika*, 13 October 1947, p. 1.
40. *Indian Express*, 4 October 1947, p. 1.
41. *CAID*, vol. 1, 1948, 3 February 1948, pp. 152–53, 173–74.
42. *CAID*, vol. 2, 1947, 5 December 1947, p. 1283.
43. *CAID*, vol. 1, 1948, 7 February 1948, p. 1948.
44. *CAID*, vol. 2, 1948, 23 February 1948, p. 1082.
45. *CAID*, vol. 1, 1949, Part I, 3 February 1949, pp. 214–15.
46. Ibid., pp. 1126, 1133–34.
47. Ibid., 16 March 1949, p. 1394.
48. Ibid., 3 February 1949, pp. 1126, 1133–34.
49. *CAID*, vol. 2, 1949, 5 March 1949, pp. 1150–51.
50. Agreements between India and Pakistan reached between inter-dominion conferences, Ministry of Education, File No. 15-7/49-A3, National Archives of India.
51. *Parliamentary Debates*, vol. 1, 1950, 2 February 1950, p. 110.
52. Ibid., 9 February 1950, pp. 379–80.
53. Ibid., 17 February 1950, pp. 618–20.
54. Parliamentary Debates, Official Report, vol. 1, 1950, 1 February 1950, pp. 27–8.
55. *Parliamentary Debates*, vol. 2, 1950, 10 April 1950, pp. 2675–78.
56. Ibid.
57. N.V. Gadgil, *Government from Inside*, Meenakshi Prakashan, 1963, p. 86.

58. B.N. Mullik, *My Years with Nehru: 1948–1964*, Allied Publishers, 1972, pp. 14–16.
59. *Parliamentary Debates*, vol. 3, 1950, 19 April 1950, pp. 3017–22.
60. Ibid.
61. B.N. Mullik, *My Years with Nehru*, pp. 15–7.

Chapter 5: Recasting the Civil Service and the Armed Forces

1.   Legislative Assembly Debates, Official Report, 15 February 1921, pp. 31–2
2.   Bisheshwar Prasad (ed.), *Expansion of the Armed Forces and Defence Organisation 1939-45*, Combined Inter-Services Historical Section, India and Pakistan, Orient Longmans, 1956, p. 54.
3.   Ibid., p. 56.
4.   Ibid., p. 209–10.
5.   Daniel Marston, *The Indian Army and the End of the Raj*, Cambridge University Press, 2014, p. 249.
6.   *Transfer of Power: 1942–7*, vol. 9, p. 117.
7.   Daniel Marston, *The Indian Army and the End of the Raj*, p. 253.
8.   Meeting of the Special Committee of the Indian Cabinet, 26 June 1947, *Transfer of Power: 1942–7*, vol. 11, p. 655.
9.   *Manchester Guardian*, 18 August 1947, p. 5.
10. *Amrita Bazar Patrika*, 1 March 1948, p. 8.
11. Daniel Marston, *The Indian Army and the End of the Raj*, p. 250.
12. *Transfer of Power: 1942–7*, vol. 9, p. 820.
13. *Transfer of Power: 1942–7*, vol. 7, pp. 80–1.
14. Mountbatten to Provincial Governors, 31 May 1947, *Transfer of Power: 1942–7*, vol. 11, pp. 29–31.
15. Minutes of Meeting, Viceroy with Indian leaders, 2 June 1947, *Transfer of Power: 1942–7*, vol. 11, p. 43.
16. *Transfer of Power: 1942–7*, vol. 9, p. 981.
17. *Transfer of Power: 1942–7*, vol. 9, p. 984.
18. Minutes of Viceroy's Fourth Staff Meeting, 28 March 1947, *Transfer of Power: 1942–7*, vol. 10, p. 35.
19. Division of the Armed Forces of India between 'Pakistan' and 'Hindustan', Note by Commander-in-Chief in India, 27 May 1947, *Transfer of Power: 1942–7*, vol. 10, p. 1005.
20. Ismay to Mountbatten, 20 June 1947, *Transfer of Power: 1942–7*, vol. 11, p. 534.
21. *CWMG*, vol. 96, pp. 9–10.
22. Constituent Assembly of India (Legislative) Debates, Official Report, vol. 1, 1947,19 November 1947, p. 206.

23. Note on Nationalisation of the Armed Forces, 16 September 1947, *SWJN*, series 2, vol. 4, p. 484.

24. Meeting of the Special Committee of the Indian Cabinet, 16 June 1947, *Transfer of Power: 1942–7*, vol. 11, p. 424.

25. *Transfer of Power: 1942–7*, vol. 12, p. 759.

26. Nehru's letter to Mountbatten, 5 July 1947, *SWJN*, series 2, vol. 3, pp. 306–7.

27. Nehru's letter to Mountbatten, 14 July 1947, *SWJN*, series 2, vol. 3, pp. 311–12.

28. Nehru's letter to Baldev Singh, 25 July 1947, *SWJN*, series 2, vol. 3, pp. 315–16.

29. Chiefs of Staff Committee 86th Meeting, 9 July 1947, *Transfer of Power: 1942–7*, vol. 12, p. 44.

30. *Transfer of Power*, vol. 12, pp. 113–14.

31. Meeting of the Special Committee of the Indian Cabinet, 26 June 1947, *Transfer of Power*, vol. 12, p. 654.

32. Viceroy's Personal Report, 18 July 1947, *Transfer of Power*, vol. 12, pp. 228–29.

33. Constituent Assembly of India (Legislative) Debates, Official Report, vol. 1, 1947, 19 November 1947, p. 199

34. *Indian Express*, 22 November 1947, p. 4.

35. Constituent Assembly of India (Legislative) Debates, Official Report, vol. 1, 1947, 19 November 1947, p. 206.

36. Constituent Assembly of India (Legislative) Debates, Official Report, vol. 2, 1949, 7 March 1949, 1171.

37. *CWMG*, vol. 96, p. 112.

38. Message to Army Officers, 27 July 1947, *CWMG*, vol. 96, pp. 156–57.

39. The Constituent Assembly of India (Legislative), Official Report, vol. 1, 1947, 27 November 1947, pp. 796–830.

40. Ibid.

41. *Indian Express*, 14 January 1949, p. 4.

42. *CWMG*, vol. 97, p. 237.

43. Outside his Field, 7 November 1947, *CWMG*, vol. 97, p. 249.

44. S.L. Menezes, *Fidelity and Honour: The Indian Army from the Seventeenth to the Twenty-first Century*, Oxford University Press, 1999, p. 459.

45. *SWJN*, series 2, vol. 23, pp. 103–4.

46. *SWJN*, series 2, vol. 26, p. 220.

47. S.L. Menezes, *Fidelity and Honour*, p. 447.

48. *Manchester Guardian*, 15 January 1949, p. 6.

49. Nehru's letter to Baldev Singh, 5 August 1948, *SWJN*, series 2, vol. 7, p. 521.

50. Constituent Assembly of India (Legislative) Debates, Official Report, vol. 2, 1949, 7 March 1949, 1171.

51. *SWJN*, series 2, vol. 25, p. 302.

52. Nehru's letter to R.S. Shukla, 18 August 1948, *SWJN*, series 2, vol. 7, p. 522.

53. Menezes, *Fidelity and Honour*, p. 450; Constituent Assembly of India (Legislative) Debates, Official Report, vol. 1, 1949, 8 February 1949, pp. 403–4.

54. Nehru's letter to General Bucher, 21 September 1948, *SWJN*, series 2, vol. 7, p. 526.

55. Nehru's letter to General Bucher, 22 September 1948, *SWJN*, series 2, vol. 7, pp. 526–27.

56. Nehru's letter to General Cariappa, 28 December 1949, *SWJN*, series 2, vol. 14, Part I, pp. 324–26.

57. All budgetary figures are from the speeches delivered by the finance minister in the relevant years.

58. Nehru's letter to John Matthai, 17 February 1950, *SWJN*, series 2, vol. 14, Part I, pp. 326–27.

59. Nehru's letter to General Cariappa, 27 March 1950, *SWJN*, series 2, vol. 14, Part I, p. 328.

60. *SWJN*, series 2, vol. 25, pp. 296–305.

61. Nehru's note to Defence Secretary, 12 May 1954, *SWJN*, series 2, vol. 25, p. 307.

62. Note to the Defence Ministry, Minister of Defence Organisation and the Defence Secretary, 30 January 1955, *SWJN*, series 2, vol. 27, pp. 495–96.

63. Rajendra Prasad's letter to Nehru, 11 August 1955, Foreign Policy of India, File No. 184/55, Office of the Secretary to the President, National Archives of India.

64. K.N. Katju's letter to Rajendra Prasad, 15 August 1955, Foreign Policy of India, File No. 184/55, Office of the Secretary to the President, National Archives of India.

65. Nehru's letter to K.N. Katju, 22 September 1954, *SWJN*, series 2, vol. 30, p. 346.

66. M.C. Chagla, *Roses in December: An Autobiography*, Bharatiya Vidya Bhavan, 1975, p. 42.

67. G.D. Khosla, *Last Days of Netaji*, Thomson Press (India) Ltd, 1974, p. 3.

68. K.P.S. Menon, *Many Worlds: An Autobiography*, Oxford University Press, 1965, p. 54.

69. K.P.S. Menon, *Many Worlds*, p. 63.

70. Interview with K.B. Lall, 26 February 1983, Cambridge South Asian Archive, Centre of South Asian Studies, University of Cambridge, https://www.s-asian.cam.ac.uk/archive/audio/

71. Minutes of Conference on 11 July held at Simla, *Transfer of Power*, vol. 8, pp. 38–40.

72. Viceroy's Journal, p. 183.

73. *Transfer of Power*, vol. 8, p. 45.

74. *Transfer of Power*, vol. 7, pp. 150–51.

75. Wavell's interview with Nehru, 13 May 1946, *Transfer of Power*, vol. 7, pp. 538–9.

76. Wavell to Pethick-Lawrence, 17 September 1946, *Transfer of Power*, vol. 8, p. 535.

77. Pethick-Lawrence to Wavell, 27 September 1946, *Transfer of Power*, vol. 8, p. 616.

78. Wavell to Pethick-Lawrence, 5 November 1946, *Transfer of Power*, vol. 9, p. 9.

79. Pethick-Lawrence to Wavell, 16 July 1946, *Transfer of Power*, vol. 8, p. 70.

80. Wavell's interview with Nehru, 22 July 1946, *Transfer of Power*, vol. 8, p. 105.

81. India and Burma Committee 3rd Meeting, 31 July 1946, *Transfer of Power*, vol. 8, pp. 152–53.

82. Pethick-Lawrence to Wavell, 26 July 1946, *Transfer of Power*, vol. 8, p. 124.

83. India and Burma Committee 3rd Meeting, 31 July 1946, *Transfer of Power*, vol. 8, pp. 151–52.

84. *Transfer of Power*, vol. 8, p. 210.

85. India and Burma Committee Paper, 10 September 1946, *Transfer of Power*, vol. 8, pp. 479–81.

86. Wavell to Pethick-Lawrence, 15 October 1946, *Transfer of Power*, vol. 8, pp. 738–39.

87. Governor-General (Home Department) to Secretary of State, 23 October 1946, *Transfer of Power*, vol. 8, pp. 792–93.

88. India and Burma Committee 6th Meeting, 13 November 1946, *Transfer of Power*, vol. 9, pp. 51–3.

89. Cabinet Conclusion, 19 November 1946, *Transfer of Power*, vol. 9, p. 106.

90. Patel's note on scheme of compensation for the services, 11 December 1946, *Transfer of Power*, vol. 9, pp. 337–41.

91. Ibid.

92. Ibid.

93. Ibid.

94. India and Burma Committee 14th Meeting, 13 March 1947, *Transfer of Power*, vol. 9, p. 936.

95. Viceroy's Personal Report No. 1, 2 April 1947, *Transfer of Power*, vol. 10, p. 90.

96. *Daily Telegraph*, 1 May 1947, p. 1; *Indian Express*, 1 May 1947, pp. 1, 6.

97. Nehru's note to the Home Ministry, 14 May 1949, Indian Administrative Service, File No. 20/21/49-G.S., Ministry of Home Affairs, Government of India, National Archives of India.

98. File No. II-I-6B, Patel Papers, National Archives of India.

99. Indian Administrative Service – Examination Regulations, File No. 45/41/47-Ests (R); Indian Administrative Service – Fixation of Cadre Strength, File No. 45/33/47-R, Ministry of Home Affairs, Government of India, National Archives of India.

100. File No. II-I-6B, Patel Papers, National Archives of India.

101. Constituent Assembly of India (Legislative) Debates, Official Report, vol. 6, 1948, 13 August 1948, pp. 1947–48.

102. The Legislative Assembly Debates, Official Report, vol. 7, 1946, 1 November 1946, pp. 383–84.

103. Legislative Assembly Debates, Official Report, vol. 1, 1947, 5 February 1947, pp. 117–18.

104. Subimal Dutt, With Nehru in the Foreign Office, Minerva Associates (Publications) Pvt. Ltd, 1977, pp. 3–5.

105. Legislative Assembly Debates, Official Report, vol. 1, 1947, 18 February 1947, p. 736.

106. Legislative Assembly Debates, Official Report, vol. 3, 1947, 11 March 1947, pp. 1697, 1703.

107. Legislative Assembly Debates, Official Report, vol. 3, 1947, 14 March 1947, p. 1907.

108. Constituent Assembly of India (Legislative) Debates, Official Report, vol. 6, 1948, 17 August 1948, p. 317.

109. Constituent Assembly of India (Legislative) Debates, Official Report, vol. 6, 1948, 31 August 1948, p. 671.

110. Constituent Assembly of India (Legislative) Debates, Official Report, vol. 3, 1948, 5 March 1948, p. 1655.

111. Jagat S. Mehta, The Tryst Betrayed: Reflections on Diplomacy and Development, Penguin, 2010, pp. 39–41.

112. Intelligence Bureau to IPI, 27 February 1945, File 1681/44, India Office Records L/P&J/12/662, British Library.

113. Telegrams exchanged between the Secretary of State and the Viceroy, 27 April 1945, File 1681/44, India Office Records L/P&J/12/662, British Library.

114. DIB's telegram to IPI, 6 July 1945 and IPI's response on 10 July 1945, File 1681/44, India Office Records L/P&J/12/662, British Library.

115. Copy of letter from the DIB, 30 October 1946, File 1681/44, India Office Records L/P&J/12/662, British Library.

116. Note by P.J. Patrick, 21 November 1946, File 1681/44, India Office Records L/P&J/12/662, British Library.

117. Note by P.J. Patrick, 21 November 1946, File 1681/44, India Office Records L/P&J/12/662, British Library.

118. Telegram from D. Monteath to G. Abell, 15 March 1947, File 1681/44, India Office Records L/P&J/12/662, British Library.

119. Christopher Andrew, *The Defence of the Realm: The Authorized History of MI5*, Penguin Books, 2009, p. 442.

120. Patel's telegram to Ramaswami Reddiar, 25 March 1947, File - Correspondence with Madras Ministers, Patel Papers, National Archives of India.

121. File No. 40/94/50-Police II, Police II Section, Ministry of Home Affairs, Government of India, National Archives of India.

122. B.N. Mullik, *My Years with Nehru: 1948–64*, Allied Publishers, 1972, p. 20.

123. Ibid., pp. 12–24.

124. Ibid., p. 25.

125. Ibid., p. 65.

126. Ibid., p. 62.

127. Ibid., p. 23.

128. For details see File No. 5/2/52-Police I (Part II), Ministry of Home Affairs, Government of India, National Archives of India.

129. Christopher Andrew, *The Defence of the Realm*, p. 445.

130. Ibid., p. 481.

Chapter 6: Nehru's Supremacy

1. Nicholas Mansergh (ed.), *Constitutional Relations between Britain and India: The Transfer of Power 1942–47*, vol. 5, Her Majesty's Stationery Office, 1974, p. 1122.

2. Penderel Moon (ed.), *Wavell: The Viceroy's Journal*, Oxford University Press, 1973, p. 98.

3. *Transfer of Power*, vol. 5. p. 1090.

4. *Transfer of Power*, vol. 5, pp. 1110–11.

5. File No. 22/56/46-Poll (I), Home Department (Political), Government of India, National Archives of India.

6. File No. 5, Ministry of Home Affairs (Political Section), Government of India, National Archives of India.

7. S. Gopal (ed.), *Selected Works of Jawaharlal Nehru* (*SWJN*), series 1, vol. 14, Orient Blackswan, 1981, pp. 525–26.

8. *Indian Annual Register 1945*, vol. 2, pp. 112–21.

9. *Indian Express*, 27 February 1946, p. 1.

10. *Indian Express*, 10 March 1946, p. 6.

11. *Indian Express*, 13 March 1946, p. 4.

12. *Indian Express*, 23 March 1946, p. 3.
13. *Indian Express*, 17 April 1946, p. 5.
14. Wavell to Pethick-Lawrence, 27 December 1945, *TOP*, vol. 6, p. 687.
15. *Indian Express*, 14 January 1946, p. 1.
16. *Indian Express*, 16 January 1946, p. 4.
17. *Indian Express*, 14 January 1946, p. 4.
18. *Indian Express*, 19 January 1946, p. 5.
19. P.N. Chopra (ed.), *Collected Works of Sardar Vallabhbhai Patel* (*CWVP*), vol. 10, pp. 159–60, 162–63, 167–68.
20. Rajmohan Gandhi, *Rajaji: A Life*, Penguin Books, 1997, pp. 222–39.
21. *Collected Works of Mahatma Gandhi* (Electronic Book) (*CWMG*), vol. 89, Publications Division, Government of India, 1999, pp. 357–58.
22. *CWMG*, vol. 89, p. 355.
23. *Indian Express*, 13 February 1946, p. 1.
24. *Indian Express*, 23 February 1946, p. 1.
25. *Indian Express*, 20 April 1946, p. 1.
26. *CWVP*, vol. 10, p. 217.
27. Durga Das (ed.), *Sardar Patel's Correspondence: 1945–50* (*SPC*), vol. 3, Navajivan Publishing House, 1972, pp. 16–7.
28. *Indian Express*, 24 April 1946, p. 1.
29. *Indian Express*, 19 May 1946, p. 3.
30. *Indian Express*, 30 April 1946, p. 1.
31. *CWMG*, vol. 90, p. 367.
32. *Indian Express*, 10 May 1946, p. 1.
33. *CWMG*, vol. 90, p. 285.
34. *Amrita Bazar Patrika*, 27 April 1946, p. 1.
35. Rajmohan Gandhi, *Patel: A Life*, Navajivan Publishing House, 2011, p. 370; Michael Brecher, *Nehru: A Political Biography*, Oxford University Press, 2005, p. 314.
36. J.B. Kripalani, *My Times: An Autobiography*, Rupa & Co., 2004, p. 612.
37. *CWMG*, vol. 81, Publications Division, Government of India, 1999, pp. 232–33.
38. *CWMG*, vol. 82, p. 218.
39. Durga Das, *India from Curzon to Nehru and After*, Rupa, 2012, p. 230.
40. Maulana Abul Kalam Azad, *India Wins Freedom*, Orient Blackswan, 2010, p. 162.
41. S. Gopal (ed.), *Selected Works of Jawaharlal Nehru*, series 2, vol. 1, Jawaharlal Nehru Memorial Fund, pp. 401–8.
42. *CWMG*, vol. 92, pp. 102, 105–7.
43. *SWJN*, series 2, vol. 1, pp. 15–25.
44. *Indian Express*, 24 November 1946, pp. 1 and 5; *CWVP*, vol. 10, pp. 290–91.

45. *CWMG*, vol. 93, pp. 211–12.
46. *CWVP*, vol. 12, pp. 4–5.
47. Jinnah to Wavell, 13 October 1946, *Transfer of Power 1942–7*, vol. 9, pp. 709-10.
48. Note by Wavell, 14 October 1946, *Transfer of Power 1942–7*, vol. 9, pp. 720–22.
49. Azad, pp. 178–79, 197; Durga Das, pp. 232–33.
50. Patel to Wavell, 16 March 1947, *CWVP*, vol. 4, pp. 534–35.
51. V.P. Menon, *Transfer of Power*, p. 351
52. Morarji Desai, *The Story of My Life*, vol. 1, S. Chand & Company Ltd, 1974, p. 271.
53. Nehru to Gandhi, 24 February 1947, *SWJN*, series 2, vol. 2, p. 53.
54. Letter to Mountbatten, 11 April 1947, *CWMG*, vol. 94, pp. 283–84.
55. Viceroy's Personal Report No. 16, 8 August 1947, *Transfer of Power*, vol. 12, p. 594.
56. Ibid.
57. *CWMG*, vol. 95, p. 206.
58. *Indian Express*, 15 June 1947, p. 1.
59. *Transfer of Power*, vol. 11, p. 67.
60. *Amrita Bazar Patrika*, 5 November 1947, p. 8.
61. *Amrita Bazar Patrika*, 29 November 1947, p. 1.
62. Nehru's letter to Mountbatten, 2 July 1947, *SWJN*, series 2, vol. 3, p. 5.
63. Nehru's letter to Mountbatten, 29 July 1947, *SWJN*, series 2, vol. 3, p. 24.
64. Minutes of Viceroy's Sixty-Fifth Staff Meeting, 28 July 1947, *Transfer of Power*, pp. 375–76.
65. Viceroy's Personal Report No. 15, 1 August 1947, *Transfer of Power*, vol. 12, pp. 451–52.
66. Viceroy's Personal Report No. 16, 8 August 1947, *Transfer of Power*, vol. 12, pp. 600–1.
67. *CWVP*, vol. 4, p. 536.
68. *CWVP*, vol. 4, p. 537.
69. Gandhi's letter to Nehru, 24 July 1947, *CWMG*, vol. 96, p. 121.
70. Viceroy's Personal Report No. 16, 8 August 1947, *Transfer of Power*, vol. 12, p. 601.
71. *Amrita Bazar Patrika*, 18 November 1946, p. 1.
72. Broadcast to the Nation, 15 August 1947, *SWJN*, vol. 3, pp. 137–38.
73. Address to Members of the AICC, 11 August 1947, *SWJN*, series 2, vol. 3, p. 431.
74. Kripalani, *My Times*, pp. 634–36.
75. *Indian Annual Register 1946*, vol. 2, p. 110.
76. Kripalani, pp. 707–9.

77. Kripalani, *My Times*, pp. 710–12.
78. *CWMG*, vol. 96, p. 279.
79. Kripalani, *My Times*, pp. 715–16.
80. *Amrita Bazar Patrika*, 18 November 1947, p. 1.
81. *Amrita Bazar Patrika*, 15 January 1948, p. 1.
82. Dr Krishnalal Shridharani, Gandhiji Back to Leadership, *Amrita Bazar Patrika*, 21 November 1947, p. 5.
83. Address to Congress Workers, 12 March 1948, *SWJN*, series 2, vol. 5, p. 345.
84. *CWVP*, vol. 4, pp. 550–51.
85. *Ananda Bazar Patrika*, 16 November 1947, p. 5.
86. *Ananda Bazar Patrika*, 3 December 1947, p. 5.
87. *Ananda Bazar Patrika*, 8 December 1947, p. 1.
88. *CWVP*, vol. 4, pp. 554–56.
89. *CWMG*, vol. 96, p. 424.
90. Rajendra Prasad to Patel, 29 September 1947, *CWVP*, vol. 4, pp. 539–40.
91. Motion Regarding Food Policy of the Government of India, Constituent Assembly of India (Legislative) Debates, 10 December 1947, pp. 1627–31.
92. Motion Regarding Food Policy of the Government of India, Constituent Assembly of India (Legislative) Debates, 10 December 1947, pp. 1627–31.
93. Motion Regarding Food Policy of the Government of India, Constituent Assembly of India (Legislative) Debates, 10 December 1947, p. 1671.
94. *Amrita Bazar Patrika*, 16 December 1947, p. 1.
95. *Amrita Bazar Patrika*, 17 December 1947, p. 8.
96. *Amrita Bazar Patrika*, 3 November 1947, p. 1.
97. Nehru's letter to Chief Ministers, 27 September 1950, *SWJN*, vol. 15, Part I, p. 143.
98. Speech at prayer meeting, 17 October 1947, *CWMG*, vol. 97, p. 105.
99. *Amrita Bazar Patrika*, 3 November 1947, p. 2.
100. *Amrita Bazar Patrika*, 19 December 1947, p. 1.
101. The Bihar Abolition of Zamindaris Repealing Act, 1950, Bihar Gazette, Extraordinary of the 18th January 1950.
102. *Amrita Bazar Patrika*, 4 November 1947, p. 8; 13 November 1947, p. 5; 22 November 1947, p. 5.
103. *Amrita Bazar Patrika*, 3 December 1947, p. 1.
104. *SWJN*, series 2, vol. 6, p. 312.
105. *SWJN*, series 2, vol. 6, p. 313.
106. *Amrita Bazar Patrika*, 7 April 1948, pp. 1, 8.
107. *SWJN*, series 2, vol. 6, pp. 297–304.
108. Ibid.
109. *SWJN*, series 2, vol. 4, p. 519.

110. Patel's letters to Iengar and Nehru, 23 December 1947, *SPC*, vol. 6, pp. 8–10.

111. Nehru to Patel, 23 December 1947, *SPC*, vol. 6, pp. 10–12.

112. Patel to Nehru, 24 December 1947, *SPC*, vol. 6, pp. 12–3.

113. Ibid.

114. Letters exchanged between Patel and Nehru, 23 December 1947, *SPC*, vol. 1, pp. 121–22.

115. N.V. Gadgil, *Government from Inside*, Meenakshi Prakashan, 1963, pp. 145–47.

116. Diary of Manibehn Patel, cited in Rajmohan Gandhi, *Patel*, p. 458.

117. *Amrita Bazar Patrika*, 13 December 1947, p. 1.

118. V. Shankar, *My Reminiscences of Sardar Patel*, vol. 1, p. 160.

119. *Amrita Bazar Patrika*, 13 January 1948, p. 1.

120. *Amrita Bazar Patrika*, 13 January 1948, p. 8.

121. Diary of Manibehn Patel, cited in Rajmohan Gandhi, *Patel*, pp. 462–63.

122. Ibid.; V. Shankar, *Reminiscences*, vol. 1, p. 160.

123. Patel to Gandhi, 13 January 1948, *SPC*, vol. 6, pp. 25–6.

124. Diary of Manibehn Patel, cited in Rajmohan Gandhi, *Patel*, pp. 462–63. Several issues of *Amrita Bazar Patrika* of this period.

125. *Amrita Bazar Patrika*, 14 January 1948, p. 8.

126. Speech at Prayer Meeting, 15 January 1948, *CWMG*, vol. 98, p. 238.

127. *CWVP*, vol. 13, p. 87.

128. Ibid., p. 91.

129. 'As an Indian Sees It', *Pittsburgh Courier*, 31 May 1947.

130. D.G. Tendulkar, *Mahatma: Life of Mohandas Karamchand Gandhi*, vol. 8, pp. 302–3.

131. Letter to Prema Kantak, 16 January 1948, *CWMG*, vol. 98, p. 243.

132. Sampurnanand, *Memories and Reflections*, Asia Publishing House, 1962, pp. 158–59.

133. Draft Constitution of the Congress, 29 January 1948, *CWMG*, Vol. 98, pp. 333-4.

134. *Amrita Bazar Patrika*, 16 February 1948, p. 1.

135. *Amrita Bazar Patrika*, 24 February 1948, p. 1.

136. *Jugantar*, 11 February 1957, p. 1.

137. *Jugantar*, 15 February and 16 February 1947, p. 1.

138. *CWVP*, vol. 5, pp. 199–209. Various issues of *Indian Express* from 12 February 1947 to 22 March 1947.

139. *Indian Express*, 1 April 1949, p. 1.

140. *Indian Express*, 14 March 1948, p. 1.

141. Letter to Sampurnanand, June 1947, *CWVP*, vol. 12, pp. 99–100.

142. Letter to Ram Manohar Lohia, 18 June 1947, *CWVP*, vol. 12, pp. 110–11.

143. *Amrita Bazar Patrika*, 21 January 1948, p. 5.

144. Jaya Prakash Narayan, Will the Socialists Leave the Congress? *Amrita Bazar Patrika*, 14 January 1948, pp. 4, 8.
145. Ibid.
146. Ibid.
147. *Indian Express*, 18 March 1948, p. 1.
148. Patel to Nehru, 15 June 1948, *CWVP*, vol. 13, pp. 137–38.
149. Interview with Stephen David, 2 October 1948, *CWVP*, vol. 13, p. 216.
150. *CWVP*, vol. 14, pp. 142–44.
151. *SWJN*, series 2, vol. 9. pp. 413–14
152. Letter to V.K. Krishna Menon, 24 February 1949, *SWJN*, series 2, vol. 10, p. 209.
153. *Amrita Bazar Patrika*, 15 June 1949, p.1.
154. Nehru to Patel, 14 June 1949, *SWJN*, series 2, vol. 11, pp. 167–68.
155. Address to the Delhi Provincial Political Conference, 19 June 1949, *SWJN*, series 2, vol. 11, pp. 171–75.
156. V. Shankar, *Reminiscences*, vol. 1, pp. 48–51; Durga Das, *From Curzon to Nehru*, pp. 31–2.
157. Nehru to V.K. Krishna Menon, 25 August 1950, *SWJN*, series 2, vol. 15, Part I, pp. 101–3.
158. Nehru to Purushottamdas Tandon, 8 August 1950, *SWJN*, series 2, vol. 15, Part I, pp. 90–2.
159. *SWJN*, series 2, vol. 15, Part I, p. 97.
160. *SWJN*, series 2, vol. 15, Part I, p. 105.
161. V. Shankar, *Reminiscences*, vol. 1, pp. 108, 110–12; Durga Das, *From Curzon to Nehru*, p. 303; Brecher, *Nehru*, p. 431; Rajmohan Gandhi, *Patel*, p. 493.
162. Parliamentary Debates, vol. 1, 1950, Official Report, 28 February 1950, p. 1010
163. Brecher, *Nehru*, p. 520.
164. *Indian Express*, 16 March 1950, p. 1.
165. *SWJN*, series 2, vol. 14, Part I, pp. 370–72.
166. Brecher, *Nehru*, p. 515; *SWJN*, series 2, vol. 14, Part I, p. 17.
167. Brecher, *Nehru*, p. 521.
168. Review of the First Five Year Plan, May 1957, Planning Commission, Government of India, passim.
169. *Indian Express*, 23 May 1950, p. 1.
170. *SWJN*, series 2, vol. 15, Part I, p. 147.
171. Kripalani, *My Times*, pp. 738–43.
172. *Jugantar*, 14 November 1950, p. 1.
173. Myron Weiner, *Party Politics in India*, Princeton University Press, 1957, pp. 73–4.
174. *SWJN*, series 2, vol. 16, Part II, pp. 131–78.; Brecher, *Nehru*, pp. 433–35, *Jugantar*, 10 September 1951, p. 1.

175. Interview to the Press, 16 September 1951, *SWJN*, series 2, vol. 16, Part II, p. 182.

176. *Indian Express*, 1 June 1950, p. 1.

177. *Indian Express*, 2 June 1950, p. 1.

178. *Indian Express*, 3 June 1950, p. 1.

179. *Indian Express*, 4 June 1950, p. 1.

180. Parliamentary Debates, Part II, vol. 16, 1951, 11 October 1951, columns 4733–34.

181. Parliamentary Debates, Part II, vol. 16, 1951, 11 October 1951, columns 4642–45, 4731–37.

182. *Manchester Guardian*, 12 October 1951, p. 6.

183. Legislative Assembly Debates, 26 March 1921, pp. 1584, 1603.

184. Chitra Sinha, *Debating Patriarchy: The Hindu Code Bill Controversy in India (1941–56)*, Oxford University Press, 201, pp. 48-51. Report of the Hindu Law Committee, 1947, Government of India, p. 40.

185. Chitra Sinha, *Debating Patriarchy*, pp. 55–63; Report of the Hindu Law Committee, 1947, Government of India, p. 40.

186. Report of the Hindu Law Committee, 1947, Government of India, pp. 1–4.

187. Ibid., pp. 37–9.

188. Legislative Assembly Debates, 11 April 1947, vol. 5, 1947, p. 3327.

189. The Constituent Assembly of India (Legislative) Debates, 9 April 1948, vol. 5, 1948, pp. 3628–29.

190. Chitra Sinha, *Debating Patriarchy*, p. 70.

191. Rajendra Prasad's letters to Nehru on 21 and 24 July 1948; Note of 31 July 1948 for party meeting and Nehru's replies on 22 and 27 July 1948, *SPC*, vol. 6, pp. 399–404.

192. Ibid.

193. Ibid.

194. Ibid.

195. The Constituent Assembly of India (Legislative) Debates, 5 April 1949, vol. 3, 1949, Part II, p. 2341.

196. Letters between Rajendra Prasad and Patel, 4 December, and 5 December 1949, *SPC*, vol. 9, pp. 109–11.

197. Nehru's letter to Ambedkar, 19 February 1951, *SWJN*, vol. 15, Part II, pp. 196–97.

198. *SWJN*, vol. 16, Part II, pp. 377–80.

199. Nehru's note to Satya Narayan Sinha, Minister of State for Parliamentary Affairs, 14 September 1951, *SWJN*, vol. 16, Part II, p. 383.

200. Letters exchanged between Nehru and Rajendra Prasad, 15 September 1951, *SWJN*, vol. 16, Part II, pp. 384–86.

201. Parliamentary Debates, vol. 15, 1951, Part II, 17 September 1951, columns 2681–82.

202. Parliamentary Debates, vol. 16, 1951, Part II, 26 September 1951, columns 3451–52.

203. Statement by Dr B.R. Ambedkar in explanation of his resignation, Vasant Moon (ed.), *Dr Babasaheb Ambedkar: Writings and Speeches*, vol. 14, Part II, Dr Ambedkar Foundation, 2013, 10 October 1951, pp.1317–27.

204. *Manchester Guardian*, 17 May 1951, p. 8.

205. *SWJN*, second series, vol. 16, p. 153.

206. The Constitution (First Amendment) Act, 1951, National Portal of India, https://www.india.gov.in/my-government/constitution-india/amendments/constitution-india-first-amendment-act-1951.

207. Ibid.

208. Parliamentary Debates, Official Report, vol. 7, 1951, 16 May 1951, columns 8814–56.

209. Ibid.

210. Ibid.

211. Ibid.

212. Ibid.

213. *Report on the First General Elections in India: 1951–52*, vol. 1, Election Commission of India, 1955, pp. 20–2.

214. Appointment of Sri Sukumar Sen as Chief Election Commissioner, File No. 30/50, National Archives of India.

215. *Report on the First General Elections in India: 1951–52*, vol. 1, pp. 22–3.

216. Nehru's letter to Chief Ministers, 1 April 1950, *SWJN*, vol. 14, Part I, p. 418.

217. Ibid., pp. 25–6.

218. Ibid., p. 27.

219. *SWJN*, vol. 16, Part II, pp. 161–71.

220. Ibid.

221. Ibid.

222. Speech at an emergency secret meeting of the AICC, Delhi, 8 September 1951, *SWJN*, vol. 16, Part II, pp. 172–73.

223. For instance, letters to the chairmen and presidents of the Pradesh Congress Committees, 19, September, 24 September, 8 October 1951, *SWJN*, vol. 16, Part II, pp. 33–7, 192–94, 202–5.

224. Letter to Anugrah Narayan Sinha, 7 October 1951, *SWJN*, vol. 16, Part II, pp. 199–200.

225. Nehru's letter to presidents of PCCs, 19 September 1951, *SWJN*, vol. 16, Part II, pp. 38–9.

226. Bal Raj Madhok, *Portrait of a Martyr: A Biography of Dr Shyama Prasad Mookerjee*, Rupa & Co., 2009, pp. 125–6; Craig Baxter, *The Jana Sangh: A Biography of an Indian Political Party*, University of Pennsylvania Press, 1969, p. 70.

227. *Jugantar*, 29 April 1951, p. 5; P.K. Chatterji, *Syama Prasad Mookerjee and Indian Politics*, Foundation Books, 2010, pp. 284–85.

228. Craig Baxter, *The Jana Sangh*, pp. 77–8.

229. Press Conference in New Delhi, 3 November 1951, *SWJN*, vol. 17, p. 6.

230. Ibid., p. 3.

231. P.K. Chatterji, *Syama Prasad Mookerjee*, p. 272.

232. *Akhil Bharatiya Ram Rajya Parishad Ke Uddyeshya Vidhan Evam* Niyam, Allahabad, undated (free translation).

233. Swami Shri Karpatriji Maharaj, *Adhunik Rajniti Aur Ram Rajya Parishad*, Akhil Bharat Ram Rajya Parishad (loose translation).

234. Ibid.

235. Werner Levi, India's Political Parties, in *Far Eastern Survey*, 10 October 1951, vol. 20, no. 17, p. 171.

236. Myron Weiner, *Party Politics in India*, pp. 98–100.

237. Myron Weiner, *Party Politics in India*, pp. 34, 100–2.

238. *Manchester Guardian*, 2 November 1951, p. 6.

239. Nehru's letter to Vijayalakshmi Pandit, 13 October 1951, *SWJN*, vol. 16, Part II, p. 45.

240. Nehru's letter to Morarji Desai, 27 October 1951, *SWJN*, vol. 16, Part II, p. 56.

241. Nehru's letter to Morarji Desai, 22 October 1951, *SWJN*, vol. 16, Part II, p. 48.

242. Statistical Report on General Elections, 1951, to the First Lok Sabha, Election Commission of India.

243. Statistical Report on General Elections, 1951, to the Legislative Assemblies, Election Commission of India.

244. Nehru to U.S. Malliah, 21 January 1952, *SWJN*, vol. 17, p. 93.

245. Note to the Congress Working Committee, 31 January 1952, *SWJN*, vol. 17, pp. 100–6.

246. Ibid.

247. *SWJN*, vol. 19, p. 515.

248. Myron Weiner, *Party Politics in India*, pp. 199–210.

249. Hari Kishore Singh, *A History of the Praja Socialist Party: 1934–59*, Narendra Prakashan, 1959, pp. 162–64.

250. Myron Weiner, *Party Politics in India*, pp. 109–11.

251. Myron Weiner, *Party Politics in India*, pp. 104–7.

252. Nehru's remarks at a press conference, 4 October 1952, *SWJN*, vol. 19, pp. 510–11.

253. Nehru's letter to Jayaprakash Narayan, 17 March 1953, *SWJN*, vol. 21, pp. 432–36.

254. Ibid.

255. Hari Kishore Singh, *A History of the Praja Socialist Party*, pp. 183–92.

256. *Indian Express*, 17 June 1953, p. 3.
257. *Jugantar*, 19 April 1952, p. 1.
258. Parliamentary Debates, House of the People, 12 March 1953, Part II, Parliament Secretariat, column 1890.
259. *Jugantar*, 24 September 1953, p. 1.
260. Brecher, *Nehru*, p. 473, Lok Sabha Debates, vol. 3, 1956, Part II, 29 March 1956, Lok Sabha Secretariat, columns 3776–803.
261. *Indian Express*, 29 May 1953, p. 1.
262. *Indian Express*, 24 August 1953, p. 1.
263. Nehru to C.M. Trivedi, 7 September 1953, *SWJN*, vol. 23, pp. 208–10.
264. *Indian Express*, 26 September 1953, p. 1; Hari Kishore Singh, *A History of the Praja Socialist Party*, pp. 194–96.
265. *Indian Express*, 2 October 1953, p. 1.
266. Parliamentary Debates, House of the People, 5 May 1954, vol. 5, 1954, Part II, Parliament Secretariat, columns 6643–44; *Los Angeles Times*, 7 November 1954, p. 20; *Jugantar*, 7 November 1953, p. 1; *Indian Express*, 26 March 1953, p. 8.
267. *Juagantar*, 10 March 1955, p. 1.
268. Nehru's letter to Vijayalakshmi Pandit, 5 March 1955, *SWJN*, vol. 28, pp. 507–10.
269. Ibid.
270. Nehru's letter to Mathai, 14 September 1949, *SWJN*, second series, vol. 13, p. 31
271. Draft Resolutions for the Avadi Congress, *SWJN*, second series, vol. 27, p. 255.
272. Speech while moving the resolution on 'Socialistic Pattern of Society', 21 January 1955, *SWJN*, vol. 7, pp. 279–83.
273. Speech on the economic policy resolution, 22 January 1955, *SWJN*, vol. 7, p. 285.
274. Michael Brecher, *Nehru*, p. 529.

Chapter 7: Foreign Relations

1. Sisir Bose and Sugata Bose (eds), Netaji Collected Works, vol. 9, p. 199.
2. Nehru's letter to Wavell, 28 August 1946, *SWJN*, series 1, vol. 15, pp. 567–69.
3. *Daily News*, 9 December 1946, p. 3; Resolution 44 (1), Adopted on the Report of the Joint First and Sixth Committee, 8 December 1946, http://www.worldlii.org/int/other/UNGA/1946/52.pdf
4. Nehru's message to W.L. Clayton, 20 September 1946, *SWJN*, series 2, vol. 1, p. 486.

5. Nehru's cable to Pethick-Lawrence, 19 September 1946, *SWJN*, series 2, vol. 1, pp. 484–85.

6. Exchange of diplomatic missions between India and the USSR, File No. 20 (4)-EUR/47, Ministry of External Affairs and Commonwealth Relations, Government of India, National Archives of India.

7. Note by Nehru, 6 September 1946, *SWJN*, series 2, vol. 1, pp. 481–82.

8. Nehru's letter to V.M. Molotov, 21 September 1946, *SWJN*, series 2, vol. 1, pp. 486–87.

9. Nehru's letter to V.K. Krishna Menon, 2 October 1946, *SWJN*, series 2, vol. 1, pp. 508–9.

10. Pethik-Lawrence to Wavell, 4 October 1946, Nicholas Mansergh (ed.), *Constitutional Relations Between Britain and India: The Transfer of Power: 1942–7*, vol. 8, Her Majesty's Stationery Office, 1979, p. 669.

11. External Affairs Department, Government of India to Secretary of State, 10 October 1946, *Transfer of Power*, vol. 8, pp. 686–87.

12. Nehru's note to K.P.S. Menon, 10 October 1946, *SWJN*, series 2, vol. 1, p. 514.

13. Nehru's letter to V.K. Krishna Menon, 13 October 1946, *SWJN*, series 2, vol. 1, p. 520.

14. Exchange of diplomatic missions between India and the USSR, File No. 20 (4)-EUR/47, Ministry of External Affairs and Commonwealth Relations, Government of India, National Archives of India.

15. Nehru's letter to Georges Bidault, 10 December 1946, *SWJN*, series 2, vol. 1, p. 552.

16. Nehru's letter to V.K. Krishna Menon, 12 April 1947, *SWJN*, series 2, vol. 2, p. 449.

17. Nehru's letter to Ernest Bevin, 17 May 1947, *SWJN*, series 2, vol. 2, p. 472.

18. *Amrita Bazar Patrika*, 22 October 1946, p. 10.

19. *Indian Express*, 2 December 1946, p. 3.

20. *Indian Express*, 7 December 1946, p. 1.

21. Nehru's letter to G.S. Bajpai, 5 December 1946, *SWJN*, series 2, vol. 1, pp. 549–50.

22. Nehru's letter to Asaf Ali, 21 December 1946, *SWJN*, series 2, vol. 1, pp. 556–57.

23. Nehru's letter to Y.D. Gundevia, 20 October 1946, *SWJN*, series 2, vol. 1, pp. 525–30.

24. *Indian Express*, 4 January 1947, p. 1; 6 January 1947, p. 2; 7 January 1947, p. 3; 9 January 1947, p. 1.

25. *Indian Express*, 9 January 1947, p. 1.

26. Nehru's note to H. Weightman, 13 January 1947, *SWJN*, series 2, vol. 1, pp. 564–65.

27. Note by Nehru, 29 January 1947, series 2, vol. 1, pp. 584–85.

28. *Indian Express*, 15 November 1946, p. 5.

29. Nehru's letter to Sjahrir, 21 January 1947, *SWJN*, series 2, vol. 1, pp. 573–74.

30. *Sydney Morning Herald*, 29 March 1947, p. 9.

31. Nehru's speech at the plenary session of the Asian Relations Conference, 23 March 1947, *SWJN*, series 2, vol. 2, pp. 503–9.

32. *Sydney Morning Herald*, 29 March 1947, p. 9.

33. Nehru's telegram to K.P.S. Menon, 14 March 1947, *SWJN*, series 2, vol. 2, p. 502.

34. Nehru's speech at the closing plenary session, 2 April 1947, *SWJN*, series 2, vol. 2, p. 512.

35. Nehru's letter to Abdur Rahman, 24 May 1947, *SWJN*, series 2, vol. 2, pp. 474–75.

36. *Manchester Guardian*, 1 December 1947, p. 5.

37. Recognition of Israel with effect from 18 September 1950, File No. 46 (15)-AWT/48, Vol. V, Ministry of External Affairs, Government of India, National Archives of India.

38. Nehru's letter to V.K. Krishna Menon, 13 January 1947, *SWJN*, series 2, vol. 1, pp. 562–63.

39. *Indian Express*, 7 December 1946, p. 1.

40. File.

41. File.

42. File.

43. *Amrita Bazar Patrika*, 4 August 1947, p. 8.

44. *Amrita Bazar Patrika*, 8 August 1947, p. 1.

45. File.

46. Nehru's letter to Asaf Ali, 18 June 1947, *SWJN*, series 2, vol. 3, pp. 330–31.

47. *Amrita Bazar Patrika*, 20 July 1947, p. 1.

48. *Amrita Bazar Patrika*, 22 July 1947, p. 1.

49. Nehru's letter to V.K. Krishna Menon, 22 July 1947, *SWJN*, series 2, vol. 3, pp. 341–42.

50. Nehru's letter to J.B. Kripalani, 25 July 1947, *SWJN*, series 2, vol. 3, pp. 344–46.

51. Nehru to Lord Listowel, 8 July 1947, *SWJN*, series 2, vol. 3, pp. 363–64.

52. Nehru's statement to the press, 24 July 1947, *SWJN*, series 2, vol. 3, pp. 359–60.

53. *Amrita Bazar Patrika*, 31 July 1947, p. 1.

54. *Manchester Guardian*, 2 August 1947, p. 5.

55. Nehru's letter to N. Ragahavan, 8 October 1947, *SWJN*, series 2, vol. 4, pp. 629–30.

56. Nehru's statement in the Constituent Assembly of India (Legislative), 12 December 1947, *SWJN*, series 2, vol. 4, pp. 618–21.
57. Mountbatten to V.K. Krishna Menon, 10 July 1947, p. 70; Nehru's letter to Attlee, 11 July 1947, pp. 110–11, *Transfer of Power*, vol. 12.
58. Durga Das, *India from Curzon to Nehru and After*, Rupa, 2012, p. 289.
59. Stanley Wolpert, *Shameful Flight: The Last Years of the British Empire in India*, Oxford University Press, 2006, pp. 144, 154.
60. V.K. Krishna Menon's letter to Mountbatten, 4 June 1947, *Transfer of Power*, vol. 11, p. 109.
61. Listowel to Mountbatten, 18 July 1947, *Transfer of Power*, vol. 12, p. 251.
62. Mountbatten to Listowel, 25 July 1947, *Transfer of Power*, vol. 12, p. 331.
63. Listowel to Mountbatten, 9 August 1947, *Transfer of Power*, vol. 12, p. 251.
64. Nehru's letter to Sudhir Ghosh, 3 August 1947, *SWJN*, series 2, vol. 3, pp. 32–3.
65. Nehru's letter to V.K. Krishna Menon, 23 February 1947, *SWJN*, series 2, vol. 2, pp. 414–15.
66. Nehru's letter to V.K. Krishna Menon, 23 August 1947, *SWJN*, series 2, vol. 4, p. 433.
67. Nehru's letter to K.P.S. Menon, 12 October 1947, *SWJN*, series 2, vol. 4, p. 584.
68. Menon, Vengalil Krishnan Krishna, File No. KV 2/2509, vol. 1, National Archives, UK.
69. *Transfer of Power*, vol. 8, p. 858.
70. J. Colville to Pethick-Lawrence, 2 December 1946, *Transfer of Power*, vol. 8, p. 244.
71. Record of interview between Mountbatten and V.K. Krishna Menon, 17 April 1947, *Transfer of Power*, vol. 10, pp. 310–13.
72. Note by Nehru, 18 January 1947, *SWJN*, series 2, vol. 1, p. 472.
73. Constituent Assembly of India (Legislative) Debates, Official Report, vol. 2, 1947, 4 December 1947, pp. 1243–65.
74. Constituent Assembly of India (Legislative) Debates, Official Report, vol. 3, 1948, 8 March 1947, pp. 1746–72.
75. Note by Nehru, 12 September 1948, *SWJN*, series 2, vol. 7, p. 611.
76. Constituent Assembly Debates, Official Report, vol. 1, 19 December 1946, p. 141.
77. Constituent Assembly Debates, Official Report, vol. 2, 20 January 1947, p. 270.
78. Constituent Assembly Debates, Official Report, vol. 2, 22 January 1947, p. 321.
79. Nehru's letter to Baldev Singh, 8 April 1947, *SWJN*, series 2, vol. 2, pp. 369–70.

80. Nehru's letter to Baldev Singh, 14 April 1947, *SWJN*, series 2, vol. 2, pp. 370–72.

81. Nehru's letter to Clement Attlee, 18 April 1948, *SWJN*, series 2, vol. 6, pp. 470–72.

82. Speech at a reception by the India League, London, 12 October 1948, *SWJN*, series 2, vol. 8, p. 363.

83. Interview with Terence Shone, 13 August 1948, *SWJN*, series 2, vol. 7, pp. 623–25.

84. File No. 40/21/49, Ministry of Home Affairs, Government of India, National Archives of India; Nehru's letter to V.K. Krishna Menon, 30 December 1948, *SWJN*, series 2, vol. 9, pp. 185–86.

85. DIB's Report on Mr V.K. Krishna Menon, File No. 2/301, National Archives of India.

86. India and Commonwealth: HPM's visit to London for the London Conference of PMs, File No. II-L-44-7, Patel Papers, National Archives of India.

87. Nehru's letter to Rob Lockhart, 29 October 1948, *SWJN*, series 2, vol. 9, p. 185.

88. The Constituent Assembly of India (Legislative), Official Report, vol. 2, 1949, 4 March 1949, p. 1258

89. India and Commonwealth: HPM's visit to London for the London Conference of PMs, File No. II-L-44-7, Patel Papers, National Archives of India.

90. India and Commonwealth: HPM's visit to London for the London Conference of PMs, File No. II-L-44-7, Patel Papers, National Archives of India.

91. The Constituent Assembly of India (Legislative) Debates, Official Report, vol. 3, 1949, 31 March 1949, pp. 2015–16.

92. The Constituent Assembly of India (Legislative) Debates, Official Report, vol. 3, 1949, 29 March 1949, pp. 2086–87.

93. India and Commonwealth: HPM's visit to London for the London Conference of PMs, File No. II-L-44-7, Patel Papers, National Archives of India.

94. India and Commonwealth: HPM's visit to London for the London Conference of PMs, File No. II-L-44-7, Patel Papers, National Archives of India.

95. India and Commonwealth: HPM's visit to London for the London Conference of PMs, File No. II-L-44-7, Patel Papers, National Archives of India.

96. *Amrita Bazar Patrika*, 29 April 1949, p. 1.

97. Constituent Assembly Debates, Official Report, vol. 8, 16 May 1949, pp. 2–10.

98. Constituent Assembly Debates, Official Report, vol. 8, 16 May 1949, pp. 2–10.

99. *Indian Express*, 25 December 1948, p. 1.

100. *Indian Express*, 26 December 1948, p. 1.

101. *Indian Express*, 24 January 1949, p. 1; *Manchester Guardian*, 24 January 1949, p. 5.

102. *Manchester Guardian*, 29 January 1949, p. 5.

103. *Manchester Guardian*, 1 March 1949, p. 8.

104. *Manchester Guardian*, 3 November 1949, p. 8.

105. Note by Nehru, 12 September 1948, *SWJN*, series 2, vol. 7, p. 610.

106. Nehru's note to Foreign Secretary, 5 December 1948, *SWJN*, series 2, vol. 8, pp. 416–17.

107. Nehru's letter to Vijayalakshmi Pandit, 1 July 1949, *SWJN*, series 2, vol. 12, pp. 408–9.

108. Nehru's note to Secretary General, Ministry of External Affairs, 9 July 1949, *SWJN*, series 2, vol. 12, pp. 416–17.

109. Nehru's note to Secretary General, Ministry of External Affairs, 9 July 1949, *SWJN*, series 2, vol. 12, pp. 416–17.

110. Nehru's letter to Thakin Nu, 7 January 1950, *SWJN*, Vol. 14, Part I, series 2, p. 505.

111. Nehru's letter to John Matthai, 10 September 1949, *SWJN*, series 2, vol. 13, p. 260.

112. Proceedings of the meeting of the Standing Committee of the Central Legislature for the Ministry of External Affairs, 17 December 1949, *SWJN*, series 2, vol. 14, Part I, p. 519.

113. Elections for Non-Permanent Members of the Security Council: A Comprehensive Review 1946–2018, https://www.securitycouncilreport.org/atf/cf/%7B65BFCF9B-6D27-4E9C-8CD3-CF6E4FF96FF9%7D/Elections%20Table%201946-2018.pdf

114. *Manchester Guardian*, 3 October 1949, p. 5.

115. Nehru's letter to Premiers of the provinces, 16 September 1949, *SWJN*, series 2, vol. 13, p. 200.

116. Government of India's Recognition of the Central People's Government, File No. 751-CJK/50, Ministry of External Affairs, National Archives of India.

117. Appointment of Shrimati Vijayalakshmi Pandit as Ambassador in USA, File No. 33(50)-EII/48, Ministry of External Affairs and Commonwealth Relations, National Archives of India.

118. Nehru's note to Foreign Secretary, 12 August 1948, *SWJN*, series 2, vol. 7, pp. 629–30.

119. Nehru's letter to Vijayalakshmi Pandit, 8 June 1949, *SWJN*, series 2, vol. 11, pp. 356–57.

120. *Los Angeles Times*, 13 October 1949, p. 36.

121. Record of talk with Dean Acheson, Secretary of State, 12 October 1949, *SWJN*, series 2, vol. 13, pp. 295–98.

122. Dean Acheson, *Present at the Creation: My Years in the State Department*, W.W. Norton & Company,1969, pp. 335–36.

123. *SWJN*, Vol. 14, Part I, series 2, p. 28.

124. Michael Brecher, *Nehru: A Political Biography*, Oxford University Press, 1998, pp. 391–92.

125. Nehru's letter to C. Rajagopalachari, 26 October 1949, *SWJN*, series 2, vol. 13, pp. 345–46.

126. Nehru's letter to Vijayalakshmi Pandit, 9 May 1950, *SWJN*, series 2, vol. 14, Part II, p. 379.

127. *Manchester Guardian*, 9 January 1950, p. 5.

128. *Manchester Guardian*, 14 January 1950, p. 7.

129. Nehru's letter to B.N. Rau, *SWJN*, series 2, vol. 14, Part II, p. 314.

130. Vijayalakshmi Pandit papers, Nehru Memorial Museum and Library, cited in Anton Harder, Not at the Cost of China: New Evidence Regarding US Proposals to Nehru for Joining the United Nations Security Council, March 2015, Working Paper #76, Cold War International History Project, https://www.wilsoncenter.org/sites/default/files/media/documents/publication/cwihp_working_paper_76_not_at_the_cost_of_china.pdf

131. *Indian Express*, 26 June 1950, p. 1; *Manchester Guardian*, 26 June 1950, p. 7.

132. Nehru's cable to V.K. Krishna Menon, 27 June 1950, *SWJN*, series 2, vol. 14, Part II, p. 307.

133. *Manchester Guardian*, 28 June 1950, p. 7; S. Gopal, *Jawaharlal Nehru: A Biography*, Oxford University Press, 1979, p. 100.

134. *Indian Express*, 29 June 1950, p.1.

135. Loy Henderson's record of talks with Nehru, 28 June 1950, *SWJN*, series 2, vol. 14, Part II, pp. 307–8.

136. Footnote to Nehru's letter to Radhakrishnan, 8 July 1950, *SWJN*, series 2, vol. 14, Part II, p. 342.

137. Nehru's letter to B.N. Rau, *SWJN*, series 2, vol. 14, Part II, p. 314.

138. S. Gopal, *Jawaharlal Nehru*, p. 100.

139. Nehru's statement at a press conference, 7 July 1950, *SWJN*, series 2, vol. 14, Part II, p. 322.

140. Messages to Stalin and Dean Acheson, 12 July 1950, *SWJN*, series 2, vol. 14, Part II, pp. 347–8.

141. Nehru's message to Vijayalakshmi Pandit, 18 July 1950, *SWJN*, series 2, vol. 14, Part II, pp. 350–51.

142. Nehru's message to V.K. Krishna Menon, 31 July 1950, *SWJN*, series 2, vol. 14, Part II, pp. 360.

143. *Indian Express*, 3 August 1950, pp. 1, 5; *Manchester Guardian*, 2 August 1950, p. 5.

144. *Indian Express*, 3 August 1950, pp. 1, 5; *Manchester Guardian*, 2 August 1950, p. 5.

145. Nehru's message to B.N. Rau, 10 August 1950, *SWJN*, series 2, vol. 15, Part I, pp. 360–61.

146. Nehru's note to the Secretary General, Ministry of External Affairs, 12 August 1950, *SWJN*, series 2, vol. 15, Part I, pp. 367–70.

147. Nehru's cable to K.M. Panikkar, 31 August 1950, *SWJN*, series 2, vol. 15, Part I, p. 385; Note to Secretary General, MEA, 7 September 1950, *SWJN*, series 2, vol. 15, Part I, p. 389.

148. *Manchester Guardian*, 12 September 1950, p. 7.

149. *Manchester Guardian*, 20 September 1950, p. 7.

150. Nehru's message to B.N. Rau, 23 September 1950, *SWJN*, series 2, vol. 15, Part I, p. 393.

151. Footnote. Nehru's note to Secretary General, MEA, 24 September 1950, *SWJN*, series 2, vol. 15, Part I, p. 395.

152. Footnote. Nehru's note to Secretary General, MEA, 24 September 1950, *SWJN*, series 2, vol. 15, Part I, p. 397.

153. Nehru's message to V.K. Krishna Menon, 28 September 1950, *SWJN*, series 2, vol. 15, Part I, p. 403–4.

154. Nehru's message to Chou En-lai, 27 September 1950, *SWJN*, series 2, vol. 15, Part I, pp. 397–99.

155. Footnote. Nehru's message to Ernest Bevin, 27 September 1950, *SWJN*, series 2, vol. 15, Part I, p. 400.

156. Footnote. Nehru's cable to B.N. Rau, 30 September 1950, *SWJN*, series 2, vol. 15, Part I, p. 405.

157. Nehru's cable to B.N. Rau, 7 October 1950, *SWJN*, series 2, vol. 15, Part I, p. 411.

158. *Manchester Guardian*, 6 November 1951, p. 5; 15.2, p. 407

159. 15.2, p. 408.

160. 4 December 1950, 15.2, p. 421.

161. 8 December 1950, 15.2, p. 450.

162. 12 December 1950, 15.2, p. 453.

163. 15 December 1950, 15.2, p. 454.

164. 22 December 1950, 15.2, p. 458

165. Commonwealth, 9 January 1951, 15.2, pp. 467–68.

166. London 10 January 1951, 15.2, p. 468.

167. 15 January 1951, 15.2, p. 476.

168. 18 January 1951, 15.2, p. 478.

169. *Manchester Guardian*, 31 January 1951, p. 5.

170. T.N. Kaul, *Diplomacy in Peace and War*, Vikas Publishing House, 1979, pp. 8–15.

171. Nehru's letter to Vijayalakshmi Pandit, 19 August 1948, *SWJN*, series 2, vol. 7, p. 666.

172. Nehru's letter to V.K. Krishna Menon, 26 June 1948, *SWJN*, series 2, vol. 6, pp. 463–66.

173. Nehru's letter to V.K. Krishna Menon, 19 August 1948, *SWJN*, series 2, vol. 7, p. 667.

174. Note of meeting with M. Novikov, 12 September 1948, *SWJN*, series 2, vol. 7, p. 670.

175. Nehru's note to Secretary General, 14 February 1949, *SWJN*, series 2, vol. 6, pp. 466–68.

176. Nehru's letter to Radhakrishnan, 25 November 1949, *SWJN*, series 2, vol. 14, Part I, pp. 541–42.

177. Nehru's letter to Radhakrishnan, 6 August 1950, *SWJN*, series 2, vol. 15, Part I, p. 463.

178. Nehru's letter to S.S. Dhawan, 10 December 1951, *SWJN*, series 2, vol. 17, p. 572.

179. K.P.S. Menon, *Many Worlds: An Autobiography*, Oxford University Press, 1966, pp. 267–68.

180. K.P.S. Menon, *Many Worlds*, p. 281.

181. Subimal Dutt, *With Nehru in the Foreign Office*, Minerva Associates (Publications) Pvt. Ltd, 1977, pp. 72–90; *SWJN*, second series, vol. 15, Part I, p. 434–36.

182. *SWJN*, second series, vol. 15, Part I, p. 429.

183. Dutt, *With Nehru in the Foreign Office*, pp. 72–90. *SWJN*, second series, vol. 15, Part I, p. 440.

184. Dutt, *With Nehru in the Foreign Office*, pp. 72–90.

185. Dutt, *With Nehru in the Foreign Office*, pp. 72–90. *SWJN*, second series, vol. 15, Part II, pp. 347–48.

186. Dutt, *With Nehru in the Foreign Office*, pp. 72–90.

187. N.V. Gadgil, *Government from Inside*, Meenakshi Prakashan, 1963, p. 84.

188. Durga Das, *From Curzon to Nehru and After*, Rupa, 2012, p. 337.

189. Dutt, *With Nehru in the Foreign Office*, pp. 72–90.

190. Ibid.

191. *SWJN*, second series, vol. 15, Part I, p. 442.

192. *SWJN*, second series, vol. 24, pp. 596–97.

193. Dutt, *With Nehru in the Foreign Office*, pp. 72–90.

194. T.N. Kaul, *Reminiscences: Discreet and Indiscreet*, Lancers Publishers, pp. 169–70.

195. *Indian Express*, 29 June 1954, p. 1; Dutt, *With Nehru in the Foreign Office*, pp. 72–90.

196. *Story of SEATO*, published by SEATO, undated.

197. *SWJN*, second series, vol. 27, p. 3.

198. *SWJN*, second series, vol. 27, p. 79.

199. Dutt, *With Nehru in the Foreign Office*, pp. 95–6; *SWJN*, second series, vol. 27, pp. 107–12.

200. Dutt, *With Nehru in the Foreign Office*, p. 97.

201. Das, *From Curzon to Nehru*, p. 341; Dutt, *With Nehru in the Foreign Office*, pp. 98–101.

202. Dutt, *With Nehru in the Foreign Office*, pp. 102–6.

203. Menon, *Many Worlds*, pp. 282–86.

204. Menon, *Many Worlds*, p. 286; Dutt, *With Nehru in the Foreign Office*, pp. 192–201; *SWJN*, second series, vol. 29, p. 231.

205. Dutt, *With Nehru in the Foreign Office*, pp. 192–201.

206. Maharajakrishna Rasgotra, *A Life in Diplomacy*, Penguin Books.

207. *SWJN*, second series, vol. 27, p. 34.

208. *SWJN*, second series, vol. 36, p. 542.

Chapter 8: Seeds of Disruption

1. Viceroy's Personal Report No. 10, 27 June 1947, Penderel Moon (ed.), *Constitutional Relations between Britain and India: The Transfer of Power 1942–7*, p. 688.

2. V.P. Menon, *Integration of the Indian States*, Orient Blackswan, 2014, p. 354.

3. Patel to Ramchandra Kak, 3 July 1947, *SPC*, vol. 1, p. 33.

4. Patel to Hari Singh, 3 July 1947, *SPC*, vol. 1, pp. 32–3.

5. Nehru to Patel, 27 September 1947, *SPC*, vol. 1, pp. 45–6.

6. *Amrita Bazar Patrika*, 7 October 1947, p.1.

7. V.P. Menon, *Integration of the Indian States*, p. 356.

8. Ibid.

9. Nehru's letter to Meherchand Mahajan, 21 October 1947, *SWJN*, series 2, vol. 4, p. 272.

10. V.P. Menon, *Integration of the Indian States*, p. 357.

11. Meherchand Mahajan to Patel, 25 October 1947, *SPC*, vol. 1, p. 63.

12. Nehru's cable to Attlee, 25 October 1947, *SWJN*, series 2, vol. 4, pp. 274–75.

13. V.P. Menon, *Integration of the Indian States*, p. 357.

14. Nehru's letter to Liaqat Ali Khan, 28 October, *SWJN*, series 2, vol. 4, pp. 288–89.

15. Nehru's letter to Meherchand Mahajan, 31 October, *SWJN*, series 2, vol. 4, pp. 292–94.
16. *Amrita Bazar Patrika*, 28 October 1947, p. 1.
17. V.P. Menon, *Integration of the Indian States*, p. 357.
18. Ibid., p. 364.
19. Nehru's letter to Patel, 30 October 1947, *SWJN*, series 2, vol. 4, pp. 290–91.
20. *Amrita Bazar Patrika*, 12 November 1947, p. 1.
21. V.P. Menon, *Integration of the Indian States*, p. 357.
22. N.S. Sarila, *The Shadow of the Great Game: The Untold Story of India's Partition*, HarperCollins, 2009, p. 358.
23. V.P. Menon, *Integration of the Indian States*, p. 357.
24. Nehru's letter to Hari Singh, 13 November 1947, *SWJN*, series 2, vol. 4, pp. 324–27.
25. *Amrita Bazar Patrika*, 17 November 1947, p. 1.
26. Nehru's letter to Dalip Singh, 21 November, 1947, *SWJN*, series 2, vol. 4, pp. 330–33.
27. Record of Mountbatten's Meeting with Nehru and Liaquat Ali Khan, 26 November 1947, *SWJN*, series 2, vol. 4, pp. 347–48.
28. Record of a meeting convened by Mountbatten, 8 December 1947, *SWJN*, series 2, vol. 4, p. 361.
29. Nehru's letter to M.C. Setalvad, 20 December 1947, *SWJN*, series 2, vol. 4, pp. 379–80.
30. Minutes of meeting between Nehru, Mountbatten and Liaquat Ali Khan, 21 December 1947, *SWJN*, series 2, vol. 4, pp. 381–87.
31. V.P. Menon, *Integration of the Indian States*, p. 357.
32. Statement at a press conference, 2 January 1948, *SWJN*, series 2, vol. 5, pp. 167–68.
33. DIB's Report on Conditions in West Pakistan, File No. 2/199, Patel Papers, National Archives of India.
34. Nehru's cable to Clement Attlee, 8 February 1948, *SWJN*, series 2, vol. 5, p. 211.
35. Nehru's letter to Vijayalakshmi Pandit, 16 February 1948, *SWJN*, series 2, vol. 5, p. 218.
36. Footnote. Nehru's cable to N. Gopalaswamy Ayyangar, 10 April 1948, *SWJN*, series 2, vol. 6, p. 155.
37. Nehru to the President of the Security Council, 5 June 1948, *SWJN*, series 2, vol. 6, pp. 171–72.
38. *Indian Express*, 8 July 1948 and 13 July 1948, p. 1.
39. *Indian Express*, 8 September 1948, pp. 1, 6.
40. Nehru's cable to V.K. Krishna Menon, 18 November 1948, *SWJN*, series 2, vol. 9, p. 47.

41. Nehru's letter to Sheikh Abdullah, 31 December 1948, *SWJN*, series 2, vol. 9, p. 226–27.

42. V.P. Menon, *Integration of the Indian States*, p. 370.

43. *Indian Express*, 29 April 1949, p. 1.

44. *SWJN*, series 2, vol. 11, p. 146.

45. Nehru's letter to Sheikh Abdullah, 10 May 1949, series 2, vol. 11, p. 115

46. *SWJN*, series 2, vol. 11, p. 125.

47. Nehru's letter to Patel, 17 April 1949, *SPC*, vol. 1, pp. 261–63.

48. Patel's letter to Nehru, 11 May 1949, *SPC*, vol. 1, p. 268.

49. Nehru's letter to Sheikh Abdullah, 18 May 1949, *SWJN*, vol. 11, pp. 120–21.

50. Constituent Assembly Debates, Official Report, vol. 10, 17 October 1949, p. 424.

51. Nehru's letter to N. Gopalaswami Ayyangar, 12 April 1952, *SWJN*, vol. 18, p. 383.

52. Nehru's letter to Maulana Abul Kalam Azad, 12 April 1952, *SWJN*, vol. 18, p. 383.

53. Nehru's letter to Indira Gandhi, 9 August 1953, *SWJN*, vol. 23, p. 311.

54. *Indian Express*, 10 August 1953, p. 1.

55. *Indian Express*, 11 August 1953, p. 1.

56. Gandhi's letter to the Chairman, AICC, 25 September 1920, *CWMG*, vol. 21, p. 298.

57. Constituent Assembly (Legislative) Debates, vol. 1, 1947, 27 November 1949, pp. 793–94.

58. Constituent Assembly Debates, vol. 11, 19 November 1949, p. 703.

59. Draft Constitution, footnote, p. 159.

60. B. Shiva Rao (ed.), *The Framing of India's Constitution: Select Documents*, vol. 4, Indian Institute of Public Administration, 1968, p. 475.

61. Report of the Linguistic Provinces Committee Appointed by the Jaipur Congress (December 1948), p. 15.

62. Note on linguistic provinces, 2 October 1949, *SWJN*, second series, vol. 13, p. 167.

63. Gopal, pp. 257–58.

64. Nehru's letter to Rajgopalachari, 28 May 1952, *SWJN*, second series, vol. 18, p. 255.

65. Lok Sabha Debates, 7 July 1952, *SWJN*, second series, vol. 18, pp. 265–66.

66. Rajya Sabha Debates, 21 July 1952, *SWJN*, second series, vol. 19, pp. 403–8

67. Nehru's letter to N. Sanjiva Reddy, 16 June 1952, *SWJN*, second series, vol. 18, p. 259.

68. Nehru's letter to V.V. Giri, 8 June 1952, *SWJN*, second series, vol. 18, p. 256.

69. Nehru's letter to Rajagopalachari, 3 December 1952, *SWJN*, second series, vol. 20, p. 235.

70. Nehru's letter to Rajagopalachari, 3 December 1952, *SWJN*, second series, vol. 20, p. 236.

71. Reply to an adjournment motion in Lok Sabha, 8 December 1952, *SWJN*, second series, vol. 20, p. 238.

72. Parliamentary Debates, House of the People, Official Report, vol. 4, 16 December 1952, columns 2439–43.

73. Nehru's letter to Rajagopalachari, 16 December 1952, *SWJN*, second series, vol. 20, p. 250.

74. Nehru's letter to the chief ministers of states and Statement in the Lok Sabha, 19 December 1952, *SWJN*, second series, vol. 20, pp. 256–57.

75. Terms of Reference of the SRC, 22 December 1953, *SWJN*, second series, vol. 24, pp. 253–54.

76. *SWJN*, second series, vol. 31, footnote, p. 153.

77. Gopal, *Jawaharlal Nehru*, p. 261.

78. Ibid.; Brecher, *Nehru*, pp. 484–85.

79. Gopal, *Jawaharlal Nehru*, pp. 264–69; Brecher, *Nehru*, pp. 484–85.

80. Appendix C, Constituent Assembly Debates (CAD), vol. 7, 4 November 1948, p. 101.

81. Ibid., pp. 107–8.

82. Ibid., pp. 109–10.

83. Ibid.

84. Ibid., pp. 145–47.

85. Ibid., p. 165.

86. Ibid., p. 155.

87. Parliamentary Debates, Official Report, vol. 1, 1950, 8 February 1950, pp. 313–14.

88. Website of Government of Arunachal Pradesh, http://arunachalpradesh.nic.in/rural/html/glance.htm

89. Nehru's letters to Jairamdas Doulatram, 25 January and 2 February 1951, *SWJN*, second series, vol. 15, Part II, pp. 181–82.

90. B.N. Mullik, *My Years with Nehru: 1948–1964*, Allied Publishers, 1972, p. 297.

91. Ibid., p. 299.

92. Sanjib Baruah, *In the Name of the Nation*, pp. 39–40.

93. *SWJN*, second series, vol. 22, pp. 221–23.

94. Ibid.

95. Mullik, *My Years with Nehru*, pp. 308–9.

96. Ibid., pp. 310–11.

97. Reply to questions in Lok Sabha, 30 May 1956, *SWJN*, second series, vol. 33, pp. 186–87.
98. Note by Nehru, 23 May 1956, *SWJN*, second series, vol. 33, pp. 182–83.
99. Mullik, *My Years with Nehru*, pp. 311–12.
100. Appraisal of Naga situation, 19 May 1956, *SWJN*, second series, vol. 33, pp. 178–79.